Cartels Diagnosed
New Insights on Collusion

Edited by

JOSEPH E. HARRINGTON, JR.
University of Pennsylvania

MAARTEN PIETER SCHINKEL
University of Amsterdam

CAMBRIDGE
UNIVERSITY PRESS

Shaftesbury Road, Cambridge CB2 8EA, United Kingdom

One Liberty Plaza, 20th Floor, New York, NY 10006, USA

477 Williamstown Road, Port Melbourne, VIC 3207, Australia

314–321, 3rd Floor, Plot 3, Splendor Forum, Jasola District Centre, New Delhi – 110025, India

103 Penang Road, #05–06/07, Visioncrest Commercial, Singapore 238467

Cambridge University Press is part of Cambridge University Press & Assessment, a department of the University of Cambridge.

We share the University's mission to contribute to society through the pursuit of education, learning and research at the highest international levels of excellence.

www.cambridge.org
Information on this title: www.cambridge.org/9781009428484

DOI: 10.1017/9781009428460

© Cambridge University Press & Assessment 2024

This publication is in copyright. Subject to statutory exception and to the provisions of relevant collective licensing agreements, no reproduction of any part may take place without the written permission of Cambridge University Press & Assessment.

When citing this work, please include a reference to the DOI 10.1017/9781009428460

First published 2024

Printed in the United Kingdom by CPI Group Ltd, Croydon CR0 4YY

A catalogue record for this publication is available from the British Library

Library of Congress Cataloging-in-Publication Data
Names: Harrington, Joseph E., Jr., 1957- editor. | Schinkel, Maarten-Pieter, editor.
Title: Cartels diagnosed : new insights on collusion / edited by Joseph E. Harrington Jr., University of Pennsylvania, Maarten Pieter Schinkel, Universiteit van Amsterdam.
Description: Cambridge, United Kingdom ; New York, NY, USA : Cambridge University Press, 2024. | Includes bibliographical references and index.
Identifiers: LCCN 2024012508 | ISBN 9781009428484 (hardback) | ISBN 9781009428453 (paperback) | ISBN 9781009428460 (ebook)
Subjects: LCSH: Cartels.
Classification: LCC HD2757.5 .C38 2024 | DDC 338.8/7–dc23/eng/20240603
LC record available at https://lccn.loc.gov/2024012508

ISBN 978-1-009-42848-4 Hardback
ISBN 978-1-009-42845-3 Paperback

Cambridge University Press & Assessment has no responsibility for the persistence or accuracy of URLs for external or third-party internet websites referred to in this publication and does not guarantee that any content on such websites is, or will remain, accurate or appropriate.

Contents

List of Figures		*page* vii
List of Tables		x
List of Contributors		xii
Introduction		1

1. Entry Barriers, Personal Relationships, and Cartel Formation 12
   Generic Drugs in the United States
   EMILY CUDDY, ROBERT H. PORTER, AMANDA STARC, AND THOMAS G. WOLLMANN

2. "Now You Are Asking for a Real War!" 44
   Private Alarm Systems in Norway
   KURT BREKKE AND LARS SØRGARD

3. Coordinating Fuel Surcharges 73
   Air Cargo Worldwide
   ZHIQI CHEN

4. Price Fixing or Fixing Competition? 94
   Bread in Israel
   CHAIM FERSHTMAN AND YOSSI SPIEGEL

5. The Role of Platforms for Facilitating Anticompetitive Communication 131
   Retail Gasoline in Australia
   DAVID P. BYRNE, NICOLAS DE ROOS, A. RACHEL GRINBERG, AND LESLIE M. MARX

6 Collusion with Non-express Communication   171
   Retail Gasoline in Norway
   JOSEPH E. HARRINGTON, JR.

7 Cartel Instability and Price Wars   192
   Retail Gasoline in Canada
   ROBERT CLARK, MARCO DUARTE, AND
   JEAN-FRANÇOIS HOUDE

8 Coordinated Rebate Reductions and Semi-collusion 222
   Retail Gasoline in Sweden
   FRODE STEEN AND LARS SØRGARD

9 Average Bid Auction Format Facilitates Bidding Rings 249
   Construction Tenders in Italy
   FRANCESCO DECAROLIS

10 The Challenges of Cartelization with Many Products
   and Ongoing Technological Advancements   272
   Liquid Crystal Displays Worldwide
   DENNIS CARLTON, MARK ISRAEL, IAN MACSWAIN,
   AND ALLAN SHAMPINE

11 Two Cartels in the Supply Chain   317
   Raw Tobacco in Spain
   THILO KLEIN, HELDER VASCONCELOS, AND
   ELENA ZOIDO

12 Is It Collusion or Competition behind Price
   Parallelism?   342
   Steel Manufacturing in Greece
   YANNIS KATSOULACOS AND MARC IVALDI

Figures

1.1	Price increases rollout over eighteen months	*page* 20
1.2	The cartel increased the prices of cartelized drugs by an average of 50 percent	29
1.3	Estimated effects on annual expenditures across collusive drug markets, 2012–2015	31
1.4	Profit margins for major generic drugmakers rise sharply upon cartel formation	32
2.1	Turnover and EBITDA of Sector and Verisure, 2008–2017	50
2.2	Timeline of documented key events and meetings between the CEOs of Sector and Verisure	52
2.3	Monthly customer churn from Sector to Verisure and smaller rivals, 2009–2017	64
4.1	Ratio of the retail price and the retail price cap of sliced dark bread, by store type, 2009–2011	120
4.2	Ratio of the retail price and the retail price cap of challah, by store type, 2009–2011	120
5.1	Visual representation of suburban and city center stations	139
5.2	Daily price cycles	147
5.3	Price restoration in April 2017	148
5.4	Station-level price cycles and restorations at hourly frequencies	150
5.5	Location of signaling stations	154
5.6	Signaling propensity and precision across retailers	158
5.7	Characteristics of stations that send price signals	165
6.1	Average retail price for six major brands	174
6.2	Screenshot from Circle K website showing recommended prices	177

6.3	Recommended price changes on the websites of Circle K and YX	178
7.1	Québec City: Fuel stations' location and net traffic flow	195
7.2	Evolution of retail prices, margins, and sales around the 2000 price war in Québec City	201
7.3	Difference in share of cumulative sales between 1999 and 2000	206
7.4	Eko stations' daily margins and sales during the price-war period	209
7.5	Evolution of margin dispersion	216
7.6	Distribution of gasoline prices in the south and east regions of Québec relative to the modal price in Québec City	218
8.1	Development in pump prices: Illustration of a drawing by a firm representative made for internal use during a cartel meeting	227
8.2	Rebate reduction illustration from November 1999: Actual price development for gasoline in 1999 (daily data) and the predicted "normal" price	236
8.3	Rebate reduction illustration May 1995: Actual prices and predicted "normal" prices (daily prices)	238
8.4	Price development as suggested by the dynamic price model	240
9.1	Example of an ABA with nineteen bids	253
9.2	Bids from an ABA in the Turin trial case	263
9.3	Outcomes of the participation test for two cartels	267
10.1	LCD panel value curve	278
10.2	2005 flat-panel display shares by application	280
10.3	LCD sales and shares by application	281
10.4	LCD vs. CRT monitor unit sales	282
10.5	17" SXGA monitor panel average price	283
10.6	Instances of Crystal Meetings	284
10.7	Example of a spreadsheet memorializing production figures	286

10.8	Example of a spreadsheet memorializing prices	287
10.9	Prices communicated at Crystal Meetings and actual transaction prices, 15″ monitor	291
10.10	Prices communicated at Crystal Meetings and actual transaction prices, 15″ monitor, XGA resolution	292
10.11	LCD panel fab generations and motherglass size	296
10.12	Share of TFT-LCD capacity by fab generation	297
10.13	Quarterly industry capacity	298
10.14	Alleged cartel member revenue shares, monitors	306
10.15	Plaintiff LCD price indices	307
10.16	Average price/cost for notebook, monitor, television, and phone panels	310
11.1	Volume of tobacco produced in Extremadura between 1985 and 2005 (tons)	320
11.2	Raw tobacco supply chain	320
11.3	A typical year of negotiations between the two cartels	328
11.4	Prices paid to the producers, by tobacco variety	331
11.5	Processors' market shares for all the available years	334
12.1	Final prices vs. list and imported prices	360
12.2	Domestic market size, level of productions, and capacities	362
12.3	Capacity utilization and market share for firm A	363
12.4	Capacity utilization at the industry level	363

Tables

0.1	List of cartel case studies	page 4
1.1	The probability of collusion varies with the number and composition of active firms	23
2.1	Acquisitions by Sector and Verisure notified to the Norwegian Competition Authority	48
3.1	The Lufthansa mechanism	80
4.1	Regulated price cap of sliced dark bread in NIS, 2008–2013	101
4.2	Distribution of sales in tons of sliced dark bread and challah, by store type, 2008–2015	103
5.1	Timeline for price signaling and restoration in April 2017	152
5.2	Sparsity in station-level restoration price signaling by retailer	156
5.3	Characteristics of stations that send price signals	167
7.1	Demand response to prices during price-war period	211
7.2	Fraction of stations pricing at the minimum	213
10.1	Revenue of monitor and notebook panels around the time of Crystal Meeting price discussions	289
10.2	Share of industry revenue at transaction prices below midpoint or lowest price communicated at Crystal Meetings, by panel	293
10.3	Share of industry revenues by manufacturer (all applications)	302
10.4	Average price/cost for alleged conspiracy period and post period	309
11.1	Processor market shares in Extremadura, 1997–2001	322
11.2	Summary of descriptive statistics on prices paid to the producers by variety	333

11.3	Data sources for the analysis of prices paid to the producers	337
11.4	Data sources for the computation of processors' market shares in Extremadura	338
12.1	Product X market shares	357
12.2	Estimated values of the marginal utility of income under the assumption of binding capacity constraints	365
12.3	Own-price elasticities of demand under the assumption of binding capacity constraints	366
12.4	Estimated markups under the assumption of binding capacity constraints	367
12.5	Own-price elasticities of demand under the assumption of nonbinding capacity constraints	368
12.6	Markups under the assumption of nonbinding capacity constraints	369
12.7	Estimated marginal costs under the assumption of nonbinding capacity constraints	370
12.8	Estimated parameters under the assumption of binding capacity constraints	380
12.9	Estimated parameters under the assumption of nonbinding capacity constraints	381

Contributors

Kurt Brekke, Professor, Department of Economics, Norwegian School of Economics

David P. Byrne, Professor, Department of Economics, University of Melbourne

Dennis W. Carlton, David McDaniel Professor of Economics, Emeritus, Booth School of Business, University of Chicago; Senior Managing Director, Compass Lexecon; Research Associate, National Bureau of Economic Research

Zhiqi Chen, Chancellor's Professor, Department of Economics, Carleton University

Robert Clark, Professor, Stephen J. R. Smith Chair in Economic Policy, Department of Economics, Queen's University

Emily Cuddy, Assistant Professor, Department of Economics, Duke University

Nicolas de Roos, Professor, School of Management, University of Liverpool

Francesco Decarolis, Professor, Department of Economics, Bocconi University

Marco Duarte, Assistant Professor, Department of Economics, University of North Carolina-Chapel Hill

LIST OF CONTRIBUTORS

Chaim Fershtman, Professor Emeritus, The Eitan Berglas School of Economics, Tel Aviv University

A. Rachel Grinberg, Partner, Bates White Economic Consulting

Joseph E. Harrington, Jr., Patrick T. Harker Professor, Department of Business Economics and Public Policy, The Wharton School, University of Pennsylvania

Jean-François Houde, Juli Plant Grainger Distinguished Chair of Economics, Department of Economics, University of Wisconsin-Madison; Research Associate, National Bureau of Economic Research

Mark Israel, Senior Managing Director, Compass Lexecon

Marc Ivaldi, Professor of Economics, Toulouse School of Economics; Academic Affiliate, NERA Economic Consulting

Yannis Katsoulacos, Professor Emeritus, Athens University of Economics and Business; Affiliated Chair Professor, Jiangxi University of Finance and Economics; Chair, Scientific Committee and Coordinator, CRESSE

Thilo Klein, Executive Vice President, Compass Lexecon

Ian MacSwain, Executive Vice President, Compass Lexecon

Leslie M. Marx, Robert A. Bandeen Professor, Fuqua School of Business, Duke University

Robert H. Porter, William R. Kenan, Jr. Professor, Department of Economics, Northwestern University

Maarten Pieter Schinkel, Professor, Department of Economics and Business, University of Amsterdam

Allan Shampine, Executive Vice President, Compass Lexecon

Yossi Spiegel, Louise Lea Flack Chair in Game Theory and Interactive Decisions, Coller School of Management, Tel Aviv University

Amanda Starc, Associate Professor of Strategy, Kellogg School of Management, Northwestern University; Research Associate, National Bureau of Economic Research

Frode Steen, Professor, Department of Economics, Norwegian School of Economics; Research Fellow, Centre for Economic Policy Research

Lars Sørgard, Professor, Department of Economics, Norwegian School of Economics

Helder Vasconcelos, Professor, Department of Economics, Porto University; Senior Vice President, Compass Lexecon

Thomas G. Wollmann, Associate Professor of Economics, Booth School of Business, University of Chicago; Research Associate, National Bureau of Economic Research

Elena Zoido, Executive Vice President, Compass Lexecon

Introduction

At the start of the 1990s, the world was still a relatively hospitable place for cartels. Many enforcers, such as the US Department of Justice's Antitrust Division, viewed cartels as largely operating in local or at most domestic markets and that senior executives of major corporations were not so audacious as to operate a global cartel. Turning to the European Commission, it pursued several national business arrangements that affected trade between the member states as part of its European integration objective, but mostly with injunctive relief, and not punishing fines. Some of its countries, such as The Netherlands, did not even have a competition law prohibiting cartels. However, by the end of the 1990s, the DOJ's Antitrust Division and the European Commission's Directorate-General for Competition were aggressively prosecuting a slew of international cartels that had been operating for years,[1] while the Netherlands had at long last

---

[1] "[T]he Division currently has roughly 30 grand juries investigating suspected international cartel activity. Similarly, at the time of the lysine investigation [in 1993], less than 2 percent of our corporate defendants were foreign-based, as compared to nearly 50 percent of our corporate defendants last year." Scott D. Hammond, Director of Criminal Enforcement, Antitrust Division, US Department of Justice, "Fighting Cartels: Why and How? Lessons Common to Detecting and Deterring Cartel Activity" (The 3rd Nordic Competition Policy Conference, 12 September 2000) www.justice.gov/atr/speech/fighting-cartels-why-and-how-lessonscommon-detecting-and-deterring-cartel-activity. "In recent years the Commission has made great strides in fighting cartels. Between 2000 and 2005 the Commission adopted 38 infringement decisions. That is an average of 6 decisions per year, twice the average of the previous 30 years. We have targeted both European and worldwide cartels, and imposed total fines of €4.4 billion. The average fine per addressee also increased significantly." Neelie Kroes, European Commissioner for Competition Policy, Directorate-General for Competition, European Commission, "Delivering on the crackdown: recent developments in the European Commission's campaign against cartels" (The 10th Annual Competition Conference at the European Institute, Fiesole, Italy, October 13, 2006) https://ec.europa.eu/commission/presscorner/detail/en/speech_06_595.

adopted a competition law and were prosecuting a massive construction cartel with hundreds of members.[2]

These anecdotes from our respective countries exemplify the sea change over the last three decades which has created an anti-cartel enforcement tsunami. During that time, almost all countries came to have competition laws,[3] more than fifty jurisdictions adopted leniency programs,[4] and over thirty countries criminalized collusion[5]. Furthermore, government fines were systematized in fining guidelines and have grown significantly in magnitude, customer damage litigation is now expanding to more countries, competition authorities are increasingly engaged in cartel screening, and the list of enforcement enhancements goes on. The result has been that new cartel cases are continuously being brought around the globe and are pursued more aggressively and effectively.

Despite this progress, cartels continue to form at a concerning rate, and even in jurisdictions with the toughest laws, the most effective enforcement, and the harshest penalties. There are also signs of some regress, as leniency applications have declined in recent years in the EU, USA, and other jurisdictions.[6] Though that could be good news if it is due to fewer cartels, it may also be an indication that cartels have managed to avoid using leniency programs.[7] Challenges for public and private enforcement are also growing as cartels engage in more diverse practices including colluding on list prices, reference prices, rebates, and surcharges. They have coordinated using more

---

[2] Zembla documentary "The Dutch Construction Cartel," November 12, 2006. www.bnnvara.nl/zembla/artikelen/the-dutch-construction-cartel.

[3] "By 2010, 126 countries had adopted a competition law, most of them within the last three decades." Bradford and Chilton, (2018), 393.

[4] Borrell, García, Jiménez, and Ordóñez-de-Haro (2019), 1–13.

[5] Shaffer, Nesbitt, and Waller (2015). However, it is a rare few countries that have incarcerated cartelists.

[6] Over 2015–21, leniency applications declined by 65 percent globally and 58 percent in OCED jurisdictions. "The Future of Effective Leniency Programmes: Advancing Detection and Deterrence of Cartels," OECD Competition Policy Roundtable Background Note, 2023.

[7] Beaton-Wells and Tran (2015).

subtle methods such as public announcements and price signaling, and facilitated collusion through information exchanges with the assistance of third parties. A growing concern is that algorithmic pricing may advance collusion, whether it is firms agreeing to the use of a supracompetitive pricing algorithm or adopting a common algorithm supplied by a third party that results in higher prices. There is even the prospect that algorithms could learn to collude autonomously without the intent of companies' employees which, should it occur, would escape existing competition laws. The last thirty years of cartel enforcement can be succinctly summarized as: Progress has been made but challenges remain.

Cartels continue to adapt and innovate and so must enforcers, as in a game of cat and mouse. At the root of more effective enforcement is knowledge about cartels' core features and mechanisms, for the more that is known about cartels, the better equipped the agencies will be in designing and implementing policies to deter them from forming, and detecting and shutting them down when they do form. With that in mind, the objective of this volume is to advance our understanding of why and how cartels form, how they operate, and how effective they are in restraining competition. To achieve this objective, we draw on a largely untapped pool of knowledge: an economist's careful examination of a particular cartel episode in association with a legal case or academic research. Typically, this knowledge is not widely disseminated because it is presented in an expert witness report for an agency, plaintiff, or defendant or, when part of an academic study, does not fit into the format of a formal theoretical or empirical analysis required for economics journals. We believe this is a squandering of valuable information for these episodes often have a novel and insightful economic story to tell. This volume was created to provide a venue for case studies that convey those stories.

Candidate episodes were screened for those that had the greatest potential to shed light on some unique or underexplored dimension to collusion, and are written by leading economic scholars and practitioners with intimate knowledge about the cartel episode. The case

Table 0.1 *List of cartel case studies*

Market	Location	Years of conduct
Air cargo	Global (Canada)	1999–2006
Average bid auctions	Italy (Turin)	2000–2003
Bread	Israel	2010
Gasoline	Australia (Melbourne)	2009–2014
Gasoline	Canada (Québec City)	1997–2000
Gasoline	Norway	2017–2019
Gasoline	Sweden	1999
Generic drugs	United States	2013–2015
Private alarm systems	Norway	2011–2017
Liquid crystal displays	Global (United States)	1996–2006
Raw tobacco	Spain	1996–2001
Steel	Greece	2002–2011

study format was designed to most effectively communicate this new insight by making that insight the focus of the discussion, while eschewing a comprehensive economic and legal review of the cartel episode. Case studies are concise, enlightening, and easy to read.

The twelve case studies in this volume span nine products or services from ten countries, as shown in Table 0.1. The cartels and the markets in which they operated vary in many respects, yet by and large these cartels occurred in markets where firms' offerings are highly similar, as is consistent with the extensive record of cartels. Though casting a wide net in terms of products and services when soliciting cases, our trawling yielded four cases in retail gasoline markets, perhaps indicative of the commonality of collusion there. But those four gasoline cartels are highly diverse as they involved distinct collusive practices and the four studies deliver different lessons about collusion.

In terms of the collusive practices, seven of the cartels coordinated final prices, with explicit collusion used in bread, gasoline (Canada), generic drugs, liquid crystal displays, and raw tobacco, and tacit collusion in two gasoline cases (Australia, Norway). Rather than coordinate final prices, firms coordinated fuel surcharges in air cargo and rebates in gasoline (Sweden). Forsaking any coordination with respect to prices, a market-sharing collusive arrangement was used in the market for private alarm systems. The one bidding ring episode in the volume (which involved a common set of players: a public procurer and construction companies) is novel in examining collusion in the context of the average bid auction format. Finally, the case study of the Greek steel market is one of mistaken identity as what looked like collusion to the competition authority turned out to be competition upon closer economic study. It serves as a reminder that not all suspicious conduct is the product of a cartel.

Spanning the collection of case studies, insight is delivered into cartel formation, cartel practices, cartel efficacy, and anti-cartel enforcement. While it does not do justice to the richness and depth of these case studies, the ensuing summary highlights some of the lessons learned.

I.1   CARTEL FORMATION

Several new pieces of insight are delivered regarding the birth and formation of cartels. The generic drugs cartel case offers a rich description of the critical role of interpersonal relationships in forming a cartel. A sales person was hired by the world's largest drugmaker, Teva Pharmaceuticals, for her strong industry contacts and tasked with "price increase implementation." For each rival company, she assessed their relevant employees in terms of perceived receptiveness to collude and entered those ratings into an Excel spreadsheet. Cartels were formed in about 90 percent of the markets where she had contacts with favorable ratings and only 20 percent in markets where such contacts were absent.

Some cartels are born out of a price war. The Israeli bread cartel may be one, but could also have been about restoring competitive prices from subcompetitive levels rather than adopting supracompetitive prices. The incident involved a baker from Haifa, Mr. Davidovitz, who aggressively priced challah in retaliation for some bakers from Jerusalem entering his home market. As discussed in the case study, it is not clear whether the "normal" conduct which the agreement restored was one of genuine competition or of a tacit agreement involving an allocation of geographic markets which the entry by Jerusalem bakeries violated. Even when the practice itself is conventional and unambiguous in its effect, what is driving it may be more nuanced than initially appreciated.

The Spanish raw tobacco case describes how the birth of an upstream cartel spawned the defensive creation of a downstream cartel. In order to support higher prices for upstream tobacco producers in Extremadura, the government induced the growers to control production volumes, which then created rents that led the downstream tobacco processors to form their own cartel to counterbalance the one upstream. Government regulation was responsible for not one but two cartels; a reminder of how poorly designed policy rules and regulations can breed collusion.

I.2 CARTEL PRACTICES

Communication and information is key to colluding, and the four gasoline cartels exemplify the variety of methods used. Two of the gasoline cartels (in Canada and Sweden) involved canonical express, direct, and private communications that flagrantly violate competition law. The cartel in Québec City communicated and coordinated pump prices. With the Swedish cartel, a plan was drawn up on the back of a napkin to coordinate a reduction in rebates for large customers while simultaneously adjusting prices at the pump. Two other cases (in Australia and Norway) entailed more subtle means. In the Australian gasoline case, a data subscription service provided by the company Informed Sources offered gasoline sellers access to competitors' real-time prices. Each subscribing company provided its prices at a high-frequency (on the order of every fifteen to thirty minutes) to the Informed Sources online platform and was given access to all subscribers' prices on that platform. This information exchange facilitated coordinating on high prices – by allowing for low-cost signaling of future prices – and monitoring for compliance with those high prices. As in many gasoline markets, prices cycled in the Norwegian gasoline market. One of the companies, Circle K, used a coded message on its publicly accessible website to signal to other gasoline companies when to raise prices and initiate the next cycle. This it did by changing the "valid from date" for a "recommended price" to the current date which then caused all firms, in a matter of hours, to raise their prices to Circle K's recommended price.

The outcome on which firms coordinated are novel in some cases. The episode explored in the Swedish gasoline market focused on suppliers coordinating the removal of rebates provided to large customers, such as transport and taxi companies, where the final price paid was the pump price less the rebate. The story is one of semi-collusion whereby, prior to the episode described, the gasoline sellers were colluding on pump prices and competing on rebates to the point that they felt a need to coordinate the removal of those rebates. In its defense, the cartel claimed compensatory decreases in pump prices when it eliminated those rebates, so no customers were harmed. However, the case study provides evidence that the intent and effect of the cartel was to raise prices for all consumers.

Similarly, there was collusion on only some price components in the market for worldwide air cargo services, where the price paid by customers was the sum of the freight rate and various other charges including a fuel surcharge. When the International Air Transport Association stopped publishing a fuel price index after being warned the practice was likely in violation of competition laws, Lufthansa continued to publish the identical index on its publicly accessible website. It did so as part of an explicit scheme to coordinate fuel surcharges but no other components of price. Since what should matter to a customer is the total price, colluding only on surcharges would seem futile because airlines could still compete by offsetting the higher surcharges with lower freight rates. This case study explains how the delegation of pricing authority within a company can cause colluding on surcharges to result in supracompetitive total prices.

A multitude of products can make collusion challenging. Given the many applications for liquid crystal display (LCD) screens and the speed of technological change, the members of the global LCD cartel faced substantial challenges in designing an effective collusive arrangement. Involving a dozen manufacturers who sold hundreds of products, they coordinated prices for only a small subset of products, focusing on the highest selling products and at a level of aggregation which did not fully take account of quality differences. Nevertheless, the cartel proved durable as it met as often as eight times a quarter for a period of ten years and, while the case study finds a small overcharge, it was still able to deliver billions of dollars in additional profits.

Idiosyncratic market features can facilitate collusion. The two main providers of home alarm systems in Norway, Sector and Verisure, did not agree on prices, but rather took advantage of a natural feature of their market to implement a no poaching agreement which would then reduce price competition. As is standard practice in markets for residential security systems, a company places a sign in front of a home using its services. For door-to-door sales, the collusive agreement was for each company's sales representatives to avoid approaching residences with a sign showing it is served by its main competitor. Compliance with the no poaching agreement was generally monitored using measures of customer churn. However, in one instance, Sector's CEO personally witnessed a deviation when a Verisure sales representative appeared at his Sector-signed residence to try to get him to switch from Sector to Verisure! Though leading to a harsh email exchange between the two CEOs, calm was soon restored and a cartel breakdown avoided.

I.3 CARTEL EFFICACY

Even largely successful cartels can be plagued by periodic disruption. After maintaining collusive prices for a long time, gas stations in and around Québec City found themselves in a year-long price war. The episode started when an independent retailer defected by lowering its price in order to increase sales volume and benefit from a price-support clause it had with an upstream supplier. The subsequent price war caused margins to shrink to nearly zero. The case study explains that the price war proved difficult to terminate because the high price-elasticity of firm demand made it costly for any firm to take the lead and raise prices, for a price hike of just two cents per liter above neighboring prices could result in a 36 percent decline in sales. This obstacle was compounded by one of the leading firms having a low-price guarantee which tied its price to the lowest price in the market. Nevertheless, the gas stations eventually re-established supracompetitive prices which, in fact, were higher than those prior to the price war.

In the market for private alarm systems, the acquisition of some smaller (non-cartel) companies by cartel member Sector created a disagreement over the collusive outcome which ultimately led to a temporary departure from the no poaching agreement. Sector felt that the customers of the acquired companies ought to be part of its collusive allocation and thus come under the no poaching agreement. A different view was taken by the other cartel member, Verisure, who continued to try to acquire those companies' customers, which both companies were doing prior to the acquisitions. Consequently, there was some aggressive business stealing of customers but the CEOs eventually resolved the matter and returned to their market-sharing arrangement.

In contrast to the aforementioned sources of internal instability, a potentially disruptive force in the generic drugs cartel was from an external source: entry by new suppliers. The significantly higher prices under collusion attracted entrants to some of the cartelized markets though there was a delay of two to four years before production started, partly due to regulatory impediments. Furthermore, supracompetitive prices were found to persist long after the end of the generic drugs conspiracy. Even with the cartel's shut down due to government investigations, the case study shows that prices far exceeded competitive levels for several years thereafter.

1.4 ANTI-CARTEL ENFORCEMENT

On matters of enforcement, the case study of public works tenders in Turin, Italy explains how the average bid auction is almost an ideal format for supporting a stable collusive arrangement. As a rough description, this format has the contract awarded to the bidder whose bid is nearest the average bid. So susceptible to collusion were these auctions that contractors from all over the region flogged to the city to share in its rents. And, so as to manipulate the average bid in its favor, multiple cartels formed and competed. The case study underscores the critical role of auction design and goes on to show how economic analysis can be used to design collusive markers to detect bidding rings.

Finally, the Greek steel market case study reminds us that parallel price movements in a concentrated market may be suggestive of collusion but could well be the product of competition. In this episode, there was some striking evidence of near-simultaneous changes in list prices by the three main domestic steel manufacturers which led the Hellenic Competition Commission to pursue an investigation. In spite of this suspicious pattern, the evidence put forth in the case study is more supportive of competition than collusion. Common price movements are explained to be the result of an import price which acted as a reference price for the three producers and it is that which drove parallel movements in domestic list prices. The case study also offers methods for distinguishing between collusion and competition which is a crucial component of effective enforcement.

1.5 CONCLUDING REMARKS

One overarching lesson that emerges from these case studies is that often some quite particular circumstances are the key to understanding how a cartel emerged, how it operated, and how successful it was. Examples of such circumstances are special contractual clauses, well-intended government regulations, and advances in communication technologies. In some situations, the firms were endowed with these facilitating circumstances, and in other situations they helped create them. Another general lesson is that cartels that appear relatively innocuous and constrained because they coordinate only a small subset of products or dimensions of competition can still manage to be profitable and durable. Competition agencies should have a keen eye for the importance of such subtleties when seeking to detect and investigate suspected cartels. Novel cartel morphologies are also promising areas for the development of advances in the theory of collusion.

The intended audience for this volume spans economists and lawyers in academia, enforcement agencies, and the business community. Case studies are written to be accessible to all scholars, practitioners, and students. The knowledge they offer could serve as the basis for developing new collusive theories and improving empirical modeling. In the classroom, case studies can be used to illustrate properties of cartels and their conduct. In the realm of practice, the volume's insight can assist competition authorities, economic consultancies, and law firms in identifying cartels, distinguishing collusion from competition, formulating theories of harm, and designing models for measuring that harm. In the development of this volume, our aspiration has been to expand what we know about cartels and to disseminate this new knowledge within the community of practitioners and scholars who wrestle with the challenges of collusion. We have certainly learned from these case studies, and it is our hope and belief that you will too.

REFERENCES

Beaton-Wells, C. and C. Tran, eds. (2015) *Anti-cartel Enforcement in a Contemporary Age: Leniency Religion*, Hart Publishing.

Borrell, J.-R., C. García, J. L. Jiménez, and J. M. Ordóñez-de-Haro (2019) "25 Years of Leniency Programs: A Turning Point in Cartel Prosecutions," *CPI Antitrust Chronicle*, 1–13.

Bradford, A. and A. S. Chilton (2018) "Competition Law around the World from 1889 to 2010: The Competition Law Index," *Journal of Competition Law & Economics*, 14, 393–432.

Shaffer, G. C., N. H. Nesbitt, and S. W. Waller (2015) "Criminalizing Cartels: A Global Trend?" in *Research Handbook on Comparative Competition Law*, A. Duke, J. Duns, and B. Sweeney, eds., Edward Elgar.

1 Entry Barriers, Personal Relationships, and Cartel Formation
Generic Drugs in the United States*

Emily Cuddy, Robert H. Porter, Amanda Starc, and Thomas G. Wollmann

1.1 INTRODUCTION

In July 2014, a *New York Times* article titled "Rapid Price Increases for Some Generic Drugs Catch Users by Surprise" caught the attention of Mike Cole, supervisor of the Connecticut AG office's unit of antitrust and fraud. The article highlighted how the prices of several generic drugs had risen sharply over the prior year. Curiously, the increases could not be attributed to ingredient shortages or manufacturing troubles. "On a hunch," according to the *Connecticut Post*, Cole forwarded the article to a staff attorney, who began issuing subpoenas (Pazniokas, 2019). This marked the start of the case against "the largest domestic corporate cartel in our nation's history" (Office of the Connecticut AG, 2020).

The ensuing investigation, which combined witness testimonies, private communications within and between the rival drugmakers, and internal documents outlining pricing strategies, reached three broad conclusions. First, the sharp increases cited by the *Times*, such as the doubling of the price of levothyroxine, were by no means unique. Second, instead of reflecting fluctuations in costs or disruptions in supply, the price hikes were the result of explicit collusion

---

* None of the authors has played any role in any of the investigations nor in any litigation relating to this matter, nor have they received any compensation from any of the parties mentioned in this article. We benefited from the superb research assistance provided by Paloma Avendano and Paulo Ramos, as well as extensive discussions with Doni Bloomfield.

among key salespeople at many of the world's largest generic drugmakers.[1] Third, and perhaps most striking, while many firms took measures to soften competition in the generic drug industry, most of the large, abrupt price hikes could be traced to a single personnel decision. Namely, in April 2013, Teva Pharmaceuticals, the world's largest generic drugmaker, hired NP,[2] a salesperson with especially strong industry relationships, and tasked her with "price increase implementation."[3]

In the eighteen months between her joining Teva and the government publicizing its investigation, NP and co-conspirators cartelized over 100 markets for generic drugs (i.e., substance-delivery-release-strength combinations). During that period, the scheme generated $12 billion of additional profit for the drugmakers (Cuddy, 2020), and even more in the years that followed. Details came to light when Connecticut, joined by forty-two other states and Puerto Rico, sued nineteen firms and fifteen individuals. The legal case *Connecticut et al. v. Teva Pharmaceuticals USA Inc. et al.* (2019, Complaint hereafter), which was filed on May 10, 2019, alleges that the defendants violated Section 1 of the Sherman Act, which prohibits price fixing. Other claims based on these and related allegations have been made by the US Department of Justice, which has obtained grand jury indictments against a subset of the defendants, and various private plaintiffs, who are seeking to recover billions in damages.

In this case study, we examine collusive behavior catalyzed by NP joining Teva by combining the rich array of facts presented in

---

[1] We use terms such as "collusion," "cartel," and "price fixing" throughout to characterize the conduct of certain firms and their employees. This usage reflects our interpretation of events described in the May 10, 2019 Complaint, which we assume are truthfully reported. However, the litigation against many of these organizations and individuals is ongoing (see Section 1.4). From the court's perspective, the conduct of those defendants is merely "alleged." Further, with respect to criminal charges against them, those defendants are innocent until proven guilty.

[2] Since their names are unimportant to our analysis, we refer to individuals by their initials.

[3] See page 158 of the Complaint, which is referenced in the following paragraph.

the Complaint with data from generic drug markets. To do so, we exploit unique features of our setting that are especially conducive to diagnosing cartels. First, the hiring of NP by Teva does not coincide with any discrete changes in the industry, and the cartels rolled out in quick succession shortly after she joined the firm. Hence, collusion represents an abrupt "shock" to conduct that is plausibly independent of outcomes we wish to examine. Second, at the point at which NP joined Teva, the firm operated in a large number of drug markets that differed from one another in ways that can be easily measured. We can use these differences to test theoretical predictions. For instance, we can use variation in the number of firms competing with Teva in each market to study how much easier it is to form a cartel when fewer firms need to reach an agreement. Third, although the Complaint was initially released with redactions, the original was unsealed by the court the following month. It contains internal spreadsheets, call logs from wireless service providers, and private messages exchanged within and between the firms that provide novel insight into how cartels operate internally. For example, we not only learn that NP factors the cooperativeness of other drugmakers into her decision to cartelize a market but we also observe the quantitative measure she personally ascribed to each.

In Section 1.2, we describe the vertical relationships and contracting arrangements in the retail pharmacy industry. Section 1.3 contains a discussion of the formation of the cartel and the factors that were conducive to collusion. In Section 1.4, we recount how state and federal investigators unearthed the cartel and summarize the ensuing litigation. Section 1.5 contains an assessment of the initial price effects of the cartel, and how vertical relationships affected the incidence of the price increases. In Section 1.6, we discuss the role of entry in response to the price increases. Section 1.7 considers the aftermath of the investigation, focusing on civil lawsuits and research investigating strategic behavior by manufacturers. In Section 1.8, we conclude.

1.2 CHARACTERISTICS OF GENERIC DRUG MARKETS

Generic drugs represent over 90 percent of prescription drug fills by volume in the USA. Although generics are bioequivalent to branded drugs,[4] they are often significantly cheaper due to competition among firms that sell generic drugs. As a result, once marketing exclusivity of a branded drug ends after patent expiration and subsequent FDA approval of a generic entrant, the market for that molecule effectively is taken over by generic formulations. The rapid transition is facilitated not only by drug insurance formulary design, which subsidizes generic use through reduced patient cost sharing, but also by law in many states, which require pharmacists to dispense the generic drug by default (NCSL Health Program, 2019).

Once market exclusivity restrictions lapse, generic drug markets allow for competition between manufacturers. Most markets have multiple manufacturers producing generic versions of the branded molecule. The majority of the collusive activity was concentrated among solid-dose drugs (e.g., capsules and tablets). Solid-dose drugs witnessed higher levels of generic entry than other drug forms (e.g., injectables and topical products). Berndt et al. (2017) found that solid-dose markets had between two and three more manufacturers on average between 2004 and 2016. These manufacturers often specialize in the production of generic molecules and are multinational. While some firms specialize in the production of a handful of similar drugs (e.g., those in the same therapeutic class), others offer a comprehensive portfolio that includes hundreds of unique molecules.

The vertical aspects of generic drug markets are similar to those of other health care products and services. In the retail prescription market, manufacturers sell to both large retail pharmacy chains (e.g., CVS) and wholesalers (e.g., McKesson Corporation), which, in turn,

---

[4] A generic drug must be bioequivalent, i.e., the generic drug must have an equivalent rate and extent of absorption of the active ingredient as the branded drug. That said, they may include different inactive ingredients.

supply independent pharmacies.[5] Although mail-order prescriptions are increasing in popularity, the majority of prescription drug fills still take place at retail pharmacies. Starc and Swanson (2021) document substantial concentration within the retail pharmacy market. In their sample, four companies – CVS, Walgreens, Rite Aid, and Walmart – account for 51 percent of retail prescription revenues. These retail pharmacies then sell to consumers, who are at the bottom of the vertical chain. Consumers visit their preferred pharmacy and are given their prescription, which is manufactured by the firm that has contracted to supply that particular retail pharmacy.

Most consumers have insurance coverage with a prescription drug benefit. These benefits typically favor the use of generic drugs via low coinsurance or a small copayment. As a result, many consumers pay little or nothing at the point-of-sale for generic prescription drugs. However, some insurers may attempt to steer consumers to some distribution channels or retail pharmacies. For example, within the Medicare Part D program, which covers elderly Americans, preferred pharmacy networks are common. These plans offer consumers additional discounts when filling their prescription drugs at an in-network pharmacy. Starc and Swanson (2021) show that consumers are willing to switch pharmacies and travel further to obtain these discounts.

Insurance plans reimburse retail pharmacies for each prescription fill. In many contracts, the reimbursement is calculated as an ingredient cost plus a dispensing fee. Dispensing fees are typically similar for drugs within a plan-pharmacy bargaining pair, but ingredient costs vary across drugs. Historically, average wholesale costs have been used to estimate acquisition costs and served as a benchmark for ingredient costs. Thus, wholesale costs were used by large payers to determine

---

[5] As of this writing, direct purchasers of generic drugs, including drug purchasing cooperatives (e.g., GPOs) and retail pharmacy operators, indirect purchasers (e.g., independent pharmacies), and end-payers (e.g., employee benefits funds, labor unions, and private insurance firms) have filed complaints against the cartel. See MDL 2724 from the United States District Court for the Eastern District of Pennsylvania for a summary.

reimbursement. However, wholesale costs were unverified numbers self-reported by generic manufacturers. These wholesale prices have been shown to be imperfect and manipulable, akin to "sticker prices" (Alpert et al., 2013). Recently, bolstered by the creation of the Center for Medicare and Medicaid Services (CMS) National Average Drug Acquisition Cost (NADAC) Survey, both public and private payers began indexing ingredient costs to the true acquisition costs of retail pharmacies and wholesalers, often using fixed reimbursement caps or so-called maximum allowable costs (MACs).[6] Nevertheless, NADAC indexing is imperfect, with considerable lags in cost updates. As we discuss below, imperfect indexing exposes retail pharmacies to fluctuations in wholesale prices. In summary, deciding which products from generic manufacturers to stock is strategically important: pharmacies earn profits from the "spread" between contractual reimbursement and the true cost of acquiring the drugs.

Wholesalers and most large chains, such as CVS and Walgreens, purchase drugs directly from manufacturers. In the early 2000s, most purchasers relied on relationship-based contracting. There was a rapid shift to auction-based procurement in the years preceding the formation of the cartel. In practice, each large purchaser solicits bids to supply a particular drug from all generic firms that have the requisite marketing rights. However, such requests are erratic, insofar as they are prompted by an unexpected change in the market, such as a new firm receiving marketing rights from the FDA or an incumbent firm exiting the market. Generic drugs are highly regulated and quasi-homogeneous goods. The resulting competition among manufacturers for a given contract is predominantly on price, where purchasers award their contracts to the lowest bidder, and the winning bid effectively becomes the pharmacy's acquisition cost.

Under this procurement mechanism, the entry (exit) of a new generic firm typically leads to a reduction (increase) of the average

---

[6] See, for instance, the Federal Upper Limit Program (FUL) and state maximum allowable costs (MAC), a fixed maximum reimbursement cap.

market price. For example, a 2019 FDA study found that the average market price of a generic molecule (relative to the brand molecule) is 39 percent lower with a single generic producer, 54 percent lower with two generic producers, and more than 95 percent lower with six or more generic producers (Center for Drug Evaluation and Research, 2019). As we explain in the next section, the formation of the cartel and the subsequent manipulation of this procurement mechanism brought an abrupt end to the typical price patterns in many generic drug markets.

1.3 CARTEL FORMATION

In this section, we describe the formation of the cartel and discuss the features of generic drug markets that may have facilitated collusion. We divide our discussion between factors that explain variation across generic drug markets in the incidence of collusion and factors that are common to all markets in the generic drug industry.

Although there may be many reasons why the cartel formed, lagging profits across the generics segment likely accelerated firms' willingness to participate in the conspiracy. For instance, at Teva, net income was down 26 percent in the first quarter of 2013. Ultimately, at least nineteen generic drug firms joined the cartel, including many of the world's largest, e.g., Actavis, Apotex, Dr. Reddy's, Glenmark, Heritage, Lupin, Mylan, Sandoz, Taro, and Teva. In effect, they formed a bidding ring, where the bidders varied across the different product markets due to their different portfolios – for instance, Teva, Lupin, and Mylan colluded in the market for fenofibrate whereas only Teva and Mylan colluded in the market for tolterodine ER because Lupin did not market that drug. According to the Complaint, "the shared objective ... [was] to attain a state of equilibrium, where no competitors are incentivized to compete for additional market share by eroding price." In manipulating the outcomes of retailer auctions, the ring's scheme was twofold – one, allocating market share for a particular drug product (e.g., across retail customers) between incumbents and new entrants (their so-called fair share principle) and, two, avoiding price erosion and/or raising prices. These allocations were greatly simplified due to the high level of concentration in the pharmacy sector: each ring member would be allocated enough retail pharmacy chains to reach their desired market share for a particular product, e.g., a 60 percent market share might entail winning the CVS and Walgreens contracts. Because the Complaint contains detailed information about Teva's participation in the ring, it is possible to trace out its role in greater detail than its co-conspirators. Thus, we focus on Teva in what follows; however, we note that Teva was not involved in all product markets where ring members colluded.

The proximate cause of Teva's involvement was that Teva hired NP on April 22, 2013 as the Director of Strategic Customer Marketing and tasked her with "price increase implementation" (Complaint, page 158). Besides the job description, the event was pivotal for at least two other reasons. First, Teva had been the world's leading generic drugmaker for several years. In early 2013, it manufactured over 500 different tablets, capsules, and solutions. Second, NP had close ties to key salespeople at nearly all of the major generic drugmakers as a result of her previous employment. Immediately prior to joining Teva, she spent eight years at Amerisource Bergen, one of the largest US drug distributors, where she most recently served as its Director of Global Generic Sourcing.

Within days of joining Teva, NP determined which markets were candidates for price hikes. First, around May 1, she assigned each of Teva's rivals a score ranging between −3 and +3 based on the strength of her relationships with salespeople at these other generic drugmakers. NP called this score the "quality" of the competition, since it measured the likelihood that a firm would cooperate with her.[7] Most large generic drugmakers received high scores,

---

[7] The Complaint alleges that "as part of her process of identifying candidates for price increases, Patel started to look very closely at Teva's relationships with its competitors, and also her own relationships with individuals at those competitors" (page 160). Based on other facts presented in the Complaint, we believe that "Teva's relationships" refers to ties between her colleagues with individuals at other firms.

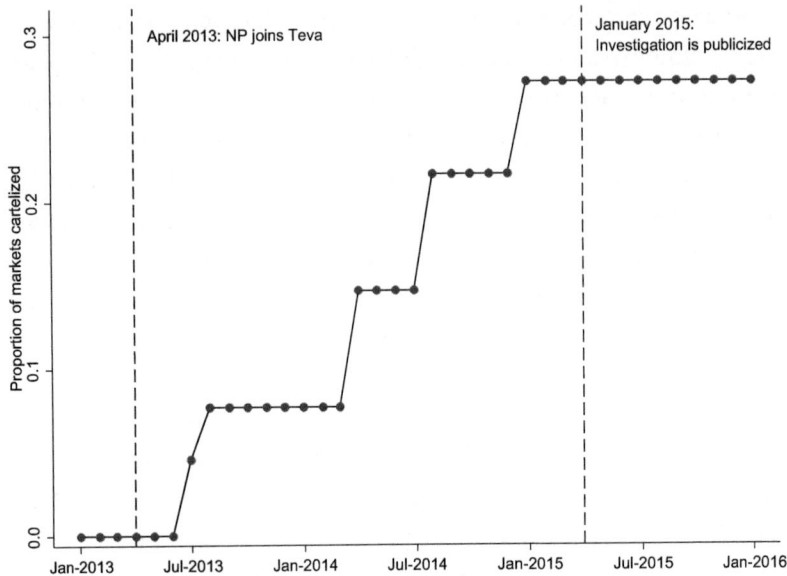

FIGURE 1.1 Price increases rollout over eighteen months.
In this figure, we plot the cumulative proportion of drug markets that have been cartelized on the y-axis against calendar quarter on the x-axis. We date market cartelization by the month of the first price increase. The proportion is calculated with respect to all drugs manufactured by Teva in the first quarter of 2013, which is the period that immediately precedes NP joining the firm. Source: Authors' calculations from the Complaint and FDA's National Drug Code Directory.

presumably reflecting frequent interactions in her prior role. For example, due to her relationships with executives later named in the complaint, Taro, Mylan, Sandoz, and Upsher-Smith all received scores of 3. Next, NP ranked each drug produced by Teva based on these scores and "certain other factors" (Complaint, page 162). On May 24, she selected a subset of drugs, entered them in a spreadsheet titled "Immediate [Price Increase] File," and sent the document to her superiors. Finally, on July 3, in concert with other cartel members, Teva began announcing price increases.

Figure 1.1 illustrates how the price increases rolled out across markets over time. The first round occurred just four months after NP joined Teva and was followed almost immediately by more price increases the following month. The final round occurred eighteen months later, just prior to when NP learned that state and federal investigators were scrutinizing the cartel members' behavior (see Section 1.4). After the initial two rounds, the remaining rounds were evenly spaced, with the exception that no increases occurred between September 2013 and March 2014. According to the Complaint, the hiatus has an obvious explanation: NP was on maternity leave at this time. The cartel increased the prices of 122 drugs altogether, or in 29 percent of the markets in which Teva operated just prior to NP joining the firm.

1.3.1 Drug-Specific Determinants of Collusion

Since Teva was active in a large number of heterogeneous markets when it hired NP, our setting provides a rare opportunity to study determinants of collusion with rich variation across markets in terms of their characteristics. We focus our attention on two of these determinants, the number and average "quality" of the other firms in the market. Both criteria differ across markets, and they should affect the dynamic incentives associated with maintaining collusion. Moreover, both were carefully considered by NP when she selected markets to cartelize, which is evident from internal communications presented in the Complaint.

Market structure may be correlated with firms' ability to initiate and sustain collusion (Harrington, 2017). Since an illegal collusive scheme cannot be enforced by binding contracts, firms must rely on dynamic incentives to enforce compliance. Successful collusion entails raising price above competitive levels, which creates a short run incentive to cheat and undercut one's co-conspirators. A collusive scheme will be stable if cheating is detected and punished relatively quickly, limiting the gains from cheating. Punishment might involve the collapse of the agreement, thereby relinquishing future collusive profits. The more firms in a market, the greater are the gains from cheating relative to the consequent foregone share of future collusive profits, and hence the less likely is a cartel to form.

The role of rival "quality" in supporting collusion is less standard. However, the literature on the formation of trading relationships in the absence of legally enforceable contracts is related. Greif (1993) and Greif et al. (1994) describe how establishing reputations and sharing information within a coalition might facilitate contract enforcement absent legal recourse. The strength of relationships is highlighted in the Complaint:

> From September 17–19, for example, high-level executives from Defendants Teva, Apotex, Actavis, Amneal, Lannett, Par, Zydus and others were invited to a gathering at a country club in Bowling Green, Kentucky where they would play golf all day and socialize at night ... At the conclusion of the outing, one of the executives – Defendant [KO] – sent an e-mail to the other attendees, stating: "This is a crazy biz but I am grateful to have friends like all of you!!!! Happy and honored to have you all as 'fraternity brothers.'"
> *(Complaint, page 31)*

To study these relationships, we base our analysis on information that is similar to what NP had available to her at the time she decided which markets to cartelize. Mirroring her selection process, our analysis is at the drug level. Sales data yields the list of drugs produced by Teva in early 2013 and the market shares of each firm, while the Complaint reports the competition quality score assigned to each firm and the list of drugs for which prices were fixed. Using this information, we calculate the average competition quality of each drug and the number of firms (other than Teva) that manufacture the drug, and we construct an indicator for collusion.

In Table 1.1, we report how the probability of collusion varies with the composition and number of other firms in the market. Two important patterns emerge. First, cartelization is much more likely to form in a market where NP has strong relationships. For instance, consider markets in which Teva and up to two other firms are present. Cartels form in 86 percent of the markets where NP assigns the other drugmakers her highest competition quality of score of 3. Yet, cartels

Table 1.1 *The probability of collusion varies with the number and composition of active firms*

Competition quality	Number of active firms			
	1 other	2 others	3 others	4+ others
{−3, −2, −1}	15% (13)	15% (20)	15% (20)	15% (27)
0	22% (9)	38% (21)	31% (13)	12% (33)
1	57% (7)	50% (24)	28% (18)	17% (23)
2	50% (8)	57% (14)	67% (6)	0% (6)
3	85% (13)	89% (9)	60% (5)	0% (1)

The sample consists of drugs manufactured by Teva in the first quarter of 2013. The row variable measures the quality of the competition (i.e., the strength of NP's relationships with the other producers of the drug). The column variable measures the number of firms other than Teva that produce the drug. To compute quality, we (a) start with the scores assigned to each firm by NP, (b) calculate their average at the drug-quarter level, weighted by the firms' market shares, and (c) select the maximum value between the quarter NP is hired and the quarter the government's investigation is publicized. The quarter that corresponds to the maximum value is the quarter for which we calculate the number of active firms. Each cell contains the proportion of markets that were cartelized. Alongside it, we report the number of markets in the cell. Source: Authors' calculations from the Complaint and the FDA's National Drug Code Directory and Orange Book.

form in only 22 percent of the markets with negative competition quality scores. Second, cartelization is much more likely to form in a market with fewer drugmakers. To illustrate, consider markets to which NP assigns positive average competition quality. Cartels form in 68 percent of the markets with just one other firm, 59 percent of markets with two others, 45 percent of markets with three others, and just 13 percent of markets with four or more others.

Consistent with these findings, new opportunities to form cartels arose over time when drug makers' competition quality scores were revised upwards. Leadership changes at rival drug makers' sales departments provided one source of these revisions. For example, NP originally assigned Zydus a competition quality score of –3. This score was sufficiently low that the firm's presence effectively precluded collusion, as evidenced by Table 1.1. However, in November 2013, KP, a colleague of NP at Teva, moved to Zydus, prompting her to raise the firm's competition quality score to +2. Clarithromycin ER tablets, Warfarin sodium tablets, and Topiramate Sprinkle capsules were included in the next round of price increases. All three were produced by both Teva and Zydus.

1.3.2 *Industry-Wide Factors Conducive to Collusion*

As just described, variation in the traits of drug markets can help explain variation in cartelization. At the same time, there are many factors conducive to collusion which were common to all generic drug markets.

1. **Firms compete mostly on price via manipulable procurement auctions.** The allocation mechanism is best described as a scoring auction, with buyers evaluating bids along several dimensions (e.g., fill rates, frequency of recalls, accuracy of invoices, timeliness of deliveries, and backhaul utilization) (Cardinal Health (2020)). However, many, if not all, of the non-price characteristics are pre-specified, since they reflect historical operating performance and/or large fixed capital investments. A cartel need only coordinate submission and bid decisions, and not other characteristics of the product, which simplifies its operations.
2. **Cartel members could detect "cheating" from collusive agreements quickly.** Confusion in the market for Moexipril Hydrochloride tablets provides a clear example. Teva and Glenmark cartelized the market around July 2013. On August 5, 2013, Teva learned that Glenmark undercut its price to a major distributor (apparently due to internal miscommunication within Glenmark). That afternoon, a Teva employee sent NP an email whose subject line was "Loss business on Moexipril" and whose only contents were "???". Five minutes later, NP emailed her colleague back, stating that she was aware of the loss and had "made the call already." The following day, NP spoke to her contact at Glenmark. Later that same day, Glenmark withdrew its bid to the distributor, and a

colleague of NP reported that "[t]oday is a new day and today ... [the distributor] has now informed me that they will NOT be moving the Moexipril business to Glenmark" (Complaint, page 134).

3. **Cartel members could also retaliate quickly against "bad citizenship."** Most buyers acted on their own, with procurement decisions for individual drugs spread throughout the year. The staggered letting of contracts (as opposed to all contracts for a given buyer being let together, for example) allows cartel members to adjust bidding behavior over time to allocate market shares. Together with rapid detection, swift retaliation enables the cartel to punish defection quickly, making it easier to sustain cooperation.

4. **Demand is relatively insensitive to the price charged.** Since aggregate demand is price-inelastic (Starc and Wollmann, 2022), revenues increased substantially following the 2013–2015 cartel-induced price hikes. In turn, profits rose sharply (see Cuddy (2020) and our Figure 1.2, described below). Internal documents show that Teva explicitly forecasted the effect of these price changes on cash flow (Complaint, page 221), which is presumably what motivated its employees to participate in the collusion despite the legal risk.

5. **Demand is stable.** Demand in mature generic prescription drug markets exhibits steady, acyclic growth, which ensures that threats of future retaliation in response to deviations are credible and severe.

6. **Markets are clearly defined.** Buyers define the markets, which correspond to particular drugs. For instance, internal communications reveal that simply by referencing "ranitidine tabs," everyone understands this to mean "ranitidine hydrochloride tablets in 150 or 300 milligrams." Clearly defined markets make it easier to communicate and make agreements.

7. **Entry was slow and expensive due to the regulatory approval process.** Beyond the typical setup costs associated with entry, generic drugmakers must receive substance-delivery-release specific authorization from the FDA to begin production. The entire process costs between $1 million and $12 million and takes between two and five years (Starc and Wollmann, 2022) and was exacerbated by a backlog of applications to the agency (Cuddy, 2020). If cartel nonmembers could enter quickly and cheaply, then their free-riding would reduce the profitability of collusion, and the scheme might have unraveled. (Igami and Sugaya (2022) describe such a dynamic in the context of the vitamin cartel.) The costs and delays associated with generic drug entry facilitated cartel stability.

8. **Firms have similar cost structures.** Manufacturers typically pay about the same amount for the chemical ingredients, and they use much the same technology to produce, package, and deliver. We would also expect incremental costs to be constant and similar across suppliers. The similarity of potential suppliers makes it more likely that a group of firms could come to an agreement on joint behavior.
9. **Firms have good information about competitors' costs.** Since most cost changes affect all firms similarly, there are unlikely to be substantial informational advantages in the market. Symmetric information also makes it easier to reach an agreement on joint behavior.
10. **Cartel members encounter one another in more than one market.** Contact between competitors in multiple markets means defection in one market can be punished in another, facilitating collusion (see Bernheim and Whinston, 1990). The more severely members can punish cheating, the more incentive firms will have to cooperate.
11. **Salespeople met socially on a regular basis to discuss issues of mutual interest.** According to the Complaint, agreements were refined and coordinated at regular lunches, parties, golf outings, "girls' nights out" (commonly abbreviated "GNOs" by the participants), and "Women in the Industry" dinners. Besides the exchange of competitively sensitive information, social gatherings might have caused the participants to form strong bonds, further strengthening the cartel, as illustrated by the "fraternity brothers" quotation above. Meetings could also be a place to resolve disputes, or to come to agreement about how to respond to changing market conditions.

1.4 INVESTIGATION AND GOVERNMENT LITIGATION

Shortly after the July 2014 *New York Times* article appeared, the Connecticut Attorney General's office filed subpoenas, obtaining thousands of internal documents, an "industry-wide phone call database" comprising more than 11 million records, cooperation from several as-yet-unidentified witnesses, and the assistance of forty-eight other states and US territories (Complaint, page 3). Around the same time as the states' civil investigations, the US Department of Justice opened a criminal investigation into Sherman Act violations, followed a few years later by a civil investigation into False Claims Act violations.

By early 2015, the conspirators became aware of the investigations because "the government was showing up on people's doorsteps" (Complaint, page 341). Around that time, DR, NP's superior, warned her to be careful when communicating with competitors. Following that conversation, NP deleted text messages exchanged with co-conspirators and stopped cartelizing new drug markets. According to the Complaint, the last cartel-induced price increase occurred on January 28, 2015 (see Figure 1.1).

State attorneys general have filed a series of complaints against the cartel members. The first, filed in December of 2016, targeted six firms in two markets, but concurrent public statements by investigators at the time implied that collusive conduct was more pervasive than the first claim suggested. Then-Connecticut Attorney General George Jepsen stated, "I can't stress enough this is just the tip of the iceberg" (Aiello, 2017). Consistent with his assessment, a second lawsuit – "the Complaint" – with over more than one hundred products was filed against twenty firms in May 2019. The unsealed version of the second indictment included 524 pages of internal communications acquired via the investigation, and it serves as the source text for much of the content of this chapter, as well as the academic studies by Cuddy (2020) and Starc and Wollmann (2022). A third complaint arrived just over a year later in June 2020, revealing a further conspiracy in the topical-formulation market. While most litigation is still pending as of this writing, several states – including Arkansas, Georgia, Louisiana, Mississippi, and Texas – have settled independently with certain indicted firms.

The first federal lawsuit was filed in December 2016. It charged two former Heritage executives with fixing prices, rigging bids, and allocating customers. The Justice Department subsequently obtained grand jury indictments against six other firms – Apotex, Glenmark, Rising, Sandoz, Taro, and Teva – as well as several of their senior executives. At the time of writing, many parties have settled. The two former Heritage executives and one former Sandoz executive have pled guilty. All await sentencing. Moreover, all seven firms have admitted to fixing prices of at least certain drugs in their portfolios and have agreed to both civil and criminal fines via deferred prosecution agreements. In total, the Department of Justice has collected over $681 million in criminal penalties as of August 2023. Additionally, the firms entered into five-year integrity agreements that include internal monitoring and price transparency provisions. Violations of these agreements would lead to prosecution, and if convicted, firms would be debarred from all Federal health care programs. Additional federal and civil litigation is also ongoing (Department of Justice, 2023).

1.5 CARTEL EFFECTS

Once the cartel became active in mid- to late-2013, its members immediately began increasing prices by manipulating the outcomes of retailer procurement auctions for drug products in the portfolios of cartel members. Executives coordinated significant increases through a flurry of communication. They met their "fair share" market allocation objective by divvying up "the market for an individual drug based on the number of competitors and the timing of their entry so that each competitor obtains an acceptable share of the market" (Complaint, pages 39–40). Then, with winners predesignated, they raised prices via bid rotation and cover bidding.

With the drugs marketed jointly by cartel members numbering in the hundreds, the collusive scheme led to an immediate divergence in price from the drugs still subject to competitive pricing. Figure 1.2 plots the changes over calendar time of average drug prices in Teva's portfolio, differentiating between drugs now identified as collusive targets and those that were not. Before 2013, all markets – including those that were to be cartelized and those that were not – experienced similar price declines, on the order of 8 percent per year. Prices in uncartelized markets continued to fall after 2013, by approximately 20 percent through 2017. In contrast, the average price of cartelized drugs increased more than 30 percent between 2013 and 2015, and remained high thereafter. The relative price of drugs in cartelized markets therefore increased by 50 percent by 2015.

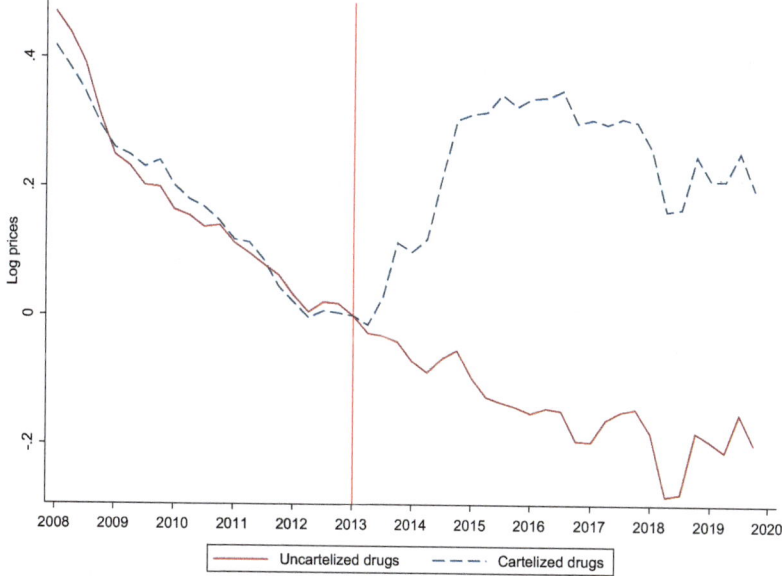

FIGURE 1.2 The cartel increased the prices of cartelized drugs by an average of 50 percent.

In this figure, we plot log prices on the y-axis against calendar time on the x-axis. The sample consists of all drugs manufactured by Teva in the first quarter of 2013. Prices are normalized to zero in that period, which is marked with a vertical line. Log prices are an unweighted average across drugs within each group. If each drug is weighted by the number of prescriptions filled in the year prior to NP joining Teva, similar price paths are observed, at least until 2015. Starting around 2016, the weighted average price of cartelized drugs falls faster than the unweighted price due to cartel-induced entry, which primarily occurs in large markets (see section 7). Source: Authors' calculations from the Complaint, Medicaid State Drug Utilization Data, and IQVIA's National Prescription Audit.

Given these large price increases, what were the likely effects and by whom were they borne? The initial effects were predominantly financial and concentrated among the firms that purchased drugs from these collusive firms, that is, large pharmacy chains and wholesalers. However, the harm eventually spread down the vertical supply chain, including payers. As a result, the price hikes affected numerous market participants and yielded both financial and non-financial repercussions. We describe this progression next.

1.5.1 Initial Effects

Quantifying the effects from the cartel's activities depends crucially on the extent to which one can plausibly estimate what prices would have been in the absence of any collusive activity. So far, both structural and reduced form approaches have been used to evaluate financial effects.

Cuddy (2020) adopts a structural approach, modeling the retail drug procurement process itself, where generic manufacturers bid to supply national pharmacies and wholesalers with their drugs. She estimates the model using an estimator for aggregate data of firms' winning bids as captured in the monthly NADAC survey data, which allows her to estimate firms' costs of goods delivered. She uses these cost estimates to reconstruct a counterfactual competitive price series for the collusive drugs. With this price series, she can quantify the extent of overcharge among a large set of drugs affected by the collusive ring's activities and also determine how the FDA's concurrent application backlog may have exacerbated these effects.

Among her sample of over one hundred collusive markets, she estimates total effects exceeding $12 billion over the eighteen months when the cartel was documented as most active – July 2013 to January 2015. As in Clark et al. (2021), she finds that there is significant dispersion in the amount of overcharge across markets: from negligible (or even negative) to nearly 4000 percent. On average, the unweighted average (median) overcharge is nearly 350 (60) percent. As shown in Figure 1.3, she demonstrates how the dispersion in price effects translates to dispersion in annual expenditures effects across collusive drug markets.

In their analysis, Clark et al. (2021) adopt a reduced-form approach, leveraging quarterly Medicaid data from 2011 to 2018 and a difference-in-differences methodology using a group of carefully selected competitive control drugs. They focus on six solid-dose drug markets (doxycycline monohydrate, meprobamate, nystatin,

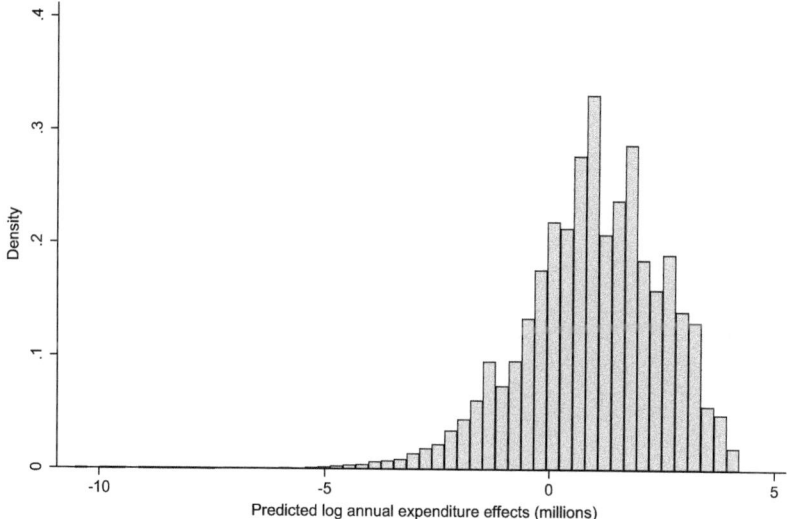

FIGURE 1.3 Estimated effects on annual expenditures across collusive drug markets, 2012–2015.

In this figure, the distribution of simulated effects across collusive drug markets is plotted. Source: Authors' calculations from the Complaint, FDA's National Drug Code Directory and Orange Book, and the pharmacy claims of a large private health insurance provider. See Cuddy (2020) for more detail.

paromomycin, theophylline, and verapamil). They estimate that collusion led to price increases of between 0 percent and 166 percent for each of the six drugs and damages of between $0 and $3 million for the Medicaid market, which are consistent with the product-level estimates from Cuddy (2020).

Of course, the immediate losses to direct purchasers were the immediate gains to cartel members. Profitability estimates are unavailable for the universe of cartel members, but the available evidence confirms that they enjoyed historic profits upon the instigation of their illegal operation. Figure 1.4 shows the profit margins over calendar time for the generic drug divisions of three key cartel members, Teva, Mylan, and Actavis. The profit margins all increased substantially after 2013. The reported margins understate the increase in profit margins in cartelized markets, insofar as the measures are average margins across all markets served by the colluding firms.

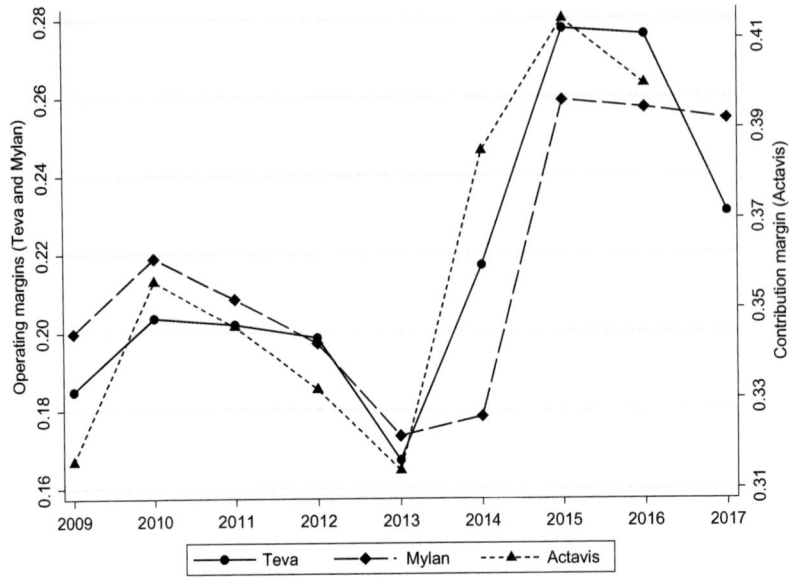

FIGURE 1.4 Profit margins for major generic drugmakers rise sharply upon cartel formation.

In this figure, profit margins are plotted in calendar time for the generic drug divisions of key cartel members. The primary y-axis measures operating income as a percentage of sales, which Teva and Mylan report, while the secondary y-axis measures "contribution" as a percentage of sales, which Actavis reports. Operating income equals net sales less the cost of goods sold, selling and marketing expenses, and research and development expenditures. Contribution is similarly defined except that all R&D costs and certain product costs (i.e., impairments of intangibles related to product rights) are explicitly excluded. Actavis was acquired in 2016, so results of its operations are not available for 2017. Mylan reports firm-wide rather than generic drug division profit margins, but generics account for the vast majority of its sales. Source: Authors' calculations from annual reports filed by Teva, Mylan, and Actavis with the Securities Exchange Commission.

Another striking implication of Figure 1.4 is the extended time frame for elevated manufacturer profits. It suggests that the effects were likely not confined to the aforementioned effects on direct purchasers of the collusive drugs. Recall that payments to pharmacies are based on an ingredient cost (plus a dispensing fee), which reflects the average acquisition cost in the market, albeit with a lag. Accordingly, over time reimbursement schemes adjust to the new, collusive market price, and upon adjustment, the direct purchasers pass on the price increases to third-party payers, ranging from the government (both state and federal) to private insurers, which are the next link in the vertical supply chain. While it is still too early to estimate empirically the extent of pass-through to third-party payers and, in turn, consumers, we next discuss how they may have been affected.

1.5.2 Pass-Through Effects

Existing reimbursement rules for generic drugs meant that pass-through from direct purchasers to third-party payers was mechanical, even if it took some time to phase in. A natural question, therefore, is why private insurers were not more attuned to the possibility of such price hikes and more strategic in their reimbursement contracting.

One obvious explanation is that generic drug price instability may not have been a first-order managerial concern before 2014. Despite large price hikes on a subset of drugs in the years preceding the creation of the cartel, generic drugs had been a "good deal" overall. Only 5 percent of generic drugs experienced price increases greater than 1 percent in 2013 (Joyce et al., 2018). The average price of a generic prescription actually decreased between 2006 and 2015 in both Medicare and Medicaid. Simultaneously, the use of generics had been increasing over time just as branded drug prices were rising, leading to greater savings relative to branded competitors (Congressional Budget Office, 2022). In a single high-profile example, several drugs for the treatment of Hepatitis C were released during our time period that cost the Medicare Part D program $4.7 billion – nearly four percent of the total annual program spending. Unsurprisingly, several payers noted in financial documents shortly thereafter that controlling *specialty* drug spending, rather than generic drug spending, was an important strategic goal.[8]

---

[8] United Health Care 2013 10-K.

That said, there was some awareness of potential issues in the generic market. At least one payer remarked that "in recent years, there has been significant consolidation within the generic manufacturing industry, and it is possible that this dynamic may enhance the ability of manufacturers to sustain or increase pricing of generic pharmaceuticals and diminish our ability to negotiate reduced acquisition costs," indicating awareness of the threat of rising prices.[9] This is especially important as pharmacies' gross profit margins are often higher for generic drugs than branded ones (Sood et al., 2017).

What about consumers? To what extent could rising upstream drug prices translate to higher out-of-pocket costs? This is an important question for at least two reasons. On the one hand, the demand side may discipline price increases and restrain the cartel. On the other hand, consumers may reduce drug consumption in response to higher out-of-pocket costs, even if doing so puts them at risk of negative health consequences.[10]

To quantify the potential scope of out-of-pocket changes, we need to understand the source and nature of prescription drug coverage. Nearly 18 percent of Americans have coverage through the Medicaid program, which has limited cost sharing because of its low-income enrollees (Keisler-Starkey and Bunch, 2021). Out-of-pocket costs will not increase for this group. Another 18 percent of people are eligible for Medicare, which subsidizes private drug coverage through Medicare Part D (Keisler-Starkey and Bunch, 2021). A recent study notes that, initially, a "relatively small portion of the price increases was passed on directly to Medicare beneficiaries in the form of higher out-of-pocket costs" (Joyce et al., 2018). This may change over time, as plans change formularies (the list of covered drugs) or move from fixed copayments to coinsurance (i.e., a fixed percentage of the upstream price).

---

[9] CVS 2013 10-K.
[10] See, e.g., Chandra et al. (2021) in the context of out-of-pocket increases in Medicare and Barkley (2022) in the context of cartel-induced insulin price increases in Mexico.

Outside of public health insurance, the majority of Americans obtain privately sponsored coverage from their employers. Most employer-sponsored plans have prescription drug coverage (Kaiser Family Foundation, 2020). These plans typically include tiered cost sharing with generic drugs on the "lowest" (cheapest) tier, as insurers want to encourage their use. Fixed dollar copayments are the most common form of cost sharing. In the case of copayments, consumers will be insured against upstream price increases. Of course, payers may increase premiums and employers may reduce wages in response to higher drug costs.

Taken together, our description of the supply chain illuminates the incidence of price increases. In the short- to medium-run, variable profits fall for the companies who are direct purchasers. Over time, price indices will evolve to account for rising prices, and insurers will face rising prices for generic drugs. We note that both government and private insurers face these rising costs but may react differently. In particular, private insurers may respond by altering plan design, such that a subset of consumers face higher out-of-pocket costs. From an economic perspective, it is interesting to note that while direct purchasers may switch suppliers, the aggregate demand response is likely to be small. This has a countervailing impact on welfare, as it limits the possible negative health consequences while implying a limited ability to discipline the cartel.

1.6 MARKET-BASED REMEDIES

Cooperatively raising prices to the extent shown in Figure 1.2 can clearly affect drugmakers' incentives. Stigler (1964) argues these changes tend to work toward mitigating harm caused by the cartel, giving the market a natural safeguard against collusive behavior. Two such mechanisms exist. One involves secret deals, that is, discounts off the collusive price. Conceptually, as a cartel hikes price, each unit sold generates greater profit, so members' incentives to undercut one another in an effort to win additional business rise as well. However, as we discussed in Section 1.3.2, cheating is unprofitable in generic drug markets because detection and retaliation are almost immediate. Consistent with this view, if one holds the number of suppliers fixed, then collusive prices are very stable in the years following the formation of the cartel. The other mechanism involves entry. Conceptually, when a cartel raises a price, it also makes the market more attractive to entrants, whose efforts to gain market share may undermine the members' agreement. Starc and Wollmann (2022) find that entry plays an important role in the evolution of cartelized generic drug markets. Three patterns in the data support this claim.

The first relates to the filing of Abbreviated New Drug Applications (ANDAs). For background, generic manufacturers must file a drug-specific ANDA to the Food and Drug Administration and gain the agency's approval before entering a market. Thus, ANDA filings provide the most immediate measure of entry. Similar to the path of prices plotted in Figure 1.2, ANDA filings for cartelized and uncartelized drugs track closely prior to NP joining Teva but diverge sharply thereafter, with cartelized markets experiencing a 30–40 percent increase in this measure of entry compared to uncartelized markets.

Second, entrants faced long delays. For example, between 2013 and 2019, the time from ANDA filing to approval typically exceeded two years. As a result, most cartelized markets did not experience *actual entry* until three to five years after cartel formation. An interesting exception, though, are markets with "dormant" ANDAs.[11] In these cases, the drug manufacturer is not currently active in the market but is authorized to manufacture the drug, so it could restart production at any time. Cartel formation induced almost immediate re-entry in many of these cases, but there were a limited number of firms holding inactive approvals (Starc and Wollmann, 2022).

The third relates to price effects. In theory, entry can destabilize cartels, precipitating their demise. This idea is not without precedent.

---

[11] Firms often obtain approval to produce a drug and begin manufacturing it, but then discontinue production, presumably because it is no longer profitable.

For instance, Igami and Sugaya (2022) argue that expansion of production by fringe entrants employing nascent technology caused some vitamin cartels to unravel in the 1990s. However, absent a competitive advantage on the part of potential entrants, such as lower costs, entrants are unlikely to earn economic profits if their entry causes the cartel to collapse and prices revert to competitive levels. (If such entry were profitable under competitive prices, then it would have been profitable prior to cartel formation, so it would have occurred already.) Alternatively, entrants could be brought into existing collusive agreements, resulting in little to no price effect. This scenario is equally unlikely, since NP lacked relationships with about two-thirds of post-cartel entrants. Finally, the cartel could survive entry, with entrants' behavior resembling that of incumbents. Since nonmembers best respond to cartel prices, one can reasonably expect prices to decline.

Empirically, entry exerted downward pressure on prices. One way to illustrate the effect of entry is to restrict attention to cartelized drugs and compare small markets to large ones. Since the decision to enter hinges on whether the discounted sum of expected future profits exceeds up-front investments, large markets should experience more entry than small ones whereas their price paths absent entry should not otherwise differ. If entry disciplines cartel prices but most entrants experience delays, then one should observe two patterns in the data. First, directly after cartel formation, the average prices of small- and large-market drugs should rise by similar amounts. Second, several years after cartel formation, the average price in small markets, which experience little entry, should remain stable, while average prices in large markets, which experience significant entry, should decline substantially. Starc and Wollmann (2022) show that entrants are drawn almost exclusively to large markets, and that prices exhibit both of the aforementioned patterns.

1.7 AFTERMATH

In light of the tremendous profits earned by cartel members and the price effects suffered by their customers, it is not surprising that in addition to the government proceedings described above, private parties have also sought damages under antitrust laws. For example, direct purchasers such as Kroger and other grocery chains as well as health insurers like Humana and UnitedHealthcare are currently suing Mylan, Teva, Endo, and other manufacturers. The plaintiffs allege that the defendants conspired to "fix, increase, stabilize, or maintain prices of the specified generic pharmaceutical drugs." At the time of writing this case study, the litigation is ongoing.

Legal action has also expanded beyond downstream buyers. Taro shareholders argued that the firm misled investors. The lawsuit states, "Defendants repeatedly told investors that 'Taro's sales and earnings growth [was] attributable to upward price adjustments and a prudent lifecycle management of [the Company's] product portfolio[;]' that '[t]here [was] a very strong market mechanism which we believe is fully in operation[;]' and that margins 'largely depend[ed] on competitive intensity which is not in our hands' while Defendants knew or recklessly disregarded that Taro was fixing prices – eliminating competition between the Conspirators for the Drugs" (brackets in original text). Further, it alleges that defendants "concealed the fact that they were threatening the Company with substantial liabilities from Taro's ongoing antitrust violations" (*Speakes* v. *Taro Pharmaceutical Industries et al.*, 2017).

Outside of the legal system, both direct purchasers and private insurers have amended contracts in an effort to hasten the pass-through of manufacturer-induced price increases. As noted above, both wholesale prices and maximum allowable charges evolve over time, shifting the burden of price increases. Small pharmacies are especially supportive of policy change, perhaps because they are the most likely to experience short-run damages. For example, the National Community Pharmacists Association has supported a wide range of reforms (National Community Pharmacists Association). Among these are the new maximum allowable cost (MAC) transparency rules, which require clear criteria for inclusion in MAC lists and frequent updating. Updating MACs is especially important for pharmacies in the event that anti-competitive manufacturer behavior leads to sudden price increases. On the insurer side, many generic drugs have been moved to higher tiers over time where coinsurance – rather than copayments – applies (Sloan and Young, 2021). In addition, more consumers are now in high-deductible health plans. While only 20 percent of workers were in HDHPs in 2013, the number has increased to approximately 30 percent in 2020 (Kaiser Family Foundation, 2021).

What about the drugmakers' response? Did the discovery of the cartel cause it to unravel? While the government's investigations stopped new cartels from forming, it does not appear to have affected existing collusive agreements. As Figure 1.2 shows, prices of cartelized drugs were relatively stable throughout the investigatory period, and, as Figure 1.4 shows, profit margins reported by cartel members far exceeded pre-2013 levels through at least 2017. The durability of high prices despite limited potential for communication (i.e., after the firms were under surveillance) suggests that the frictions that make it difficult for firms to coordinate initially are also likely to be important in sustaining the collusive agreements (see Asker and Nocke (2021) for additional discussion). Indeed, as NP states, once coordination is achieved, "price increases tend to stick and markets settle quickly" (Complaint, page 160).

Taken together, it becomes clear that the financial effects discussed in Section 1.5 were just one dimension of the harm the cartel caused. In some sense, one could make the argument that the non-financial repercussions of the cartel's activities may yield the most lasting impact on the generic drug market. For example, the contractual adjustments to drug insurance expose far more consumers to any future short-term price volatility than ever before.

1.8 LESSONS LEARNED

The US generic drug cartel provides a unique opportunity to study the origin and impact of collusion in an economically important market. Some aspects of behavior in this market are likely to be unique to the setting. For instance, the vertical industry structure muted aggregate demand responses to price hikes. However, most aspects are common to many markets, meaning the lessons presented here apply quite broadly.

One key takeaway is that interpersonal relationships can be critical to cartel formation. In this setting, we are fortunate to observe a quantitative measure, based on a ringleader's own assessment, of how close she was to the key salesperson at each drug manufacturer. Although this factor is rarely emphasized in the economics literature, it plays a pivotal role here. Perhaps most strikingly, cartels form in about 90 percent of markets where NP has close ties to all of the other market participants, but only about 20 percent of markets where she lacks such relationships.

Another key takeaway is that the effects of collusive behavior may persist long after explicit communication between the cartel members has ended. The conspirators learned in early 2015 that they were being investigated by the government. They severely limited direct communication with one another thereafter. That response prevented new cartels from forming in other generic drug markets. However, the data strongly suggests that collusive prices persisted for many years afterwards. In all likelihood, high prices were sustained by a tacit understanding that if any cartel member were to undercut the others then the market would revert to much lower prices. This view is consistent with remarks made by the cartel ringleader, which imply that collusion is hard to initiate but easy to maintain in generic drug markets. Given the estimated magnitude of the damages between 2013 and 2015, sustained price fixing probably produced significant additional harm.

Finally, our setting illustrates that cartels attract entrants that undercut collusive prices, in an effort to gain market share. However, it also highlights the limitations of entry in regulated markets, where firms must endure high costs and long delays before beginning production. As a result, many cartelized markets did not attract any entry, and in markets that did attract entry typically two to four years passed before entrants began production. Notably, the FDA has introduced reforms that aim to reduce the entrance delay, which have resulted in the elimination of 90 percent of the pre-2017 backlog of ANDAs. However, new ANDA applications also grew rapidly, so backlogs persist.

REFERENCES

Aiello, C. (2017) "Connecticut AG on Generic Drug Price-Fixing Suit: 'this is just the tip of the iceberg,'" CNBC, October. www.cnbc.com/2017/10/31/connecticut-ag-on-generic-drug-suitjust-the-tip-of-the-iceberg.html.

Alpert, A., M. Duggan, and J. K. Hellerstein. (2013) Perverse Reverse Price Competition: Average Wholesale Prices and Medicaid Pharmaceutical Spending. *Journal of Public Economics*, 108, 44–62.

Asker J. and V. Nocke (2021) *Collusion, Mergers, and Related Antitrust Issues*. Handbook of Industrial Organization, volume 5, Elsevier, 177–279.

Barkley, A. (2022) "The Human Cost of Collusion: Health Effects of a Mexican Insulin Cartel." Working paper.

Berndt, E. R., R. M. Conti, and S. J. Murphy (2017) The Landscape of US Generic Prescription Drug Markets, 2004–2016. Working Paper 23640, National Bureau of Economic Research.

Cardinal Health (2020) "Manufacturer Reference Manual." www.cardinalhealth.com/content/dam/corp/web/documents/Manual/cardinalhealth-pharma-supplier-guidebook.pdf.

Center for Drug Evaluation and Research (2019) "New Evidence Linking Greater Generic Competition and Lower Generic Drug Prices." www.fda.gov/about-fda/center-drug-evaluation-and-research-cder/generic-competition-and-drug-prices.

Chandra, A., E. Flack, and Z. Obermeyer (2021) The Health Costs of Cost-Sharing. Working Paper 28439, February, National Bureau of Economic Research.

Clark, R., C. A. Fabiilli, L. Lasio, et al. (2021) Collusion in the US Generic Drug Industry. Working Paper 1474, Queen's University.

Congressional Budget Office (2022) "Prescription Drugs: Spending, Use, and Prices." www.cbo.gov/system/files/2022-01/57050-Rx-Spending.pdf.

Connecticut et al. v. Teva Pharmaceuticals USA Inc. et al. (2019) "1 F. Supp. 160 D. Conn.., 2019)." https://ag.ny.gov/sites/default/files/gdms_complaint_5.10.19._final_redacted_public_version.pdf.

Cuddy, E. (2020) "Competition and Collusion in the Generic Drug Market," Working paper, Mimeo.

Department of Justice (2023) "Major Generic Drug Companies to Pay Over Quarter of a Billion Dollars to Resolve Price-Fixing Charges and Divest Key Drug at the Center of Their Conspiracy. The United States Department of Justice." www.justice.gov/opa/pr/major-generic-drug-companies-pay-over-quarter-billion-dollars-resolve-price-fixing-charges.

Greif, A. (1993) "Contract Enforceability and Economic Institutions in Early Trade: The Maghribi Traders' Coalition," *The American Economic Review*, 525–548.

Greif, A., P. Milgrom, and B. R. Weingast (1994) "Coordination, Commitment, and Enforcement: The Case of the Merchant Guild," *Journal of Political Economy*, 102(4), 745–776.

Harrington, J. Jr. (2017) The Theory of Collusion and Competition Policy, MIT Press.

Igami, M. and T. Sugaya (2022) "Measuring the Incentive to Collude: The Vitamin Cartels, 1990–99," *The Review of Economic Studies*, 89(3), 1460–1494.

Joyce, G., L. E. Henkhaus, L. Gascue, and J. Zissimopoulos (2018) "Generic Drug Price Hikes and Out-of-Pocket Spending for Medicare Beneficiaries," *Health Affairs*, 37(10), 1578–1586.

Kaiser Family Foundation (2020) "Employer Health Benefits Survey: Prescription Drug Benefits." www.kff.org/report-section/ehbs-2020-section-9-prescription-drug-benefits/.

Kaiser Family Foundation (2020) "Employer Health Benefits Survey - Section 8: High-Deductible Health Plans with Savings Option." www.kff.org/report-section/ehbs-2020-section-8-high-deductible-health-plans-with-savings-option/.

Keisler-Starkey, K. and L. N. Bunch (2020) Health Insurance Coverage in the United States: Sep 2021. https://usatrade.census.gov/content/dam/Census/library/publications/2021/demo/p60-274.pdf.

Kroger Co. et al. v. Actavis Holdco U.S. et al. (2018) "1 F. Supp. 2 (E.D. Pa., 2018)." https://s3.amazonaws.com/assets.fiercemarkets.net/grocerylawsuit.pdf.

National Community Pharmacists Association. "PBM Reform. NCPA. URL." https://ncpa.org/pbm-reform.

NCSL Health Program (2019) "Generic Drug Substitution Laws." www.ncsl.org/portals/1/documents/health/Generic_Drug_Substitution_Laws_32193.pdf.

Office of the Connecticut Attorney General (2020) "Attorney General Tong Leads Coalition Filing 3rd Complaint in Ongoing Antitrust Price-Fixing Investigation into Generic Drug Industry." Press release, Office of the Connecticut Attorney General.

Pazniokas, M. (2019) "Drug Price-Fixing Lawsuit Pushes CT Probe Into National Spotlight." *CT Post*, May.

Rosenthal. E. (2014) "Rapid Price Increases for Some Generic Drugs Catch Users by Surprise." *New York Times*, July.

Sloan C. and J. Young (2021) "For the First Time, a Majority of Generic Drugs Are on Non-Generic Tiers in Part D." *Avalere Health*, June. https://avalere.com/insights/for-the-first-time-a-majority-of-generic-drugs-are-on-non-generic-tiers-in-part-d.

Sood, N., T. Shih, K. V. Nuys, and D. Goldman (2017) "The Flow of Money through the Pharmaceutical Distribution System." Health Affairs Blog,.

Speakes v. Taro Pharmaceutical Industries et al. (2017) "F. Supp. 8 (S.D.N.Y, 2017)." https://storage.courtlistener.com/recap/gov.uscourts.nysd.464413/gov.uscourts.nysd.464413.29.0.pdf.

Starc, A. and A. Swanson (2021) "Preferred Pharmacy Networks and Drug Costs." *American Economic Journal: Economic Policy*, 13(3), 406–46.

Starc, A. and T. G. Wollmann (2022) "Does Entry Remedy Collusion? Evidence from the Generic Prescription Drug Cartel." Working Paper 29886, National Bureau of Economic Research.

Stigler, G. J. (1964) "A Theory of Oligopoly." *The Journal of Political Economy*, 72(1), 44–61.

2 "Now You Are Asking for a Real War!"

*Private Alarm Systems in Norway**

Kurt Brekke and Lars Sørgard

2.1 INTRODUCTION

More than 20 percent of private homes in Norway have an alarm system (approx. 400,000 homes), which happens to be one of the highest penetration rates in the world.[1] During the years 2008–2011, the private alarm market experienced a significant consolidation through a wave of mergers and acquisitions. The market structure became essentially a duopoly comprising companies Sector and Verisure with a joint market share of more than 80 percent that increased to over 90 percent, and a Herfindahl index of almost 4500 (at the national level) by 2019. While there is local geographic variation, Sector and Verisure are both present in most regions across Norway.

In June 2017 the Norwegian Competition Authority (NCA) did a dawn raid at the premises of Sector and Verisure. Essentially based on extensively documented direct communications between the two companies' CEOs, the investigation revealed a collusive market-sharing agreement. The market sharing was related to door sales, which is a key marketing channel in the private alarm market. More

---

* We are indebted to Joseph Harrington and Maarten Pieter Schinkel for very helpful comments to earlier drafts. Disclaimer: Both authors were at the Norwegian Competition Authority (NCA) during the investigation of the cartel case presented in this case study. Sørgard was Director General (2016–2022) and Brekke was Chief Economist (2016–2020). Views and opinions are solely those of the authors and should not be attributed to the NCA. The same applies to possible errors in describing the case.

[1] This information is reported in the NCA's decision letter dated November 25, 2020, which can be downloaded at www.konkurransetilsynet.no.

specifically, the two companies had agreed to abstain from door sales to private homes marked with the rival company's sign indicating it provided alarm services. Deviation from the agreement was detected by monitoring customer churn across the private alarm companies (and, in two instances, when a Verisure sales representative knocked on the door of the home of Sector's CEO!).

The NCA found that Sector and Verisure had violated the prohibition against harmful collusive practices (§ 10) in the Norwegian competition law, which essentially is harmonized with EU competition law (Art. 101). For this violation, which is dated from August 2011 to the dawn raid in June 2017, the NCA imposed a combined record-high fine of NOK 1.2 billion (€ 120 million) on the two companies. There was no leniency notice or settlement procedure applied in this case. Five days after the Statement of Objection in 2019, Sector announced that it would pay its fine of NOK 467 million. Verisure first challenged the NCA's decision but eventually paid the full fine of NOK 766 million after the Competition Appeal Tribunal upheld the decision in late 2021.

This cartel case offers a unique opportunity to understand how illegal collusive agreements are formed and sustained in practice. We know from economic theory that for a cartel to succeed, it has to overcome several challenges.[2] Seen in retrospect, the collusive agreement between Sector and Verisure had important prerequisites for success. First, external instability was not a serious threat. Shortly before the cartel formed, the private alarm market had effectively turned into a duopoly by a series of acquisitions, and entry (or expansion) of potential competitors was deterred by an aggressive customer win-back strategy by both companies. Second, the market-sharing rule was simple and transparent. Door sales was the key sales channel to private homes. Homes fitted with an alarm system were marked with highly visible logo shields of the alarm company, which were meant to deter burglars.

---

[2] See, for instance, the overview in Harrington (2023).

After the series of mergers prior to the start of the cartel, Verisure and Sector each had about half of the private homes with an alarm system under contract. By abstaining from knocking on doors marked with the rival company's sign, the two companies implemented a simple and effective market allocation scheme. As far as we know, the two companies never coordinated on prices; they simply agreed not to poach each other's customers using the door sales channel.

The remaining challenge for Sector and Verisure was making sure the collusive agreement was internally stable. Given a market-sharing arrangement, it is always tempting to deviate by stealing a customer from the rival. To understand how the two companies managed to ensure internal stability of their collusive agreement, we will examine in detail the extensive communications between the CEOs. We will also describe the various measures that Sector and Verisure took to monitor compliance and how they punished deviations from the market-sharing agreement. Interestingly, there are two episodes of collusion breakdown, or "war" (as it was referred to by the CEOs), during the cartel period, which helps us understand what can trigger a punishment phase and how companies manage to re-establish the collusive outcome.

This chapter is structured as follows. Section 2.2 describes the industry and how the cartel started. Section 2.3 presents briefly the core elements of internal stability for cartels in general, the challenges in this case, and how the two firms communicated. With that as background, Section 2.4 examines the communication, monitoring, and punishment observed in this cartel case in the context of the criteria for internal stability. Finally, Section 2.5 concludes with the lessons learned from this case study and a discussion on implications for competition policy in detecting collusive market-sharing agreements.

2.2 THE INDUSTRY AND HOW IT ALL STARTED

The market for alarm systems in Norway has been growing sharply in the past few decades and achieved an annual turnover in 2021 of more than NOK 2.4 billion (USD 240 million) or NOK 480 (USD 48) per capita.

The private and business segments of this market are quite different. Business customers require more complex equipment and services than private customers. Companies serving the business segment have higher costs, which makes them uncompetitive in the private segment. Thus, the alarm companies tend to specialize in one market segment, as is the case in the Norwegian market. Relevant to understanding this cartel, Sector and Verisure do not compete actively for business customers, and vice versa for the alarm companies in the business segment.

The private alarm market is subscription based, where customers pay (usually) a monthly fee for the alarm system and services offered by the alarm companies.[3] The package includes an installed (burglar and fire) alarm system that is connected to the company's alarm center. Most of the companies, including Sector and Verisure, have their own emergency guard team. When switching providers, the customers need to have an alarm system installed by the new provider, as the alarm systems are not compatible across providers. For new customers, the companies typically offer the installation of the alarm system for free or at subsidized prices with a minimum period contract for their security services. Thus, the switching costs for customers are low.

The key sales channel to win new customers in the alarm market is door sales. Each company has a team of traveling sales agents who visit the premises of prospective customers and knock on doors. Phone sales are also used but mainly as a reactive sales channel for customers that check alternative offers or to convince customers that are considering switching providers to stay (which is referred to as win back). Advertising can also cause consumers to approach companies for an offer.

At the start of 2008, the private alarm market in Norway comprised four large companies – Sector, Verisure (named Securitas Direct

---

[3] There exist a few smaller companies that sell alarm systems that customers can buy and install themselves, without extensive alarm services offered. These companies have a negligible market share in the private alarm market and are ignored in the case study.

Table 2.1 *Acquisitions by Sector and Verisure notified to the Norwegian Competition Authority*

Year	Acquisitions
August 2008	Verisure (Securitas Direct) acquires Hafslund (private alarm company)
December 2011	Verisure (Securitas Direct) acquires Personal Service and Sikkerhet
December 2011	Sector acquires G4S (private alarm customer portfolio)
March 2012	Sector acquires Nokas (private alarm customer portfolio)
June 2012	Sector acquires BKK Marked (private alarm customer portfolio)
June 2012	Verisure (Securitas Direct) acquires ISS Facility Service (customer portfolio)
August 2012	Verisure (Securitas Direct) acquires Vaktvesenet
May 2016	Verisure acquires Lyse Alarm
October 2016	Verisure acquires Falck Alarm

Source: Norwegian Competition Authority (www.konkurransetilsynet.no)

until 2014), Hafslund, and G4S – and a range of small companies. However, during the ensuing years, Sector and Verisure gradually acquired a series of both small and large rivals. Table 2.1 summarizes the acquisitions by the two companies that were above the merger control thresholds and thus the NCA was notified.

Among the list of acquisitions in Table 2.1, two stand out. The first is the acquisition of Hafslund's private alarm customer base by Verisure in 2008. This acquisition made Verisure by far the largest firm in the industry. Sector was the second largest, and G4S the third largest. In early 2011 the three companies had a joint market share of almost 80 percent – Verisure (43.6 percent), Sector (19.1 percent), and G4S (16.2 percent).[4]

---

[4] These market shares are for the first quarter of 2011 and were collected by the industry association NHO Service. See paragraph 155 in the SO the NCA sent to Verisure and Sector, dated 17.06.2019: Varsel-offentlig-versjon-Sector-Alarm-AS-

The second major acquisition is Sector's acquisition of G4S's private alarm customer base at the end of 2011. This acquisition essentially turned the market into a duopoly where Sector and Verisure had a joint market share of more than 80 percent with a competitive fringe of smaller rivals having the remaining 20 percent.[5] After the 2011 merger, the split of market shares between the two companies was fairly symmetric with Verisure having only a slightly larger share than Sector. By 2019 the joint market share of Verisure and Sector had increased to approximately 90 percent and become less symmetrically distributed, as Sector had 34 percent and Verisure had 56–57 percent. The third largest company was Nokas, with a market share of around 2 percent.[6]

Figure 2.1 shows that both Sector and Verisure had strong growth in sales revenues (solid lines) from 2008 to 2017, with two significant jumps. The first jump is for Verisure from 2008 to 2009, which reflects the acquisition of Hafslund. This major acquisition almost doubled the annual turnover for Verisure. The other significant jump is for Sector from 2011 to 2012, doubling the company's annual sales revenues by acquiring G4S. The sales revenues of both Sector and Verisure continued to grow in parallel, partly due to further acquisitions of smaller rivals by both companies. These mergers contributed to creating a market structure that was more conducive to collusion.

Figure 2.1 also displays the development in the two companies' earnings (EBITDA), which are reported as a percentage of sales revenues. We see that their operating profits are increasing at a faster rate

---

Isanor-Invest-AS-Verisure-AS-Verisure-Midholding-AB-ileggelse-av-overtredelsesgebyr-etter-konkurranseloven-§-29-jf.-§-10-og.pdf (konkurransetilsynet.no).

[5] The competitive fringe consists mainly of small companies with only a local geographic presence. There is one larger player, Nokas, but this company is mainly present in the business segment and had only a few private customers. These companies did not have a door-to-door salesforce like that in Sector and Verisure.

[6] Tveit and Solberg (2019) report market shares of Sector at 34 percent and Nokas at approximately 2 percent, and a Herfindahl index of 4444. Given this information, we deduce that Verisure's market share must have been 56–57 percent.

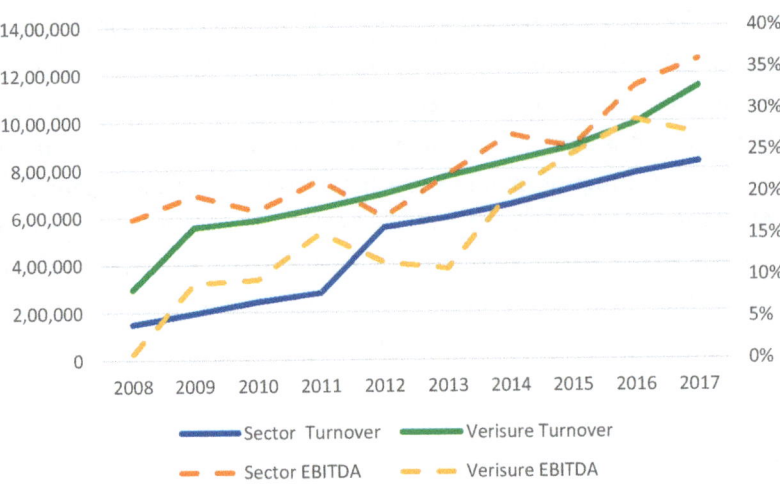

FIGURE 2.1 Turnover and EBITDA of Sector and Verisure, 2008–2017.

than their sales revenues. The increase in their earnings has been substantial for both companies over this period, as was the level of EBITDA of 30–35 percent at the end of the period. There is, however, an interesting break in this trend around 2012 and 2013, which coincides with the two periods where the collusive market-sharing agreement between Sector and Verisure breaks down ("war") before it is re-established later in 2013.

How did the collusive market-sharing practice between Sector and Verisure start? In 2009, shortly after the acquisition of Hafslund, Verisure hired a CEO, who soon after his accession launched a new sales force called SWOT. This sales force was targeted with attracting customers from rivals through door sales. While Sector had used door sales as their key sales channel since the 1990s, the establishment of SWOT in 2009 marked a more proactive door sales strategy for Verisure. The CEO of Verisure said about the launch of SWOT:

> It was a big change for Sector when Verisure went from being kind and stable to this innovation [SWOT] with very aggressive sellers.

> Verisure tripled sales in a very short time. They had a new technology [SWOT]. ... They [Verisure] were not as afraid of knocking on competitors' doors as one had been traditionally in the alarm market. They did not control so much [of the sales behavior] from the head quarter as before. ... They [Verisure] thought they would take everything and then see what the consequences were as they went forward.[7]

According to the NCA's decision, around the same time the two CEOs were in contact for the first time:

> This new approach [establishment of the SWOT team] by the biggest firm in the industry led to reaction from rivals. According to the CEO of Verisure, the CEO of Sector did early on contact him because Sector as the second largest firm was very interested in everything Verisure did.[8]

As we will describe later, this resulted in frequent, long-lasting communications between the CEOs of the two companies, involving email, phone, and even personal meetings in the coming years. Verisure's competitive move to develop more door sales contributed to cartel formation between the two companies.

Sector's new CEO from 2007 had previously worked at Hydro. According to Verisure CEO's later testimony, he came from an industry where it was common to talk with competitors.[9] In October 2009 Sector's CEO had sent an email to an employee of Verisure stating that "this is probably not in line with the industry's attitude towards 'business stealing.'"[10] This email was triggered by the fact that Verisure had started acquiring customers from Sector through door sales. After a meeting between the two CEOs in January 2010 (organized by the industry association for other legitimate purposes), Sector's CEO wrote to the chairman of the company's board: "I think

---

[7] Paragraph 142 in the NCA's decision. [8] Ibid.
[9] Paragraph 148 in the NCA's decision. [10] Paragraph 136 in the NCA's decision.

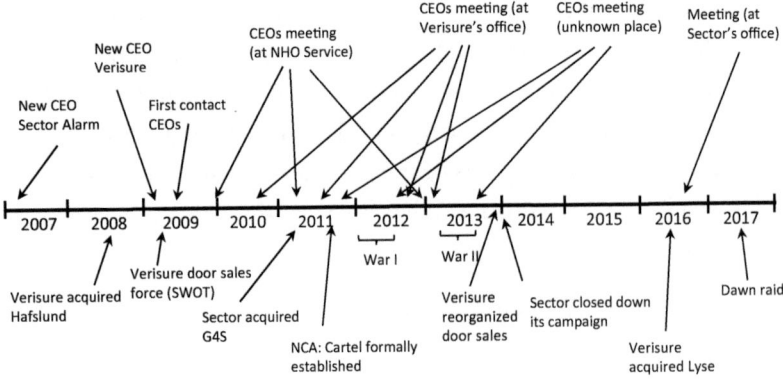

FIGURE 2.2 Timeline of documented key events and meetings between the CEOs of Sector and Verisure.

we have the right contact in Direct [Verisure] now and we agree on the rules of the game. I will handle this."[11]

After that, the two CEOs communicated frequently for years to come. They often did so through not only emails but also phone calls and face-to-face meetings. In Figure 2.2 we show a few of the important events in this industry, including the major acquisitions, periods of war, and some of the known meetings between the CEOs.

As indicated in Figure 2.2, and based on legal standard and evidence, the NCA defines the collusive market-sharing practice between Sector and Verisure to be established on August 17, 2011. The verdict refers to a fascinating start of the collusive conduct where on that day a salesperson from Verisure knocks on the door of Sector's CEO, trying to sell him a Verisure alarm. Sector's CEO immediately sends an email to Verisure's CEO informing him that his house is well marked with Sector signs and asking why they sent their salespersons to Sector's customers. Verisure's CEO responds the same evening first by asking, "Did you buy?" But then he says they had an internal ban but cannot perfectly control their salesforce, and anyhow Sector started it all by capturing Verisure's customers. However, he ends his email by conveying that they prefer to approach customers

---

[11] Paragraph 153 in the NCA's decision.

without an alarm system and not customers served by another company. The episode initiated a series of email exchanges between the two CEOs, which, according to the NCA's decision, established the collusive market-sharing agreement between Sector and Verisure that lasted until the dawn raid in 2017.

2.3 COLLUSIVE PRACTICE AND INTERNAL STABILITY

To sustain a collusive outcome, firms must agree on the specifics of one, achieve internal and external stability, and avoid detection by the competition authority. While obviously the collusive agreement between Sector and Verisure eventually failed as regards the last condition, it lasted several years.

The alarm market has features that make it easy to coordinate on a collusive outcome. Specifically, the companies are actively approaching customers, and the allocation of customers is public information for it is indicated by an external marker at a customer's home. In contrast to other retail markets, where consumers approach suppliers, there is potential for a no-poaching agreement simply by agreeing to not approach the doors of other firm's customers.

External stability was served by the pre-cartel acquisitions of many smaller rivals and the win-back strategy of Sector and Verisure. Since the market for alarm services is subscription based, the original provider would be notified if a house owner decides to switch to another provider, as this involves a termination of contract. This notification facilitates an effective monitoring of customer churn across providers. The providers are thus informed about the identity of the new supplier and can, before the subscription is canceled, give a matching offer to the customer.[12] By having such a win-back strategy, they will, in many cases, have prevented a new supplier from

---

[12] If, say, a customer of Sector cancels their subscription, a sales agent would call to ask why they canceled and try to convince them to stay on by, for instance, matching the other company's offer (i.e., win back). During this communication, the alarm company usually acquires information on whether the customer switched to Verisure or some other company, or simply chose not to have an alarm system. Case evidence revealed that this monitoring (and win back) practice was common to both companies.

capturing their customers. This aggressive strategy toward rival firms explains why the two companies did not lose market share after the cartel was established. In fact, their joint market share increased from 80 to 90 percent during the years they colluded.

The key challenge for Sector and Verisure, however, was to ensure the internal stability of the collusive agreement. The colluding firms had adopted an arrangement that incentivized compliance with the agreed-upon no-poaching outcome. This involved two key elements. First, they had a punishment for deviating from the collusive agreement and this punishment must be severe enough that the expected profits from complying with the agreement are higher than the expected profits from deviating. Second, deviations were observable to the collusive firms, so that punishment can be implemented quickly, thereby ensuring the expected profit from cheating remained low.

Monitoring is a key element of most collusive schemes as it facilitates the detection of noncompliance by a cartel member. Helpful for monitoring, the private alarm market in Norway is transparent along several dimensions, as pointed out in the NCA's decision and by the parties themselves. When a private house owner signs a contract with one of the alarm companies, the firm installs the alarm system and puts a sign on the house. The sign states explicitly that an alarm is installed in the house and names the company that provides the alarm system. Obviously, the main reason for marking the house with a sign is to deter potential burglars from breaking into the house. But, as we will see, the sign can also be used as a signal to a rival firm's sales agents to abstain from knocking on the door and move on to another house. In other words, the alarm sign on a house can be an effective coordination mechanism.

Verisure and Sector used the monitoring information of customer switches to calculate the customer churn (usually at monthly level) for their closest rivals. When a customer filed a cancelation, a sales person would contact this customer (usually by phone) before the cancelation was effective. During this conversation the sales person would ask why the customer canceled and what they could do to convince the customer to stay, such as matching a rival's offer or lowering the price. From this communication, the two companies also had a precise record of how many customers they took from their rivals. The companies also knew that the rival was monitoring customer churn. The CEO of Verisure explained it this way:

> V1 [CEO Verisure] said that he thinks that S2 [CEO Sector] knows in the same second as Securitas Direct [Verisure] stops [capturing consumers from Sector], then Sector stops losing consumers. S2 knows just as well as V1 when he loses consumers or not, it is no secret.[13]

In many markets, including the private alarm market, prices are not directly observable to rival firms, as they may be personalized or include individual rebates. In such cases, monitoring is made easier if the collusive outcome is determined as a market allocation scheme, for example assigning specific customers to each cartel member as in this particular case. Since the rivals are very small, any customer switching is very likely to be between Sector and Verisure, so each firm can assume that the loss of sales is very likely due to cheating by the other firm. But even in this case there is no guarantee that cheating took place, since it could be that some customers are leaving the market or other customers are entering the market.

With deviation effectively monitored, cartel stability also requires some prospects for a punishment taking place that would deter the firms from deviating in the first place. To make such a threat effective, several conditions should be met. First, the punishment must be simple and easy to understand, so the cartel members will know exactly what to expect and can easily calculate the consequences of cheating. Second, it should be a credible threat so each firm can expect the punishment will be imposed. Third, the

---

[13] Paragraph 382 in NCA's decision.

punishment must be tough enough to make deviation unprofitable and at the same time designed such that it is possible to return to a collusive outcome.

While the collusive agreement between Sector and Verisure was clear and simple (i.e., do not knock on doors of the rival's customers), there were some challenges with the interpretation of the customer churn data. Sales of alarm systems could be done in other ways than through door sales. It could be by phone sales or by trade fair sales, implying that there could be some customer churn, even if they complied with not knocking on the doors of the other company's customers. Thus, the churn numbers had to be interpreted with some care in terms of whether they truly reflected deviations from the market-sharing agreement.[14]

There was also a potential agency problem for the companies, as the remuneration of the sales agents was partly based on their sales volume. Thus, sales agents had an incentive to knock on all doors, including those of the rival. This could generate unintended customer churn because of lack of compliance by each company's sales force. It was particularly Verisure that had its sales force on such contracts. To deal with this challenge, the company monitored its sales agents and sent clear instructions to its sales force to avoid Sector customers. There are several telling examples of such internal communications.

2.4 CARTEL COMMUNICATIONS AND CONDUCT

So far we have explained that the collusion involved a simple coordination device which was supported by detailed monitoring. But to illustrate how they managed to punish deviations, we need to look into the communications between the two firm's CEOs. Let us first describe those communications, and then discuss the cartel's strategy concerning deviations and punishments.

---

[14] Indeed, the two companies had a lower bound of customer churn that was acceptable without any further measures like communication of threats or straightforward retaliation (such as instructing sales personnel to now knock on rival doors and offer lower prices).

2.4.1 Communications between Sector and Verisure

During 2010 the CEOs of the two companies communicated on several occasions regarding sales activities. In July 2010 the CEO of Sector was informed by his sales manager that sales agents from Verisure were knocking on Sector customers' doors and offering to pay for the disassembling of the alarm. He sent the following email to the CEO of Verisure:

> Hi! Thanks for last time we met! Got an email from my sales manager, see below. I guess it is a misunderstanding or a "creative" sales agent, but it would be nice to get it confirmed by you. So that I can reassure my organization. I wish you a nice summer.

The CEO of Verisure replied the same day:

> Hello, cannot rule out that someone in our organization has done this, but we have neither a "competitor campaign" nor such routines. Have a wonderful summer.

During 2010 and until the end of September 2011, the two CEOs complained about each other engaging in business stealing. The first known instance where they referred to a tit-for-tat response is a February 2011 email from Sector's CEO to Verisure's CEO[15]:

> We measure quite exact and if you steal ... customer from us we have to take back 1 for 1. It is unfortunate for the industry this since still ... % of the homes have no alarm in Norway and we should all concentrate on them, but it must of course be free competition.

This email was passed on from the CEO to the general management in Verisure. This activity could well reflect Verisure's sales force SWOT's periodic difficulties with reaching their sales goals. It was then tempting for them to knock on the doors of Sector's customers.

---

[15] Tit-for-tat is an expression meaning "equivalent retaliation."

In August 2011 the two CEOs communicated with each other in emails that their sales agents had a ban on knocking on the rival's customers' doors, but that this changed when they observed business stealing. On August 17 the CEO of Sector reported to the CEO of Verisure that a Verisure seller had knocked on his door (see Section 2.2). The CEO of Verisure wrote in an email to the CEO of Sector:

> ... We had an internal ban on knocking on your customers' doors until you launched a substantial business stealing. This is a situation you have initiated. We prefer to knock on new doors'

The CEO of Sector replied:

> My sellers have been ordered not to knock on houses with Verisure signs, but even though we go on doors with Hafslund signs [acquired by Verisure] which are not connected to an alarm center. So I do not agree on who initiated this.

The reference to Hafslund indicates that although the Sector CEO claimed that they abstained from knocking on doors marked with Verisure signs, he admitted that they approached Hafslund customers even after Verisure had acquired the company. Verisure considered this to be a violation of their agreement, whereas Sector argued that they approached only Hafslund customers that had not yet been switched to Verisure's alarm system and thus did not have the Verisure sign on their door.

The day after, as a response to the previous email, Sector's CEO sent an email to Verisure's CEO referring to evidence that sales agents from Verisure had approached Sector customers: "Now you are asking for a real war!" This can be seen as a signal of a possible tough punishment in response to a deviation.

The next month this aggression gradually escalated, but then suddenly calmed down so it never turned into what could be characterized as a war. The two CEOs had frequent communications about what they regarded as deviations from their collusive agreement during this period, including also a direct phone call on August 23,

2011. Internal emails at Verisure during September 2011 showed that the company implemented several measures to limit the stealing of customers from Sector.

One of the highlights of these communications is the following email from Sector's CEO to Verisure's CEO on December 6, showing that a Verisure seller for the second time knocked on the door of the CEO of Sector: "Had a seller from you on my door right now! My house is very good marked [with a Sector sign]." The CEO of Verisure responded two days later: "Hi, sorry about that, but I hope the number of such incidences is substantially reduced."

This mutual understanding was explained in an internal Verisure email from December 14, 2011:

> The big issue is to restrict our rivals from stealing our customers in a targeted way. Our action has been "an eye for eye." When Sector established their own team that knocked on [our doors], then we sent [our sales agents] that knocked on houses with signs from Sector. Here we ended up with an unofficial agreement that this is not the way we behave in this industry. That implied less active business stealing the last months.

At the end of 2011, Sector had increased its sales by acquiring the private alarm customer base of G4S, and shortly after registered a sharp increase in churn to Verisure. It turned out that Verisure sales agents were aggressively knocking on the doors of G4S customers, which Sector interpreted as a breach of their collusive agreement. In a Sector internal email, it was stated that "it is time to take off our silk gloves now." Sector responded aggressively and clearly signaled it by sending a fax to Verisure showing terminated contracts of customers that Sector had stolen from Verisure. This escalated to a full-scale war between the two companies, as illustrated by this statement by Verisure's CEO:

> At a certain point of time, a Friday afternoon, Sector sent terminated contracts to Verisure via fax, a clear signal that they

were tired of Verisure stealing costumers from them. Verisure had no campaign or so, so we thought Sector had gone nuts. We decided that we should send our terminated contracts to Sector the week after.

A sales director in Verisure explained that "this was a direct provocation ... and we responded with an all-out attack." The all-out attack came in July 2012 and is apparently in contrast with the tit-for-tat strategy. It was clearly a part of a punishment according to an internal email sent by Verisure's CEO:

> As you might know, we have an ever so small war with Sector right now. ... We cannot accept such action [by Sector], and we are running a hefty campaign in July. ... It is very important that you do not communicate anything with Sector or persons that talks to Sector, because we want them to experience great uncertainty concerning our plans and how long it will last.

The initial plan of Verisure was to have a campaign in only July, but it lasted to mid-August. Sector's CEO tried several times during this period to get in touch with Verisure's CEO, but he did not respond. In an internal email dated August 1, Verisure's CEO wrote an email to Sector's CEO saying that "I have a couple of voicemails on my phone but will not listen to them before well into August." The customer churn between the two companies peaked at a record-high level in this period. The deviations by Sector and Verisure from their collusive agreement had resulted in a fierce battle for customers.

Eventually, on August 14 the two CEOs met. Two days later the CEO of Verisure sent an internal email to his sales managers: "The Sector war has come to an end. ... The war ended 10-1 to Verisure."

We have no exact information about how the two companies succeeded in returning to the no-poaching collusive outcome after this breakdown of collusion though we do know the two CEOs met face-to-face.

At a meeting of Sector's senior management on February 26, 2013, it was decided:

> Take back the number of customers that has been stolen. . . . Inform [Verisure] so they understand what is going on. Earliest start is after April 1. Prepare a plan B in case the activity should increase.

Sector started knocking on Verisure customers' doors as of April 2, and Verisure clearly knew this according to internal emails in Verisure. In response, Verisure decided to launch a campaign to capture customers which lasted from May 1 to September 1. As of June, Verisure had an all-time high number of new consumers. At the same time, Sector was very active.

Internally, Verisure recognized that Sector had increased its capacity to fight, and on August 26, 2013 the CEOs of Sector and Verisure met to discuss whether they should end the war. On September 2, Verisure's CEO sent an internal email: "It will unfortunately not be the same speed ahead. We end our war and go into a more normal pace." After that, communication continued between the two CEOs as they conveyed a tough response if there was any escalation by the other firm.

The management team in Verisure decided on December 11, 2013 that they should change the sales organization in order to move from the current campaign to a more normal one with less active acquisition of rivals' customers. At the same time, Sector decided to scale down its campaign against Verisure starting on December 31.

From that point on and until the NCA's dawn raid in June 2017, there were no new wars between Verisure and Sector. Apparently they had in mind the experiences from the two previous wars, as illustrated by an internal email in Sector to the sales force on February 17, 2014:

> We see few cancellations now that are due to Verisure acquisitions, so we must not "pour gasoline on the fire" that starts a new war, which is not in the interest of any of us.

It is also clear that they were aware of the incentives to lie about any possible deviation. There are numerous instances where the two CEOs received some information, and then used alternative sources to check whether it was true. In particular, whether business stealing was part of a management-orchestrated campaign or just an aberration by a sales agent.

In response to Verisure acquiring Lyse in May 2016, Sector's CEO internally communicated:

> We cannot and shall not attack Lyse/Verisure by knocking on doors. ... We continue to defend ourselves by knocking on their customers' doors if they do that, else not.

At the same time there were some internal rumors within Verisure that Sector planned a campaign to acquire Lyse customers. After communicating with Sector's CEO, the CEO of Verisure wrote in an internal email that he had checked, and Sector had no such plans.

In June 2017, the NCA conducted a dawn raid at the premises of both Sector and Verisure. To our knowledge, there were no more emails or any other communication either internal to a firm or between firms that related to the collusive arrangement.

2.4.2 Conduct: Deviations and Punishments

This case illustrates the challenges cartels face in sustaining their agreements, even in a setting with two firms, a rather simple and transparent coordination mechanism, and the absence of any serious threats from non-cartel members.

That they started coordinating their behavior around 2011 makes sense given acquisitions resulted in those two firms controlling almost 80 percent of the market for alarm systems for residential homes. And a win-back strategy led to a quite tough response to those outsiders trying to capture their consumers and thereby stopped them from growing and being a threat to the cartel. A system of regular communication between the two CEOs was established already right after the new Verisure CEO arrived in

2009.[16] In 2010 there were instances where they asked whether the rivals' business stealing is a misunderstanding, for example caused by an overly ambitious sales agent, or was instead part of a new business strategy. In early 2011 we then see the first reference to a tit-for-tat strategy concerning existing customers, combined with an encouragement to go after only new consumers (no business stealing).

According to the NCA's decision, the cartel started after the CEOs explicitly informed each other, on August 17, 2011, that they had instructed their sellers to abstain from knocking on rival doors. This market-sharing mechanism could easily be implemented, since a customer with an alarm has signs on their house with the name of the alarm company. Note, though, that there is really no clear date on when the cartel started. The two CEOs had increasingly engaged well before, while communicating their strategy to each other and signaling a market-sharing mechanism – a common understanding of not knocking on each other's customers' doors.

Even in such a transparent market, there is still some uncertainty about what is going on. As far as we see, deviations arose from two different sources. First, there is constantly a question whether sales personnel chose to deviate on their own. Approaching the rival's customers could enable them to meet their sales targets. Second, after the acquisition of a small rival, deviations could emerge because of uncertainty as to whether those new customers for the acquiring firm are part of the no-poaching agreement.

The deviations perpetrated by sales personnel are illustrated by some of the communications between the CEOs as, for example, when one asks the other whether there is a new campaign initiated by the rival or just a sales agent operating on their own. At play here is a fundamental principal–agent problem, where incentives for each sales agent to acquire new customers can make it tempting to knock

---

[16] The CEOs had regular contact on more legitimate issues like meetings of the Confederation of Norwegian Enterprises (NHO) and violations to marketing regulations.

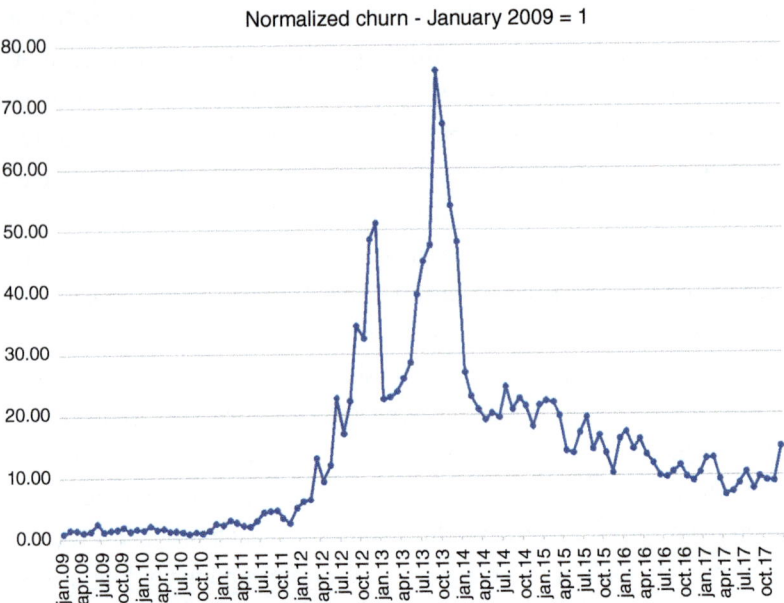

FIGURE 2.3 Monthly customer churn from Sector to Verisure and smaller rivals, 2009–2017 (divided by the churn level in January 2009).
Source: The Norwegian Competition Authority

on a house with the rival's sign. It also indicates that they are aware that cheating can take place and that each has the incentive to not inform the other firm about cheating, and that they have to work to verify the reason for a customer switching providers.

The customer churn between Sector and Verisure varied a lot during the cartel period. This is illustrated in Figure 2.3 which displays the monthly customer churn from Sector to Verisure (and a few smaller rivals) over 2009–2017 normalized at the churn level in the first month of observation (which is January 2009).[17]

---

[17] For business privacy reasons, we were not provided access to the raw customer churn data between Sector and Verisure. Therefore, the monthly customer churn for Sector is normalized by the first month of observation and aggregated across all rivals. However, the figure gives a strong indication of changes in customer switching between the two companies during the cartel period. Recall that Sector and Verisure had a joint market share of 80 to 90 percent over this period.
As explained in Section 2.3, customers exiting the market were identified by call-

Figure 2.3 shows a striking pattern. The customer churn for Sector is stable at a low level until spring 2012 when it sharply increases and peaks by a factor of more than 50 by the fall of 2012. The monthly churn then drops significantly during spring 2013 before it peaks again in fall 2013 by a factor of almost 80 by fall 2013. These changes are massive.

Interestingly, the sharp increases in customer churn from Sector to Verisure and smaller rivals correspond precisely with the two war periods between the companies, which we described in detail above.

The first war broke out in February–March 2012. This illustrates our second source of deviation, the acquisition of a small rival. This war was triggered by Sector's acquisitions of the private alarm customer bases of several rivals, including GS4, Nokas, and BKK. As a response to these acquisitions, Verisure started a campaign to attract customers of the companies that Sector had acquired. Prior to the acquisition, Verisure could have competed for those customers, but now those customers were supplied by Sector and, from Sector's perspective, were not up for grabs. In essence, Sector's acquisitions had caused there to be a disagreement between Sector and Verisure about the market allocation scheme.

Given Sector considered Verisure's campaign to be a hostile maneuver that violated their market-sharing agreement, it chose to respond aggressively by going after Verisure's customers. To signal that this was retaliation (or punishment) and not a deviation, Sector sent a fax to Verisure with all the customers they had stolen from Verisure in the previous week. If it had instead been a deviation from the collusive outcome, as opposed to a punishment as part of the collusive arrangement, Sector would have kept that information hidden from Verisure.

ups from the companies when ending the subscription. Thus, the raw data should be quite precise, implying that Figure 2.3 gives an accurate picture on customer churn between the companies.

An interesting observation is that, during the punishment phase, Sector and Verisure did not follow a tit-for-tat strategy but instead switched to an *all-out attack* on its rival. During the summer of 2012, when the first war escalated, there was no more "an eye for an eye" between the two companies. And the war lasted longer than initially planned. Verisure's original plan was to fight until the end of July, but the war continued for several more weeks. Verisure also blocked all communication with Sector which, according to Verisure, created uncertainty about the toughness of the punishment and how long it would last. Although we do not know what determined the length of Verisure's aggression, one possible explanation is that their plan was to acquire a certain number of customers before approaching Sector to end the war.

During the first war, it seems that Verisure fought more intensely than Sector, as illustrated by the fact that Sector's CEO was the one trying to ask for "good weather and grace." However, he was not able to get in touch with Verisure's CEO by email or phone. Eventually they had a face-to-face meeting right before that the war ended, and it seems that Verisure had captured more customers from Sector than Sector had acquired from Verisure. Although we do not know what the CEOs talked about during that meeting, it appears that a physical meeting or at least close communication was needed to return to the tit-for-tat strategy they had before the war.

The second war was in the first half of 2013 and seems to be the result of a gradual escalation, where the tit-for-tat strategy led them to gradually steal more customers from each other. At some point, this led to an all-out war, where both firms launched campaigns to steal customers from each other. As in the first war, the approach was not tit-for-tat, but rather a punishment where each of them was apparently trying to grab as many customers from their rival as they could. One interesting distinction from the first war seems to be that Sector was more aggressive. Verisure noticed this, and there were internal discussions in Verisure on whether they would gain from ending the war. Right after that, the two CEOs met and the war ended.

One can interpret this conduct as consistent with an extended version of the classic tit-for-tat strategy or a combination of tit-for-tat strategy and a stick-and-carrot strategy with a tough punishment phase.[18]

First, they took into account unintentional errors, as not every deviation brought a retaliatory response. Communication was critical in several instances, in particular when one CEO asks the other about the reason for some business stealing. It can facilitate collusion to be able to identify the deviations that are, in fact, a mistake and thus do not warrant an aggressive response.

Second, deviations could vary a lot in terms of how many customers are taken from the other company. There was always some business stealing going on in this market, even after the companies both had declared that the war is over. It seems as if they strived to keep business stealing to a minimum, while recognizing that it would not entirely disappear.

Third, there was a systematic departure from the tit-for-tat strategy when the companies entered into a war with a punishment tougher than tit-for-tat. One interpretation is that the punishment is as severe as it can be, and then the question is how long will it last. In the first war, Sector was the one that had to back down, while in the second war it seems that Verisure had to give in. In this respect, it was more of a stick-and-carrot strategy with a tough punishment phase, rather than a tit-for-tat strategy.

Fourth, direct communication seems to have been crucial for this cartel to succeed. The mere scope of the communication – through emails, phone calls and face-to-face meetings – reveals their importance for internal stability. In particular, the evidence shows how reversion to the no-poaching outcome can be difficult to do just by signaling through market behavior. Indeed, a meeting where the CEOs met in person was apparently the turning point both in fall 2012 and fall 2013 when they ended the two wars.

---

[18] While tit-for-tat refers to equivalent retaliation, stick-and-carrot refers to intense competition (stick) followed by a return to a collusive outcome (reward).

Finally, the two wars they fought seem to have been very important for the subsequent coordinated behavior. From internal emails we see that they referred to earlier wars, and told each other that such an outcome should be avoided. Less frequent direct communications are observed after the two wars, indicating that they had a better understanding of each other's strategy. The price structure they both used – providing free alarm installation to new customers – reduced the switching costs new customers would face. It is then no surprise that they refer to earlier wars, since low switching costs can lead to tough competition when they fight for customers. The prospect of intense competition in response to evidence of noncompliance can deter deviations and support a stable collusive outcome.

2.5 LESSONS TO BE LEARNED

From the perspective of competition law enforcement, it is relevant to ask what can be learned from this particular cartel. It is well known that having fewer firms in an industry may increase the risk for (tacit or explicit) collusion and thus lead to a larger scope for a cartel to succeed. As a result, merger control can and should play an important role in industries with a potential for collusion.[19] This case supports that point, though in an unfortunate way. The two cartel members made numerous acquisitions that were notified to the NCA, and at least two of these acquisitions were decisive for the industry to be dominated by those two firms. Although we have no indication that the mergers were part of a plan to form a cartel, still the success of the cartel in this industry was at least partly due to the NCA allowing a market structure to form that facilitated collusion.

Another lesson is that the market share of a cartel that is not industry wide can increase, even though independent fringe competitors can benefit from their umbrella effect to raise prices. In this case,

---

[19] Merger control was introduced in Norway in 1988, and from the start it was possible to intervene both due to unilateral as well as coordinated effects. The latter means that they could intervene in a merger if it made collusion more likely. The relationship between collusion and mergers is discussed in Asker and Nocke (2021).

the joint market share of the colluding firms increased (from 80 to 90 percent) during the cartel period. This is usually not consistent with standard theory of explicit collusion when the cartel does not involve all firms in the market.[20] In that case, non-colluding firms would usually benefit from the cartel by increased market share and higher margins. However, in this case the collusive agreement between Sector and Verisure applied only to customers of the two companies. Competition between them and other small suppliers for customers of rivals (or customers without an alarm system) remained, and indeed both companies competed aggressively to steal customers from non-colluding companies. This explains the rising joint market share of Sector and Verisure.

Another lesson is that explicit coordination may be more often necessary than sometimes thought. Considering the industry characteristics in the Norwegian private alarm market, there is a large potential for coordinated behavior: just two large firms, great transparency of sales, and a simple market-sharing device. Such a setting should be expected suitable for (lawful) tacit collusion rather than (unlawful) explicit collusion (see, for example, Fonseca and Norman, 2012). But that is not what happened in the Sector–Verisure case. Coordination in the real world might require express communication even in a setting with considerable potential for tacit understanding. Note also that there is, as far as we know, no communication between the parties about prices, only a no-poaching arrangement.

Let us think about some collusive markers suggested by the Sector–Verisure case that could be used for other markets. In subscription-based markets, like the alarm market, customer churn can be an informative indicator for a possible collusive agreement, at least when the market ticks off the boxes in terms of being suitable for collusion. In such circumstances, competition authorities may look for patterns in customer churn similar to the ones in this case.

---

[20] See Bos and Harrington (2010), where they show that a firm experiences a drop in its sales when it joins a cartel consisting of some firms in an industry.

In particular, if one observes periods with high and unstable churn being followed by periods with low and stable churn, this may suggest that a collusive arrangement has been implemented by the companies. Usually, such data are not publicly available, which means that competition authorities would need to collect this information either from third parties or from the parties themselves. Still, this could be a useful *ex officio* strategy.

Another insight from this case study is that direct communication can be extremely important in order to implement and sustain a collusive agreement. When monitoring is imperfect – as churn is not solely due to business stealing but may have other sources like opportunistic sales agents, customers entering or exiting the market, or simply natural variations – then communication plays an important role. Indeed, communication can be used to signal that you see the rival engaging in a deviation and then putting forward threats of retaliations, but also clarifying misunderstanding that may avoid a mistaken and very costly war. Equally important, communication might serve as a tool to re-establish the collusive agreement from a breakdown due to deviations and retaliations. Given this important role of communication, it is likely that competition authorities may find evidence of such, though more sophisticated ways of communication may make it difficult to detect in other cases.

This case also shows that once a cartel is established, there might be less need for direct communication. In this particular case we observe that after two wars the companies both realized what might happen if they deviated, and direct communication happened less frequently. This observation points to how difficult it can be to shut down a cartel once it has achieved internal stability. Cartel detection and enforcement through high fines might not be enough, since direct communication might no longer be needed to maintain the agreement. This calls for other means, for example director disqualifications and imprisonment to try to change the culture in the corporation and thereby induce competitive conduct. Another alternative could be structural remedies, such as a sale of assets, which is already in use in merger control in many countries and a few monopolization cases in the USA. As we observed in this case, acquisitions preceded cartel formation and it may take the sale of assets to destabilize the cartel.[21]

By way of conclusion, we would like to mention that we also believe this case study provides insights for future research on collusive strategies. Indeed, the switch from a tit-for-tat strategy to one more similar to a stick-and-carrot strategy was observed in this case. To re-establish the collusive agreement, the alarm companies implemented an even harsher punishment than tit-for-tat. As conveyed by one of the CEOs: *"now you are asking for a real war."*

REFERENCES

Asker, J., and V. Nocke (2021) "Collusion, Mergers and Related Antitrust Issues," in K. Ho, A. Hortacsu, and A. Lizzeri eds., *Handbook of Industrial Organization*, vol. 5, Elsevier, 177–279.

Axelrod, R. (1980) "Effective Choice in the Prisoner's Dilemma," *Journal of Conflict Resolution*, 24(1), 3–25.

Bos, I., and J. E. Harrington, Jr. (2010) "Endogenous Cartel Formation with Heterogenous Firms," *RAND Journal of Economics*, 41(1), 92–117.

Competition Appeal Tribunal (2021) "Decision letter to Verisure, November 25, 2021." Konkurranseklagenemndas-vedtak-i-sak-2021-1051-Offentlig-versjon.pdf (klagenemndssekretariatet.no).

Fonseca, M. A., and H.-T. Normann (2012) "Explicit vs. Tacit Collusion: The Impact of Communication in Oligopoly Experiments," *European Economic Review*, 56(8), 1759–1772.

Harrington, Jr., J. E. (2018) "A Proposal for a Structural Remedy for Illegal Collusion," *Antitrust Law Journal*, 82, 335.

Harrington, Jr., J. E. (2023) "The Practical Requirements of a Successful Cartel," in P. Whelan (ed.), *Research Handbook on Cartels*, Edward Elgar, 5–21.

Norwegian Competition Authority (2019) "Decision letter to Sector, July 4, 2019." VedtakV2019–18–SectorAlarmAS/InsanorInvestAS–ileggelseavovertredelsesgebyr–krrl§29jf§10ogEØS-avtalenartikkel53-Konkurransetilsynet.

---

[21] See Harrington (2018) for a discussion of structural remedies in cartel cases.

Norwegian Competition Authority (2020) "Decision letter to Verisure, November 25, 2020." VedtakV2020–32–VerisureAS/VerisureMidholdingAS-ileggelseavovertredelsesgebyr–krrl§29jf§10ogEØS-avtalenartikkel53-Konkurransetilsynet.

Tveit, S. T., and S. O. Solberg (2019) "Minority Acquisitions under Merger Control Scrutiny in Norway: Key Learnings from the Recent Sector Alarm/Nokas Case," Kluwer Competition Law Blog, July 19, 2019. competitionlawblog.kluwercompetitionlaw.com/2019/07/19/minority-acquisitions-under-merger-control-scrutiny-in-norway-key-learnings-from-the-recent-sector-alarmnokas-case/.

3 Coordinating Fuel Surcharges
Air Cargo Worldwide[*]
Zhiqi Chen

3.1 INTRODUCTION

From late 1999 to 2006, over twenty airlines around the world colluded on the setting and implementation of fuel and other surcharges for international air cargo services.[1] The events leading up to this cartel can be dated back to August 1997, when the International Air Transport Association (IATA), a trade group for airlines, adopted a draft resolution that would have established a mechanism that linked a fuel surcharge to a fuel price index. While the draft resolution never officially took effect, IATA published and updated the index value until March 2000 when the US Department of Transportation refused IATA's application for approval and antitrust immunity for the resolution. After IATA abandoned the index, one of the airlines, Lufthansa, began to publish a fuel price index that was identical to the IATA index. Meanwhile, starting from late 1999, a group of airlines communicated with each other regarding the fuel surcharge. Executives of these airlines regularly contacted each other to coordinate on the application and modification of the fuel surcharge mechanism as well as on changes to fuel surcharge rates. Over time, more airlines joined the group. After the 9/11 terrorist attacks in 2001, coordination among airlines was expanded to include the introduction and implementation of a security surcharge, ostensibly to cover increased costs due to enhanced security measures and higher

---

[*] I would like to thank Iwan Bos, Joseph Harrington, Thomas Ross, and Maarten Pieter Schinkel for helpful discussions and comments. I worked as an economics expert for a Canadian government agency on the international air cargo cartel case from 2012 to 2015. My academic work on this subject started only after my involvement in the case ended.

[1] European Commission (2010) and US Department of Justice (2008b).

insurance premiums for cargo shipments. The cartel was ended in February 2006 when competition authorities in the USA and EU simultaneously raided the offices of major airlines.

For their roles in the cartel, the airlines were forced to pay fines in the USA, EU, and several countries in other parts of the world.[2] In the USA, the fines on the airlines totaled $1.8 billion.[3] With the most recent decision by the EU's General Court, the total amount of EU fines stood at €740 million.[4] Moreover, twenty-one airline executives were charged by the US Department of Justice, and eight of them were sentenced to serve prison time.[5] Many airlines also paid damages to purchasers of air cargo services following class action suits in several countries including the USA, UK, and Canada. In the USA alone, settlements from class action suits totaled $1.2 billion.[6]

This cartel has a number of interesting features, of which the most fascinating is that the airlines colluded on only one component of the full price for air cargo services: surcharges. The other (and usually larger) price component, the freight rate, continued to be set independently by the airlines. Since what matters to a customer should be the sum of the freight rate and surcharges, colluding on surcharges without fixing the freight rate would seem futile for raising the total price because the higher surcharges could simply be offset by lower freight rates as airlines compete for customers. This

---

[2] These other countries include Australia, Canada, South Korea, New Zealand, and South Africa (US District Court 2014, p. 10).

[3] US Department of Justice (2020).

[4] This total amount consists of the fine on Qantas imposed by the European Commission in 2010 (€8.88 million) and the fines on the other eleven companies after the adjustments in the 2022 judgement by the General Court (€730.87 million). After the European Commission's first decision on this case in November 2010, eleven of the twelve companies subject to the decision challenged it before the EU's General Court. In December 2015, the General Court annulled the Commission's decision against the eleven companies. In response, the Commission adopted a new decision and re-established the fines on these companies in March 2017 (European Commission 2017a). The eleven companies again filed an application challenging the decision, on which the General Court issued a judgement in March 2022 (Court of Justice of the European Union 2022). Qantas was the only company that did not appeal the 2010 decision (European Commission 2017a).

[5] US Department of Justice (2020). [6] Hausfeld (2016).

preliminary assessment then raises the question whether this cartel could have had any significant impact on the actual price paid for international cargo services.

In this case study, I review the history and operation of the international air cargo cartel.[7] Moreover, I discuss theories that shed light on the price effects of this cartel. In particular, the theoretical analyses by Chen (2017, 2023) demonstrate that colluding on surcharges without coordination on base prices can be an effective way of raising the full price of a product. This anti-competitive effect is driven by the division of pricing authority between the head office and a firm's local offices. By delegating the decision on base prices to each local office and tying the latter's performance measure to only this price component, a firm weakens the local office's incentive to reduce base price in response to an increase in surcharge. This gives the firm a way to raise the full price *via* a higher surcharge. In the absence of coordination on surcharges, however, the head office of each firm still has the incentive to undercut its rivals through a lower surcharge. By colluding on surcharges, the firms eliminate the competition on surcharges among the head offices, thus achieving a higher level of full prices.

The remainder of this paper is organized as follows. After some relevant background information about international air cargo services is presented in Section 3.2, the history and operation of the international air cargo cartel is reviewed in Section 3.3. I then offer my observations about the interesting features of this cartel in Section 3.4 and discuss the theories of its anti-competitive effects in Section 3.5. Section 3.6 concludes.

---

[7] This review draws information from the public records about the cartel, including the decisions by the European Commission (2010, 2017b), the Federal Court of Australian (2014) and the US District Court (2014). While I had additional knowledge about this cartel from my own work as an economics expert for a Canadian government agency during 2012–2015, I am not able to share much of this knowledge due to confidentiality. Nevertheless, it helped the development of the views expressed here.

3.2 INTERNATIONAL AIR CARGO SERVICES

International air cargo services involve the transportation of industrial and consumer products by air across national borders. These services are provided by airlines (carriers) from an airport of origin to an airport of destination using the cargo hold (also known as the bellyhold) of passenger aircrafts or dedicated air freighter aircrafts. The direct purchasers of air cargo services are usually freight forwarders.[8] They act on behalf of shippers, who are the actual importers or exporters of the goods to be transported. Typically, an air cargo carrier is responsible for transporting the freight between the origin and destination airports while the purchaser of such services is responsible for the ground transportation of the cargo from the shipper to the origin airport and from the destination airport to the ultimate recipient.

An airline offers international air cargo services through its local cargo sales offices at individual airports. In locations where the airline's cargo business volume is too small to justify dedicated cargo sales offices, the airline may appoint General Sales Agents (GSAs) or General Sales and Service Agents (GSSAs) to perform the airline's sales and marketing function.[9] An airline's local sales office or GSA at an airport is the point of contact for freight forwarders who need to ship goods from the airport.[10] An important task performed by a local sales office or GSA is the negotiation of freight rates with freight forwarders.[11] These negotiated freight rates may be for shipments during a period of time (typically one traffic season which is six months), or for just one particular shipment (the "spot rates").[12]

---

[8] European Commission (2017b, para 14).
[9] Federal Court of Australia (2014, para 103). A GSSA differs from a GSA in that it also performs ground handling services in addition to sales and marketing. Henceforth I will combine GSAs and GSSAs and refer to them collectively as GSAs.
[10] Federal Court of Australia (2014, para 107).
[11] European Commission (2017b, para 17).
[12] European Commission (2017b, para 17) and Federal Court of Australia (2014, para 98).

Note that the freight rate is only one component of the price for the carriage of freight. During the period of the international air cargo cartel, the price was the freight rate plus applicable surcharges (e.g., fuel surcharge). The surcharges were set by the airlines' management and were not negotiable.[13] In other words, while a local cargo sales office or GSA did not have the authority to alter the surcharges, it had flexibility in negotiating freight rates with individual freight forwarders. It therefore did have considerable discretion over the total final prices that freight forwarders paid.

The price of carrying freight by air for each route is normally expressed in terms of per kilogram of "chargeable weight" of a shipment. The chargeable weight is the higher of the actual weight in kilograms or the volumetric weight calculated using a formula that accounts for volume of low-density cargo.[14]

3.3 HISTORY AND OPERATION OF THE CARTEL

The events leading up to the international air cargo cartel can be dated back to August 1997, when IATA adopted a draft resolution that would have established a mechanism linking the fuel surcharge rate to a fuel price index. Recognizing that fuel costs represented a significant portion of airlines' operating costs, IATA had been monitoring the price of aviation fuel beginning in 1990.[15] As the fuel price increased substantially in the eighteen months leading up to January 1997, the Cargo Tariff Coordinating Conferences (one of the IATA's working committees) organized a meeting in Geneva that led to a proposed resolution known as "Resolution 116ss."[16] After some refinements, Resolution 116ss was passed by mail vote in August 1997.[17]

---

[13] European Commission (2017b, para 17) and US District Court (2014, p. 72).
[14] Federal Court of Australia (2014, para 51) and European Commission (2017b, para 17).
[15] Federal Court of Australia (2014, para 493).
[16] Federal Court of Australia (2014, para 494).
[17] Federal Court of Australia (2014, para 495).

Resolution 116ss established a fuel price index to be used as the basis for the setting and adjustments of fuel surcharge by member airlines. Specifically, the index was based on the average weekly spot prices of aviation fuel from published oil industry sources, with the average fuel price in June 1996 assigned a value of 100. The rate of fuel surcharge was then tied to three threshold values of the fuel price index: 110, 130, and 150. If the index value exceeded 130 for a period of two consecutive weeks, IATA members were advised to implement a fuel surcharge of $0.10 per kilogram (or its equivalent in local currency). If the index then fell below 110 for two consecutive weeks, the surcharge would be suspended. If it rose above 150 for two consecutive weeks, IATA would convene a special meeting of the Cargo Tariff Coordinating Conferences to review the amount of fuel surcharge.[18]

However, Resolution 116ss never went into effect because it did not receive regulatory approval in the USA and several other countries.[19] Nevertheless, IATA routinely published and updated the fuel index value until March 2000, when the US Department of Transportation (DOT) refused IATA's application for approval and antitrust immunity for the resolution.[20] When informing its members of the DOT's decision, IATA warned them of potential antitrust liability associated with the use of the IATA index: "If the carriers were to coordinate pricing by reference to the Index, whether pursuant to this disapproved Resolution or simply through de facto parallel pricing actions, this could be regarded as an illegal conspiracy in violation of applicable Competition laws..."[21]

---

[18] US District Court (2014, p. 5) and European Commission (2017b, para 114).

[19] Federal Court of Australia (2014, para 497).

[20] Federal Court of Australia (2014, para 497). The DOT rejected IATA's application on the basis that "[t]he uniform, industry-wide index mechanism proposed here appears fundamentally flawed and unfair to shippers and other users of cargo air transportation" (as quoted in US District Court 2014, p. 6). To be more specific, the DOT's objections to the index mechanism included its failure to readjust as quickly when prices moved down and its failure to take into account the airlines fuel hedging programmes (Federal Court of Australia 2014, para 501).

[21] As quoted in US District Court (2014, p. 6).

After IATA abandoned the index, one of the major air cargo carriers, Lufthansa, began to publish its own fuel price index on its publicly available website. This "Lufthansa Index" was identical to the IATA index, with the same threshold values and the same two-week lag for any adjustment of the surcharge.[22] The Lufthansa Index is notable because it was used subsequently by not only Lufthansa but other airlines to determine the timing and the fuel surcharge rate.[23] Even in instances where some airlines developed their own fuel price indices, they were modeled after the Lufthansa Index.[24] As a result, there was little difference between the various fuel surcharge mechanisms used by the airlines.[25]

The air cargo cartel essentially involved the coordination among the airlines on the setting and implementation of fuel and other surcharges for international air cargo services. Evidence shows that such coordination started from at least December 1999.[26] At that time, the IATA index had exceeded 130 for two consecutive weeks, which was the trigger for the imposition of fuel surcharge in Resolution 116ss.[27] Even though Resolution 116ss was never declared effective, a group of airlines contacted each other to discuss whether and how fuel surcharge should be implemented.[28] These discussions were followed by the introduction of a fuel surcharge of $0.10/kg (or

---

[22] Federal Court of Australia (2014, para 12). Lufthansa initially sought IATA's permission to publish the IATA index at Lufthansa's website, but IATA refused. Subsequently, Lufthansa published the same index but renamed it as the "Lufthansa Index" (US District Court 2014, p. 5).

[23] US District Court (2014, p. 7).   [24] US District Court (2014, p. 7).

[25] European Commission (2017b, para 115).

[26] European Commission (2017b, para 703). While not ruling out the possibility that some airlines communicated about fuel surcharges between August 1997 (when Resolution 116ss was passed) and December 1999, I would note that no airlines introduced a fuel surcharge during this period.

[27] Federal Court of Australia (2014, para 498).

[28] To be clear, these discussions were not under the auspices of IATA. While the IATA index was used by the airlines to coordinate fuel surcharges from December 1999 to March 2000, IATA itself did not participate in the cartel activities. In early December 1999, a number of airlines contacted IATA about fuel surcharges but each was advised by IATA that Resolution 116ss was not effective (Federal Court of Australia 2014, para 499).

Table 3.1 *The Lufthansa mechanism: Revised in January 2002*

		Lufthansa index value	
Level	Fuel surcharge rate	Implementation/increase	Suspension/decrease
1	EUR/USD 0.05/kg	115	110
2	EUR/USD 0.10/kg	135	120
3	EUR/USD 0.15/kg	165	145
4	EUR/USD 0.20/kg	190	170

Source: Federal Court of Australia (2014, para 504).

its local currency equivalent) by a number of airlines, including Air France, Lufthansa, Cargolux, Korean Air, and Air Canada.[29]

After the introduction of a fuel surcharge, the airlines continued to contact each other regularly to coordinate on the application and modification of the fuel surcharge mechanism as well as on changes to the fuel surcharge rate. Over time, more airlines joined the group.[30] As the aviation fuel prices rose and fell in the ensuing years, the airlines adjusted the fuel surcharge rate in line with the Lufthansa Index (or other similar indices).[31] For its part, Lufthansa revised its mechanism for the determination of the fuel surcharge rate several times by adding and adjusting the threshold values of the index that would trigger an increase or decrease of fuel surcharges. In January 2002, for instance, Lufthansa announced a revised mechanism as shown in Table 3.1. This mechanism specified four levels for the fuel surcharge rate, ranging from €/$0.05/kg to €/$0.20/kg, along with the trigger points for the implementation and suspension of each level. For example, the Level 2 fuel surcharge rate (€/$0.10/kg) would be applied if the value of Lufthansa Index exceeded 135 (but was below

---

[29] Federal Court of Australia (2014, para 500) and US District Court (2014, p. 5).
[30] European Commission (2017b, para 2).
[31] See section 4.3 of European Commission (2017b) for a detailed discussion of the airlines' activities in coordinating the adjustments of fuel surcharge rates between 2000 and 2006.

165) for two consecutive weeks, and it would be removed (and replaced by the Level 1 fuel surcharge rate) if the index value fell below 120 (but was above 110) for two consecutive weeks. Note that this revised mechanism involved more levels for the fuel surcharge rate and different trigger points than the initial Lufthansa mechanism (which was copied from the IATA mechanism described in Resolution 116ss).

As alluded to above, airlines coordinated fuel surcharge rates through bilateral and multilateral contacts. These communications were conducted by telephone, email, fax, and in-person meetings.[32] The meetings could be between executives of just two airlines, in small groups of them, and in some instances in large forums.[33] For example, the Cargo Sub-Committee of the Board of Airline Representatives (BAR) in Hong Kong held repeated meetings to coordinate fuel surcharge rates.[34]

The objective of the cartel was to ensure that airlines throughout the world adopted the same fuel surcharge rate (adjusted for local currencies) at about the same time.[35] Accordingly, the cartel needed to coordinate two dimensions: the fuel surcharge rate and the timing of its implementation. This was a challenging task considering the large number of airlines and cargo routes around the world. The cartel accomplished it *via* a complex network of contacts among airline executives at the headquarters and in individual countries or regions.[36] There were some idiosyncrasies in the operation of this

---

[32] US District Court (2014, p. 7) and European Commission (2017b, para 704).
[33] European Commission (2017b, para 111).
[34] Federal Court of Australia (2014, paras 508–509).
[35] European Commission (2017b, para 109).
[36] European Commission (2017b, para 704). We can get a sense about the managerial levels of airline executives who participated in the cartel activities from the list of individuals who served jail sentences in the USA. For example, Keith Packer was Commercial General Manager for British Airways World Cargo (US Department of Justice 2008c), Maria Christina Ullings was Senior Vice President of Cargo Sales and Marketing of Martinair Cargo (US Department of Justice 2020), Bruce McCaffrey was Qantas Airways' Vice President of Freight for the Americas (US Department of Justice 2008a), and Timothy Pfeil was SAS Cargo's Area Director of Sales for North America (US District Court 2008).

cartel network in different parts of the world.³⁷ But generally speaking executives at the headquarters were involved in the coordination on the fuel surcharge mechanism and the setting of fuel surcharge rates, while lower level executives coordinated on the timing of the adoption of the rate set by the headquarters as well as monitoring other airlines for compliance with the agreement.

Notably, however, the local sales offices and GSAs of the airlines at individual airports were not involved in the decisions regarding the rate and timing of fuel surcharge. They had no authority to alter the fuel surcharge when they dealt with freight forwarders, though they had flexibility to adjust freight rates. Generally speaking, the airlines were not accused of fixing the freight rates during this period.³⁸ Indeed, the local sales organizations of different airlines continued to compete for customers by offering discounts off freight rates even while the executives at higher levels colluded on fuel surcharges. Consistent with this division of rate-setting power, the performance of local sales offices was usually evaluated based on the freight revenues they generated but not on surcharge revenues.

After the 9/11 terrorist attacks in 2001, air cargo carriers in addition introduced the security surcharge (also known as insurance and security surcharge) ostensibly to cover increased costs due to enhanced security measures and higher insurance premiums for cargo shipments.³⁹ As in the case of the fuel surcharge, the airlines discussed and coordinated on the introduction of the security surcharge.

---

[37] In Hong Kong, for example, an airline's fuel surcharge rate had to be approved by the local regulator, the Hong Kong Civil Aviation Department (Federal Court of Australia 2014, para 447). The Hong Kong BAR Cargo Sub-Committee organized meetings to determine the fuel surcharge rates that would be submitted to the regulator for approval in joint applications by all cargo carriers (Federal Court of Australia 2014, paras 508–511). But this was not the case in most other parts of the world where contacts among airline executives regarding fuel surcharge were more ad hoc.

[38] An exception is the Indonesian airline Garuda which allegedly colluded with several airlines on freight rates for outbound routes to Sydney and Perth in Australia in 2001 (Federal Court of Australia 2014, paras 1149–1155).

[39] Federal Court of Australia (2014, para 2) and European Commission (2017b, para 577).

Their discussions covered various dimensions, including whether and when to introduce the surcharge, in what form, and at what rate.[40] After the surcharge was introduced in October 2001, the airlines continued their coordination on the security (and fuel) surcharge rate until the cartel broke down in 2006.[41]

In December 2005, the international air cargo cartel had caught the attention of competition authorities after Lufthansa submitted a leniency application.[42] In February 2006, competition authorities in the USA and EU simultaneously raided the offices of major airlines, including British Airways, Air France–KLM, Cargolux, SAS, Cathay Pacific Airways, Japan Airlines International, LAN Airlines, and Singapore Airlines.[43] This event marked the end of the cartel.[44]

3.4 NOTABLE FEATURES OF THE CARTEL

The collusion over air cargo surcharges is a very interesting case study of cartel operations for at least four notable features.

1. Collusion on one component of the full price

    Perhaps the most interesting feature of this cartel is that the airlines colluded only on surcharges. Generally speaking, the cartel imposed no restrictions on the airlines' freedom to set their own freight rates. During the cartel period, the local sales offices and GSAs of these airlines continued to compete for customers by offering discounts off freight rates.

---

[40] European Commission (2017b, para 579).
[41] European Commission (2017b, para 579).
[42] European Commission (2017b, para 77). Lufthansa's in-house legal team became aware of the air cargo cartel after the company implemented a competition law compliance programme in 2004. Some employees came forward and disclosed information about price-fixing activities in air cargo operations to their compliance officers. After an internal investigation revealed that the activities were widespread throughout the company, Lufthansa decided to seek amnesty in December 2005 (Bergman and Sokol 2015, p. 310).
[43] European Commission (2017b, para 79).
[44] It is interesting to note that the dissolution of this cartel did not necessarily lead to lower fuel surcharges. Turner (2022) finds that post-cartel fuel surcharge rates closely resemble those implied by the Lufthansa methodology. He concludes that cartel detection caused a switch from explicit to tacit collusion, but not a reduction in prices.

This collusive practice naturally raises a question about its effectiveness in pushing up the full price of air cargo services since higher surcharges achieved through collusion could simply have been offset by lower freight rates as the airlines competed for customers.[45] This central question regarding the cartel's impact will be explored in the next section.

2. Collusion on a simple variable

Another notable aspect of the fuel surcharge is that the rate was on a per kilogram basis and was, generally, independent of the distance of shipments.[46] It means, for example, the amount of fuel surcharge charged on a shipment from New York to Paris was the same as that on a shipment of the same (chargeable) weight from New York to Tokyo.

This feature of the cartel is noteworthy because the fuel surcharge was supposed to help the airlines recoup the lost profits due to higher costs of aviation fuel. Yet the revenue generated by such a fuel surcharge would not have been proportional to the increases in fuel costs because it did not depend on the distance of shipments. As such, the fuel surcharge was not an effective scheme for the recoupment of increased fuel costs. While this feature raises questions about the claimed benign purpose of the surcharges for the recovery of exceptional cost, one might also wonder whether the cartel had colluded on a poorly designed variable.

However, in spite of these remarkable features, this simple flat rate had merit for the airlines because, in my opinion, its simplicity substantially reduced the costs of coordination among them. A distance-dependent surcharge scheme would have entailed a myriad of rates for the thousands of different cargo routes around the world, and the resulting complexity would have made it more difficult for the cartel members to reach an agreement and to monitor each other's compliance with the agreement.[47] In contrast, a single surcharge rate (adjusting for local

---

[45] Indeed, several airlines made this type of argument in their defence against antitrust damages claims. See US District Court (2014, p. 73).

[46] One exception was the outbound fuel surcharge rate from Hong Kong, where the airlines implemented two different fuel surcharge rates, one rate for intra-Asia shipments and the other rate for "long-haul" shipments to the rest of the world (Federal Court of Australia, paras 523–547).

[47] To be more specific, if the airlines had chosen to collude on a surcharge rate on the basis of $x per kilogram and also per kilometer, it would have been more difficult for an airline to estimate the additional revenue to be generated by the surcharge because it would have had to take into account the distance of different routes and the volume of cargo for each route. This, along with differences in airlines' network

currency exchange rates) appears to have been much simpler for the airlines to negotiate and implement on a global scale. While it is true that the flat fuel surcharge rate was a less precise instrument for recouping fuel costs, my belief is that the real goal of the cartel was to increase the airlines' revenues (and hence profits) and rising fuel prices were an opportunistic cover for the introduction of the surcharge.[48]

3. Index as a facilitating device

A third interesting feature of this cartel is the use of the Lufthansa Index to coordinate on the fuel surcharge rate. Recall that this index was the core element of a mechanism that specified a target level of the fuel surcharge rate as a function of changes in the price of aviation fuel. For example, the Lufthansa mechanism announced in January 2002 (reproduced in Table 3.1) had a fuel surcharge rate of €/$0.10/kg to be applied if the value of Lufthansa Index exceeded 135 (but was below 165) for two consecutive weeks, and it would be removed (and replaced by a lower rate of €/$0.05/kg) if the index value fell below 120 (but was above 110) for two consecutive weeks.

It should be noted that the airlines did not automatically adopt the fuel surcharge rates as prescribed by the Lufthansa mechanism. Rather, they used the index value as a signal for initiating another round of communication and coordination. Specifically, when the index value was approaching a trigger point for rate adjustment, airline executives would contact each other to discuss their intentions and plans for implementing the anticipated rate change. These discussions, in turn, ensured that the rate specified in the Lufthansa mechanism would be adopted in a coordinated way. Therefore, the Lufthansa mechanism did not dictate the

structure, would have made it harder for them to reach an agreement on the rate. Moreover, it is standard practice in this industry to quote prices in terms of origin-destination pair (e.g., from New York to Frankfurt) rather than per kilometer. To implement a cartel agreement on a per-kilometer surcharge rate, each airline would have had to convert it into a rate for each origin-destination pair so that the surcharge rate and freight rate were expressed on the same basis. With thousands of cargo routes around the world, this would have made it more difficult for the cartel to detect undercutting of the collusive fuel surcharge rate.

[48] My belief is based on the observation that the choice of the initial fuel surcharge rate in IATA's Resolution 116ss was not founded on any serious analysis of the actual cost impact of higher fuel prices, and that the implementation of this rate and the subsequent rate adjustments were tied to the value of the Lufthansa Index (or similar indices) which, as I will explain below, did not reflect the actual unit cost of fuel incurred by the airlines.

airlines' actions on fuel surcharge rates, but it did facilitate their coordination by providing an anchor for their expectations about the timing and the amount of rate adjustment to be implemented.[49]

One interesting detail about the Lufthansa Index and its predecessor – the IATA fuel price index – is that it was tied to the spot prices of aviation fuel. But the spot prices were not necessarily the prices at which the airlines purchased their fuel. Since most airlines had long-term fuel contracts and employed hedging to manage their fuel costs,[50] the value of the Lufthansa Index did not typically reflect the actual unit cost of fuel incurred by the airlines. Consequently, the fuel surcharge revenues generated by this mechanism need not have born a close relationship to the airlines' actual costs of fuel.

4. Complex web of contacts

While illicit communication among competitors is a typical component of cartel operations, the international air cargo cartel is notable in the complexity of its network of contacts. These contacts involved airline executives at different corporate levels and in different parts of the world.[51] While, in some instances, coordination was centralized through a multilateral forum,[52] for the most part it was done through bilateral contacts, with executives of different airlines regularly contacting each other to discuss their intentions and plans, share information, and urge compliance with an agreed course of action.[53] With more than twenty airlines participating, this complex web of bilateral contacts supported decentralized coordination.

On the surface, this complexity may appear inefficient for a cartel, but it worked for this cartel because of the particular characteristic of the international air cargo business that cooperations among airlines are needed as part of their normal operations. This need exists because no

---

[49] For example, the index value had exceeded 135 for two weeks by September 5, 2002 (Federal Court of Australia 2014, para 631). Since this was the trigger point for the fuel surcharge rate to be raised to €/$0.10/kg, it promoted discussions among the airlines about the timing of a rate increase. As detailed in European Commission (2017b, paras 245–257), these discussions facilitated the implementation of the higher surcharge rate by the airlines in late September and early October 2002.
[50] Wilke and Michaels (2006).   [51] European Commission (2017b, para 107).
[52] For example, the Cargo Sub-Committee of BAR in Hong Kong organized meetings to coordinate their members' actions on surcharges (Federal Court of Australia 2014, paras 508–509).
[53] European Commission (2017b, paras 109 and 706).

airline has a large enough network to reach all major cargo destinations in the world.[54] To expand their network coverage and improve their schedule, it is common for airlines to enter into interlining agreements with each other.[55] The interlining agreements and other cooperations among the airlines created an environment where airline executives communicated regularly with each other about operational issues. It is perhaps not surprising then that the same channels of communications were used by the airlines to coordinate their actions on surcharges. The difference, of course, is that coordination on prices among competitors is illegal, a fact to which some participants in the air cargo cartel seemed to pay little attention.[56]

3.5 ANTI-COMPETITIVE EFFECTS OF THE CARTEL

The arguably most interesting feature of this cartel is that the airlines colluded on only one component of the full price for cargo services. Through the lens of the standard theory of collusion, it is not obvious that such collusion could have any significant impact on the full price (freight rate plus surcharges) because supracompetitive surcharges could simply be offset by a lower freight rate as the airlines compete for a customer's business. In this section, I address this issue by discussing theories about the possible anti-competitive effects of collusion on surcharge.

Before I present these theories, I would note that in many countries it is not necessary for the competition authorities to show

---

[54] European Commission (2017b, para 16).
[55] Interlining occurs when the freight of one airline is carried using the capacity of a different airline (Federal Court of Australia 2014, para 84).
[56] Keith Packer, one of the executives who served jail time for their roles in the international air cargo cartel, attended competition law training in October 2004, in the midst of the cartel (Larson 2010). But the training had no apparent impact on him as he continued to participate in price-fixing activities afterwards. In an article after his release from jail, Packer observed, "competition law training was typically delivered to large commercial audiences by inhouse or external legal teams via PowerPoint presentations of the law itself with some actual case studies to try to make it more relevant. Compliance can be a very dry, boring subject for commercial executives who view the training as very much a 'tick the box' exercise and easily let their minds drift to their many other priorities during the presentations" (Packer 2011).

actual anti-competitive effects in order to convict a cartel. In the United States, for example, agreements among competitors to fix any prices are per se illegal.[57] In the European Union, there is no need to consider the actual effects of a cartel agreement when the object of the agreement is proven to be anti-competitive.[58] Consequently, in their legal proceedings against the international air cargo cartel, there was very little analysis on the actual or likely anti-competitive effects of the collusion. Indeed, in its decisions on this case, the European Commission stated that it made no assessment of the cartel's anti-competitive effects.[59]

A number of academics, however, have proposed theories that help shed some light on the likely effects of this cartel. Of particular relevance are two theories developed by Chen (2017, 2023).[60] Relevant to the air cargo cartel, these theories explain how it can be profitable for firms to collude on surcharges while competing on base price, and showing effect on final prices that their customers pay.

While there are some differences in the two models analyzed in Chen (2017, 2023), they share a common element by taking account of a firms' internal pricing hierarchy. In both models, the full price of a product consists of two components: a base price and a surcharge. Consistent with the practices in the air cargo industry, it is assumed the surcharge is decided by a firms' head office, while the base price is set at a firm's local office. By itself, this division of pricing authority within the firm does not necessarily imply a higher full price. If the head office and the local office are incentivized to maximize the same objective (such as profit), both will want to achieve the same full price

---

[57] Federal Trade Commission and US Department of Justice (2010).
[58] European Commission (2017b, para 917).
[59] European Commission (2017b, para 917).
[60] Other theories demonstrating that collusion on surcharges has anti-competitive effects include Garrod (2006) and Ross and Shadarevian (2021). These theories, however, do not offer an explanation for why firms would collude on surcharges but not on base prices. Instead, they assume that firms collude on base prices. Therefore, these theories do not explain how it can be profitable for firms to collude on surcharges while competing on base prices, which is an important characteristic of the international air cargo cartel.

that maximizes it. In such a situation, the local office would respond to a higher surcharge by reducing the base price by an equal amount, leaving the full price unchanged. By that argument, collusion on surcharges without coordination on base prices would have no effect on equilibrium full prices.

This is where another feature in these models becomes important: the local office is incentivized to maximize a different objective than that of the head office. Specifically, the head office has the standard objective of maximizing the firm's profit, but the local office is incentivized to maximize the (net) revenue generated by the price component it controls which is the base price. This feature is consistent with the practice in the air cargo industry that the performance of local sales offices is usually evaluated based on the freight revenues they generate but not on the surcharge revenues.

Chen (2017, 2023) demonstrates that with such an incentive contract for the local office, a larger surcharge will lead to a higher full price. The contract weakens the local office's incentive to reduce the base price in response to a larger surcharge because its performance measure is tied to only the revenue generated by the base price. Consequently, even though the base price may still fall in response to a rise in surcharge, the decrease in base price does not completely offset the increase in surcharge.[61] This property enables the head office of a firm to influence the full price *via* the surcharge it sets.

---

[61] To understand the intuition behind this result, consider the familiar trade-off a firm faces when raising the (full) price of a product. On the one hand, a higher price enables a firm to earn a larger profit margin on each unit sold. On the other hand, a higher price reduces the units sold and the firm forgoes the profit it could have earned on the lost units. The firm's profit-maximizing price is the one that balances these two effects. Note that this price does not depend on whether or how the price is divided between a surcharge and a base price. For this reason, if the local office is incentivized to maximize profit, it will want to keep the full price at the profit-maximizing level, and it can achieve this by reducing the base price to exactly offset an increase in surcharge. However, if the local office's performance is tied to only the revenue generated by the base price, it will no longer be concerned about the reduction in surcharge revenue caused by the lost sales due to a higher full price. Consequently, it will not lower the base price to the point of completely offsetting

However, when firms compete with each other, each firm faces the usual incentive to undercut its rival. While the incentive contract restrains a local office's temptation to reduce the base price, the head office of each firm still has the incentive to cut its surcharge to attract customers from its rivals. By colluding on surcharges, on the other hand, the firms eliminate the competition on surcharges among the head offices, thus raising the full prices *via* supracompetitive surcharges.

The models in Chen (2017, 2023) differ in the exact mechanisms used by firms to set base prices. In Chen (2017), a local office negotiates a base price with each buyer individually, while in Chen (2023), a local office sets a uniform base price that all buyers take as given. This difference in pricing mechanism has a quantitative impact on the level of full prices achieved by collusion on surcharges. In the case where the base price is determined through bilateral bargaining, collusion on only surcharges leads to higher full prices than if firms collude on full prices. In the case where each local office sets a uniform base price, collusion on only surcharges achieves the same level of full prices as collusion on full prices. Therefore, collusion on only surcharges is as harmful to buyers as collusion on full prices when the base price is uniform (Chen, 2023), and it is actually more harmful than collusion on full prices when the base price is negotiated (Chen, 2017).

Note that the way base prices are set in Chen (2017) is consistent with the practice in the air cargo industry that freight rates are often negotiated between airlines' local sales offices and their customers. This suggests that surcharge-fixing by the international air cargo cartel was likely more harmful than if the airlines had colluded on freight rates without imposing the surcharges. It is worth noting that the amount of restitution awarded by courts to customers indicates that the magnitude of anti-competitive harm was substantial. For

the increase in surcharge. Thus, with such an incentive contract a higher surcharge leads to a higher full price.

example, direct purchasers of international air cargo services in the USA obtained $1.2 billion in settlements with more than thirty airlines. These settlements represented from 2 percent to more than 10 percent of these airlines' sales to and from the USA during the relevant period.[62]

3.6 CONCLUSION

Several features of the international air cargo conspiracy make it an interesting case study of cartels. They include the choice of a simple variable to collude on, the use of a price index as a facilitating device, and the reliance on a complex web of contacts by which cartel members communicated and coordinated. Most interesting of all is that the airlines colluded on only one price component (surcharges) and not on other components (specifically, freight rates). Such a collusive practice seems poorly designed because, as airlines compete for customers, supracompetitive surcharges could have been offset by lower freight rates. However, a careful analysis of this cartel suggests otherwise. Given the airlines' actual practices for the setting of surcharges and freight rates, colluding on surcharges without coordinating on base prices could be an effective way of raising the full price. Essentially, the local offices did not have the authority, nor incentives to fully offset the surcharges with lower base prices. In fact, the simplicity of coordinating on a fuel surcharge and the use of a fuel price index showed ingenuity in the collusive scheme implemented by the international air cargo cartel.

REFERENCES

Bergman, H. and D. D. Sokol (2015) "The Air Cargo Cartel: Lessons for Compliance," in Caron Beaton-Wells and Christopher Tran (eds.), *Anti-Cartel Enforcement in a Contemporary Age: Leniency Religion*, London, Bloomsbury Publishing.

[62] Hausfeld (2016).

Chen, Z. (2017) "Colluding on Surcharges," unpublished manuscript, Carleton University.

Chen, Z. (2023) "Partitioned Pricing and Collusion on Surcharges," *The Economic Journal*, 133 (655), 2614–2639.

Court of Justice of the European Union (2022) "Cartel on the Airfreight Market: The General Court Rules on Actions Brought by Multiple Airlines," Press Release No 53/22, Luxembourg, March 30, 2022.

European Commission (2010) "Commission Decision of 9.11.2010 Relating to a Proceeding under Article 101 of the Treaty on the Functioning of the European Union, Article 53 of the EEA Agreement and Article 8 of the Agreement between the European Community and the Swiss Confederation on Air Transport, Case COMP/39258 – Airfreight," Brussels, November 9, 2010.

European Commission (2017a) "Antitrust: Commission Re-adopts Decision and Fines Air Cargo Carriers €776 Million for Price-Fixing Cartel," European Commission Press release, Brussels, March 17, 2017.

European Commission (2017b) "Commission Decision of 17.3.2017 Relating to a Proceeding under Article 101 of the Treaty on the Functioning of the European Union, Article 53 of the EEA Agreement and Article 8 of the Agreement between the European Community and the Swiss Confederation on Air Transport, AT.39258 – Airfreight," Brussels, March 17, 2017.

Federal Court of Australia (2014) "Australian Competition and Consumer Commission v Air New Zealand Limited [2014] FCA 1157," October 31, 2014.

Federal Trade Commission and US Department of Justice (2010) "Antitrust Guidelines for Collaborations among Competitors," April 2000.

Garrod, L. (2006) "Surcharging as a Facilitating Practice," Centre for Competition Policy Working Paper 06-17, University of East Anglia.

Hausfeld (2016) "Hausfeld Announces Final Settlement in Decade-Long Air Cargo Price Fixing Litigation," Globe Newswire, May 19, 2016.

Larson, E. (2010) "Ex-BA Executive Shares Prison Tales to Sway Violators," Bloomberg, October 22, 2010.

Packer, K. (2011) "A Cautionary Tale: How a Competition Law Breach Led to a Jail Term for One BA Exec," Legalweek.com, September 22, 2011.

Ross, T. W. and V. Shadarevian (2021) "Partitioned Pricing and Collusion," unpublished manuscript, University of British Columbia.

Turner, D. C. (2022) "The Impact of Cartel Dissolution on Prices: Evidence from the Air Cargo Cartel," unpublished manuscript, available at SSRN: https://ssrn.com/abstract=4114672.

US Department of Justice (2008a) "Former Qantas Airline Executive Agrees to Plead Guilty to Participating in Price-Fixing Conspiracy on Air

Cargo Shipments," United States Department of Justice news release, May 8, 2008.

US Department of Justice (2008b) "Major International Airlines Agree to Plead Guilty and Pay Criminal Fines Totaling More Than $500 Million for Fixing Prices on Air Cargo Rates," United States Department of Justice news release, June 26, 2008.

US Department of Justice (2008c) "Former British Airways Executive Agrees to Plead Guilty to Participating in Price-Fixing Conspiracy on Air Cargo Shipments," United States Department of Justice news release, September 30, 2008.

US Department of Justice (2020) "Extradited Former Air Cargo Executive Pleads Guilty for Participating in a Worldwide Price-Fixing Conspiracy," United States Department of Justice news release, January 23, 2020.

US District Court (2008) "Plea Agreement, *United States of America v. Timothy Pfeil*, 08-cr-227-JDB," United States District Court for the District of Columbia, August 29, 2008.

US District Court (2014) "In re Air Cargo Shipping Services Antitrust Litigation, 06-MD-1175 (JG)(VVP)," United States District Court Eastern District of New York, October 15, 2014.

Wilke, J. R. and D. Michaels (2006) "Lufthansa to Co-operate in Air-Cargo Investigation," *The Globe and Mail*, March 8, 2006, B.13.

4 Price Fixing or Fixing Competition?
*Bread in Israel**

Chaim Fershtman and Yossi Spiegel

4.1 INTRODUCTION

We study a price-fixing agreement between the four largest industrial bakeries in Israel which took place from mid February 2010 to the end of May 2010. The agreement involved the prices of standard bread and challah that are subject to price cap regulation.[1] Combined, the bakeries – Angel Bakeries Ltd., J&E Berman Group Ltd., Davidovitz and Sons Bakery Ltd., and the Dganit Group – account for 90–95 percent of the sales of these products. The conspiracy ended when the Israel Competition Authority (ICA) started an open investigation of the affair and conducted a dawn raid of the bakeries' offices and arrested their CEOs at the end of May 2010. The ICA viewed the case as one of its flagship cases,[2] and the popular press – which referred to the case as the "Bread Cartel" – described it as "one of the most serious affairs uncovered by the

---

* Disclaimer: Chaim Fershtman submitted an economic expert opinion in the case on behalf of Dganit Ein Bar's executives and Yossi Spiegel submitted an economic expert opinion on behalf of Dganit Ein Bar in a regulatory proceeding. We thank Yaron Angel, Itai Ater, David Gilo, Mazor Matkevich, Menachem Perlman, Yaron Yehezkel, and especially the editors of this volume, Joe Harrington and Maarten Pieter Schinkel, for many helpful comments.

[1] Challah is a special bread, usually braided and typically eaten on Shabbat. For details about the case, see Criminal Case Number 28192-08-12, *The State of Israel* v. *Angel and Others*, https://tinyurl.com/3y5suf5p (henceforth "*The State of Israel* v. *Angel and Others*").

[2] See "The bread cartel: hitting the pocket and not the prison," Avner Finkelstein, Calcalist, March 22, 2017, www.calcalist.co.il/Ext/Comp/ArticleLayout/CdaArticlePrint1280/0,16492,3710149,00.html.

Antitrust Authority" and one that came at the expense of the "weak and needy."[3]

In the process of its investigation, the ICA wiretapped the phones of the bakeries' executives, including those of the CEOs of the four large bakeries, for ninety days from the beginning of February 2010 (before the agreement started) until the end of April 2010. This gave the ICA access to hundreds of phone conversations, and provides us with a unique perspective on the inner workings of the agreement, right from its inception.

Among other things, the ICA found that during the relevant period, the four CEOs had met at the offices of a leading Tel Aviv law firm, lower-level managers had met in a gasoline station on the Trans-Israel highway, and the bakeries' executives had hundreds of phone conversations about prices and customers. In these meetings and phone conversations, the executives agreed to raise the price of sliced dark bread and challah in some stores and to stop competing for each other's customers. The evidence indicates that, by and large, the bakeries complied with these agreements.

In July 2015 and November 2017, the Jerusalem District Court found the four large bakeries and their executives guilty of conspiring to fix prices and divide the market for sliced dark bread and challah.[4] The Court held that "Both agreements, by their content and essence, posed a significant potential harm to competition,"[5]

---

[3] See "The bread cartel affair: The bakeries committed offenses under aggravating circumstances," Ela Levi-Weinrib, Globes, July 9, 2015, www.globes.co.il/news/article.aspx?did=1001051611 or "The serious bread cartel is well organized by senior officials – on the backs of the weak and the needy," Ora Koren and Amit Ben-Aroya, Haaretz, May 25, 2010, www.haaretz.co.il/misc/2010-05-25/ty-article/0000017f-dbda-d856-a37f-ffdabbc10000.

[4] The Berman Group Ltd., the Davidovitz and Sons Bakery Ltd., and their executives were found guilty in July 2015. Angel Bakeries, the Dganit Group and their executives were found guilty only in November 2017 following a plea bargain.

[5] *The State of Israel* v. *Angel and Others*, Paragraph 580.

and convicted the bakeries and their executives of violating the Israeli Economic Competition law under "aggravating circumstances."[6] The executives were then sentenced to four to twelve months in jail, which were unprecedented criminal sentences in Israel for price fixing.[7]

Although the bakeries' executives admitted to most of the charges, they had a different interpretation of the events, which was relevant for determining whether the offense was committed under aggravating circumstances. In particular, the executives claimed that their agreements were intended to stop a "price war" that erupted at the end of 2009 and the beginning of 2010 mainly in ultra-orthodox neighborhoods.[8] They also argued that the agreement to stop competition for each other's customers was incidental to the main agreement to raise prices and was intended to ensure that the price war would not erupt all over again. On these grounds, the Davidovitz and Sons Bakery (henceforth "Davidovitz"), Mr. Davidovitz, and the CEO of the Berman Group (henceforth "Berman") appealed the District Court's decision to convict them under aggravating circumstances to the Supreme Court. The State of Israel also appealed the sentences of the two executives, arguing that they were not severe enough.[9] The Supreme Court rejected the

---

[6] "Aggravating circumstances" are defined in Section 47A of the Israeli Economic Competition law as "circumstances in which significant harm may be caused to business competition." The maximum sentence for criminal offenses of the Israeli competition law is five years of imprisonment rather than three if the offense was committed under aggravating circumstances.

[7] Mr. Angel, the CEO of Angel Bakeries and a partial owner was sentenced in 2017 to five months in jail after reaching a plea bargain, the CEO of Dganit Group got four months of community service, and the chairman of the board of Dganit Group got a monetary fine due to personal health circumstances.

[8] Specifically, the Court mentioned neighborhoods in Jerusalem, Bnei Brak, Beit Shemesh, Beitar, Elad, and Kiryat Sefer. See *The State of Israel* v. *Angel and Others*, Paragraph 53.

[9] See Criminal Case Appeals Numbers 1656/16, 1665/16, and 1674/16 *Davidovitz and Others* v. *The State of Israel and J&E Berman Ltd*.
https://tinyurl.com/j5xa2y9h
(henceforth *"Davidovitz and Others* v. *The State of Israel"*).

appeals in March 2017 and stated in the lead opinion that "... the present case is indeed one of those exceptional cases in which the harm to competition is particularly severe."[10] Nonetheless, it reduced the executives' sentences to three months in jail and three months of community services.

Several important features of this case are worth emphasizing. First, sliced dark bread and challah, which are at the center of the case, are subject to price cap regulation, which is designed to cover the bakeries' costs, including their cost of capital. However, due to the considerable market power that retail chains have vis-à-vis the bakeries, the retail prices of sliced dark bread and challah are on average 5–15 percent below their retail price caps. As a result, the bakeries sell them to retailers at a loss.[11] The bakeries argue that these losses are a price they are forced to pay in order to sell other bread products to retailers, on which they make positive margins. Although sliced dark bread and challah were already sold at a loss, a few months before the bakeries reached their agreements, Davidovitz had started offering them in some stores at a special deal of "3 loaves for 10 NIS," (henceforth "3 for 10"); these deals triggered a price war.

To appreciate these deals, one should bear in mind that the regulated retail price cap at the time was 6.66 NIS for sliced dark bread and 4.84 NIS for challah and the corresponding wholesale price caps, which do not include VAT (16 percent at the time), were 5.07 NIS for sliced dark bread and 3.72 NIS for challah. These prices reflects the bakeries' costs plus a fair rate of return on invested capital. A "3 for 10" deal implies a retail price of 8.62 NIS net of VAT for three loaves; once a retail margin is accounted for, the effective wholesale price per loaf is then substantially below the regulated wholesale price. Importantly, the "3 for 10" deals were offered only in a limited number of stores, mainly in ultra-orthodox neighborhoods in the

---

[10] *Davidovitz and Others* v. *The State of Israel*, Paragraph 94.
[11] *The State of Israel* v. *Angel and Others*, Paragraph 422.

Jerusalem area, which is the "home turf" of Angel Bakeries (henceforth "Angel") and Berman. Angel and Berman reacted by also offering "3 for 10" deals in some stores. The deals are attractive to ultra-orthodox families, which tend to be very large and consume a lot of bread, and are typically low income.

Second, although the bakeries agreed to stop the "3 for 10" deals on dark sliced bread and challah and raise retail prices to "2 for 10" on sliced dark bread and "3 for 11" for challah, these prices were still substantially below the regulated price caps and were also below the average retail prices across all stores in Israel at the time (6.30 NIS for sliced dark bread and 4.61 NIS for challah).[12]

Third, the bakeries agreed to stop the "3 for 10" deals in stores that had offered these deals, rather than raise the prices of all types of bread in all stores (or a subgroup of stores). In fact, the bakeries argued that the "3 for 10" deals had been offered in only about forty stores. Although the Court was unable to verify this claim, it nonetheless agreed that the number of stores that had offered these deals was not substantially different.[13]

Fourth, as already mentioned, the main disagreement between the ICA and the bakeries was how to interpret the price-fixing agreement. The ICA argued that prior to the agreement, the bakeries had engaged in "fierce competition" over market shares, which involved low prices, promotions, and attempts to acquire new customers. It also argued that the bakeries had formed a cartel, intended to raise prices and divide the market in order to boost the bakeries' profits at the public's expense.[14] The ICA also claimed that, but for the cartel, the competitive actions of the bakeries would have continued for a

---

[12] It might be argued that selling regulated bread at low prices was part of competition to get access to stores, where the bakeries sell unregulated bread at positive margins. However, the "3 for 10" deals were exclusively offered in stores where the bulk of the demand is for regulated bread and where customer loyalty is very low.

[13] *The State of Israel* v. *Angel and Others*, Paragraph 66.

[14] See the prosecution's Summary of Arguments in *The State of Israel* v. *Angel and Others*, Paragraphs 6, 28, 58, 703, 732.

long period of time.[15] The bakeries argued instead that the motivation for the agreements was to stop a price war that had erupted in some stores and prevent it from spreading to other stores and that the price war was in any event short-lived and would have stopped on its own. They also argued that the agreement to stop competing for customers was an ancillary agreement, "rooted in the desire to bring about the cessation of the '3 for 10' deals"; that is it was incidental to the main agreement to raise prices.[16] The Court on its part, argued in its summary of events, that the "3 for 10" deals were driven by the bakeries' attempt to invade each other's territories and gain market shares, as well as by a "deterrent–punitive element" in response to the competitive initiatives of the rival bakeries.[17]

In this paper, we review the bread case. We begin in Section 4.2 by reviewing the Israeli bread market and its relevant characteristics for the case. In Section 4.3 we describe the price-fixing agreement in detail, and in Section 4.4 we discuss the possible interpretations of the events. We conclude in Section 4.5.

4.2 THE ISRAELI BREAD MARKET

The Israeli bread market can be divided into three main segments.

a) Standard bread (dark and white bread, sliced and unsliced) and challah, which are subject to price cap regulation at the wholesale and retail levels by the inter-ministerial Price Committee of the Ministry of Finance and the Ministry of Economy and Industry which operates under the 1996 Supervision of Prices of Goods and Services Act.
b) Other types of bread (e.g., whole-grain bread, multigrain bread, light bread, and rye bread) and various types of challah (e.g., sweet challah, light challah, and spelt challah) which are not subject to price controls and sold at about twice or even three times the price of price-controlled bread.[18]
c) Pita bread and rolls.

---

[15] See the prosecution's Summary of Arguments in *The State of Israel* v. *Angel and Others*, Paragraph 299.
[16] *The State of Israel* v. *Angel and Others*, Paragraph 134–136.
[17] *The State of Israel* v. *Angel and Others*, Paragraphs 32 and 473.
[18] For instance, an Excel sheet in "The Consumer Council's Inspection: Where are the Best Deals on Bread?" June 26, 2016, www.consumers.org.il/item/semel_030716

There are strong indications that price-controlled bread is a distinct market, including the large gap between its price and the price of other types of bread and various indications for a limited degree of substitutability between these breads (Price Committee, 2021). Indeed, the Court determined that price-controlled bread is the relevant market for the case.[19] In what follows, we will therefore focus on this market.

4.2.1 The Market for Price-Controlled Bread

Similarly to traditional rate of return or price cap regulation, the price cap on standard bread and challah is set to cover the firms' costs and ensure investors a fair return on their investment. By design then, the wholesale price cap reflects the average total cost of bread (including its cost of capital), and the retail price cap is equal to the wholesale price cap plus a normal retail margin and VAT.[20] Table 4.1 shows the wholesale and retail price caps on dark bread (sliced and unsliced) and challah, which account for nearly all sales of price-controlled bread. As the table shows, the regulated price caps were adjusted several times during the 2009–2011 period due to exogenous cost shocks such as changes in the price of flour or energy, or due to changes in VAT.[21]

As we discuss below, due to the considerable market power that retail chains have vis-à-vis the bakeries, the price caps are not binding: in 2009–2011, the retail prices of dark bread and challah were 5–15 percent below their retail price caps, which suggests that these products were sold at below cost (including a fair rate of return on investments).

---

shows that on average, the price of special breads within the same supermarket chain was 2.1–2.9 times higher than the price of price-controlled bread.

[19] *The State of Israel* v. *Angel and Others*, Paragraphs 309–321.

[20] An important caveat is that the price cap is based on data that is averaged across bakeries and hence may exceed the average cost of one bakery, but be below the average cost of another.

[21] The rate of VAT was raised from 15.5 percent to 16.5 percent on July 1, 2009 and was lowered to 16 percent on January 1, 2010.

Table 4.1 *Regulated price cap of sliced dark bread in NIS, 2008–2013*

Effective date	Sliced dark bread		Dark bread		Challah	
	Wholesale price (excl. VAT)	Retail price (incl. VAT)	Wholesale price (excl. VAT)	Retail price (incl. VAT)	Wholesale price (excl. VAT)	Retail price (incl. VAT)
December 4, 2008	5.33	6.96	3.60	4.64	3.91	5.07
March 12, 2009	5.10	6.66	3.44	4.44	3.74	4.84
June 22, 2009	5.26	6.88	3.56	4.59	3.86	5.00
July 1, 2009	5.26	6.94	3.56	4.63	3.86	5.05
October 29, 2009	5.07	6.69	3.43	4.46	3.72	4.86
January 1, 2010	5.07	6.66	3.43	4.44	3.72	4.84
August 5, 2010	5.25	6.90	3.55	4.60	3.86	5.02
October 3, 2010	5.44	7.15	3.68	4.77	3.99	5.20
February 8, 2011	5.63	7.38	3.80	4.92	4.13	5.37
August 14, 2012	5.99	7.87	4.05	5.24	4.40	5.72

Based on data from Israel's Central Bureau of Statistics, as of 2012, price-controlled bread accounted for 15 percent of the total sales of bread in Israel in NIS (Price Committee, 2021, table 1).[22] The share of price-controlled bread in the total sales of the four large bakeries is much higher though. For instance, in 2010, price-controlled bread accounted for 38–43 percent of the total sales of bread in NIS at Angel – the largest bakery in Israel – and 35–40 percent of its total sales in NIS; this share dropped to 30–34 percent by 2015.[23] The share of price-controlled bread in the total sales of Berman and Davidovitz – the second and third largest bakeries in Israel – was similar.[24]

A breakdown of sales in tons of price-controlled bread by store type, based on data from StoreNext,[25] indicates that in 2008–2013, sliced dark bread accounted on average for 65 percent of the sales of price-controlled bread, challah accounted for 19 percent, and dark loaves of bread for 15 percent. The sales of white bread are negligible and indeed, the agreements between the bakeries did not directly involve the price of white bread.

Table 4.2 shows a breakdown of the sales in tons of sliced dark bread and challah by store type, again based on StoreNext data. There are four store types in our data: the first two, "main local chains" and "main hard discount (HD) chains," belong to the main supermarket chains. HD stores are large and carry a large assortment of products; local stores are smaller, carry fewer products, and tend to charge higher prices. The third category, "other HD chains," refers to HD

---

[22] The figures for earlier years should probably be somewhat higher, as the share of price-controlled bread in the total sales of bread in NIS declined steadily over time and dropped from 15 percent in 2012 to 8.2 percent by 2018.

[23] See Salomon A. Angel Ltd., Financial Statements for 2010, Sec 26.1 (in Hebrew), and Salomon A. Angel Ltd., Financial Statements for 2015, Sec 27.2 (in Hebrew).

[24] *The State of Israel* v. *Angel and Others*, Footnote 55.

[25] StoreNext is a market research company that collects data directly from the cash registers of over 3,000 stores, mainly in the Jewish sector. The data covers around 80 percent of the market, including most of the major supermarket chains, as well as about 60 percent of all minimarkets. The data is extrapolated to reflect sales in the entire market.

Table 4.2 *Distribution of sales in tons of sliced dark bread and challah, by store type, 2008–2015*

	Main local chains (%)	Main HD chains (%)	Other HD chains (%)	Small stores (%)
Dark bread	35	60	2	3
Sliced dark bread	22	45	12	21
Challah	25	59	8	8

stores that belong to smaller HD supermarket chains. The last category, "small stores," includes minimarkets, grocery stores, and convenience stores. Table 4.2 shows that most of the sales are in the main supermarket chains and especially their HD stores. It should be noted that most stores that offered the "3 for 10" deals were in the small stores category.[26]

Since the late 1980s, the price-controlled bread market in Israel has gone through a consolidation process that involved a series of mergers and acquisitions. As of the early 2000s, Angel, Berman, Davidovitz, and Dganit are the largest industrial bakeries in Israel and account for about 50 percent of the total sales of bread in Israel, and 90–95 percent of the sales of price-controlled bread.[27] The consolidation of industrial bakeries is not unique to Israel: a similar process took place in the USA and the UK (see Appendix 7.2 in Sutton, 1991), and in South Africa (Mncube, 2013).[28]

As we will discuss in detail below, the bread market has an important geographic dimension. At a national level though, the largest bakery in Israel is Angel, with an estimated market share of

---

[26] Sales at "small stores" may be biased downward, however, as small stores are underrepresented in the StoreNext data.
[27] The only other bakery that supplies price-controlled bread is the Agami Bakery, located midway between Tel Aviv and Haifa. See *The State of Israel* v. *Angel and Others*, Paragraph 335. The market for non-industrial bread is much more fragmented and even today there are "hundreds of bakeries" in Israel (Price Committee, 2022).
[28] Interestingly, Block, Nold and Sidak (1981) report that during the 1960s and 1970s, bread cases were the most common among DOJ's food price-fixing cases.

around 20 percent as of 2010.[29] Angel owns bakeries in Jerusalem, Lod (the center of Israel), and Netivot (the south of Israel), 50 percent of a bakery in Kfar Hahoresh (south east of Haifa), and a pastry factory in Beit Shemesh (near Jerusalem). Berman is the second largest group and owns bakeries in Jerusalem, Ramat Hasharon, Holon, and Bat Yam (the last three are in the Tel Aviv metropolitan area). The third largest group is Davidovitz; it owns bakeries in Kiryat Ata (east of Haifa) and Holon (the Tel Aviv metropolitan area). The fourth largest bakery is Dganit, which owns the Dganit Ein Bar bakery in Kibbutz Einat (center of Israel) and the Merhavit Bakery in Kiryat Shmona (upper Galilee in the north of Israel). The last two bakeries have cross ownership links: Davidovitz holds 50 percent of the voting rights and 33 percent of the cash flow rights in the Merhavit Bakery, which in turn holds 50 percent of the Dganit Ein Bar bakery (the remaining 50 percent are held by Kibbutz Einat).

4.2.2 Important Characteristics of the Bread Market

The Israeli price-controlled bread market has several characteristics that are important for understanding the case. First, the market is highly competitive because standard bread and challah are homogeneous products and consumers are price sensitive with little brand loyalty (Price Committee, 2021, pp. 10–11).[30] In addition, the supply of price-controlled bread is highly elastic because the four large bakeries have excess capacity and can easily expand their production levels (Price Committee, 2021, p. 11), and because bread is delivered to stores on a daily basis, so the bakeries observe the retail prices of breads produced by competing bakeries and can respond to these prices in real time.[31] Another factor that makes the industry highly

---

[29] See Salomon A. Angel Ltd., Financial Statements for 2010, sec 1.2 (in Hebrew).
[30] For instance, Mr. Davidovitz testified that at least in ultra-orthodox neighborhoods where price competition is intense and product's loyalty is low, "I cannot sell for even one minute after I raise the price." *The State of Israel* v. *Angel and Others*, Paragraph 399.
[31] Although the bakeries cannot observe the wholesale prices of competing bakeries, our understanding is that they can infer them fairly reliably from the retail prices.

competitive is that most retailers source bread from only one or two bakeries (Price Committee, 2021, p. 10), so if a bakery is not selected by a given store as a designated supplier, it cannot sell bread at all at that store. Moreover, absent long-term supply contracts, retailers can fairly easily switch bakeries.

A second important characteristic of the bread industry is that the four large bakeries produce and sell both standard bread and challah, which are subject to price controls, as well as other types of bread that are not subject to price controls. Although the agreements between the bakeries involved only the prices of sliced dark bread and challah, it is conceivable that other segments of the market may have also been affected due to unilateral effects.[32] However, since the Court did not address this possibility explicitly, we will restrict our attention only to the price-controlled bread market.

Third, evidence presented in court indicates that retail chains have considerable market power vis-à-vis the bakeries.[33] Similarly, the Price Committee report (Price Committee, 2021, p. 10) argues that:

> "The bakeries have difficulty negotiating with the retailers and are required to give them large discounts, in order to ensure that the supply agreements, which can be canceled at any time without reservations or preconditions, are not cancelled".

Indeed, the large bakeries have complained for years that due to the discounts that they are forced to give large supermarket chains, standard bread and challah are sold at a loss at prices that are well below their regulated price caps. The bakeries claim that they are willing to sustain these losses because supermarket chains require them to offer all types of bread. That is, the losses on standard bread and challah are in effect a price that they are forced to pay in order to be able to sell

---

[32] There is no evidence that the bakeries discussed any bread types other than those involved in the "3 for 10" deals, i.e., sliced dark bread and challah.
[33] *The State of Israel* v. *Angel and Others*, Paragraphs 193–194.

other bread products in supermarket chains. In fact, the interministerial Price Committee found that the bakeries' profitability is low or even negative (Price Committee, 2021, p. 13), and the committee's head from 1995 to 2011, Mrs. Zvia Dori, testified in court that during her entire time in office as a government official, standard bread and challah were always sold at a loss to retailers.[34] Moreover, an audit by an accountant hired by the Price Committee found that in 2010, Berman lost "millions of NIS" on sales of standard bread and challah.[35]

Fourth, historically, the bread market tended to be localized. This tendency was driven by the need to deliver fresh bread to stores early in the morning on a daily basis. Moreover, when serving a particular store, closer bakeries have a cost advantage over more distant bakeries due to lower costs of distribution which gives them a strategic advantage. Thus, the bakeries' cost functions depend not only on their output levels, but also on the structure of the network of retailers that each of them supplies. Not surprisingly then, Angel and Berman, which were originally located in Jerusalem, dominated the Jerusalem area and the south of Israel; Davidovitz, which is located near Haifa, was the dominant industrial bakery in the north of Israel; and Dganit, which is located in the center of Israel, operated mainly in that area.

Over time, however, the industrial bakeries expanded into new geographic areas. This geographic expansion was driven by several factors. First, the bakeries started using an enzyme that preserves the freshness of bread for several days and allows them to ship it over longer distances. Second, the four large bakeries increased their production facilities and had excess capacity; moreover they acquired bakeries in other geographic areas, which made it possible to serve larger geographic areas. In particular, Angel and Berman started to expand in the north of Israel, where Davidovitz had been the

---

[34] *The State of Israel* v. *Angel and Others*, Paragraph 422.
[35] *The State of Israel* v. *Angel and Others*, Paragraph 426.

dominant bakery. Angel entered the Haifa market following a merger with Oranim Bakery in 2001, and Berman started expanding in the north and made low price offers to some of Davidovitz's customers. Davidovitz in turn, tried to expand in the Jerusalem area, which was the "home turf" of Angel and Berman, as part of a strategy that began about five years before the "bread cartel."[36] A third factor that contributed to the geographic expansion of the bakeries was the geographic expansion of supermarket chains that had exclusive deals with some of the bakeries. For example, Rami Levy, which is by now the second largest supermarket chain in Israel, and at the time was selling exclusively Angel's bread, expanded into the Haifa region in 2009 and started selling Angel's bread in an area that was until then dominated by Davidovitz.[37]

4.3 THE BAKERIES' AGREEMENTS

In this section we describe the bakeries' agreements; in doing so, we rely on the decisions of the Jerusalem District Court and the Supreme Court.[38]

4.3.1 The Background to the Agreements

As mentioned earlier, historically the bread market tended to be localized, but over time, the industrial bakeries started to "invade" each other's territories. A number of executives testified in court that while the bakeries had constantly been trying to acquire new customers, competition in the industry featured "ebbs and flows" with waves of intense competition, followed by periods of less intense competition.[39] It appears from the evidence that at the end of 2009 and the beginning of 2010, competition for new customers was

---

[36] *The State of Israel* v. *Angel and Others*, Paragraphs 35–36.
[37] Based on private communication with Yaron Angel.
[38] We rely mainly on *The State of Israel* v. *Angel and Others* and on *Davidovitz and Others* v. *The State of Israel*.
[39] *The State of Israel* v. *Angel and Others*, Paragraph 49. Although the ICA has argued that these fluctuations in the intensity of competition were not necessarily natural and entirely spontaneous, the Court did not have sufficient evidence to

at a peak and was especially intense between Davidovitz and Berman. In fact, a contractor of Davidovitz testified that competition during that period was "the longest and most difficult war we have ever had."[40]

Specifically, it appears that in January–February 2010, Berman made extensive efforts to expand in the north and transferred two additional salesmen to the north to support these efforts.[41] Berman's CEO testified that these "aggressive" efforts to penetrate dozens of stores that were previously served mostly by Davidovitz were a retaliation against Davidovitz, after Davidovitz "took" from Berman seventeen stores in the north. He also testified that while these efforts were costly, they were meant to convey a message to Davidovitz that "there is a price for every harm done to us."[42] A sales and marketing manager at Berman testified that the motivation for these efforts was twofold:

> "If someone has slapped me, he will receive a slap, so things are focused in the direction of Davidovitz... It is both a desire to expand and the desire to retaliate."[43]

The manager also testified that Berman's CEO gave an instruction to recover the sales that were lost to Davidovitz from "another place," and explained that the efforts were focused on Davidovitz rather than other bakeries, because "it is impossible to fight with everybody." Moreover he testified that this was competition at full force and hence he instructed his own men to "charge ahead."[44]

Davidovitz decided to retaliate and expanded its operations in the Jerusalem area and started offering "3 for 10" deals on sliced dark

---

substantiate the argument at the level required in a criminal trial, see *The State of Israel* v. *Angel and Others*, Paragraph 52.

[40] *The State of Israel* v. *Angel and Others*, Paragraph 29.
[41] *The State of Israel* v. *Angel and Others*, Paragraph 27.
[42] *The State of Israel* v. *Angel and Others*, Paragraph 28.
[43] *The State of Israel* v. *Angel and Others*, Paragraphs 28–29.
[44] *The State of Israel* v. *Angel and Others*, Paragraph 29.

bread and challah (and in some cases "4 for 10" deals on challah) in ultra-orthodox neighborhoods. Mr. Davidovitz testified that:

> "[Berman] will understand once and for all that there are no strong and weak here ... there is a limit to everything ... They [Angel and Berman] need to understand that Jerusalem ... is not another fortress of Angel and Berman and that's it ... they need to understand it like it took me years to realize that I was alone in and around Haifa and all of a sudden you come and see the shelves stocked with everyone's [bread]".[45]

Moreover, Mr. Davidovitz testified that as far as the "3 for 10" deals are concerned,

> "I'm not in a hurry. I have intended to invest millions. I have no intention of stopping until they give me back what they took from me in the north".[46]

A regional manager at Davidovitz testified that had Berman not penetrated areas that were dominated by Davidovitz, she probably wouldn't have gone after "every other" customer of Berman. She added that although she is always interested in new customers, the normal mode of operation is to offer new customers "prices that are a little lower than what you usually offer in the current market." However, during the relevant period, "Berman offered unprecedented prices and discounts ... so what do you do? Counterattack."[47]

The Court concluded that Davidovitz's aggressive actions in Jerusalem, including the "3 for 10" deals, were part of a strategy to penetrate the Jerusalem market in order to strike a competitive balance against Angel and Berman – which had penetrated the Haifa region and the north – and prevent Davidovitz from being pushed

---

[45] *The State of Israel* v. *Angel and Others*, Paragraph 30.
[46] *The State of Israel* v. *Angel and Others*, Paragraph 398.
[47] *The State of Israel* v. *Angel and Others*, Paragraphs 40–46.

out of the market.[48] There was evidence that Angel and Berman also offered "3 for 10" deals in some stores.[49]

Importantly, the "3 for 10" deals were offered mainly in ultra-orthodox neighborhoods in Jerusalem, Bnei Brak, Beit Shemesh, Beitar, Elad, and Kiryat Sefer.[50] In these neighborhoods, families tend to be very large, so buying three loaves of bread (which weigh 750 grams each) at once is natural, and over half of the community is below the poverty line (Israel Democracy Institute, 2016, Chapters 1 and 3).[51] Indeed, in ultra-orthodox communities like Bnei Brak, price-controlled bread accounts for 70 percent of the sales of bread, while in Tel Aviv, where the ultra-orthodox community is very small, it accounts for merely 30 percent.[52]

There are also indications that the "3 for 10" deals were offered only in a limited number of stores. For instance, Davidovitz argued that the "3 for 10" deals had been offered in only forty stores.[53] Although the Court was unable to verify this claim, it did point out that the totality of the evidence suggests that the actual number of stores that had offered the deals was not significantly different. In particular, the Court held that the "3 for 10" deals had not been offered in the large supermarket chains.

The concern that the "3 for 10" deals would spread to other stores, and especially retail chains, led to the executives' meeting.[54] According to the ICA, the CEOs of the four large bakeries first met on February 23, 2010 at the office of a leading law firm in Tel Aviv.[55]

---

[48] *The State of Israel* v. *Angel and Others*, Paragraph 31.
[49] For instance, see *The State of Israel* v. *Angel and Others*, Paragraph 91.
[50] *The State of Israel* v. *Angel and Others*, Paragraph 53.
[51] Between 2012 and 2014, the total fertility rate (number of children potentially born to a woman during her childbearing years) averaged 6.9 children per woman in the Haredi (i.e., ultra-orthodox) community. A majority of Haredi families are living in poverty, and the share of Haredi children defined as poor is 67 percent. See Israel Democracy Institute, 2016, ch. 1 and 3.
[52] *The State of Israel* v. *Angel and Others*, Paragraph 65. This finding is not surprising since standard bread is a classic example of an inferior good.
[53] *The State of Israel* v. *Angel and Others*, Paragraph 66.
[54] *The State of Israel* v. *Angel and Others*, Paragraph 392.
[55] Ironically, the slogan of the law firm is "Where Clients Make Partners."

The first part of the meeting was legitimate and lasted for about an hour; the rest of the meeting, however, took place without the presence of lawyers and lasted for several hours.[56] Eventually, the CEOs reached two agreements.

4.3.2 The First Agreement

The first agreement reached by the CEOs was to stop the "3 for 10" deals. They also agreed that in stores served by more than one bakery, the dominant supplier will raise its prices first ("the strong one raises first") and that the other suppliers will not use this price increase to increase their own sales at the expense of the dominant supplier.[57]

More specifically, the CEOs agreed that, as a first step, the minimal price of sliced dark bread and challah would be "3 for 10" as of February 28, 2010.[58] In later meetings between various executives from the different bakeries, that were held a few days after the CEOs' meeting, the minimal price was raised to "2 for 10" for sliced dark bread and "3 for 11" for challah as of March 3 or in some cases as of March 10, 2010.[59] There is evidence that the bakeries kept discussing the implementation of the first agreement until the agreement ended in late May 2010.[60]

Following the first agreement, prices started to increase at the beginning of March 2010 to "3 for 12," "2 for 8," or even "2 for 10."[61]

---

[56] See the prosecution's Summary of Arguments in *The State of Israel* v. *Angel and Others*, Paragraphs 12–13. According to the press, the purpose of the meeting was to discuss regulatory matters. See "After the intervention of the 'system' Davidovitz did not deliver bread and the customer remained frustrated," Tomer Ganon, Anat Roeh, and Zohar Shahar-Levy, Calcalist, January 30, 2014, www.calcalist.co.il/local/articles/0,7340,L-3623013,00.html.

[57] *The State of Israel* v. *Angel and Others*, Paragraph 76.

[58] *The State of Israel* v. *Angel and Others*, Paragraph 75.

[59] *The State of Israel* v. *Angel and Others*, Paragraph 75.

[60] The last meeting on record was held on May 20, 2010 between a sales manager at Angel and a marketing manager at Davidovitz in a gasoline station on the Trans-Israel highway. See *The State of Israel* v. *Angel and Others*, Paragraph 126.

[61] *The State of Israel* v. *Angel and Others*, Paragraphs 78, 82, 91, and 113. Note that these offers are retail prices and include VAT. Accounting for VAT and retail

This was true especially after Passover 2010 (March 29–April 6).[62] There is even evidence that Davidovitz committed to stop supplying stores that did not raise prices and that Berman conditioned its wholesale price on the stores' retail prices in order to induce them to raise prices.[63]

Although the Court found that the agreement to raise prices was substantially implemented and led to a significant increase in retail prices in the relevant stores,[64] it did point out difficulties in implementing the agreement, at least before Passover. For example, Mr. Davidovitz was quoted in court as complaining that "To tell you the truth, I'm tired of these meetings. Nothing comes out of them."[65]

One obstacle to implementing the agreement was the fact that it involved retail prices, which are set by retailers, who were not parties to the agreement. For instance, some retailers had already advertised the "3 for 10" deals and were unable or unwilling to raise prices,[66] while others decided unilaterally to offer these deals.[67] A possible reason why the bakeries' agreement concerned the retail price of bread (rather than its wholesale price), despite the fact that the bakeries do not control it directly, is that the retail price is easily observable. By contrast, wholesale prices, including discounts and various payments between the bakeries and stores, are confidential and hard to verify.

4.3.3 The Second Agreement

Apart from agreeing to stop the "3 for 10" deals, the bakeries also agreed to stop competing for one another's existing customers; the

---

margins, the associated wholesale prices are still substantially below the regulated wholesale price.

[62] During Passover, which is celebrated for eight days, bakeries do not produce nor supply bread. Passover is then a natural break in the bread market.
[63] *The State of Israel* v. *Angel and Others*, Paragraphs 98 and 114.
[64] *The State of Israel* v. *Angel and Others*, Paragraph 132.
[65] *The State of Israel* v. *Angel and Others*, Paragraph 206, Footnote 46.
[66] *The State of Israel* v. *Angel and Others*, Paragraph 94.
[67] *The State of Israel* v. *Angel and Others*, Paragraphs 56 and 364.

Court referred to this agreement as "the second agreement." The Court accepted the bakeries' claim that the second agreement was triggered by the desire to stop the "3 for 10."

The Court held that the overall picture that emerges from the evidence is that the bakeries had actively and vigorously implemented the second agreement and developed an effective mechanism for investigating complaints about violations of the agreement.

For example, Yellow, which is a large chain of 250 convenience stores served by Berman, had negotiated a supply contract with Davidovitz just before the agreement was reached. Berman's CEO complained to Dganit's CEO, who also served as the chairman of the bakers' association, and demanded that Davidovitz stops selling to Yellow. Although Mr. Davidovitz argued that the relationship with Yellow began prior to the second agreement and that he could not break the contract with Yellow, he nonetheless asked Dganit's CEO to tell Berman's CEO that "if I take something from him, then I will give him something somewhere else."[68] When Dganit's CEO delivered this message, Berman's CEO replied:

> "No, we don't have such an agreement, it's not true, and I have also signed all sorts of things and didn't come to anyone with any demands; I folded like a shmock, that's all".[69]

In a later conversion, Mr. Davidovitz asked Dganit's CEO to remind Berman's CEO that Berman also took a chain from Davidovitz after the agreement was reached, and that he, Mr. Davidovitz, "didn't say anything to him, and I didn't call you or anyone."[70] Moreover, a marketing manager at Davidovitz said that he has a list of stores that he can enter as a retaliation in case Berman will react to Davidovitz's sales to Yellow.[71] The Court's decision does not mention how the dispute over Yellow ended.

---

[68] *The State of Israel* v. *Angel and Others*, Paragraphs 161–171.
[69] *The State of Israel* v. *Angel and Others*, Paragraph 167.
[70] *The State of Israel* v. *Angel and Others*, Paragraph 167.
[71] *The State of Israel* v. *Angel and Others*, Paragraph 170.

It is worth noting that Davidovitz argued that the evidence presented in court shows that the bakeries have settled at most fourteen disputes over customers, and that most of them were in March 2010, when the agreement was still new, but that later on in April 2010, many disputes were not settled. Davidovitz also argued that half of the settled disputes concerned customers in the ultra-orthodox sector, where the "3 for 10" deals had been offered.[72]

4.4 POSSIBLE INTERPRETATIONS OF THE BAKERIES' AGREEMENTS

Price fixing is illegal according to Israeli competition law. Hence, the illegality of the bakeries' agreements was not disputed. Still, there is an open question regarding the interpretation of the two agreements.[73] There are at least two possible interpretations. The first, advanced by the ICA, views the bakeries' agreements as a standard textbook cartel aimed at stopping "concrete competitive actions that the various bakeries were about to take" and that "would have lasted for a long time" but for the cartel.[74] While the ICA did not make this argument explicit, it essentially made the case that the bakeries had engaged in "normal" competition prior to the price-fixing agreement, which was then intended to raise prices above their "normal" level.

The second possible interpretation is that the price-fixing agreement was intended to end a price war in the form of the "3 for 10" deals. The question, of course, is why the price war has erupted? The standard view of price wars is that they are part of some dynamic collusive arrangement (e.g., Slade, 1990). In our case, the arrangement could have been a market division agreement, according to which the bakeries agreed not to invade each other's territory. This possibility,

---

[72] *The State of Israel* v. *Angel and Others*, Paragraphs 252 and 254.
[73] As mentioned earlier, the interpretation was relevant for the criminal sentences imposed on the bakeries' executives.
[74] See the prosecution's Summary of Arguments in *The State of Israel* v. *Angel and Others*, Paragraphs 167 and 200. In fact, the ICA relied on Carlton and Perloff (2005) to make the case that the bakeries' agreement had features that made it stable and would have helped it to last for a long time.

however, is inconsistent with the ICA's claim that the bakeries started colluding only after the CEOs' meeting.[75] Another possibility is that the price war was part of a non-collusive market competition and the bakeries' agreement was intended to stop it. While this possibility is less standard in the IO literature, we believe that it is highly plausible and one of the reasons why the case is particularly interesting.

Although the Court mainly emphasized the ICA's interpretation of the bakeries' agreements as a standard textbook cartel, it also acknowledged the second:

> "The overall picture is that both the Berman Bakery and the Davidovitz Bakery had two motives for their competitive actions. On the one hand, there was a competitive element of market penetration, by lowering prices and increasing market share. Alongside it, there was also a deterrent – punitive element, whose purpose was to respond to the competitive actions of the opponent".[76]

Before we continue to discuss the two interpretations in more detail, it is worth noting that the two interpretations imply a different pattern of prices. According to the standard cartel story – the ICA's interpretation – prices are initially at some competitive level. When firms form a cartel, prices increase and stay high as long as the cartel is in effect. Once the cartel ends, either due to antitrust enforcement or because it internally breaks down, prices drop.[77] The alternative interpretation – the agreement was intended to end a price war in the

---

[75] *The State of Israel* v. *Angel and Others*, Paragraph 52.
[76] *The State of Israel* v. *Angel and Others*, Paragraph 32.
[77] Interestingly, there are well-documented episodes of prices remaining at supracompetitive levels even after a cartel had been shut down by the antitrust agency. For example, Figure 2 in Harrington (2023) shows that the price of Beta Carotene remained high even after guilty pleas were submitted in the vitamins cartel. By contrast, Figure 1 in Harrington (2023) shows that the price path of Vitamin A was typical: starting with the official birth date of the vitamins cartel, price gradually climbed, stabilized, and then drastically fell in association with the investigations by antitrust agencies in Europe and the USA.

form of the "3 for 10" deals – implies a different pattern of prices. Initially, prices are at some level which could be competitive or collusive. Then, prices drop when a price war erupts. When firms reach a price-fixing agreement, prices increase, but then drop again once the agreement breaks down.

4.4.1 The ICA's Cartel Interpretations

The ICA argued that the bakeries formed a "cartel" which "significantly harmed competition."[78] It described the events of the case as follows: "At the end of 2009 and the beginning of 2010, a fierce competition developed among the accused bakeries."[79] As part of this competition, Berman "had expanded the marketing of its products in the north," while Davidovitz had started competing "more intensively in the Jerusalem area and the center." Moreover, "by its very nature" competition would have spread to other areas. According to the ICA,

> The purpose of the competition that took place prior to the cartel was clear and simple – to increase the bakeries' market share by lowering prices, using promotions, and trying to attract customers in a variety of ways.[80]

The ICA also argued that the lower wholesale prices offered by the bakeries in order to gain market share allowed retailers to offer sliced dark bread and challah at "prices of 3 or 4 loaves for 10 NIS (or at a cheaper price),"[81] and that these deals would have continued for a long period of time, but for the cartel.[82] The ICA then claimed that the

---

[78] The prosecution's Summary of Arguments in *The State of Israel* v. *Angel and Others*, Paragraphs 1 and 58.
[79] The prosecution's Summary of Arguments in *The State of Israel* v. *Angel and Others*, Paragraph 4.
[80] The prosecution's Summary of Arguments in *The State of Israel* v. *Angel and Others*, Paragraph 6.
[81] The prosecution's Summary of Arguments in *The State of Israel* v. *Angel and Others*, Paragraphs 4–5.
[82] The prosecution's Summary of Arguments in *The State of Israel* v. *Angel and Others*, Paragraph 200.

purpose of the CEOs' meeting was "to stop the competition and the retail price decreases,"[83] and that the bakeries' cartel "ended competitive processes that were in their infancy," and "prevented low prices from reaching additional locations and retailers."[84]

The ICA's interpretation of the bakeries' agreements begs at least three questions. First, if the bakeries already took the trouble and risk associated with fixing the prices of sliced dark bread and challah, why did they fix them only at "2 for 10" or "3 for 11" and not at higher levels? After all, the "2 for 10" or "3 for 11" deals still imply a per-unit retail price which is significantly below the retail and even wholesale price caps (6.66 NIS and 5.07 NIS for sliced dark bread and 4.84 NIS and 3.97 NIS for challah), and accounting for VAT and retail margins, are most probably substantially below the bakeries average costs. In fact, StoreNext data that we use below to generate Figures 4.1 and 4.2 shows that in March–April 2010, the average retail prices across all stores were 6.30 NIS for sliced dark bread and 4.61 NIS for challah. At the very least, it seems odd that the bakeries decided to fix prices in some stores at a level that was substantially below the average price across all stores.

The second question is why fix only the prices of sliced dark bread and challah, which account for only a third (or less) of the bakeries' sales, and not also fix the prices of other types of bread? Indeed, the evidence does not indicate any conversations between the bakeries' executives about breads that were not subject to price controls and were sold at a profit.

A third question is why the bakeries have agreed to fix the prices of sliced dark bread and challah only in the relatively small number of stores that had offered them at the "3 for 10" deals, rather than fix prices in all stores, including the supermarket chains, which in any event account for the bulk of the sales of bread?

---

[83] The prosecution's Summary of Arguments in *The State of Israel* v. *Angel and Others*, Paragraph 12.

[84] See the prosecution's Summary of Arguments in *The State of Israel* v. *Angel and Others*, Paragraphs 703 and 732.

In other words, if the bakeries were trying to form a cartel, then it is not clear why they reached a limited agreement that fixed the prices of only two types of bread, in only a small number of stores, and at a level substantially below the average retail price across all stores, rather than fix the prices of more types of bread, in more stores, and at higher prices.

Apart from these questions regarding the nature of the agreements, there is also a question about the interpretation of the "3 for 10" deals. The ICA interprets the deals as "fierce competition" aimed at gaining market shares. But then, had the deals been part of competition rather than a price war, one would have expected to observe them again in the thirteen years since the cartel was exposed. The bakeries, however, never offered such deep discounts again since 2010.

Unfortunately, the ICA did not present any evidence about prices at the store level either before the "3 for 10" deals were offered, nor after the bakeries' agreements stopped.[85] From the court's case then, it is impossible to tell how prices have evolved over time in stores that had offered the "3 for 10" deals, in neighboring stores, and in more distant stores. The evolution of prices, however, is important because it speaks to the motivation for the agreements. To examine the evolution of prices, before, during, and after the bakeries' agreements we resort to public information on sales using StoreNext data. In particular, we use StoreNext data to examine the prices of sliced dark bread and challah from the beginning of 2009 to the end of 2011. If we divide the monthly sales in NIS by the sales in tons, and note that sliced dark bread weighs 750 grams, while challah weighs 500 grams, we get the monthly per-unit average prices.[86]

---

[85] In a criminal case it is enough to show that the bakeries' agreements led to a price increase once the "3 for 10" deals had stopped.

[86] Unfortunately, the data does not allow us to distinguish stores that were affected by the agreements (mostly stores in ultra-orthodox neighborhoods in the Jerusalem area) and stores that were not, and also does not allow us to distinguish between prices in different submarkets (e.g., the ultra-orthodox submarket), or different geographic areas (e.g., the Jerusalem area).

Recall from Table 4.1 that the regulated price cap was adjusted several times during the 2009–2011 period due to exogenous cost shocks (e.g., changes in the price of flour or energy) or changes in VAT.[87] To control for such cost shocks and changes in the VAT rate, we present in Figures 4.1 and 4.2 below the ratio of the retail prices of sliced dark bread and challah and their respective retail price caps. Since the price caps are by design set to cover the bakeries' costs, including their cost of capital, one can think of the ratios in Figures 4.1 and 4.2 as proxies for the price-cost ratios of sliced dark bread and challah.[88] We show the ratios separately for the four store types in our data: "Main HD," "Main local," "Other HD," and "Small stores." The period between the left and middle vertical lines refers to the price war between the bakeries (November 2009–February 2010).[89] The period between the middle and right vertical lines refers to the bakeries' agreements (end of February 2010–May 2010).

Figure 4.1 shows that the retail prices of sliced dark bread were below the retail price cap and their ratio declined from around 95 percent at the start of 2009, to close to 85 percent at the end of 2011, with the exception of prices at the main local supermarket chains (the dashed line) which stayed above 95 percent of the price cap. More importantly, the figure shows that retail prices at the main local supermarket chains were not affected by the price war, nor by the bakeries' agreements. Prices at the main HD chains (the solid line)

---

[87] The rate of VAT was raised from 15.5 to 16.5 percent on July 1, 2009 and was lowered to 16 percent on January 1, 2010.

[88] One should bear in mind that price cap regulation in Israel, like in many other countries, is imperfect and may involve political considerations. The price cap then is an imperfect proxy for costs. Nonetheless, during the 2009–2011 period, prices were adjusted on the basis of an indexation mechanism (rather than full-blown regulatory hearings) which is why we believe that it is a fairly reasonable proxy for costs.

[89] Notice though that the ICA did not establish when the price war broke out exactly; it merely stated that "intense competition" had developed among the bakeries "at the end of 2009 and the beginning of 2010." See the prosecution's Summary of Arguments in *The State of Israel* v. *Angel and Others*, Paragraph 4. Although the "3 for 10" deals probably started only at the beginning of 2010, we will also include November and December 2009 in the price war period.

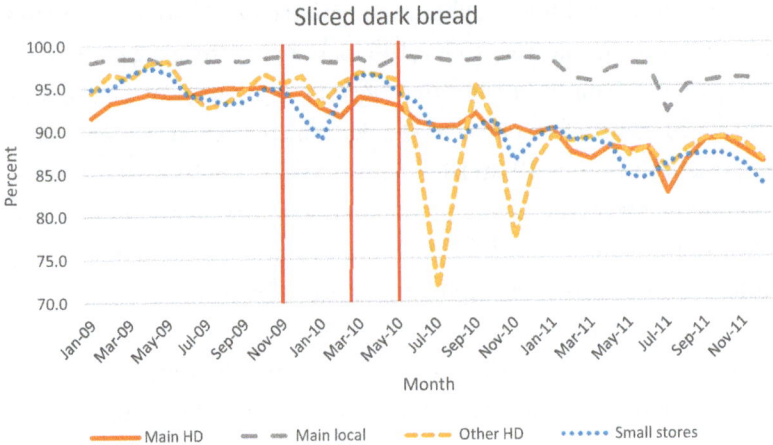

FIGURE 4.1 Ratio of the retail price and the retail price cap of sliced dark bread, by store type, 2009–2011.

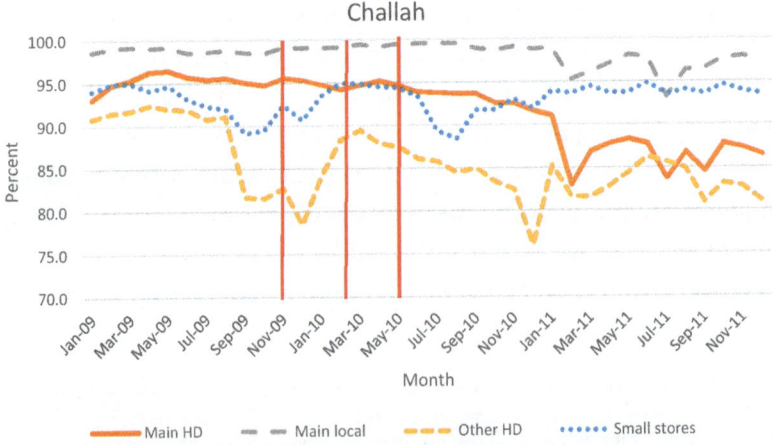

FIGURE 4.2 Ratio of the retail price and the retail price cap of challah, by store type, 2009–2011.

seem to have declined steadily over time and as in the case of prices at the main local supermarket chains, they do not seem to have been affected by the price war or the bakeries' agreements. These results are not surprising given that the evidence presented in court indicates that the price war and the bakeries' agreements involved mostly stores in ultra-orthodox neighborhoods, which do not belong to the main supermarket chains. The results are also inconsistent with the idea that Davidovitz was trying to expand its operations in the Jerusalem area, otherwise he would have probably tried to also penetrate the main supermarket chains, where the bulk of sales are. The evidence presented in court, however, does not indicate that this had been the case.

One might argue that prices at other HD chains (the square dotted line) and small stores (the round dotted line) dipped at the beginning of 2010, but then recovered from February 2010 to May 2010, before declining after May 2010. However the pattern of prices after May 2010 does not seem to be very different from that at the main HD chains, so it is hard to tell if the decline after May 2010 is due to the end of the bakeries' agreements or to more fundamental reasons. Importantly though, retail prices at other HD chains, and small stores during February 2010–May 2010 do not seem very different than they were before November 2009, which is consistent with the idea that the bakeries' agreements only eliminated the deep discounts that were offered during the price war period rather than increased prices to a supracompetitive level.

Figure 4.2 shows that similarly to sliced dark bread, the retail prices of challah were below the regulated retail price cap, and their ratio declined over time, albeit only at the main HD stores and other HD stores. Moreover, retail prices at the main local supermarket chains (the solid line) and in small stores (the round dotted line) do not seem to have been affected by the price war, nor by the bakeries' agreements. If anything, the retail prices of challah at the main HD chains and at other HD chains have only increased from the end of 2009 until March 2010, and then seem to have decreased over the March–May 2010 period (especially in the case of other HD chains). This price pattern is inconsistent with the ICA's interpretation of the bakeries' agreements as a "bread cartel."

4.4.2 The Agreements Were Intended to Stop a Price War

An alternative interpretation of the events is that the agreements were meant to stop a price war between the bakeries. As mentioned earlier, there are at least two possible reasons why a price war might have erupted. The first is that the price war was a part of some collusive arrangement, and the second is that competition in the bakery industry has unique features which are conducive to occasional price wars which can erupt even without collusive agreements. We now discuss the two reasons in detail.

The traditional view of price wars in the IO literature is that they are part of a collusive equilibrium of an infinitely repeated game (e.g., Slade, 1990).[90] However, while the Court mentioned that the bakeries had discussions about customers even before 2010, the ICA did not present the court with sufficient evidence to establish that collusion started before the CEOs' meeting on February 23, 2010.[91] Moreover, the ICA explicitly argued that the bakeries started colluding only after the CEOs had met.

Although there is no evidence for overt collusion before the CEOs' meeting, it is possible that the bakeries had already engaged in tacit collusion even before 2010, perhaps in the form of geographic market division and possibly price coordination. The price war that erupted at the beginning of 2010 could have then been, for example, a punishment phase of such a collusive agreement and the price-fixing agreement could have been a renegotiation of this punishment phase.

There are indeed some indications that the price war was a result of some geographic market division. The price war erupted when Davidovitz started offering the "3 for 10" deals mainly in ultra-orthodox neighborhoods in Jerusalem in order to show Berman and Angel that "there is a limit to everything" and that if they invade

---

[90] Slade (1990) classifies models of price wars into *imperfect-monitoring* models, in which players' actions cannot be observed; *learning* models, in which structural parameters are unknown to the players; and *cyclical* models, in which observability is perfect but business cycles affect the difficulty of colluding.

[91] *The State of Israel* v. *Angel and Others*, Paragraph 52.

Haifa, he will show them that Jerusalem "is not another fortress of Angel and Berman." Moreover, he was quoted by the court as saying that he has "no intention of stopping" the deals until Berman and Angel "give me back what they took from me in the north" and that he plans to continue with the "3 for 10" deals because "I want them to understand one thing, we are just as crazy as they are."[92]

This interpretation though has an obvious weakness: if the price war was part of an existing collusive agreement, then once the agreement was exposed by the ICA, we should have observed some change in market behavior. However, we do not observe such a change: market shares and prices in the second part of 2010 and in 2011, were similar to those during 2009 when presumably the bakeries colluded.

An alternative interpretation is that competition between the bakeries naturally involves geographic market segmentation due to the bakeries' different locations and the logistic costs of supplying stores across different geographic areas. It is plausible that in such a setting, the bakeries occasionally invade each other's territories, incumbents retaliate, and periodic localized price wars erupt. Although we are not aware of an existing model that has these features, we can nonetheless discuss how such a setting might be formalized.

Specifically, we can think of each bakery as a network, with the production facilities being the hubs, and the retailers being the nodes.[93] Due to the logistic costs of delivering bread to the stores across different geographic locations, the cost of each bakery naturally

---

[92] *The State of Israel* v. *Angel and Others*, Paragraphs 398 and 413.
[93] Recall that each of the large four bakeries has several production facilities located in different geographic areas. Angel owns bakeries in Jerusalem, Lod (the center of Israel), Netivot (the south of Israel), and holds 50 percent in a bakery in Kfar Hahoresh (south east of Haifa); Berman owns a bakery in Jerusalem and three others in the Tel Aviv metropolitan area, Davidovitz owns bakeries in Kiryat Ata (east of Haifa) and in the Tel Aviv metropolitan area, and Dganit Ein Bar bakery is located in Kibbutz Einat (center of Israel) and owns a bakery in Kiryat Shmona (upper Galilee in the north of Israel).

depends on the entire spatial structure of its network. For instance, due to economies of density, it may be cheaper to supply bread to retailers that are clustered together than to retailers that are spread over a large area. A candidate for an equilibrium in such a setting should prescribe a distribution network for each bakery (i.e., which stores are linked to the network) and a vector of prices, one for each retailer. The equilibrium conditions should then be (i) it is not profitable to link a retailer that is currently not part of the firm's distribution network and (ii) it is also not profitable to unlink a retailer that currently belongs to the network. Clearly, such an equilibrium may feature price dispersion and a network with some degree of clustering in certain geographic areas.

It is conceivable that over time networks may expand or contract due to external shocks, such as shocks to logistic costs, or to the demands of different retailers (either in the firm's network or outside it). Expansions in turn may trigger "local" price wars, which do not necessarily have to propagate to the entire network. For example, a higher demand in a certain area may induce a bakery to add trucks and perhaps salesmen to that area; this lowers the cost of supplying retailers in neighboring areas and the bakery may offer these retailers lower prices. These offers in turn may trigger retaliation by incumbents and may lead to a local price war. The bakeries' agreements were perhaps an attempt to stop such a price war.

Given this setting, it is plausible that the price war was caused by Mr. Davidovitz's decision to strike a competitive balance against Angel and Berman, and show them that he was not going to tolerate their expansion in the north.[94] There are indications that the price war escalated quickly and the bakeries feared that it would spread to the "entire market," including the large supermarket chains.[95] In fact,

---

[94] Slade (1990) argues that price wars can also be driven by "anger and irrationality." This could also explain Mr. Davidovitz's willingness to "invest millions" in the "3 for 10" deals until Angel and Berman "give me back what they took from me in the north." *The State of Israel* v. *Angel and Others*, Paragraph 398.

[95] *The State of Israel* v. *Angel and Others*, Paragraph 392.

a manager in the Davidovitz group even described the price war as a "catastrophe on a global scale."[96] It is also possible that the bakeries were concerned that if bread is sold at very low prices, there would be a pressure on regulators to decrease the regulated price further, thereby increasing the bakeries' losses from selling price-controlled bread. With this interpretation in mind, the first agreement – to stop the "3 for 10" deals – can be viewed as a "cease-fire" agreement, whereas the second agreement – to stop competing for existing customers – can be viewed as a "cessation of hostilities" agreement.

More specifically, the bakeries were interested in stopping a costly price war that was about to go out of control. However, in and of itself, the first agreement did not eliminate the cause of the price war, which was the incentive to invade the "home turf" of other bakeries and win some of their customers. It is then plausible that the bakeries realized that a "cease-fire" agreement would not hold for a long time, and in order to prevent the price war from erupting all over again, they needed a second agreement that would eliminate the reason for offering retailers deep discounts. It is also plausible that the bakeries feared that if they raise their prices, they may lose some retailers to rival bakeries. They then needed the second agreement to reassure them that raising prices will not induce retailers to switch to rival bakeries.

We believe that this interpretation is consistent with the evidence. First, Davidovitz offered the "3 for 10" deals mainly in the Jerusalem area, which is the "home turf" of Angel and Berman. Obviously then, the "3 for 10" deals were particularly damaging for Angel and Berman, as the "ripple effect" on nearby stores forced them, as Mr. Davidovitz argued, "to lower prices in all of Jerusalem."[97] At the same time, these deals were not very damaging to Davidovitz due to its limited presence in Jerusalem. In a sense then, the "3 for 10" deals are akin to a Judo strategy, whereby a smaller player chooses low

---

[96] *The State of Israel* v. *Angel and Others*, Paragraph 386.
[97] *The State of Israel* v. *Angel and Others*, Paragraph 68.

prices, which the big player finds unprofitable to match because matching them translates into a large loss of revenue due to the big player's large market share (Gelman and Salop, 1983).[98]

Second, if the "3 for 10" deals were aimed at gaining market share, as the ICA argued, then it is not clear why they were offered only in ultra-orthodox neighborhoods and not elsewhere, and in particular at the main supermarket chains, where the bulk of price-controlled bread is sold.[99] Moreover, the "3 for 10" deals were easily reversible because they were not offered through formal contracts with the relevant stores. It is hard to see how gaining market share only while selling at deep discounts (without a prospect for recoupment) can be a profitable strategy.

Third, in a typical price-fixing case, prices increase from the static equilibrium level, p^*, to some higher level p^{**}, and then return to p^* after the cartel ends. In Figure 4.1, this pattern can be observed only in the case of other HD chains and small stores. However, if one starts at the beginning of 2009, it seems that prices were at a level of p^* until around November 2009, then they dropped to p^{**} from November 2009 until February 2010, and then returned to p^* from March to May 2010. Although the ICA interpreted the increase from p^{**} to p^* as a sign of a cartel, once we take a longer perspective, the price pattern is consistent with the idea that p^{**} represents a price war, while the return to p^* seems like a "cease-fire" agreement.

Fourth, it is typically hard to know what the state of mind of decision makers is. Here, however, we have direct evidence on the motivation behind the bakeries' actions. For example, Berman's CEO

---

[98] There is an important difference, however: an entrant playing a judo strategy intentionally sets a low price to deter the incumbent from matching it. Here, it seems that Mr. Davidovitz was aware that Angel and Berman would be forced to lower their prices, but was still interested in offering the "3 for 10" deals in order to send Angel and Berman a message that they should not expand in the north.

[99] And as we already mentioned, the "3 for 10" deals are particularly attractive to ultra-orthodox families which on average have 6.9 children per family. It is hard to imagine that non ultra-orthodox families with 2–3 children will need to buy three loaves of bread at once.

testified that Berman's "aggressive" efforts to penetrate dozens of stores in the north were intended to convey a message to Davidovitz that "there is a price for every harm done to us," whereas Mr. Davidovitz testified that the motivation for the "3 for 10" deals was to ensure that Berman "will understand once and for all that there are no strong and weak here ... there is a limit to everything."[100] He also testified that he had no intention of stopping the "3 for 10" deals until Angel and Berman "give me back what they took from me in the north"[101] and that "I want them to understand one thing, we are just as crazy as they are."[102] Berman indeed perceived the "3 for 10" deals as retaliation by Davidovitz for its "combative initiative" in the north.[103]

4.5 CONCLUSION

There is no dispute that the bakeries engaged in price fixing: the hundreds of wiretapped phone conversations obtained by the ICA indicate clearly that the bakeries' executives agreed to raise the price of sliced dark bread and challah in some stores and to stop competing for each other's customers. Yet, although the executives admitted to most of the charges, the motivation for the price-fixing agreement remains an open question.

In principle, there could be different motivations for price fixing. The most common is the textbook cartel motivation: firms collude by setting prices above their static Nash equilibrium levels. But there are other possibilities. For instance, firms may be engaged in a price war, perhaps due to a "punishment phase" which is part of an existing collusive agreement, and wish to negotiate a shorter, or less severe, punishment. Another possibility is that the price-fixing agreement is intended to stop a price war that is not part of a collusive agreement, but nonetheless erupted in an otherwise competitive

---

[100] *The State of Israel* v. *Angel and Others*, Paragraph 30.
[101] *The State of Israel* v. *Angel and Others*, Paragraph 398.
[102] *The State of Israel* v. *Angel and Others*, Paragraph 413.
[103] *The State of Israel* v. *Angel and Others*, Paragraph 30.

market. Interestingly, the Court in the Israeli bread cartel case stated in its summary of events that the bakeries' price war had both "a deterrent – punitive element, the purpose of which is to respond to the rival's competitive actions," which is consistent with the second motivation, as well as "a competitive element of market penetration, by lowering prices and increasing market share," which is consistent with the third motivation.[104]

The main difference between the different motivations is the price level before and after the price-fixing agreement. According to the first interpretation, the agreement is intended to raise prices from the static Nash equilibrium level, p^*, to a higher level. According to the second and third interpretations, prices before the agreement are below p^* and the agreement is intended to raise them to p^* according to the third interpretation, and a level which is possibly still below p^* according to the second interpretation.

Although it is hard to tell which of these possibilities is the most relevant for the bakeries' case, the first possibility – firms were trying to collude on prices above the static Nash equilibrium – does not account for the fact that prior to the agreement, the bakeries had engaged in a price war that involved "3 for 10" deals in a limited number of stores. It also overlooks the fact that the agreement merely restored the prices that prevailed before the price war, rather than leading to higher prices.

The possibility that the agreement was a renegotiation of a punishment phase that was part of an existing collusive agreement – is at least in principle plausible, as the bakeries could have engaged in some tacit collusive agreement before 2010; the price war that erupted in early 2010 could have then been a "punishment phase" associated with that agreement. This interpretation, however, is inconsistent with the fact that market shares and prices after the price-fixing agreement was discovered by the ICA in May 2010 were similar to

---

[104] *The State of Israel* v. *Angel and Others*, Paragraphs 32 and 473.

those prior to the price war in early 2010 when firms were presumably colluding with each other.

It therefore appears that the possibility that the agreement was meant to stop a price war which was part of the competitive process in an industry that features a network structure seems the most plausible one. As already mentioned, the agreement to eliminate the "3 for 10" deals could then be interpreted as a "cease-fire" agreement, while the agreement to stop competing for each other's customers seems like a "cessation of hostilities" agreement intended to eliminate the incentive to give deep discounts.

We believe that the main takeaway from the Israeli bread case is the idea that price fixing can be an outcome of different types of competitive processes and not necessarily part of cartel behavior, which is meant to fix competition. The distinction between "fixing competition" and "price fixing" is not obvious or simple, but the two may have different motivations and implications for consumers and should be part of a detailed analysis of markets.

REFERENCES

Block, M. K., F. C. Nold, and J. Gregory Sidak, (1981) "The Deterrent Effect of Antitrust Enforcement" *Journal of Political Economy*, 89, 429–445.

Carlton D. and J. Perloff (2005) *Modern Industrial Organization*, 4th Edition, Pearson/Addison Wesley.

Gelman, J. and S. Salop (1983) "Judo Economics: Capacity Limitation and Coupon Competition," *The Bell Journal of Economics*, 14(2), 315–25.

Harrington J. (2023) "Competitor Coupons: A Remedy for Residual Collusion" *Journal of Competition Law & Economics*, 19 (2023), 610–627.

Israel Democracy Institute (2016) "*Statistical Report on Ultra-Orthodox Society in Israel, 2016,*" https://en.idi.org.il/haredi/2016/

Mncube, L. (2013) "Strategic Entry Deterrence: Pioneer Foods and the Bread Cartel," *Journal of Competition Law & Economics*, 9(3), 637–654.

Price Committee (2021) "Summary of the Price Committee Deliberations: Basic Review of Price-led Bread Products," www.gov.il/BlobFolder/dynamiccollector resultitem/decision_22072021/he/decision_and_directives_decision_22072021 .pdf.

Price Committee (2022) "Summary of the Price Committee Deliberations: Basic Review of Price-Controlled Bread Products," www.gov.il/BlobFolder/dynamic collectorresultitem/decision_16052022/he/decision_and_directives_decision_16052022.pdf.

Sutton, J. (1991) *Sunk Cost and Market Structure*, MIT Press.

The Knesset Research and Information Center (RIC) (2022), "Description and Analysis of the Price Regulation of Bread Products in Israel," https://fs.knesset.gov.il/globaldocs/MMM/45bc9b89-b781-ec11-8146-00155d0401c3/2_45bc9b89-b781-ec11-8146-00155d0401c3_11_19497.pdf.

Slade, M. (1990) "Strategic Pricing Models and Interpretation of Price-War Data," *European Economic Review*, 34, 524–537.

5 The Role of Platforms for Facilitating Anticompetitive Communication

*Retail Gasoline in Australia**

David P. Byrne, Nicolas de Roos, A. Rachel Grinberg, and Leslie M. Marx

5.1 OVERVIEW

In this case study, we examine the role of a platform in facilitating anticompetitive price signaling through an analysis of the *Informed Sources* matter,[1] from the Australian retail gasoline industry. The matter involves price coordination among retail gasoline stations in Melbourne, Australia, facilitated by a price information–sharing platform from a retail data and analytics company called Informed Sources. Informed Sources provides a platform that facilitates near real-time, station-level price sharing among major gasoline retailers. In 2014, the Australian Competition and Consumer Commission (ACCC) initiated proceedings against Informed Sources and major gasoline retailers that subscribed to it, contending that the platform

---

* We are grateful to Joe Harrington and Maarten Pieter Schinkel for helpful comments and to Xiaosong Wu for valuable research support. The research was supported by funding from the Australian Research Council (DP21010231 and DP200103574). Simon Loertscher and seminar participants at Monash University provided helpful comments and suggestions. Disclosures: David P. Byrne, A. Rachel Grinberg, and Leslie M. Marx were retained by the Australian Competition and Consumer Commission for the Informed Sources matter, while Nicolas de Roos was retained by 7-Eleven. Disclaimers: Everywhere collusion is mentioned in this document, it is meant in the economic and not the legal sense. The interpretations of all results are those of the authors and do not necessarily represent those of the Australian Competition and Consumer Commission.

[1] *Australian Competition and Consumer Commission* v. *Informed Sources (Australia) Pty Ltd.* was filed to the Federal Court of Australia on August 19, 2014, with the matter dating to January 1, 2011. The matter was resolved via settlement in December 2015 (ACCC 2015).

likely substantially lessened competition by enabling price signaling and monitoring.

In the ACCC's words:

> The ACCC alleges that the arrangements were likely to increase retail petrol price coordination and cooperation, and were likely to decrease competitive rivalry. ... The ACCC alleges that fuel retailers can use, and have used, the Informed Sources service as a near real time communication device in relation to petrol pricing. In particular, it is alleged that retailers can propose a price increase to their competitors and monitor the response to it. If, for example, the response is not sufficient, they can quickly withdraw the proposal and may punish competitors that have not accepted the proposed increased price.
>
> Rod Sims, ACCC Chair, August 20, 2014 (ACCC, 2014a)

Through a narrative example, we frame the Informed Sources matter and the key economic issues at play. Then, we provide evidence on how such information-sharing platforms facilitate anticompetitive conduct by reducing the cost of price signaling and enhancing its effectiveness in coordinating prices. To do so, we employ rich publicly available real-time pricing data from a separate Australian price transparency platform called FuelCheck, which shares essential features with the Informed Sources platform: the same set of major participants, comprehensive real-time price information available to all major participants, and similar pricing behavior, market structure and demographics.[2] Lastly, we discuss the matter and our empirics in the context of emerging research and antitrust cases, focusing on how cartels operate and how price-sharing platforms can serve as

---

[2] As we discuss below, real-time station-level pricing data from the Informed Sources platform are not publicly available. However, such data granularity is necessary for illustrating the nature of platform-enabled anticompetitive pricing from the Informed Sources matter. Fortunately, such information is available from the FuelCheck platform and illustrative of the key competition issues from the Informed Sources matter.

facilitating devices. In contrast to the extensive literature focusing on the role of monitoring in sustaining collusion, our results expand our understanding of how platforms enable low-cost, effective price signaling, making prices a medium of communication.

Our narrative example and examination of the FuelCheck pricing data sheds light on how anticompetitive pricing can arise not through meetings in smoke-filled rooms but through platform-enabled *signaling*. In particular, FuelCheck allows coordinating retailers to observe each other's prices, station by station, and know that the others observed these prices at high frequency (e.g., every fifteen to thirty minutes). In addition, FuelCheck allows retailers to *monitor* any deviations from their coordinated pricing strategies. Such signaling and monitoring enable companies to implement price cycles, whereby retailers: (1) infrequently signal and coordinate on large discrete price increases; with (2) frequent daily price undercutting between price jumps. Coordinated price jumps periodically restore profit margins, allowing firms to control overall average margin levels. As we detail below, all of these insights regarding signaling, monitoring, and coordinated price cycles that we derive from the FuelCheck platform were at the center of the matter involving the Informed Sources platform.

Because the economics literature has already given much attention to the role of monitoring in facilitating collusion, this case study focuses on the signaling role of the platform.[3] In particular, we examine how a price information–sharing platform enables firms to overcome otherwise significant challenges in coordinating their conduct in the face of imperfect signaling and the absence of explicit direct communication. Combining insights from the Informed Sources

---

[3] In our setting of retail gasoline, an imperfect monitoring mechanism that is potentially available to retailers is employing price spotters (such as taxi drivers) to phone in their observations on rivals' prices. Real-time price information–sharing platforms move firms toward perfect monitoring. In doing so, they allow firms to more easily and quickly detect secret price cutting and enact punishments, which facilitates collusion (Harrington, 2011; Luco, 2019).

matter with complementary rich gasoline price data from the FuelCheck platform, we illustrate how a platform facilitates anticompetitive coordination by reducing the risks and costs associated with price leadership and consensus building. In light of our results, we discuss how the signaling aspect of platforms such as Informed Sources raises particular challenges for antitrust authorities. Specifically, they allow prices to become a medium of communication, and there are difficulties associated with enjoining firms from changing their own prices.[4]

These insights from our case study add to a growing body of empirical work describing signaling and coordination practices in retail gasoline markets using station-level price data. Byrne and de Roos (2019) document evidence from Perth, Australia, that price leaders created focal points and used price signals from a small number of stations to coordinate rival prices and soften price competition over time.[5] Assad et al. (2024) document that the adoption of algorithmic pricing among German gasoline retailers led to elevated prices and margins similar to what Byrne and de Roos (2019) find. Notably, Byrne and de Roos (2019) and Assad et al. (2024) study markets with government-run price information platforms that provide real-time information to consumers and retailers. That both environments reveal an evolution toward higher, coordinated prices underlines the role of information sharing in facilitating anticompetitive conduct.[6]

---

[4] Article 101 of the Treaty on the Functioning of the European Union has policies prohibiting information exchange. In Australia, restrictions on concerted practices provided by Subsection 45(1)(c) of the Competition and Consumer Act 2010 might be relevant.

[5] In earlier work, Atkinson (2009) finds some evidence of individual stations using brief price increases to signal the price level and timing for the next market-wide price increase in the small town of Guelph, Canada.

[6] Luco (2019) also finds elevated margins after the introduction of a government-run price information platform in Chile, particularly in markets where consumers fail to use the platform. Montag and Winter (2020) find, in Germany, that the introduction of a government-run price information platform leads to lower margins, particularly in local markets where consumers more intensively engage with price information from the platform. That the effect may be ambiguous makes sense since price data is available to both the demand and supply sides of the market.

We develop our case study of the Informed Sources matter in four parts. We start by further describing the matter in Section 5.2. In Section 5.3, we provide a motivating narrative to illustrate the potential role of a platform such as Informed Sources in supporting elevated prices. In Section 5.4, we empirically describe and illustrate competitive effects of the Informed Sources platform, focusing on platform-enabled price signaling. Section 5.5 concludes the case study.

5.2 THE INFORMED SOURCES MATTER

Informed Sources is a global retail data and analytics company that provides gasoline retailers with "accurate, reliable, timely data" enabling them "to make decisions with confidence" with "a complete view of the market."[7] Informed Sources provides a price information–sharing platform to subscribing retailers as part of its services.[8] Two key aspects of the platform are that subscribers: (1) provide their station-level price data every fifteen minutes to the platform[9] and (2) have access to all prices provided to the platform. Importantly, prior to the Informed Sources matter, the platform enabled information sharing only on the *supply-side* of the market. It did not provide consumers or search apps on the *demand-side* of the market with complete, high-frequency price data to enable price search.[10]

These services have been provided to gasoline retailers in Australia since at least 2000 (Wang, 2009a). Since this time, retail gasoline prices across all major Australian cities have exhibited

---

[7] https://informedsources.com/.
[8] From their website, they also collect and provide pricing data and analytics to grocery retailers as well.
[9] The price-sharing interval for a limited number of subscribers was thirty minutes.
[10] Prior to the settlement of the Informed Sources matter, Informed Sources provided data for consumers only twice daily and with geographic restrictions. Their high-frequency station-level data was not available to the demand-side of the market, such as through third-party search apps for consumers, at any stage prior to the Informed Sources matter.

asymmetric price cycles that involve two parts: (1) infrequent large discrete price jumps; with (2) regular price undercutting between jumps. Such jumps and cuts give rise to a "sawtooth" pattern in prices over time (see Figure 5.2). Byrne and de Roos (2019) document the history of retail price cycles in Australian cities from 2001 to 2014, illustrating a change in conduct in 2009 that persists through to the Informed Sources matter.[11] Before 2009, price cycle stability and retailers' ability to coordinate price jumps were sensitive to wholesale price volatility largely due to crude oil prices. For instance, price cycles became particularly unstable in 2008–2009 amid a significant global crude oil shock. In addition, before 2009, price jumps predictably occurred on Thursdays, with regular seven, fourteen, or twenty-one-day cycle lengths between jumps.

After global crude oil prices settled in 2009, the pricing structure evolved to what exists during the Informed Sources matter. Under this new pricing structure, the price jumps unpredictably occur on all days of the week. In addition, the cycle length becomes noisier and grows to thirty to thirty-five days. Yet despite less predictable jump timing and irregular cycle lengths, price cycles and jumps remain tightly coordinated throughout 2010–2014 and are robust to wholesale price volatility. Byrne and de Roos (2019) illustrates that BP (a major retailer) used price experimentation, signaling, and leadership in 2009 to coordinate a profit-enhancing equilibrium transition to a new, robust cyclical pricing structure in Perth. To our knowledge, there are no studies on why or how coinciding equilibrium transitions occurred in other major cities like Melbourne or Sydney. But Byrne and de Roos (2019) confirm that such transitions indeed occur and that this is the pricing structure that exists throughout 2009–2014, leading into the Informed Sources matter.

Around the time of the Informed Sources matter in 2014, subscribers to Informed Sources' information-sharing service included all

---

[11] In particular, see appendix B of their paper for the history of retail pricing across Australian cities.

five major Australian gasoline retailers: BP Australia Pty Ltd (BP), Caltex Australia Petroleum Pty Ltd (Caltex), Woolworths Ltd (Woolworths), Eureka Operations Pty Ltd (trading as Coles Express), and 7-Eleven Stores Pty Ltd (7-Eleven) (ACCC, 2015). The ACCC alleged that "the price information exchange service allowed those retailers to communicate with each other about their prices, and had the effect or likely effect of substantially lessening competition for the sale of petrol in Melbourne" (ACCC, 2015). In addition, the ACCC noted the overall effect of the conduct on consumers was potentially large: "even a small increase in petrol pricing can have a significant impact on consumers overall. For example, if net petrol prices increase by 1c per litre over a year, the loss to Australian consumers would be around $190 million for the year" (ACCC, 2014a).

Outcome of the Matter

The ACCC instituted proceedings against Informed Sources and the five major gasoline retailers in August 2014, alleging that they violated Section 45 of the Competition and Consumer Act 2010, which prohibits "contracts, arrangements or understandings that have the purpose, effect or likely effect of substantially lessening competition" (ACCC, 2015). A settlement emerged sixteen months later in December 2015, which saw one of the five major retailers, Coles Express, agree to withdraw from the Informed Sources information-sharing agreement. Moreover, Informed Sources agreed to make the same high-frequency station-level price data used on its platform available to third-party consumer search apps.[12]

---

[12] "BP, Caltex, Woolworths, and 7-Eleven have agreed that they will not enter into or give effect to any price information–exchange service unless the information each receives is made available to consumers and third party organizations at the same time. Informed Sources has agreed that it will not supply the information exchange service unless the pricing information it provides to petrol retailers is made available to consumers for free and to third parties on reasonable commercial terms at the same time" (ACCC, 2015). For a general discussion on this approach to remedying platform-based coordination, see Gal (2023).

The ACCC viewed the settlement as promoting competition through supply-side and demand-side forces.[13] On the supply side, limiting coverage of Informed Sources from five to four major gasoline retailers could be expected to limit the platform's role in facilitating price signaling and coordination. On the demand side, making the platform's data available to third-party providers potentially allowed price comparison apps to enter. Through such apps, consumers could better compare prices across stations, increasing consumers' sensitivity to price differences across stations, thereby building competitive pressure for stations to undercut each other.

5.3 ANTICOMPETITIVE POTENTIAL OF INFORMATION-SHARING PLATFORMS

Before delving into the complexities of platform-enabled price signaling in practice, we develop a simplified narrative to highlight the potential role of a platform like Informed Sources in supporting the signaling of coordinated price increases.

In our narrative, there is a city consisting of a city center and outlying areas (e.g., suburbs), which we visualize in Figure 5.1. Two firms operate retail gasoline stations. Each firm has two stations, one in the city center and the other in an outer suburb. Let us imagine that the two stations in the city center are within sight of each other and in locations that allow consumers in the city center to straightforwardly compare their prices before choosing whether and where to purchase gasoline. The suburban stations are far apart in separate suburbs, so comparisons with other stations are less straightforward. The firms have similar input costs for the gasoline they sell to consumers.

Suppose both firms charge a price of $2.00 per gallon at their stations, which is close to the firms' input cost. Given the

---

[13] "Another key outcome is the availability of the retail price information to third-party service providers. This will promote innovation in the provision of petrol price information, to the benefit of consumers.... The ACCC believes that this will facilitate improved competition amongst petrol retailers" (ACCC, 2015, quoting ACCC Chairman Rod Sims).

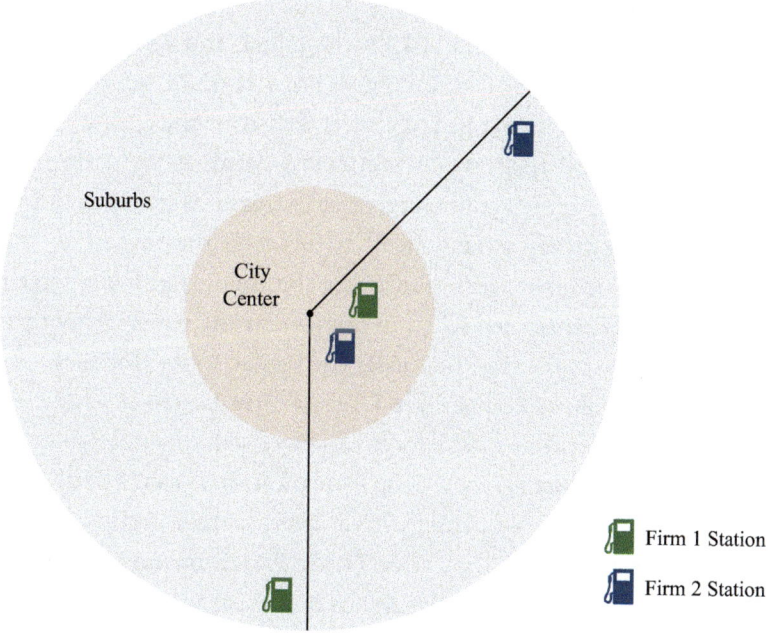

FIGURE 5.1 Visual representation of suburban and city center stations.

information available to firm 1, its target is for both firms to increase their stations' prices to $2.20 on the following day. In contrast, firm 2 considers a price of $2.18 to be the best target. In this situation, a coordinated price increase is profitable to both firms (but harms consumers). However, suppose only one firm increases its price. In that case, that firm will lose substantial business at its city center location, where consumers can readily observe the price differential between the two city center stations. In addition, the firm will likely lose business at its suburban location as consumers choose to delay purchasing in response to the higher price and perhaps become aware of its rival's lower prices in the city center and the other suburb. Thus, while the potential profitability of price increases is apparent to these firms, they face challenges in accomplishing such price increases.

Explicit Communication

Suppose the firms' managers talk on the phone and agree that each will open its stations at a compromise price of $2.19 the next day. Then, when the stations open the next day, the managers position price spotters near their rival's stations to confirm their opening prices. In this way, the coordinated price increase, which we refer to as a *price restoration*, is launched.[14] Crucial to the success of the restoration is the managers' ability to communicate about which restoration price to set and when to implement the restoration price, and their ability to confirm that their rival stuck to its promises.

At prices above competitive levels, a firm has an incentive to undercut the price of its rival later in the day (when the price spotters have gone home), thereby increasing its market share significantly but only decreasing its (above-competitive level) margin slightly. Thus, after starting the day with a price of $2.19, a firm might consider reducing its price at one or both stations to capture market share from the rival. Consumers would shift their purchasing toward lower-priced stations as they recognize the price differential. At some point, the firm with the higher price would realize that something had changed, either because it directly monitors the price of the other station (e.g., it sends a price spotter back out to check) or because it recognizes that the change in consumers' purchasing patterns must be due to a decrease in its rival's price. The firm may respond by cutting its price, which may lead to further discounting that reduces the profits of both firms.

Imperfect Signaling

Now let us suppose that to avoid running afoul of antitrust laws, the firms refrain from direct communication. In this case, the firms face the task of signaling using prices alone. Starting from prices of $2.00, suppose that firm 1 tries to signal a price restoration by increasing its

---

[14] As discussed in Section 5.4.2, the retail gasoline markets we study exhibit regular asymmetric price cycles. A *restoration* refers to the phase of a price cycle in which prices are "restored" to the cycle peak.

price in the city center to $2.20. Doing so makes it easy for firm 2 to observe firm 1's signal because firm 2, with its nearby city center station, can simply observe firm 1's price board. This quick and reliable observability is a benefit of city center signaling. However, consumers traveling in the city center, of which there are many, can also observe the price differential between the two stations and can, at little cost, divert their purchases to the lower-priced one. As a result, firm 1 risks substantial profit losses in its effort to signal a price restoration from its station in the city center.

Alternatively, firm 1 could try to signal only with its suburban station in a part of the city with fewer people. This risks firm 2 not recognizing the signal for a substantial amount of time and, with that delay, creates a risk of lost profits for firm 1. As time passes, consumers are increasingly likely to recognize the price differential with the distant stations and take advantage of it by purchasing at those other stations. These effects are exacerbated because firm 2, which benefits from the price differential, can credibly feign ignorance of the rival's signal for some time. Eventually, firm 2 might respond with a price increase of its own, but perhaps only moving its prices to its preferred $2.18, thereby initiating rounds of price undercutting.

In summary, signaling either with the city center or suburban station is costly, and the outcome is uncertain. But, if the signal at the suburban station were sure to be recognized quickly by firm 2, then suburban signaling would have the advantage that suburban consumers do not immediately see the price differential created by the signal, and they may face incremental travel costs to take advantage of that differential. Further, if the total volume of sales is lower in the suburbs than in the city center, then this would also mitigate profit losses from suburban signaling.[15] Thus, a technology that ensures that rivals promptly and reliably observe suburban signals limits the costs

---

[15] Retailers may have the incentive to vary which station is used for signaling to avoid having a station develop a reputation for being relatively high-priced because this could induce consumers to avoid that station or make more significant efforts to price compare before purchasing from that station.

associated with the signaling process. A price information–sharing platform enables precisely these properties.

5.3.3 Platform-Enabled Signaling

Let us insert a near real-time information-sharing platform like Informed Sources into our story. Once the platform is in place, firm 1 briefly increases its price to $2.20, which we refer to as a "flare," at its suburban station. Because the flare is brief and at a remote station, it limits firm 1's signaling cost in terms of lost sales. Moreover, via the platform, the flare provides a reliable and immediately identifiable signal regarding the restoration price level. A flare from firm 2 at its suburban station hitting the same price can confirm that the signal was received and seconded; flares at different price levels can function as counterproposals of the restoration price level. After a period without further flares, the pricing intentions of each firm have been communicated.

The platform then also facilitates the timing of the price restoration. Either firm can initiate the restoration by raising its price to the first proposed price or one of the counterproposals, confident that its rival will quickly be aware of its move. This time, the price increase will not be retracted. Their rival will follow with an equivalent price increase of their own, and a coordinated restoration will have been achieved.[16] Further, the platform enables reliable, prompt monitoring at a low cost because it provides searchable and sortable pricing data, making it easy for subscribers to verify compliance. The realization that undercutting will be detected essentially immediately acts as a deterrent for such undercutting in the first place.

Thus, the insertion of the platform into our narrative permits low-cost signaling using prices as a means of communication, facilitates monitoring, and ultimately promotes more frequent and

---

[16] As we document below, in the second phase of a coordinated restoration, in which prices are increased without retraction, each firm may choose to raise prices gradually across their network to further confirm their rivals are also raising prices across their networks. Byrne and de Roos (2019) similarly document gradualism as a key feature of coordinated price increases.

prolonged episodes of elevated prices. In what follows, we show that the key elements of this narrative are apparent in the data.

5.4 EFFECTS OF INFORMED SOURCES

The Informed Sources matter highlights critical aspects of collusive, platform-enabled signaling as discussed in our narrative, which we empirically illustrate in this section. Although the Melbourne data used in the Informed Sources matter are confidential, we can illustrate the main effects using publicly available data sources from nearby Sydney. The effects seen in the public data illustrate well the effects at issue in the Informed Sources matter.

Our analysis proceeds in four parts. First, in Section 5.4.1, we explain why Sydney and our publicly available gasoline price data from a separate platform called FuelCheck can shed light on the Informed Sources matter from Melbourne. In Section 5.4.2, we describe key features of gasoline price dynamics in the markets in which Informed Sources operated. We then develop an illustrative empirical example of platform-enabled price signaling in Section 5.4.3. Motivated by our example, in Section 5.4.4, we leverage our rich FuelCheck dataset to empirically document a price signaling process that parallels that from the Informed Sources matter, and we discuss the crucial role of platform-enabled price information sharing in facilitating such signaling. All of the data used in Section 5.4 is from FuelCheck for the Sydney market.

5.4.1 Sydney and FuelCheck

Sydney has three relevant features for the Informed Sources matter. First, it is the closest comparison city to Melbourne worldwide in terms of size, demographics, consumer behavior, and market structure.[17]

---

[17] Sydney and Melbourne are both on the east coast of Australia, separated by 500 miles. In 2016, the population of Sydney was 4,446,805, and the population of Melbourne was 4,485,211, and each city had an area of approximately 2,000 square kilometers that contained more than 500 people per square kilometer (Australian Bureau of Statistics, 2016 Census QuickStats, www.abs.gov.au/).

In the 2016–2017 sample period that we consider, Sydney's market, like Melbourne's, was dominated by the same five retailers that subscribed to Informed Sources before December 2015: BP, Caltex, Coles, Woolworths, and 7-Eleven. In total, these retailers operated 448 of 694 (65 percent) of all stations in the greater Sydney metropolitan area and set prices centrally across their station networks.[18] Smaller retail chains and independent stations operated the remaining 246 (35 percent) stations. Further, as shown in Byrne and de Roos (2019, online appendix), retailers in Sydney and Melbourne, as well as in Brisbane and Adelaide, have a history of employing similar pricing strategies, in particular price cycles (described momentarily). Thus, in Sydney, we observe the same players implementing similar coordinating pricing structures in a similar market setting as in the Informed Sources matter from Melbourne.

Second, in the period that we consider, August 1, 2016, to December 31, 2017, Sydney-based retailers and consumers had access to a platform called FuelCheck,[19] which provided (and continues to provide) real-time information on station-level prices.[20] The New South Wales government launched the platform in August 2016, eight months after the resolution of the Informed Sources matter.[21] In the period that we consider and the data that we analyze below, retailers in Sydney used FuelCheck to coordinate price increases in similar

---

[18] All major Australian cities have asymmetric market shares similar to Sydney, with the five major retailers operating approximately two-thirds of all stations in a given market (Byrne and de Roos, 2019; Byrne et al., 2023). These shares are stable around the Informed Sources matter, with little station entry or exit at that time (ACCC, 2014b, pp. 24–26).

[19] www.fuelcheck.nsw.gov.au/.

[20] Although FuelCheck was (and still is) available to consumers, we would not expect this to interfere with the gasoline retailers' use of FuelCheck for price signaling because consumers generally do not engage in data aggregation and analysis of fuel prices, and therefore are unlikely to observe flares and understand their information content. Moreover, successful signaling in FuelCheck (to which consumers had access) indicates that signaling was viable in the Informed Sources platform (to which they had no access).

[21] FuelCheck differs from Informed Sources in that FuelCheck provides prices to both retailers and consumers, whereas Informed Sources before December 2015 only provided high-frequency prices to retailers. As we show, this difference does not prevent Sydney retailers during our 2017 case study period from engaging in signaling similar to that of Melbourne retailers during the period at issue in the ACCC's proceedings.

ways to how they used the Informed Sources platform in the period prior to the ACCC's proceedings against Informed Sources. Thus, FuelCheck in Sydney provides a comparable technological and competitive setting to Informed Sources in Melbourne to analyze platform-enabled price signaling.

Finally, FuelCheck provides access to comprehensive historical real-time station-level gasoline prices. These data allow us to undertake a forensic analysis of retail pricing, ranging from daily prices at the retailer level to hourly prices at the station level. The richness of the data proves critical because key aspects of platform-based price signaling, as employed in the Informed Sources matter, are only observable at high frequencies at individual stations.

Given similar market structures and conduct, and sufficiently rich data for our case study, we describe pricing conduct from FuelCheck in Sydney to illustrate key issues from the Informed Sources matter in Melbourne. In doing so, we effectively presume that: (1) the Informed Sources platform could be effective for price signaling and coordinated increases and (2) given it is the same retailers in Sydney and Melbourne, the Informed Sources platform is likely to have been used for that purpose.

5.4.2 Price Cycles

Price cycles characterize retail gasoline pricing in urban markets worldwide.[22] In Australia, gasoline prices in Melbourne, Sydney, and many urban markets exhibit price cycles.[23] The ACCC describes gasoline (petrol) price cycles as follows:

---

[22] Regular asymmetric cycles in prices, sometimes referred to as Edgeworth cycles, have been observed in a variety of retail gasoline markets around the world, including in Australia (Wang, 2009a; Byrne and de Roos, 2019), Canada (Noel, 2007; Clark and Houde, 2013, 2014; Byrne et al., 2015), Europe (Foros and Steen, 2013; Linder, 2018), and the United States (Lewis, 2012; Zimmerman et al., 2013). See Eckert (2013) for a survey. In an Edgeworth cycle, price movements are sharply asymmetric over time and highly coordinated across firms. These features are evident in Figure 5.2, which shows that in each cycle, prices rise rapidly for all retailers and decline gradually until the next cycle begins.

[23] See, for example, ACCC, "Petrol Price Cycles," www.accc.gov.au/consumers/petrol-diesel-lpg/petrol-price-cycles.

A petrol price cycle is a movement in retail price from a low point (or trough) to a high point (or peak) to a subsequent low point. In these cycles, prices steadily go down for a period followed by a sharp increase. Price cycles result from deliberate pricing policies of petrol retailers and are not directly related to changes in wholesale costs.[24]

In the Informed Sources matter, the overarching price dynamics involved price cycles, which we illustrate with Figure 5.2. The figure plots daily average prices for the five major retailers and all other (smaller) retailers for all of 2017. With roughly monthly frequency, prices exhibit discrete jumps (*price restorations*) with gradual price undercutting in between the jumps (*undercutting phase*). Price restorations become more likely as retail prices approach the main time-varying component of stations' marginal cost, the wholesale terminal gate price (TGP).[25] The size of the price increase in a given cycle's restoration is thus central to determining retailers' average margins.[26]

---

[24] ACCC, "Petrol Price Cycles," www.accc.gov.au/consumers/petrol-diesel-lpg/petrol-price-cycles.

[25] From ACCC (2014b, p. 44): "TGPs are the spot prices at which petrol can be bought from a refinery or terminal. ... TGPs are calculated with reference to the IPP [Input Parity Price] and by adding excise and GST, other operating costs incurred in the wholesale sector (including storage and local transportation) and a wholesale margin....

$$TGP = IPP + excise + GST + wholesale\ operating\ costs + wholesale\ margin."$$

As stated on p. 39 of the same report, "The IPP is based on the international price of refined petrol plus other import costs and is an indicator of the notional average cost of importing refined petrol into Australia. ... In 2013–14 the international price of refined petrol accounted for over 95 percent of the IPP." And, from p. 41, the relevant international price for computing the IPP is the price of Singapore Mogas 95 Unleaded.

[26] Given the central role of cycles in shaping the market's price dynamics, we restrict our attention to stations that regularly engage in price cycles. Specifically, we focus on stations with eighteen or more dates with daily margin jumps greater than 5 cpl, identifying station-level price restorations. In other words, we focus on stations that exhibit monthly price cycles in Sydney. We classify 420 of 694 stations in the greater Sydney region as engaging in monthly cycles. The five major retailers operate 319 (76 percent) of these stations. Smaller retail chains and independent retailers operate the remaining 101 (24 percent) stations. Our results are robust to variations in identifying station-level price cycles and classifying cycling versus non-cycling stations.

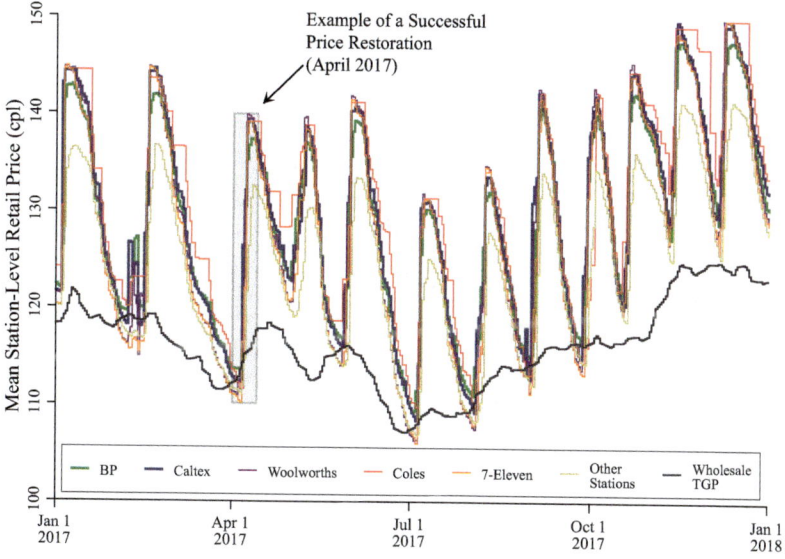

FIGURE 5.2 Daily price cycles.

Figure 5.2 further reveals cross-sectional and inter-temporal price dispersion across retailers, with smaller retailers' prices tracking with the major retailers' prices but staying below and following them. Thus, the major retailers' price leadership and ability to coordinate price restorations is central to determining both their own *and* rival price levels.

5.4.3 Price Signaling and Coordination: An Illustrative Example

The shaded box in Figure 5.2 carves out a particular price restoration from April 2017 that serves as our working example for highlighting platform-enabled signaling. We zoom in around this event in panel (a) of Figure 5.3, which plots *hourly* prices by retailer between April 1 and April 14. At this frequency and level of aggregation, BP emerges as the retailer whose prices jump first in initiating a market-wide price restoration. Panel (b) further zooms into hourly level pricing on April 6 and 7 (as indicated by the shaded box in panel (a)), which more

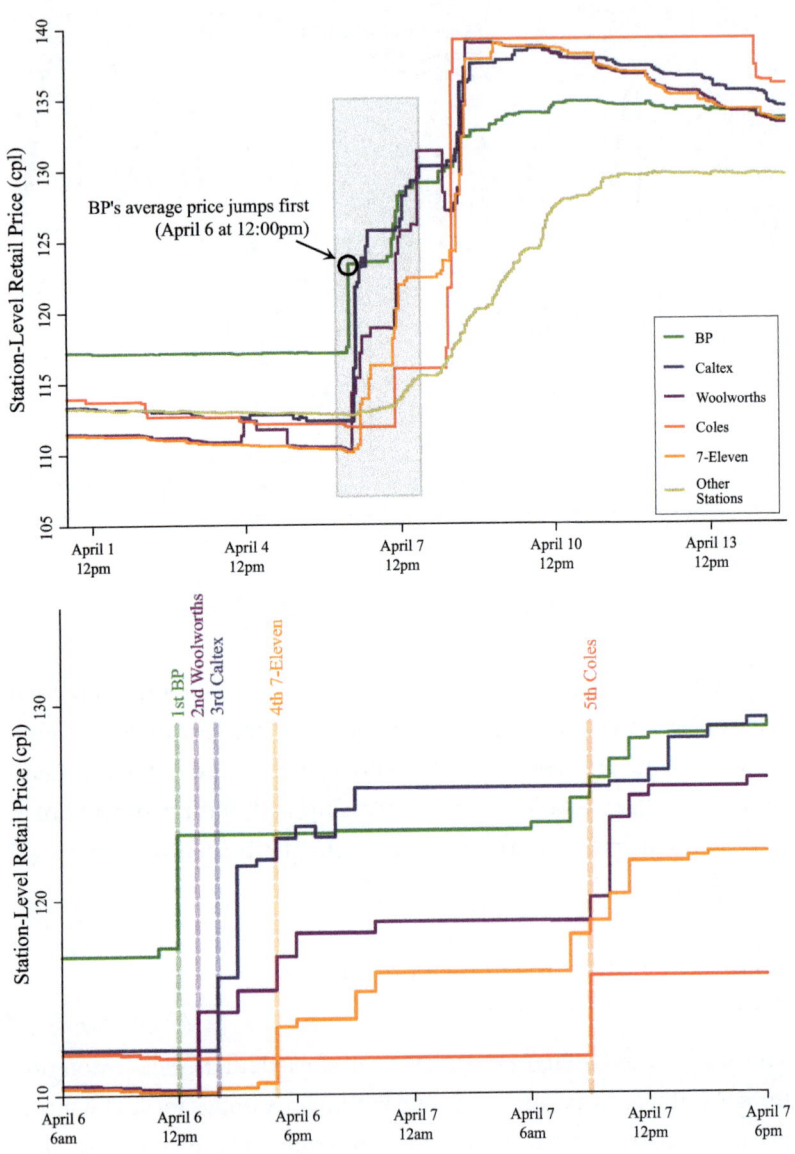

FIGURE 5.3 Price restoration in April 2017.

clearly illustrates the exact order in which retailer-level price jumps occur. BP's average price is the first to exhibit a significant jump at 12 p.m. on April 6. Woolworths and Caltex follow with significant jumps at 1 p.m. and 2 p.m., respectively. Later in the same day, 7-Eleven's average price jumps at 5 p.m. Finally, Coles' average price is the last to jump, at 9 a.m. on April 7 (the following day).

While Figure 5.3 focuses on average retailer-level prices, the FuelCheck (and, by analogy, the Informed Sources) platform allows effective signaling and confirmatory reply signaling by a retailer using the prices at individual gasoline stations. To see this, we need to unpack Figure 5.3 even further and move from the retailer level to the individual station level. Doing so, we show in Figure 5.4 that in the days leading up to the restoration on April 6, the retailers used prices at individual stations to communicate the target price level for the restoration.

In particular, Figure 5.4 plots hourly station-level prices with thin lines and average retailer prices (as in panel (a) of Figure 5.3) in thick lines. Panels (a)–(d) provide these plots for BP, Caltex, Woolworths, and Coles, respectively, from April 1 at 12 a.m. to April 14 at 12 a.m. The dashed lines and circles in the panels highlight the flares. As shown in panel (c), Woolworths is the first to flare, with one station jumping to 137.9 cents per liter (cpl) at 10 a.m. on April 4. Woolworths reinforces this signal by increasing its price at two more stations to 137.9 cpl at 11 a.m. the same day. Panel (b) reveals two subsequent flares from Caltex in response to Woolworths. The first occurs three hours after the Woolworth flares, with Caltex increasing its price at one station to 137.9 cpl at 2 p.m. and returning the station's price to its previous level at the station's opening the next day. Caltex sends a second flare at 133.9 cpl for three hours on April 5 from 1 p.m. to 4 p.m., proposing another potential restoration price.

Having observed four flares at 137.9 cpl and one flare at 133.9 cpl, at 11 a.m. on April 6, BP increases its price at one station to 137.9 cpl, signaling the imminent launch of the price restoration. An hour later at 12 p.m., BP increases its price at sixteen stations to the same

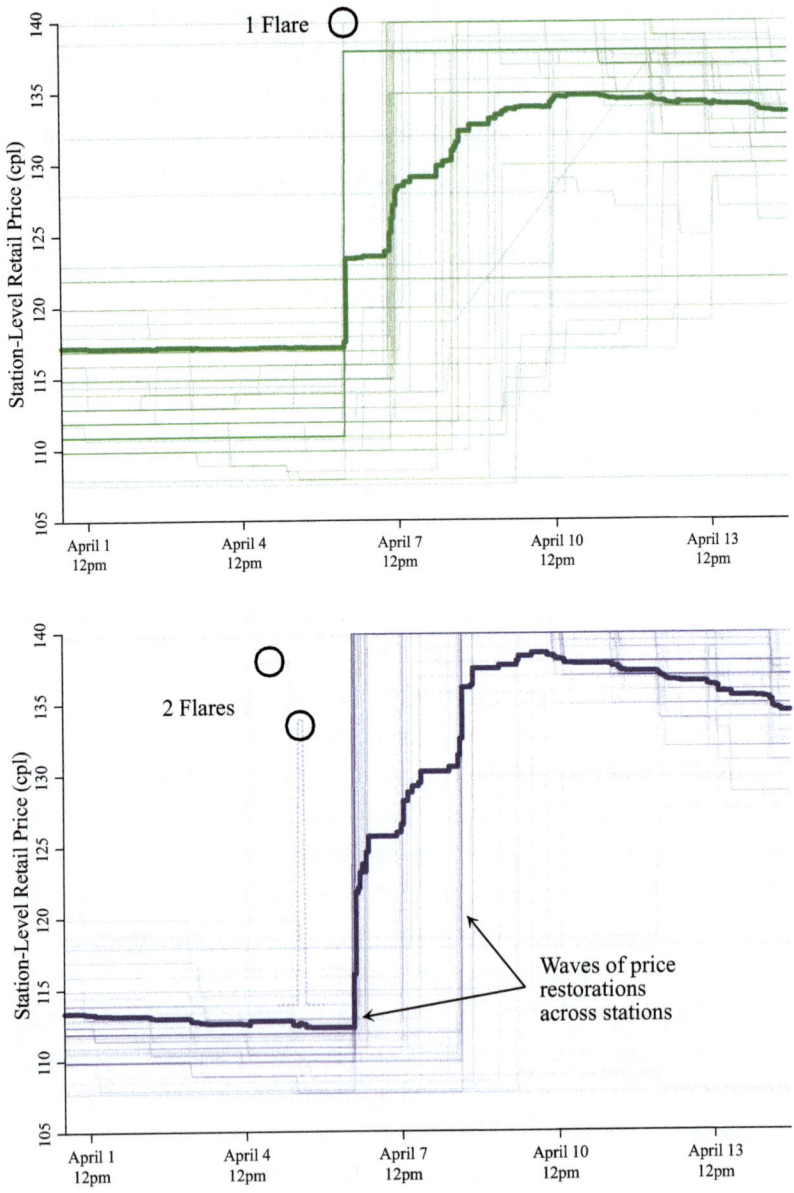

FIGURE 5.4 Station-level price cycles and restorations at hourly frequencies.
Notes: Faint thin solid lines plot station-level hourly prices for a given retailer. Faint thin dashed lines plot station-level hourly prices for selected stations whose prices temporarily jump ("flares") in advance of the market-wide price restoration. Dark thick solid lines plot average hourly prices across stations.

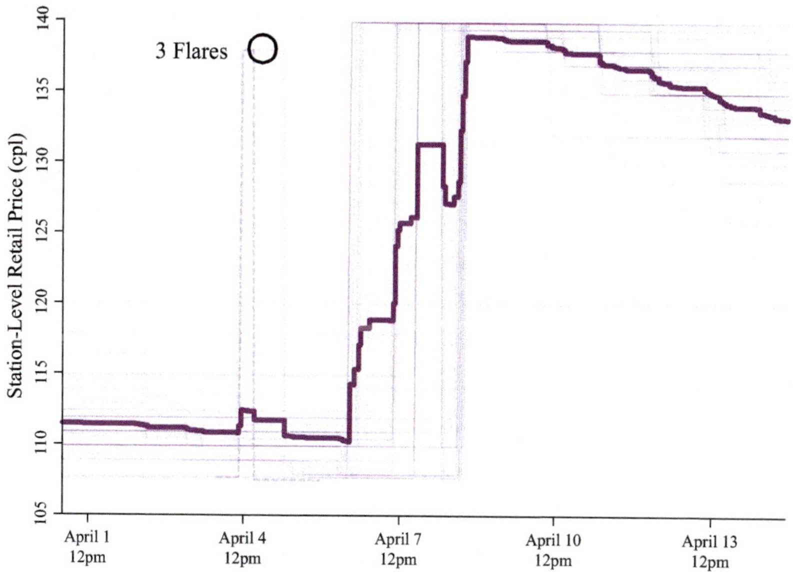

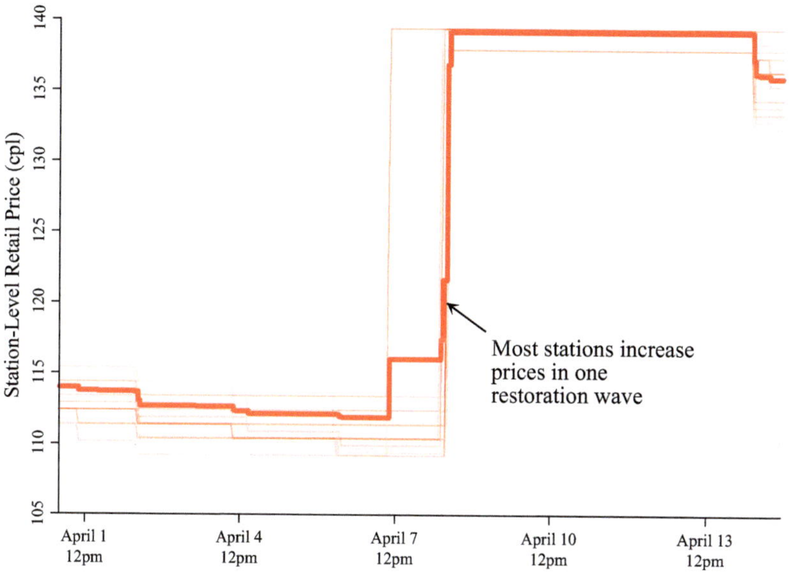

FIGURE 5.4 (cont.)

level and, interestingly, increases its price at one station to 139.9 cpl. We interpret this latter increase as a flare embedded within BP's restoration-initiating increases to 137.9 cpl at the other sixteen stations. BP's flare proves crucial as Woolworths and Caltex follow with price increases within two hours at numerous stations, all of which target 139.9 cpl. Indeed, the focal point for the remainder of the cycle's price restoration is 139.9 cpl at hundreds of stations across the market. A flare by just one BP station appears to have set this off. Table 5.1 summarizes the timeline of price signaling and coordination from our example.

Table 5.1 *Timeline for price signaling and restoration in April 2017*

Date	Time	Retailer	Action
April 4	10 a.m.	Woolworths	1 station jumps to 137.9 → flare stays up until April 5 at 6 a.m. (station open the next day)
	11 a.m.	Woolworths	2 stations jump to 137.9 → flare 1 stays up until April 4 at 5 p.m. (6 hours) → flare 2 stays up until April 5 at 6 a.m. (station open the next day)
	2 p.m.	Caltex	1 stations jumps to 137.9 → flare stays up until April 5 at 10 a.m. (station open the next day)
April 5	1 p.m.	Caltex	1 station jumps to 133.9 → flare stays up until April 5 at 4 p.m. (3 hours)
April 6	11 a.m.	BP	1 station jumps to 137.9
	12 p.m.	BP	16 stations jump to 137.9 1 station jumps to **139.9** → flare embedded within the 16 stations jumping to 137.9
	1 p.m.	Woolworths	7 stations jump to **139.9**
	2 p.m.	Caltex	8 stations jump to **139.9**

For the remainder of the cycle, the focal point for price restoration is **139.9**.

Signals in Executing the Price Restoration

An additional feature in Panel (a) of Figure 5.3 is the dip in Woolworths' average price midway between April 7 and April 10. Woolworths' price dip occurs just before the increase in Coles' average price through its largely market-wide increase in prices across its stations. While Coles increases prices at many of its stations in the signaling window highlighted in Figure 5.3(a), its more significant market-wide price increases did not occur until *after* Woolworths' price decrease, which may have served as a prompt. All of this would have been clear to the stations involved because of their participation in a price-sharing platform and the associated ability to sort, average, and analyze real-time price data.

Location of Signaling Stations

Table 5.1 contains six stations that send signals before retailers begin restoring price levels. Given our motivating narrative above, it is natural to ask about these stations' locations. Panel (a) of Figure 5.5 plots the station locations for all major retailers in Sydney, while panel (b) highlights the location of the six signaling stations from Table 5.1 with enlarged station markers. Relative to the city center, marked by the Sydney Opera House in the center-right of both panels, we find that five signaling stations are in remote suburbs. This pattern aligns with our narrative discussion above and how platforms make it possible to effectively signal price increases from relatively remote stations to help reduce the cost of signaling due to lost market share.

5.4.4 Sparsity, Precision, and Seclusion in Price Signaling

Building from our illustrative example, we now use our entire August 2016 to December 2017 sample to characterize three key aspects of platform-enabled signaling: sparsity, precision, and seclusion. Our results from this analysis confirm the insights from our illustrative example and offer new ones.

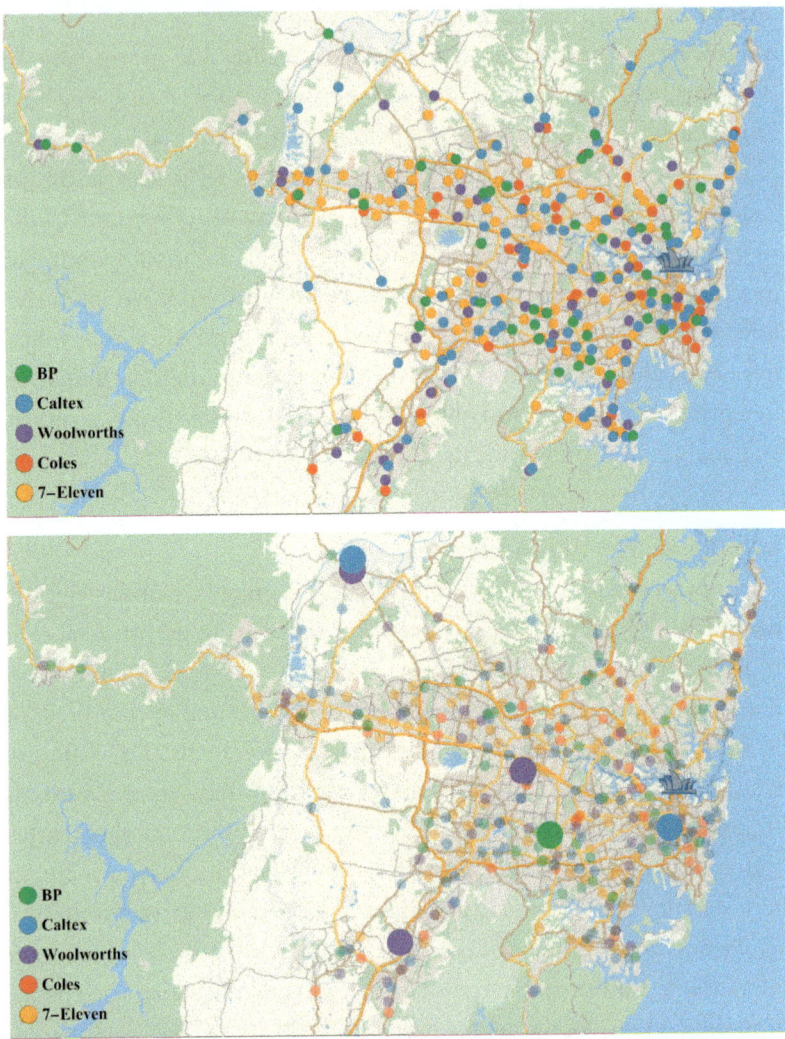

FIGURE 5.5 Location of signaling stations.

Classifying Price Restorations and Signals

For our empirical analysis, it is necessary to classify price restorations at various levels of aggregation and signals at the station-level. We do so in the following four steps (price measures are in terms of cents per liter):

1. Identify the start of *market-level price restorations*.
   Let $\overline{m}_t$ be the market-level average daily retail price – TGP margin across stations (in cpl) with $\Delta \overline{m}_t = \overline{m}_t - \overline{m}_{t-1}$. We identify the start of a market-wide price restoration on date t if $\Delta \overline{m}_t > 2$ and $\Delta \overline{m}_{t-k} < 2$ for $k = 1, 2, 3$. In words, date t is the start of a market-level price restoration if: (1) enough stations begin restoring their prices such that the market-wide average margin grows by more than 2 cpl; and (2) such market-level average margin increases are not observed in the dates just before t.[27]

2. Identify *station-level price restorations* within a market-level restoration window.
   Let p_{it} be station i's price on date t, and let τ be a date when a market-level price restoration begins (as identified in step 1). Station i's restoration price within a fourteen-day market-level restoration window around τ is computed as $p_{i\tau}^{rest} = \max(\{p_{i\tau-7}, \ldots, p_{i\tau+7}\})$. In words, a station's restoration price is the highest price that it charges within a fourteen-day window around the start of a market-level price restoration.

3. Identify *retailer-level price restorations* within a market-level restoration window.[28]
   We identify retailer r's restoration price among its n_r stations in a market-level price restoration starting on date τ as $p_{r\tau}^{rest} = \mathrm{mode}\{p_{1\tau}^{rest}, \ldots, p_{n_r\tau}^{rest}\}$. In words, retailer r's restoration price is the modal station-level restoration price within a fourteen-day market-level price restoration window around τ.

4. Identify *signaling dates* and *signals* just before market-level price restorations.
   Let $\Delta p_{it} = p_{it} - p_{it-1}$ be station i's daily price change. Date t is classified as a signaling date if: (1) it is within seven days before the start of a market-level

---

[27] Visually, Figure 5.2 shows that market-wide restorations eventually yield average daily margin increases of more than 20 cpl. However, this restoration-driven margin increase occurs once all retailers, including smaller independents, begin restoring margins, which is later in the market-level restoration phase. Using a 2 cpl margin increase threshold allows us to identify the *beginning* of market-level restorations phases, typically when major retailers restore margins at multiple stations but before the entire market starts doing so. For instance, April 6, in our example above, is classified as the beginning of a restoration phase. Our results are robust to varying the margin threshold from 1 cpl to 10 cpl.

[28] Recall from our discussion in Section 5.4.2 above that cycles occur roughly once per month. Using a fourteen-day market-level restoration window ensures that no such windows overlap across restorations and yields a sufficiently large window to capture all early and late station-level restorations around a market-level restoration.

Table 5.2 *Sparsity in station-level restoration price signaling by retailer*

Retailer	Station-level signals per restoration	Number of stations
BP	1.28	45
Caltex	1.22	80
Woolworths	1.56	48
Coles	1.94	40
7-Eleven	0.56	106

price restoration (as identified in step 1); and (2) $\Delta p_{it} > 5$ at less than fifteen stations.[29] In other words, signaling dates are just before the start of market-level price restorations when a small group of stations engages in price jumps. We classify station-level price jumps where $\Delta p_{it} > 5$ as station-level price signals on these dates. Notably, such signals do not necessarily correspond to a station's restoration price within a given market-level restoration window.[30]

Sparsity

Our classification scheme identifies eighteen market-level price restorations within our August 1, 2016, to December 1, 2017, sample from Sydney. As alluded to above, market-level restorations occur about once per month. Across the 18 restorations, we identify 132 station-level price signals, which implies 7.3 station-level price signals per market-level restoration. Table 5.2 summarizes the average number of station-level signals by retailer and compares this to the size of each retailer's station network. Retailers tend to send signals from 1 or 2 stations, yet they have station networks with 40 to 101 stations, which underlines the sparsity of station-level price signaling.

---

[29] Like our simple threshold rule for classifying the start of market-wide price restorations, this simple rule is effective in classifying periods involving pre-restoration price signaling. Our results are robust to variations on the 5 cpl and fifteen station thresholds. The threshold rule that we employ is one of several methods used in the literature to classify cyclical pricing. See Holt et al. (2022) for a discussion of the performance of a range of related methods.

[30] For instance, recall from our example above that Woolworths and Caltex had pre-restoration signals of 137.9, but their restoration price was subsequently 139.9.

This sparsity is valuable to gasoline retailers because it reduces the cost of signaling.

Precision

In our illustrative example, the 137.9 price signals from Caltex and Woolworths precipitate their 139.9 restoration prices. Their station-level signals do not perfectly correspond to the retailer-level restoration prices. To systematically investigate such signaling error, we compute a *signal error* as $e_{it} = p_{it} - p_{TT}^{rest}$, which is the difference between a given station-level signal p_{it} and station i's subsequent retailer-level restoration price within restoration window τ, p_{TT}^{rest}. If, for example, $e_{it} = 0$, then station i's signal on date t corresponds exactly to its corresponding retailer's subsequent restoration price within the market-wide restoration window that t sits within.

Empirically, we find that signals are precise and informative about retailers' restoration prices. For instance, the average signal error is $\bar{e}_{it} = 1.2$, which is small relative to a mean station-level restoration price of 137.5, and an average restoration price jump of 21.2. Of the 132 signals that we identify, 78 (59 percent) are exactly 0 cpl, with 90 percent being 4 cpl or less.

Figure 5.6 documents retailers' propensity to engage in price signaling and the precision of their signals. Panel (a) shows that retailers signal at similar rates. For instance, BP sends signals in six of eighteen (33 percent) market-level restorations, whereas 7-Eleven is the least likely to send signals, with signals in three of eighteen (17 percent) restorations.

Panel (b) shows retailers send highly informative signals about future restoration prices. Except for Caltex, retailers' signals correspond *exactly* to their restoration price levels between 71 percent and 90 percent of the time. Furthermore, statistical tests confirm at the 1 percent significance level that the proportion of signals that exactly equal a given station's retailer's restoration price level is statistically significantly different from 0. Price signals are, statistically, informative about retailers' future restoration prices.

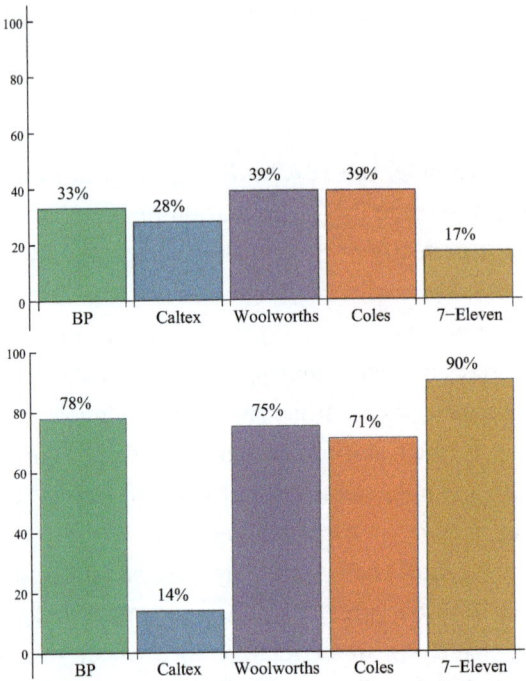

FIGURE 5.6 Signaling propensity and precision across retailers.

Caltex stands out in not sending signals that exactly correspond to its restoration prices. However, in additional calculations, we find that more than 80 percent of Caltex's station-level price signals are within 3 cpl of their future retailer-level restoration prices. So, although their signals are relatively less precise, they are informative within a 3 cpl bandwidth of future restoration prices.

In sum, the results from Table 5.2 and Figure 5.6 imply that stations send precise signals about restoration prices from just a few stations. Moreover, retailers vary their participation in sending signals across price restorations, suggesting that they share signaling costs associated with lost market share. In a market with more than 600 stations, quickly identifying precise signals about rivals' prices from a handful of station-level price jumps would be difficult without a platform. Platform-generated real-time price data and the ability to sort rivals' station-level price distributions make monitoring sparse price signals straightforward.[31]

Seclusion

Our discussion so far raises the question of whether the major retailers account for stations' proximity to competitor stations in determining from which stations to send signals.

The data show that signaling and non-signaling stations are similar in terms of their geographic proximity to the city's center; however, there are differences between signaling and non-signaling stations in terms of local competition as measured by the number of rival stations within a 1-kilometer radius (see Appendix 5A for details). Signaling stations tend to have fewer local rival stations, suggesting they are more secluded from competition.[32]

Further, we estimate an econometric model (see Appendix 5A) to formally characterize factors that influence whether a station ever sends a signal in our sample. Results show that local competition is a key determinant of whether a station sends signals, while the distance from the center of the city is not. The influence of competition is particularly localized, as one additional rival station within 500 meters yields a 5.6 percentage point drop in the probability that a station sends signals. This influence is quantitatively large, as it implies a 20 percent reduction in the probability a station ever engages in signaling relative to the sample mean probability of 28 percentage points.

---

[31] There is a precedent for these results from Perth, Australia, which also has regular price cycles and a platform that makes real-time price data available. Byrne and de Roos (2019) show that in Perth, BP, the market price leader between 2009–2013, was able to signal future price restorations and coordinate rival prices with a small number (<5) of stations. Wang (2009a) documents that retailers employ mixed strategies in leading price restorations, thereby enabling the sharing of costs (due to lost market share) among price leaders.

[32] Previous empirical retail gasoline studies find that competition is highly localized. See, for example, Hastings (2004), Verlinda (2008), Chandra and Tappata (2011), and Luco (2019).

We can also estimate the cost of price signaling in the presence of local rival stations that rationalizes retailers' decision to send signals from stations secluded from local competition. Using unique daily station-level sales data, Wang (2009b) estimates a local cross-price demand elasticity of −18 between neighboring stations in Australian retail gasoline markets with price cycles.[33] The average station-level restoration price jump, corresponding to price jumps from precise signals, is 21.2 cpl. Given an average restoration price of 137.5 cpl, an average restoration price jump represents an 18 percent price increase (21.2/(137.5-21.2)). A back-of-the-envelope calculation based on these figures implies zero sales for a station that sends signals in the presence of a nearby rival. Such a potential collapse in sales helps explain why having local rivals within 500 meters has such a large quantitative impact on whether a given station sends price signals.

Varying Which Stations Send Signals
Beyond secluding signaling stations from local competition, we also find that retailers vary which stations send signals over time. Specifically, among the eighty-nine stations that sent at least one signal, sixty-two (70 percent) only sent one signal over our eighteen-month sample period. Overall, 96 percent of all signaling stations sent three or fewer signals over this period, implying there do not exist "focal" stations from which retailers signal.

These findings further emphasize the importance of a platform for enabling price signaling. In particular, our market structure results highlight how platforms eliminate the role of geography with signaling. Consider a counterfactual scenario without a platform in which retailers want to signal with stations with nearby rivals to ensure their price signals are received. Yet, we find the *opposite* of this, consistent with geography not determining whether rivals observe

---

[33] The estimate of Wang (2009b) sits between other estimates from Canada from Houde (2012) and Clark and Houde (2013) of −15 and −30, respectively.

signals. Instead, through a platform, retailers can avoid high signaling costs while sending effective signals using stations that are secluded from nearby competitors.

To further reduce signaling costs, stations vary which isolated stations send signals, thereby limiting consumers' ability to learn which stations are high-priced "signallers" and substitute away from them.[34] At the same time, on the supply side, rivals do not require consistent "signaller" stations to monitor for signals. Instead, with access to real-time price data, a searchable platform, and pricing algorithms (Assad et al., 2024) that can quickly identify maximal prices and large price changes among rivals' stations, retailers can monitor and respond to price signals irrespective of the consistency of their geographic locations.

5.5 CONCLUSION

Informed Sources provided a mechanism for subscribing gasoline retailers to communicate effectively regarding future prices (including proposals and responses). Although the retailers used their actual prices to communicate, they were able to limit the costs of doing so because, with the facilitation of the Informed Sources platform, they could effectively communicate with only brief price changes at a small number of sites. Even more, communication sites were varied over time and strategically chosen for their limited local competition. In contrast, in other settings absent an information-sharing platform,

---

[34] Our demand-based argument for firms' incentives to vary the identities of signaling stations stems from recent empirical evidence from Wu et al. (2022). They find that gasoline consumers rapidly update their beliefs about stations' relative price levels within a given day along their commuting routes, substituting toward lower-priced stations. Given habitual commuting behavior in urban markets, like Melbourne and Sydney, we believe consumers would likewise update their beliefs about relatively "high" and "low" priced stations over time if a retailer designated a particular station to be a "signaller." Recall that such signals represent extreme, 20 percent to 30 percent, discrete price jumps relative to rival stations' prices when sent from the bottom of the cycle. Such price jumps are likely salient to consumers, particularly if a given station repeatedly sends them each month in coordinating restorations.

price-based communication could expose firms to potentially significant lost profits because a firm that signals using elevated prices risks losing substantial business to its lower-priced rivals. In sum, the Informed Sources platform facilitated anticompetitive effects by enabling the monitoring of current prices and the reliable, low-cost signaling of future prices.

It has long been recognized that price-sharing systems can serve as facilitating devices. For example, in the 1920s, the US government prosecuted several trade association cases.[35] In these cases, competitors engaged in frequent (often daily or weekly) information reporting and dissemination via a centralized information exchange system. More recently, in the 1994 Airline Tariff Publishing Company case, the US government investigated collusion in the Airline Industry.[36] Although the case settled without a judicial ruling on defendants' liability, it is regarded as a landmark case for competition policy toward treatment of information sharing via price announcements, with the US government contending that through the airline's information-sharing system (ATP), firms engaged in an "electronic dialogue" that helped them to fix prices.[37]

---

[35] Cases include: *Am. Column & Lumber Co.* v. *United States*, 257 U.S. 377 (1921); *United States* v. *Am. Linseed Oil Co.*, 262 U.S. 371 (1923); *Maple Flooring Mfrs. Ass'n.* v. *United States*, 268 U.S. 563 (1925); *Cement Mfrs. Ass'n.* v. *United States*, 268 U.S. 588 (1925). See also, Whitney (1934), Alexander (1997), and Borenstein (2004).

[36] *United States* v. *Airline Tariff Publ'g Co.*, No. 92-cv-2854 SSH (D.D.C. 1994). See also Borenstein (2004) and Miller (2010).

[37] "The ATP fare dissemination system provided a forum for the airline defendants to communicate about their prices. Using, among other things, first and last ticket dates and footnote designators, they exchanged clear and concise messages setting forth the fares each wanted the others to charge, and identifying fares each wanted the others to eliminate. Through this electronic dialogue, they conducted negotiations, offered explanations, traded concessions with one another, took actions against their independent self-interests, punished recalcitrant airlines that discounted fares, and exchanged commitments and assurances – all to the end of reaching agreements to increase fares, eliminate discounts and set fare restrictions." Competitive Impact Statement, *United States* v. *Airline Tariff Publ'g Co.*, No. 92-cv-2854 SSH (D.D.C. Mar. 17, 1994), available at www.justice.gov/file/483606/download.

In the context of historical antitrust cases involving price-sharing systems, our case study of the Informed Sources matter provides a key takeaway: digital information-sharing platforms provide a forum for an "electronic dialogue" that facilitates anticompetitive conduct.

For policymakers, our case study underlines competitive concerns associated with price-sharing platforms. In particular, the speed and reliability with which communication was possible through the Informed Source platform substantially removed the usual deterrents to firms' using prices for signaling. In resolving the Informed Sources matter, the ACCC attempted to reinsert such deterrents by requiring that the shared prices be made available to consumers and third parties for five years. Further, the ACCC's settlement with Informed Sources included that two retailers, Mobil and Coles Express, would not subscribe to Informed Sources or a similar service for five years. In concurrent research, Byrne et al. (2023) study the effectiveness of these remedies, finding that the removal of Coles from the platform was associated with an increase in prices. Intuitively, the more limited information flow to Coles slowed Coles' reaction time relative to its competitors, thereby slowing the rate of decline of prices in the undercutting phase of the price cycle.

Price-fixing conspiracies have historically created systems that share price data, making prices transparent to participating firms. The case history shows a progression from letters, telephone, fax, email, and text messages to digital platforms. Although the use of price-sharing devices is not new, the type of systems used have evolved with technological advancements. Thus, as technology advances, so do facilitating devices, and so must our appreciation for the possible anticompetitive effects of the latest advance.

How, then, might policy evolve with the rise of digital price-sharing technologies and associated signaling practices? Monitoring is a natural policy lever, particularly through the use of "big data" screens for anticompetitive conduct. Recent studies by Byrne and de Roos (2019), Miller et al. (2021) and Assad et al. (2024) leverage high-frequency panel data, like the data generated by the Informed Sources platform, to detect price signaling and transitions toward anticompetitive conduct. In principle, similar algorithms used by firms to detect and respond to rivals via platform-generated price data can also be used by antitrust authorities for monitoring conduct. Our case study underlines the importance of having high-frequency, disaggregated price data for such data-driven monitoring.

In this case study, we have illustrated that a platform that provides high-frequency, market-wide price information facilitates low-cost signaling, aiding coordination. We might expect that regulating the scope or frequency of information provision could disrupt these signaling practices. However, there are trade-offs involved. In the Informed Sources matter, removing Coles from the platform as part of the settlement effectively reduced the frequency of information flows to Coles, potentially contributing to an increase in prices (Byrne et al., 2023). In the retail gasoline market in Perth studied by Byrne and de Roos (2019), regulators restricted firms to daily price changes. While this limited the scope for low-cost signaling, the data suggest that it simplified the problem of coordinating on focal points for pricing. Given such trade-offs, policy debates regarding the regulation of digital platforms and pricing algorithms are ongoing.[38]

APPENDIX 5A DETAILS FOR ANALYSIS OF SECLUSION

As mentioned in the body of the case study, our discussion raises the question whether the major retailers account for stations' proximity to competitor stations in determining from which stations to send signals. The panels in Figure 5.7

---

[38] See Ezrachi and Stucke (2020) for an extensive discussion of public policy and regulatory debates over information sharing, pricing algorithms, and the impact of digital platforms on competitive conduct. Recent theoretical and empirical research in economics on these issues include Byrne and de Roos (2019), Luco (2019), Calvano et al. (2020), Montag and Winter (2020), Assad et al. (2024), Asker et al. (2022), Leisten (2022), Ater and Rigbi (2023), and Brown and MacKay (2023).

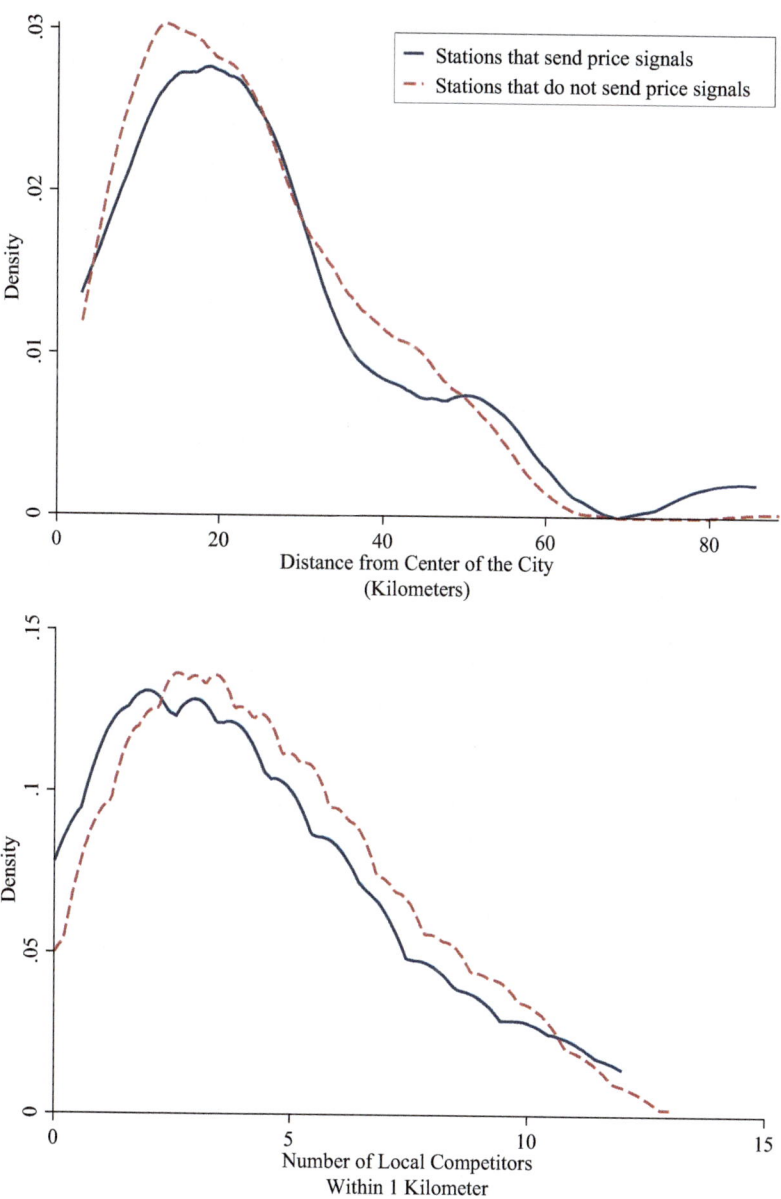

FIGURE 5.7 Characteristics of stations that send price signals.

provide visual evidence related to this question. To construct the figures, we classify a station as a *signaling station* if it sends at least one signal across any of the eighteen market-level restorations that we examine. Of the major retailers' 319 stations, 89 (28 percent) send at least one signal. Figure 5.7(a), which plots a station's distance from the center of the city (the Sydney Opera House), indicates that signaling and non-signaling stations are similar in terms of their geographic proximity to the city's center. Figure 5.7(b), in contrast, visually reveals differences between signaling and non-signaling stations in terms of local competition as measured by the number of rival stations within a 1-kilometer radius. Signaling stations tend to have fewer local rival stations, suggesting they are more secluded from competition.[39]

We use a linear probability model (LPM) to formally characterize factors that influence whether station i ever sends a signal in our sample:

$$1\{\text{signals}\}_i = \alpha_0 + \alpha_1 \text{Nrival}_i^k + \alpha_2 \text{Dist}_i + X_i\beta + \rho_r + \epsilon_{i,r}$$

where $1\{\text{signals}\}_i$ is a dummy equaling 1 if station i ever sends a signal before a restoration, Nrival_i^k is the number of rival stations within distance k of station i, Dist_i is the distance of station i from the city center (the Sydney Opera House), X_i is a vector of demographic variables for population, density, income, age, education, and language in station i's census block,[40] ρ_r is a fixed effect for retailer r operating station i, and ϵ_i is an econometric error that we allow to be heteroskedastic.

Table 5.3 contains our LPM results. The coefficient estimates for our local market structure variables (see Table 5.3) correspond to the visual evidence from Figure 5.7: local competition is a key determinant of whether a station sends signals, while the distance from the center of the city is not. The influence of competition is particularly localized, as one additional rival station within 500 meters yields a 5.6 percentage point drop in the probability that a station sends signals. This influence is quantitatively large, as it implies a 20 percent reduction in the probability a station ever engages in signaling relative to the sample mean probability of 28 percentage points.

---

[39] Our radius-based approach to defining localized markets around individual stations is consistent with the approach used in previous studies (see, e.g., Hastings, 2004; Verlinda, 2008; Chandra and Tappata, 2011; Luco, 2019).

[40] We use Statistical Area 2 (SA2) census blocks from the Australian Bureau of Statistics. SA2's correspond to well-defined suburbs across Sydney.

Table 5.3 *Characteristics of stations that send price signals*

	(1)	(2)	(3)	(4)
Local market structure				
Number of rival stations within ...				
500 meters	−0.056**			
	(0.028)			
1 kilometer		−0.032*		
		(0.017)		
2 kilometers			−0.013	
			(0.009)	
3 kilometers				−0.008
				(0.005)
Distance from city center (km)	0.003	0.003	0.002	0.002
	(0.002)	(0.002)	(0.002)	(0.002)
Population (100,000's)	−0.188	−0.175	−0.187	−0.185
	(0.291)	(0.291)	(0.292)	(0.293)
Population density (100,000's)	−1.169	−0.841	−0.584	−0.548
	(1.308)	(1.299)	(1.330)	(1.341)
Median income (100,000's)	−0.632	−0.695	−0.759	−0.761
	(0.480)	(0.480)	(0.501)	(0.514)
Average Age	0.005	0.005	0.004	0.004
	(0.008)	(0.008)	(0.008)	(0.008)
Share of people with Bachelor's degree	0.828***	0.809***	0.810***	0.804***
	(0.292)	(0.294)	(0.294)	(0.294)
Share of people English speaking	0.046	0.015	0.028	−0.070
	(0.441)	(0.440)	(0.447)	(0.440)
R-Squared	0.113	0.113	0.110	0.110
Observations	420	420	420	420

Notes: The dependent variable is a dummy variable equaling one if a station ever engages in price signaling between August 1, 2016, and December 31, 2017. The mean of the dependent variable is 0.22. Local demographics are measured at the Australian Bureau of Statistics "Statistical Area 2" (SA2) level and correspond to the SA2 in which a given station is located. All regressions include retailer fixed effects. Robust standard errors are in parentheses: ***$p < 0.01$, **$p < 0.05$, *$p < 0.1$.

REFERENCES

Alexander, B. J. (1997) "Failed Cooperation in Heterogeneous Industries under the National Recovery Administration," *Journal of Economic History*, 57, 322–344.

Asker, J., C. Fershtman, and A. Pakes (2024) "The Impact of Artificial Intelligence Design on Pricing," *Journal of Economics & Management Science*, 33, 276–304.

Assad, S., R. Clark, D. Ershov, and X. Lei (2024) "Algorithmic Pricing and Competition: Empirical Evidence from the German Retail Gasoline Market," *Journal of Political Economy*, 132, 723–771.

Ater, I. and O. Rigbi (2023) "Price Transparency, Media, and Informative Advertising," *American Economic Journal: Microeconomics*, volume 15 and pages 1–29.

Atkinson, B. (2009) "Retail Gasoline Price Cycles: Evidence from Guelph, Ontario Using Bi-Hourly, Station-Specific Retail Price Data," *The Energy Journal*, 30, 85–109.

Australian Competition & Consumer Commission (2014a) "ACCC Takes Action Against Informed Sources and Petrol Retailers for Price Information Sharing," Press Release, August 20, 2014, www.accc.gov.au/media-release/accc-takes-action-against-informed-sources-and-petrol-retailers-for-price-information-sharing.

Australian Competition & Consumer Commission (2014b): "Monitoring of the Australian Petroleum Industry: Report of the ACCC into the Prices, Costs and Profits of Unleaded Petrol in Australia," www.accc.gov.au/publications/annual-monitoring-of-the-australian-petroleumindustry/monitoring-of-the-australian-petroleum-industry-2014-report.

Australian Competition and Consumer Commission (2015) "Petrol Price Information Sharing Proceedings Resolved," Press Release, December 23, 2015, www.accc.gov.au/mediarelease/petrol-price-information-sharing-proceedings-resolved.

Borenstein, S. (2004) "Rapid Price Communication and Coordination: The Airline Tariff Publishing Case (1994)," in J. Kwoka Jr. and L. White, eds., *The Antitrust Revolution: Economics, Competition and Policy*, Oxford University Press, 233–251.

Brown, Z. Y. and A. MacKay (2023) "Competition in Pricing Algorithms," *American Economic Journal: Microeconomics*, 15, 109–156.

Byrne, D. P. and N. de Roos (2019) "Learning to Coordinate: A Study in Retail Gasoline," *American Economic Review*, 109, 591–619.

Byrne, D. P., N. de Roos, M. S. Lewis, L. M. Marx, and X. Wu (2023) "Information Sharing and Oligopoly Pricing: A Natural Experiment in Retail Gasoline," Working Paper, University of Melbourne.

Byrne, D. P., G. Leslie, and R. Ware (2015) "How Do Consumers Respond to Gasoline Price Cycles?" *The Energy Journal*, 36, 115–147.

Calvano, E., G. Calzolari, V. Denicolo, and S. Pastorello (2020) "Artificial Intelligence, Algorithmic Pricing, and Collusion," *American Economic Review*, 110, 3267–3297.

Chandra, A. and M. Tappata (2011) "Consumer Search and Dynamic Price Dispersion: An Application to Gasoline Markets," *RAND Journal of Economics*, 42, 681–704.

Clark, R. and J.-F. Houde (2013) "Collusion with Asymmetric Retailers: Evidence from a Gasoline Price-Fixing Case," *American Economic Journal: Microeconomics*, 5, 97–123.

Clark, R. and J.-F. Houde (2014) "The Impact of Explicit Communication on Pricing: Evidence from the Collapse of a Gasoline Cartel," *Journal of Industrial Economics*, 62, 191–228.

Eckert, A. (2013) "Empirical Studies of Gasoline Retailing: A Guide to the Literature," *Journal of Economic Surveys*, 27, 140–166.

Ezrachi, A. and M. E. Stucke (2020) *Virtual Competition*, Harvard University Press.

Foros, O. and F. Steen (2013) "Vertical Control and Price Cycles in Gasoline Retailing," *Scandinavian Journal of Economics*, 115, 640–661.

Gal, M. S. (2023) "Limiting Algorithmic Cartels," *Berkeley Journal of Law and Technology*, 38, 173–229.

Harrington, J. E. (2011) "Posted Pricing as a Plus Factor," *Journal of Competition Law and Economics*, 7, 1–35.

Hastings, J. S. (2004) "Vertical Relationships and Competition in Retail Gasoline Markets: Empirical Evidence from Contract Changes in Southern California," *American Economic Review*, 94, 317–328.

Holt, T., M. Igami, and S. Scheidegger (2022) "Detecting Edgeworth Cycles," Working Paper, Yale University.

Houde, J.-F. (2012) "Spatial Differentiation and Vertical Mergers in Retail Markets for Gasoline," *American Economic Review*, 105, 2147–2182.

Leisten, M. (2022) "Algorithmic Competition, with Humans," Working Paper, United States Federal Trade Commission.

Lewis, M. S. (2012) "Price Leadership and Coordination in Retail Gasoline Markets with Price Cycles," *International Journal of Industrial Organization*, 30, 342–351.

Linder, M. (2018) "Price Cycles in the German Retail Gasoline Market: Competition or Collusion?" *Economics Bulletin*, 38, 593–602.

Luco, F. (2019) "Who Benefits from Information Disclosure? The Case of Retail Gasoline," *American Economic Journal: Microeconomics*, 11, 277–305.

Miller, A. R. (2010) "Did the Airline Tariff Publishing Case Reduce Collusion?" *Journal of Law and Economics*, 53, 569–586.

Miller, N. H., G. Sheu, and M. C. Weinberg (2021) "Oligopolistic Price Leadership and Mergers: The United States Beer Industry," *American Economic Review*, 111, 3123–3159.

Montag, F. and C. Winter (2020) "Price Transparency against Market Power," Mimeo, LMU.

Noel, M. D. (2007) "Edgeworth Price Cycles: Evidence from the Toronto Retail Gasoline Market," *The Journal of Industrial Economics*, 55, 69–92.

Verlinda, J. A. (2008) "Do Rockets Rise Faster and Feathers Fall Slower in an Atmosphere of Local Market Power? Evidence from the Retail Gasoline Market," *Journal of Industrial Economics*, 56, 581–612.

Wang, Z. (2009a) "(Mixed) Strategy in Oligopoly Pricing: Evidence from Gasoline Price Cycles before and under a Timing Regulation," *Journal of Political Economy*, 117, 987–1030.

Wang, Z. (2009b) "Station-Level Gasoline Demand in an Australian Market with Regular Price Cycles," *Agricultural and Resource Economics*, 53, 467–483.

Whitney, S. N. (1934) *Trade Associations and Industrial Control*, New York: Central Book Co.

Wu, X., M. S. Lewis, and F. Wolak (2022) "Consumer Search with Learning in the Retail Gasoline Market," *RAND Journal of Economics*.

Zimmerman, P. R., J. M. Yun, and C. T. Taylor (2013) "Edgeworth Price Cycles in Gasoline: Evidence from the United States," *Review of Industrial Organization*, 42, 297–320.

6 Collusion with Non-express Communication

Retail Gasoline in Norway*

Joseph E. Harrington, Jr.

6.1 INTRODUCTION

In August 2019, the Norwegian Competition Authority (NCA) opened an investigation of Circle K and YX, two of the major retail gasoline companies in Norway, for a possible violation of the Competition Act's prohibition against anticompetitive agreements and concerted practices. The investigation stemmed from both companies posting recommended gasoline prices on their websites. The NCA claimed that this practice facilitated coordination among Circle K, YX, and other major gasoline companies in the setting of their retail prices. Circle K and YX disagreed with the NCA's competition concerns and both sides pursued remedies. In October 2020, NCA accepted the proposed remedy of Circle K and YX which was to end the practice of posting recommended gasoline prices on their websites for a period of five years.[1]

---

* The author thanks Maarten Pieter Schinkel for his constructive comments. I worked as a consulting expert for the Norwegian Competition Authority in their case against Circle K and YX. The article is not funded in whole or in part, either directly or indirectly, by the Norwegian Competition Authority or any other person or entity. No client or other interested party has a right to review, or has reviewed, this article. I alone am responsible for the content and opinions expressed here.

[1] Decision V2020-26: Circle K Norge AS (YX Norge AS) under Section 12(3), cf. Section 10 of the Norwegian Competition Act and Article 53 of the EEA Agreement; hereafter referred to as NCA Decision 2020. The link to the Circle K decision is https://konkurransetilsynet.no/decisions/vedtak-2020–26-og-vedtak-2020-27-circle-k-norge-as-og-yx-norge-as-konkurranseloven-%c2%a7-12-tredje-ledd-jf-%c2%a7-10-og-eos-avtalen-artikkel-53/ and to the YX decision is https://konkurransetilsynet.no/decisions/vedtak-2020–27-yx-norge-as-konkurranseloven-%c2%a7-12-tredje-ledd-jf-%c2%a7-10-og-eos-avtalen-artikkel-53/. The two decisions are identical.

This case study examines this communication practice as a mechanism for coordinating the retail prices of the major gasoline companies. It explains how the posted recommended prices were intended for competitors and not consumers, and identifies a well-defined coordinating signal that is clearly distinguishable from any instrument of competition. This is not a case of price signaling but rather communication in coded messages.[2]

Section 6.2 provides background information on industry structure and conduct. Section 6.3 describes the contested communication practice. Section 6.4 explains how it served to coordinate companies' retail gasoline prices and Section 6.5 discusses its effect on prices. Section 6.6 concludes.

6.2 BACKGROUND ON INDUSTRY STRUCTURE AND FIRM CONDUCT[3]

There are four major retail gasoline companies with a nationwide presence in Norway: Circle K, Certas Energy Norway (operating the brand Esso), St1 Norway (operating the brand Shell), and Uno-X Energy (operating the brands Uno-X and YX). In aggregate, the four companies have a market share of 95 percent, with the company market shares ranging from a low of 18 percent for Uno-X Energy to a high of 31 percent for Circle K.[4] In total, there are approximately 1,700 gasoline stations in Norway with around 550 dealer-owned stations and the rest being company-owned.[5]

As part of their pricing protocols, each of the four major companies initially sets a nationally recommended price relevant for all its

---

[2] For a general discussion of communication in the context of collusion, the reader is referred to chapter 3 in Kaplow (2013).
[3] Unless otherwise noted, the information in this section is from V2015 – 29 "St1 Nordic Oy – Smart Fuel AS – Competition Act 16, Decision with remedies" (merger decision of the NCA).
[4] Market shares are measured by volume of gasoline sold in 2017 (NCA Decision 2020).
[5] Number of stations is from the Norwegian Gasolineeum Association's website. www.drivkraftnorge.no/Tall-og-fakta/bensinstasjoner/.

stations, both company-owned and dealer-owned. Circle K and YX post their recommended prices on a publicly accessible website, while the other two companies internally communicate them to their stations. Companies also have locally recommended prices for each station which equal the (nationally) recommended price plus transportation cost (for getting the fuel to the station) and adjusted for nearby competitors' retail prices, which were observed by the station and reported to the company's headquarters. At company-owned stations, headquarters directly controls retail prices and sets them at each station's locally recommended price. Dealer-owned stations receive locally recommended prices and, while they are free to deviate from them, headquarters is able to exert considerable control over their retail prices by adjusting wholesale prices (Foros and Steen, 2013).[6]

Prior to November 27, 2017, this pricing process was augmented by the following communication practice. When changing its recommended prices,[7] Circle K would post them on its website the day before they were valid, usually between 7 a.m. and 4 p.m. That announcement stated the date (but not the time) at which recommended prices became valid. Routinely on Mondays and Thursdays, the companies set the retail price at company-owned stations equal to the recommended price (plus transportation cost) and induced dealer-owned stations to also do so.

These procedures produced a regularity to retail prices over the course of a week. Figure 6.1 reports the average retail price for six major brands. The top panel is representative of the pattern that was observed prior to November 27, 2017.[8] Prices would sharply increase

---

[6] The process works as follows. The dealer-owned stations pay a list price (common to all stations) net of an agreed margin (e.g., 50 øre per liter). The list price is equal to the recommended price (net of transportation costs). If competing stations start to engage in price undercutting, the dealer reports their prices to headquarters who then reduces the recommended price to the level of the competing stations and induces dealers to charge that price by reducing the wholesale price.

[7] Unless otherwise noted, "recommended price" refers to the nationally recommended price.

[8] For the top panel, the prices of the six brands moved in sync and closely tracked the average price.

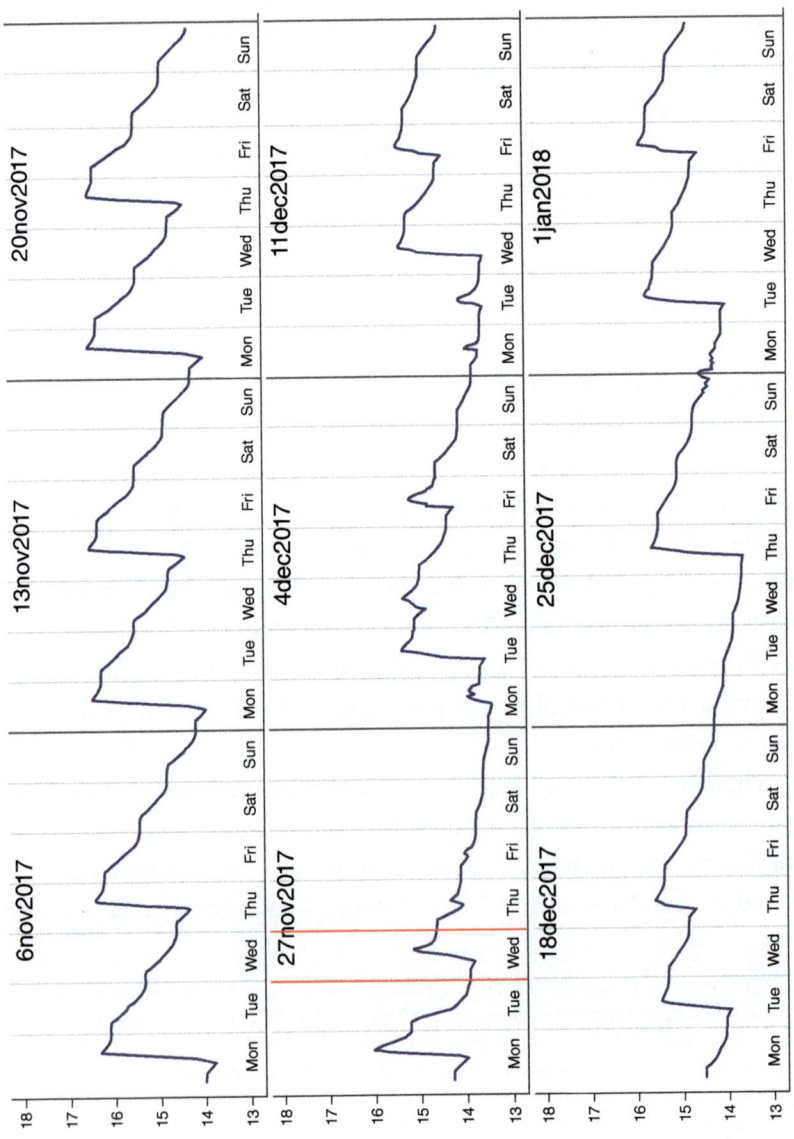

FIGURE 6.1 Average retail price for six major brands.
(*Source*: NCA Decision 2020)
For the six major brands, the vertical axis is the average price per liter in Norwegian Kroner for 95 unleaded gasoline based on hourly data.

on Monday, gradually decline over the course of the next few days (as retail prices adjusted to local market conditions), sharply increase on Thursday, and gradually decline until they were raised again on Monday. Commonly observed in retail gasoline markets, the rockets-and-feathers pattern (also referred to as the Edgeworth cycle) has prices rise like a "rocket" and fall like a "feather" (Eckert, 2013).

6.3 DESCRIPTION OF NEW PRACTICE

Though it was a Monday, Circle K did not raise its retail prices on November 27, 2017. In accordance with convention, the other companies did raise their retail prices. On November 29, 2017, Circle K issued a press release describing a new pricing policy which explained why it did not raise the price on Monday (excerpts from that press release are provided below). As shown in the middle panel of Figure 6.1, prices in the ensuing three weeks did not follow cleanly defined cycles. Furthermore, prices across companies did not move in sync. However, by the week of December 18, 2017, companies' retail prices were once again synchronized though with different timing. As seen in the bottom panel of Figure 6.1, prices were still characterized by a rockets-and-feathers pattern but the day of the week on which prices were raised was not always the same and there was variation in the time between price increases.[9]

In its press release of November 29, 2017, Circle K stated that the goal of the new pricing policy was "to get more even prices throughout the week, thus making it easier for customers to fill when it suits them best."[10] More exactly, the new policy no longer had it routinely raise prices on Mondays and Thursdays.

> The majority of Norwegian motorists want to refuel when it suits them best, rather than steering for specific days where the price is low.... A large number of customers endeavor to refuel when it is

---

[9] For the bottom panel, the prices of the six brands moved in sync and closely tracked the average price.

[10] Google translation of Press Release by Circle K on November 29, 2017. https://kommunikasjon.ntb.no/pressemelding/circle-k-vil-gjore-det-enklere-for-kundene-a-fylle-tanken-nar-de-selv-vil?publisherId=16596283&releaseId=16604904.

cheapest, first and foremost on Sunday evening and Monday morning. Then queues and crowds await gasoline stations across the country. Neither the customers nor our stations want such a pattern.[11]

As is clear from Figure 6.1, and contrary to Circle K's statement, prices were not more stable over the week. However, prices were less predictable because consumers did not know when prices would be increased.

This new policy was reflected in a change in companies' procedures when it came to announcing recommended prices. As it had previously done, Circle K continued to list a "recommended price," a "valid from" (*gjeldende fra*) date for that recommended price, and the amount of the change in the recommended price (*endring*) on its website. This information is provided for gasoline and diesel products (both regular and premium) and for manned and unmanned (*automatstasjoner*) stations. Figure 6.2 provides a screenshot from the website.

However, the timing of announcements was different. On a day in which Circle K would change the recommended prices on its website, it would do so around 8 a.m. and update the "valid from" date to the current date. There are instances in which a recommended price was not changed but the "valid from" date was still updated to the current date, and the reported change in price was "0 øre." The website would also state that the change was effective starting at 10 a.m.; hence, price changes were publicly announced about two hours prior to becoming effective. After Circle K made these changes on its website, YX would revise its website between 8:30 a.m. and 9:30 a.m. by matching Circle K's recommended prices[12] and updating its "valid from" date to the current date. Figure 6.3 documents the change in timing as it reports the time at which recommended prices were changed on the websites of Circle K and YX. After adopting the new communication practice, all announcements of a change in recommended prices occurred in the

---

[11] Ibid.
[12] From August 2018, YX matched CK's recommended price. Prior to August 2018, YX had a fixed spread to CK's recommended price.

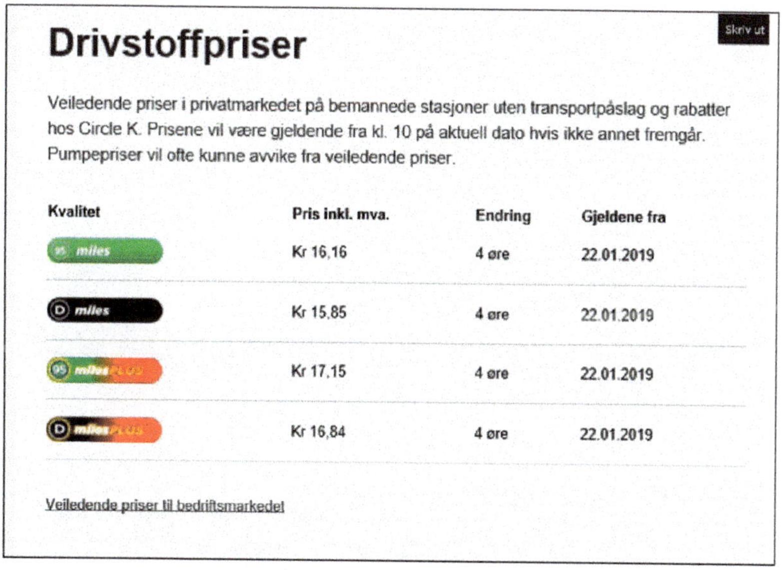

Skriv ut

Drivstoffpriser

Veiledende priser i privatmarkedet på bemannede stasjoner uten transportpåslag og rabatter hos Circle K. Prisene vil være gjeldende fra kl. 10 på aktuell dato hvis ikke annet fremgår. Pumpepriser vil ofte kunne avvike fra veiledende priser.

Kvalitet	Pris inkl. mva.	Endring	Gjeldene fra
95 miles	Kr 16,16	4 øre	22.01.2019
D miles	Kr 15,85	4 øre	22.01.2019
95 milesPLUS	Kr 17,15	4 øre	22.01.2019
D milesPLUS	Kr 16,84	4 øre	22.01.2019

Veiledende priser til bedriftsmarkedet

FIGURE 6.2 Screenshot from Circle K website showing recommended prices.
(*Source*: NCA Decision 2020)

8–10 a.m. window. Prior to it, such announcements were distributed over the day. Recall that Circle K and YX are the only chains that publicly post their recommended prices. The other chains' recommended prices were internally communicated to their stations.

At 10 a.m. on the day of an updating of the "valid from" date (whether or not recommended prices were changed), Circle K (and Best, which is a chain of dealer-owned stations connected to Circle K) and YX would change retail prices to the currently recommended prices (plus transportation costs) at all stations.[13] Later in the morning, Shell and Esso would start changing their stations' prices. An increasing number of stations would adopt the new prices over the course of the next few hours. Uno-X and Automat1 (which have

[13] Based on data from four Circle K stations in four different cities, Foros and Nguyen-Ones (2021) found that 54 percent of the price increases occurred at 10 a.m. and 45 percent at 11 a.m.

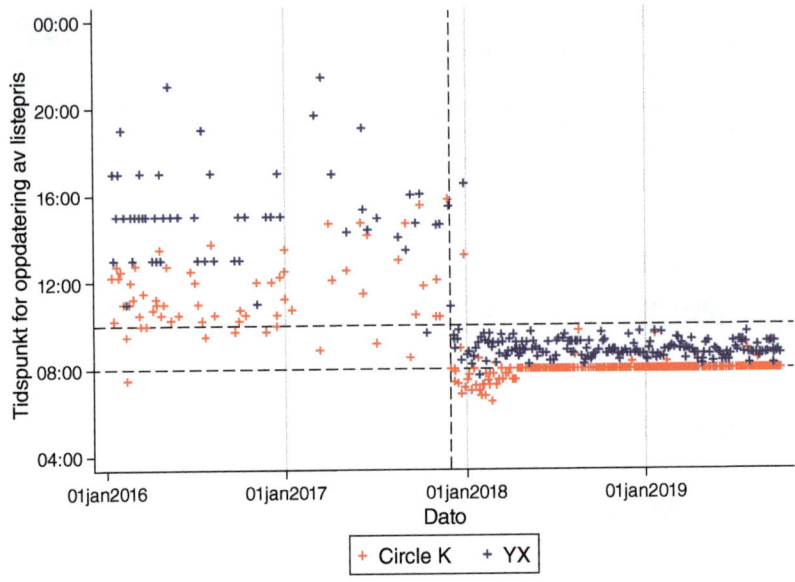

FIGURE 6.3 Recommended price changes on the websites of Circle K and YX.
(*Source*: NCA Decision 2020)
Translation of legend for vertical axis:
"The time during the day for updates of recommended prices"

unmanned stations) increased prices across their stations around 1 p.m. Retail prices would remain at this new level for a few hours, after which stations would start lowering their prices. The decline of retail prices would take place over several days (where the number of days was variable over time) until, again around 8 a.m. on a given day, Circle K would restart the price cycle by updating its "valid from" date and typically changing its recommended prices.[14]

6.4 THEORY OF COLLUSION

The communication practice to be examined is the following. Around 8 a.m. on a day in which it intends to set retail prices equal to

---

[14] For further details on and analysis of these price patterns, see Nguyen-Ones (2020) and Foros and Nguyen-Ones (2021).

recommended prices, Circle K changes information on its publicly accessible website. It updates the "valid from" date to the current date, changes the recommended prices when they are different from the previous recommended prices, and states that the change is effective at 10 a.m. Between 8:30 a.m. and 9:30 a.m., YX matches Circle K's announcement on its own publicly accessible website. At 10 a.m., Circle K and YX raise their prices to the currently recommended prices. The other companies follow in the ensuing hours by raising their prices at an increasing number of their stations. This practice was adopted as of mid December 2017.[15]

I will argue that Circle K's communication practice is a non-express means of coordinating a collective increase in prices of the four major gasoline retailers. As Circle K's announcements are public, there is the possibility that they are not intended for Circle K's competitors and thus could have a legitimate rationale. Section 6.4.1 explains the announcements were intended for competitors, not other market participants. Section 6.4.2 then explains how the announcements facilitated coordinated pricing. More specifically, Circle K's announcement was a coded signal for all companies to raise their prices.

6.4.1 Posted Recommended Prices Are Intended for Competitors

When Circle K announces a change in its recommended price on its web site, there are three sets of market participants for whom it may be intended: 1) Circle K's stations, 2) consumers, and 3) competitors (such as YX). It is obvious that this information is useful to its own stations and thus is a class of intended recipients. However, it is equally clear that Circle K intends this information not just for its own stations but for other market participants too; for if this

---

[15] I will not evaluate prior communication practices, nor the transition to this new communication practice. For establishing the theory of collusion, it is sufficient to focus on the properties and implications of the practice in place starting in mid December 2017.

information is only intended for Circle K's own stations, it would be distributed using a password-protected web site or some other private channel such as email. That option is clearly available to Circle K because this is the practice of companies other than Circle K and YX who only internally disseminate recommended prices. In general, companies tend to operate under the default of keeping strategic information – such as prices – confidential unless it benefits them from sharing the information or they are compelled by law or custom to do so. Hence, I must conclude that the public posting of recommended prices by Circle K and YX is done because the information is also intended for consumers and/or other gasoline companies, those being the only other relevant actors.

If Circle K intends consumers to learn the information then presumably it is information that is of value to them and they are aware that it is available. Given that prices can vary across stations and time, consumers would certainly benefit from receiving information about current and future prices. However, Circle K's posted recommended prices provide little or no information of value to consumers in their search for low prices. First, recommended prices are generally uninformative of current prices. When a recommended price is changed at 10 a.m. on a given day, the retail price will equal the recommended price plus transportation costs but consumers do not know the transportation costs. Furthermore, the retail price will soon depart from the recommended price (plus transportation costs) as stations begin to lower their retail prices. For all practical purposes, the posted recommended prices provide little useful information for consumers to learn about the current prices being charged at various stations. Second, recommended prices are generally uninformative of future prices. Learning future prices could be valuable to those consumers who can intertemporally shift their purchases of gasoline. More specifically, if consumers know that prices will rise in the near future, they can purchase now in order to avoid those higher future prices. (Indeed, that is what occurred under the previous pricing regime.) In principle, the posting of recommended prices does provide that opportunity. When at 8 a.m. Circle K announces a change in its recommended prices to become effective at 10 a.m., a consumer could infer that retail prices will rise at 10 a.m. as a new price cycle is started. They could then shift any planned purchases after 10 a.m. to the 8–10 a.m. window and thereby buy before the price is raised at 10 a.m. However, such conduct seems impractical for almost all consumers. For a consumer to be able to engage in such intertemporal shifting of their purchases, they would have to monitor the Circle K web site at 8 a.m. on a daily basis and, in addition, they must know that a change in the recommended price will mean the start of a new price cycle. While consumers are certainly motivated to save on how much money they spend for gasoline, it is unreasonable to expect consumers to be so astute and observant as to make use of these subtle and sporadic announcements of a change in the recommended price.

In sum, it is not credible that the online posting of recommended prices by Circle K provides useful information for consumers. In contrast, if actual retail prices at particular stations were posted online, that information would be useful for consumers in finding the stations that currently offer the lowest gasoline prices. Or if Circle K announces a future change in retail prices (well in advance of that change, such as twenty-four hours), that information might be useful for consumers in their decision as to whether to buy now or wait (though again it is unclear consumers would take the time to regularly monitor for such advance price announcements). The point is that there is information that Circle K could post online which might be useful to consumers. Given that they do not and instead post information of little value to consumers, it seems clear that the online posting of recommended prices is not intended for consumers.

Given that Circle K publicly posts its recommended prices, it must intend for that information to be received by actors other than its own stations. Given that the recommended prices are effectively useless to consumers, consumers are not the intended recipients. From these observations, it follows that Circle K publicly posts its recommended prices for the purpose of informing other gasoline companies.[16]

6.4.2 Posted Recommended Prices Coordinate Retail Prices

If gasoline companies are expressly communicating a plan to coordinate recommended prices – one company explicitly proposes to the others that they all raise their recommended prices, and the others accept that invitation – it is clear the communication is harmful and unlawful. If one gasoline company is setting the retail price and other gasoline companies are matching that retail price, such price leadership and matching is harmful but lawful. Though both practices create consumer harm, they differ in a crucial way. With express communication, messages designed to coordinate (verbal expression of an invitation to collude) can be disentangled from actions in the marketplace (prices). With price leadership and matching (or, more generally, price signaling), price is both the message to coordinate and the terms of trade for consumers. That they are intertwined prevents the practice from being prohibited.

Circle K's communication practice is neither express communication nor price signaling and is properly viewed as non-express communication for which, like express communication, there is a clearly identifiable announcement. This announcement is: *changing the "valid from" date to the current date.* Typically, a change in the "valid from" date is also accompanied by a change in the recommended price. However, there are instances in which the "valid from" date is changed but the recommended price is left unchanged. Whether or not a recommended price is changed, when Circle K updates the "valid from" date to the current date, it is a signal for all gasoline companies to raise their prices to Circle K's recommended price (adjusted for differential transportation costs).

---

[16] For a broader discussion of price exchanges among competitors, see Harrington and Leslie (2023).

How do we determine that an announcement (whether actions, words, or symbols) embodies some particular message? We cannot get inside the head of the person making the announcement to determine what they want receivers of that announcement to infer. However, we do know that when party A sends a message to party B, it is done with the intent to solicit certain conduct from party B. Thus, in some instances, party A's message can be inferred from the conduct of party B. If we claim that some announcement by party A contained a message to party B then evidence in support of that claim is conduct by party B consistent with that message. The basis for concluding that Circle K's announcement of a change in the "valid from" date contained the message that all gasoline companies are to raise their retail prices to Circle K's recommended price is that the other gasoline companies did exactly that: they raised their retail prices to Circle K's recommended price. This is true even if the recommended price did not change.

In most cases, Circle K did change the recommended prices at the same time that it updated the "valid from" date. Suppose it was possible to explain away the instances in which the "valid from" date was updated but the recommended price was left unchanged. There is still a clearly identified announcement: *Circle K changing its recommended price*. That is, the act of Circle K changing its recommended price conveyed the message: *all gasoline companies are to raise their retail prices to Circle K's recommended price*. It is crucial to understand that this practice is distinct from price signaling. If it involved not recommended prices but instead retail prices and other gasoline companies always matched Circle K's announced retail price then we could not disentangle price as a "message" (for rival companies) from price as the "terms of trade" (for consumers). However, retail prices were generally not linked to recommended prices, as reflected in retail prices typically being below recommended prices. While the recommended price might determine the initial retail prices at the start of the cycle, retail prices soon became untethered to recommended prices. Circle K changing its recommended price was a signal for all companies to raise retail prices to the recommended price and thereby initiate a new cycle.

That retail prices are not a transformation of recommended prices is evidenced by two properties. First, if the retail price was tied to the recommended price then when the recommended price goes up so would the retail price, and when the recommended price goes down so would the retail price. But that is not the case. Suppose companies' retail prices were below the recommended price on day t and, on day t + 1, and Circle K lowered the recommended price but to a level exceeding the previous day's retail prices. In response, all gasoline companies would raise their retail prices to the new recommended price even though that recommended price is below the one of the previous day; recommended prices and retail prices move in different directions. The point is that recommended prices and retail prices can move in the opposite direction or the same direction which implies the retail price is not a transformation of the recommended price; they are distinct variables.

Turning to the second property, if the retail price was tethered to the recommended price then small changes in the recommended price would result in small changes in the retail price. But that is also not the case. A small change in the recommended price typically caused a large change in retail prices. For example, suppose on day t the recommended price is 15.91 and the retail price is 14.72. If Circle K lowers the recommended price to 15.90 on day t + 1 then retail prices will rise from 14.72 to 15.90. Hence, a one øre drop in the recommended price results in a rise in the retail price which is 118 times as large. The retail price is not just responding to the recommended price but also to *Circle K's announcement that it is changing its recommended price*. It is that announcement, which is a clearly defined and distinct message from the terms of trade, that is the retail price.

The following perspective may be useful for appreciating the difference between this communication practice and price leadership. Suppose a firm knows that other firms will match its price. With that knowledge, the firm raises the price because it anticipates that other firms will follow its lead. Though pricing is coordinated – as a firm raises its price with the intent that competitors will match it – the firm's conduct is not in violation of competition law because a firm has the right to choose its price irrespective of what may be the reaction of other firms. That other firms should respond in a way that creates consumer harm is ancillary to a legitimate act: the selection of a firm's own price. While coordinated pricing as just described is lawful, *communication to facilitate coordinate pricing is unlawful.* A firm making an announcement (updating the "valid from" date on its web site) to competitors that is anticipated to have the effect of all firms raising their prices to a common level is no more lawful than a firm explicitly inviting competitors to set a common price. The anticompetitive effect of the announcement is not ancillary to a legitimate purpose; coordinated pricing is the sole purpose of the announcement.

In sum, Circle K signaled to other gasoline companies to raise retail prices to Circle K's recommended price by changing the "valid from" date and changing the recommended price on its publicly accessible web site. This change on Circle K's web page occurred around 8 a.m. along with the announcement that it is effective as of 10 a.m. I have argued that this change is a signal to coordinate on raising retail prices to Circle K's recommended price starting at 10 a.m. After receiving this message, YX would typically respond between 8:30 a.m. and 9:30 a.m. with the same recommended prices and "valid from" date.[17] One can interpret Circle K changing its "valid from" date and recommended prices on its website as an "invitation" to coordinate on raising retail prices at 10 a.m., and YX matching that change in "valid from" date and recommended prices on its website as an "acceptance" of that invitation.[18]

[17] Based on web scraping starting in the fall of 2018, the NCA determined that YX responded in this manner to Circle K in 118 out of 120 observations.

[18] "[T]he firms' actions become concerted when the firms have achieved the conditions of conscious parallelism by communication of their intent to raise prices and their reliance on one another to do the same. Crucially, the rivals need not have exchanged promises or assurances of their actions; it is enough that they have communicated their intent to act and their reliance on others to do so. If these

To further appreciate the illegality of this communication practice, consider the following alternative communication systems. Suppose Circle K posts its recommended price online and, when it wants the price cycle to restart with all companies' retail prices equaling Circle K's recommended price, it puts the following statement on its website: *all gasoline companies are advised to set retail prices equal to the recommended prices plus transportation costs.* Such a message is clearly an unlawful invitation to collude. Now suppose that the statement *all gasoline companies are advised to set retail prices equal to the recommended prices plus transportation costs* is replaced with an upward arrow ↑ on the web page along with recommended prices. If the presence of ↑ causes all companies to raise their retail prices to the recommended price, there would be no difference from the first case. With either scenario, there is an overt act of communication – either words or symbols – that resulted in the coordination of competitors' prices. In practice, Circle K did not use an ↑ but instead a change in the "valid from" date and a change in recommended prices to convey the same message: *all gasoline companies are advised to set retail prices equal to the recommended prices.*

As reflected in their conduct, gasoline companies had the following agreement based on coded messages: if the "valid from" date on Circle K's website is the current date then all companies are to coordinate on setting retail prices equal to Circle K's recommended prices. If the perspective is taken that the message is in the change in the recommended price (not the change in the "valid from" date) then gasoline companies have the following agreement: if any recommended price on Circle K's website is changed then all companies

conditions are present, then the ensuing consciously parallel actions are concerted. ... Communication of intent and reliance is a tangible, culpable action that differs from the actions of firms in an ordinary competition or in a simple conscious parallelism. The character of the communications and their proximity to parallel action in conformity with the communications distinguish them from other, benign exchanges." Page (2009), pp. 451–452.

are to coordinate on setting retail prices equal to Circle K's recommended prices. Circle K updating the "valid from" date (or changing the recommended price, even by a trivial amount) is code for raising retail prices to the recommended prices.

That there is a remedy underscores that these announcements are messages which facilitate coordination and are not part of the competitive process. Prohibiting Circle K from the online posting of recommended prices would prevent it from communicating to its competitors when to raise their prices. At the same, its prohibition would not affect communication between a company's headquarters and its stations – as that can be performed through private channels – and would not affect consumer information because the online recommended prices are not useful in their purchasing decisions.

6.5 EFFECT

The focus has been on how this communication practice allowed the gasoline companies to coordinate increases in their retail prices. Though I do not offer an analysis measuring the effect of this practice on retail prices, there are several reasons to believe that it would have harmed consumers.

The first reason for suspecting consumer harm is associated with the difficulty of predicting the initiation of a price cycle; consumers can no longer count on retail prices increasing on Mondays and Thursdays. Consequently, the intertemporal shifting of their purchases, so as to avoid the highest prices, is more difficult under the new pricing regime. Though there are still price cycles, consumers do not know when they will start and end. We would then expect a smaller share of purchases to occur when prices are lowest. Holding fixed the distribution of prices over time (which, admittedly, there is no reason to think that is true), this would imply higher average transaction prices.

The second reason why consumers are likely to be harmed is that Circle K would have only made this change if it expected to earn higher profits. Unless there are some cost efficiencies from having more stable demand over the week (which could possibly be true), higher profit is likely to require a higher average transaction price. That would certainly suggest consumers are worse off though it is possible, due to risk aversion, consumers could benefit if prices were less variable over the week. However, apparently prices were, in fact, not less variable, as exemplified in Figure 6.1.

There is a related consideration. With this new practice, the market went from a convention in which the initiation of a price cycle was not controlled by any individual firm – there was an equilibrium in which all firms increased their prices on Mondays and Thursdays – to one in which Circle K controlled the start of a new price cycle. That new institution is conducive to prices being set to maximize the profits of Circle K while making sure that the other gasoline companies are incentivized to follow Circle K's lead. Such a pricing policy would seem more likely than not to imply higher prices and, therefore, consumer harm.[19]

As I am discussing effect, this is an appropriate place to consider a possible (but misguided) efficiency defense for Circle K's conduct. As described in the press release quoted in Section 6.3, Circle K's new pricing policy had the declared goal of benefiting consumers. By making the initiation of a price cycle unpredictable – rather than predictably occurring on Mondays and Thursdays – it would avoid consumers queueing on Sundays and Wednesdays. Putting aside the open question of its impact on average transaction prices, this argument would, at best, justify Circle K's adoption of the new pricing policy, but it would not justify them making public announcements on their website that served to coordinate competitors' price increases. If it had instead used communications internal to the company (which was the practice of all companies except Circle K and YX), Circle K could have implemented the new pricing policy while avoiding communication that facilitated coordinated pricing. As the

---

[19] Some preliminary empirical analysis relevant to effect is provided in Nguyen-Ones (2020) and Foros and Nguyen-Ones (2021).

pricing policy could be implemented with or without the announcements, an efficiency defense for the pricing policy is not an efficiency defense for the announcements.

6.6 CONCLUDING REMARKS

When firms do not expressly communicate, it can be difficult for them to coordinate a price increase. In some markets, this can be done by a price leader increasing its price and then waiting for other firms to observe the higher price and match it. In the case of retail gasoline, such a mechanism is problematic because, due to the high price-elasticity of firm demand, the price leader can realize significant loss of demand until its price increase is matched. Furthermore, the need to coordinate prices is a routine phenomenon when, as in the case of retail gasoline markets in Norway, there are frequent price cycles which require coordinating on the restart of a cycle.

The first takeaway of this case study is the identification of a new method for coordinating price increases. Market leader Circle K would provide an announcement on its publicly accessible website, which it could expect competitors to regularly monitor, informing firms of an imminent increase in its price. In this way, Circle K could expect other firms to raise their prices contemporaneously with it or shortly thereafter. With that expectation, Circle K could profitably lead the industry in restarting a new price cycle.

While that takeaway is about collusive practices, the second takeaway is about prosecuting those practices. The practice of Circle K and YX is properly viewed as unlawful price fixing because there is a clearly identified announcement (specifically, a change in the "valid from" date and, most commonly, a "change in the recommended price") which allowed gasoline stations to coordinate their retail prices (setting the retail price equal to the recommended price plus transportation costs) and for which its discontinuation would not interfere with the competitive process. Circle K's announcement on its website was an invitation for YX to price at Circle K's recommended price, and YX's response in posting the same announcement on its website was acceptance of Circle K's invitation. We then have communication that formed an agreement to coordinate raising prices.

In concluding, a framework is offered for proving that firms have engaged in non-express communication to coordinate prices.

1. Identify an announcement that can be separated from price and other market variables.
2. Establish that the announcement is not intended for other market participants (e.g., consumers) by showing: i) the cost of accessing the announcement is too high; ii) the benefit from the information contained in the announcement is too low; or iii) they did not, in fact, access the announcement (which is evidence that either it was too costly to access or it was of little value).
3. Establish a theory of collusion by showing how the announcement allows competitors to coordinate their prices.
4. Show effect of the communication practice on transaction prices.

By the per se standard in the United States, the first three steps should be sufficient to establish a violation of Section 1 of the Sherman Act. Unless there is an efficiency defense under Article 101(3), the first three steps should be sufficient to establish a violation by object in the European Union under Article 101(1) of the Treaty on the Functioning of the European Union. Satisfaction of the first condition implies there is a remedy which is prohibiting firms from making those announcements. The fourth step provides additional evidence in support of the theory articulated in step 3.

REFERENCES

Eckert, A. (2013) "Empirical Studies of Gasoline Retailing: A Guide to the Literature," *Journal of Economic Surveys*, 27, 140–166.

Foros, Ø. and M. Nguyen-Ones (2021) "Coordinate to Obfuscate? The Role of Prior Announcements of Recommended Prices," *Economics Letters*, 198, 109680.

Foros, Ø. and F. Steen (2013) "Vertical Control and Price Cycles in Gasoline Retailing," *Scandinavian Journal of Economics*, 115, 640–661.

Harrington, J. E., Jr. and C. R. Leslie (2023) "Horizontal Price Exchanges," *Cardozo Law Review*, 44, 2301–2359.

Kaplow, L. (2013) *Competition Policy and Price Fixing*, Princeton: Princeton University Press.

Nguyen-Ones, M., (2020) "Price Coordination with Public Prior Announcements in Retail Gasoline Markets," working paper, Norwegian School of Economics, July.

Page, W. H. (2009) "Twombly and Communication: The Emerging Definition of Concerted Action under the New Pleading Standards," *Journal of Competition Law & Economics*, 5, 439–468.

7 Cartel Instability and Price Wars

Retail Gasoline in Canada

Robert Clark, Marco Duarte, and
Jean-François Houde

7.1 INTRODUCTION

We provide a case study of a price-war episode that took place in Québec City's retail gasoline market in 2000 between two periods of coordination.[1] Our investigation sheds light on its causes, development, and aftereffects, using detailed data on prices, sales volume, and station characteristics, along with testimony from a government investigation into the origins of the war.[2]

Despite fragmented ownership, in the years leading up to the price war, Québec City's retail gasoline market was characterized by high margins and limited price dispersion across stations within a neighborhood. These patterns resulted from a particular form of hub-and-spoke collusive arrangement in which upstream branded suppliers coordinated zone pricing between their own downstream retailers and independent branded stations operating in the same neighborhood. Upstream suppliers influenced prices charged by

---

[1] Legal disclaimer: This case study analyzes pricing in Quebec City's retail gasoline market strictly from an economic point of view. Any allegations of collusion in this market and others in the province have not been proven in a court of justice. However, for the purpose of this case study, we take collusion in investigated markets as established.

[2] The data used in this chapter come from three main sources: Kent Marketing, the leading survey company for the Canadian gasoline market, that every two months collects information on sales, amenities, brand affiliation, and a snapshot of prices for (close to) the universe of stations located in large cities relating to sales from January 1995 until June 2001; Québec's energy board's weekly survey of retail prices at a random sample of thirteen stations from December 1997 until February 2004; Market research company MJ Ervin's weekly survey of retail prices for a sample of fifteen stations from January 2001 to November 2012. We also refer to documents from the Competition Bureau and from the Régie de l'énergie, that are described in more detail in Appendix A.

independent station owners and softened retail competition by using nonlinear wholesale pricing schemes (i.e., quantity discounts) and by offering price-support clauses that guaranteed retailers a minimum profit flow. Integrated, company-owned stations were motivated to maintain high prices and avoid stealing business from other stations, but branded independents had incentive to undercut the arrangement and take advantage of the price-support clause, especially toward the end of their contracts with the upstream firm. Nonetheless, coordination was maintained throughout the late 1990s as branded independents chose the stream of profits provided by contract renewal over those from undercutting.

Conditions changed drastically in January 2000. A branded independent retailer, in the last year of its lease contract, chose to defect from the collusive arrangement by lowering its price to increase sales volume and benefit from a price-support clause it had with its upstream supplier. This event triggered a price war that caused margins to collapse from over five cents per liter (cpl) to nearly zero, with almost no dispersion in prices across the city and surrounding area. The station that instigated the price war and other stations along commuting paths were winners, experiencing large market share increases at the expense of stations in the downtown core. Suppliers also suffered significant losses, as retail margins close to zero implied large transfers to independent retailers with price-support clauses.

The price war lasted almost a full year. Specific market characteristics made it difficult for the cartel members to regroup. Using daily station-level data, we show that it was extremely costly to restart coordination because demand was very elastic: raising the price two cpl above neighboring prices could result in a 36 percent loss of volume. A low-price guarantee policy offered by one of the larger players in the market also made it difficult to transition out of the price war. In December 2000, a group of stations filed a lawsuit with the regulatory agency alleging predatory pricing from some competitors. We provide evidence that following the investigation and subsequent intervention by the government, coordination restarted, and firms transitioned to a new equilibrium in which margins were even higher and prices more unified across the entire city than they had been before the price war. The postwar pricing pattern is similar to what was observed in the retail gasoline markets of four nearby cities, where a Competition Bureau investigation uncovered evidence of an alleged hard-core cartel.[3]

This case study highlights how the vertical contracts employed in many gasoline markets to share risk and soften competition can also generate a conflict of interest between suppliers and retailers. Vertical contracts featuring price-support clauses and nonlinear pricing allow suppliers to influence buyers' pricing decisions and could potentially facilitate collusion.[4] However, these contractual features might also trigger price wars since retailers do not bear all the losses from deviating. Our analysis also illustrates how challenging it can be to restart coordination after the buyer deviates. We highlight in particular the significance of elastic demand and low-price guarantee policies, common features in many retail markets.

The rest of the case study is divided into five sections. In the first, we describe the main features of the industry that are important for understanding the incentives faced by firms in Québec's fuel industry. Section 7.3 describes the coordinated zone-pricing equilibrium that retailers and suppliers achieved before the start of the price war. In Section 7.4 we explain the causes of the price war and its dissemination. In Sections 7.5 and 7.6, we explain the challenges faced by firms attempting to restart coordination and the new collusive equilibrium they achieved afterward. Finally, in Section 7.7, we conclude.

---

[3] See Erutku and Hildebrand (2010), Clark and Houde (2013), and Clark and Houde (2014).

[4] There is a large literature studying the effect of vertical restraints on both intra and interbrand competition and how it can facilitate collusion. For an extensive discussion on that, see Rey and Vergé (2008).

RETAIL GASOLINE IN CANADA 195

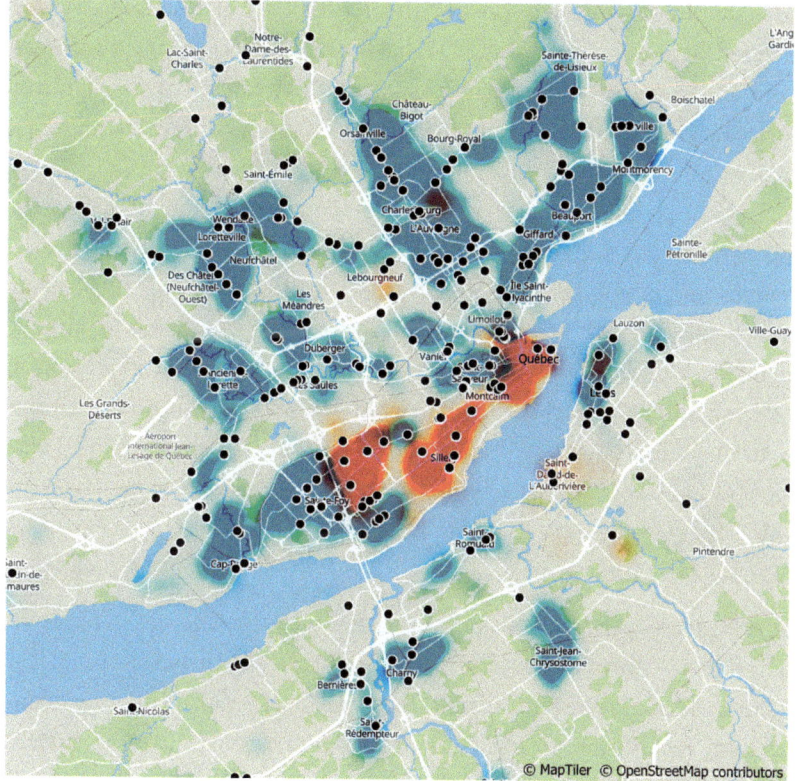

FIGURE 7.1 Québec City: Fuel stations' locations and net traffic flow.

7.2 SETTING

In the late 1990s, there were just over 300 stations in Québec City and surrounding areas. Figure 7.1 shows the geographical distribution of the stations and highlights the main traffic patterns of consumers. The figure provides a heat map of the net traffic in each neighborhood (i.e., destination – origin), with positive net traffic in red and negative net traffic in blue.[5] As can be seen, traffic flows from the outer regions

---

[5] Information is from the Ministère des Transports et de la Mobilité durable's 2001 origin-destination survey. Net traffic for a given geographical zone 'x' corresponds to the number of respondents claiming displacement to 'x' minus the number of displacements from 'x.' There are 950 zones.

toward the downtown core on the North side of the St Lawrence River.[6] Before the price war, stations located in non-commuting areas and the downtown core had posted the highest prices, with lower prices posted in the peripheral neighborhoods and along commuting paths.[7]

Three different types of stations operate in the market, namely stations owned by (i) national fuel chains (brands), (ii) independent companies with brand affiliations (contracts), and (iii) unbranded independent companies. In the 1990s, station ownership was fragmented, with around ten different fuel brands and with independent branded stations making up a significant share of the ownership of stations associated with the four major fuel suppliers: 49 percent, 24 percent, 41 percent, and 40 percent of Esso, Petro Canada, Shell, and Ultramar stations, respectively.

7.2.1 Vertical Contracts

Branded independent stations operate under two different types of contracts – commission-based and cross-lease. Both types of vertical contracts are negotiated every three to five years, reflecting local market conditions. Commission-based contracts are used primarily by one of the larger chains operating in the market, Ultramar, which at the time owned the nearest refinery. Under these contracts it controls the inventory and sets retail prices, with the station owner receiving a commission. Rather than using this arrangement, most independent retailers operating branded stations sign long-term cross-lease contracts with an upstream supplier. The structure of these contracts differs across stations and brands, but the idea is that the independent retailer leases the facility to a supplier, who leases it back to the retailer under various terms and conditions. The main reason

---

[6] For more details on commuting patterns in Québec City and their impact on demand for retail gasoline, see Houde (2012).

[7] Based on Kent database, for the period between 1997 and 1999, the average gasoline price was 59.42 cpl at areas south of the St. Lawrence River (Levis), 58.92 at the downtown core north of the river (Quebec, Sainte-Foy, Sillery, and Cap-Rouge), and 58.48 at other neighborhoods.

for the existence of these contracts is that they allow the upstream supplier to maintain access to the site in the event the station owner sells the property. Stations operating under cross-lease contracts are responsible for setting the retail price but face a nonlinear compensation scheme (namely quantity discounts).[8] The cross-lease contract specifies a "lease" paid to the station operator, which is expressed on a per-volume basis (e.g. 1.6 cpl), but not the wholesale price, since it is not contractible due to fluctuations in oil prices. Cross-lease contracts also specify a minimum quantity that the retailer needs to purchase from the supplier every period. Failure to meet this volume target leads to financial penalties. As a result, profit margins are random and subject to important downside market risk. When the market price falls, because of a price war for instance, stations must earn small or negative gross margins to avoid penalties.

Because of borrowing constraints and the presence of large fixed costs, retailers are particularly sensitive to the risk of earning negative profits during periods of low margins. To transfer part of this risk to the supplier, cross-lease contracts between station operators and oil companies are characterized by price-support clauses that establish a lower bound on the gross margin earned by retailers. These clauses, also known as minimum margins, are negotiated at the beginning of the contract and then held fixed. They ensure owners of a positive profit margin on gasoline sales even if gasoline is sold at cost (such as in the event of a price war). Although the exact nature of vertical contracts is unknown, several witnesses confirmed the existence of price-support clauses among independent stations operating under three of the four vertically integrated brands.[9] These sorts of arrangements have been used in many other retail gasoline markets throughout the world, including those in Australia, Norway, and the Netherlands.[10]

---

[8] These agreements specify what equipment must be installed at the facility (e.g. pumps and convenience store), and determine the structure of the retailer's compensation.

[9] See Régie (2000).

[10] See Wang (2009), Foros and Steen (2013) and Faber and Janssen (2019).

7.2.2 Retail Price Floor

Prices in the province are regulated by the law on petroleum products (Loi sur les produits pétroliers), which was enacted at the start of 1997 and administrated by the Régie de l'énergie du Québec (hereafter the Régie). The law stipulates a weekly floor price equal to:

$$MEP_{mt} = \omega_t + \tau_{mt} + T_{mt}, \qquad (1)$$

where, for market m during week t, ω_t is the minimum wholesale price at the terminal, τ_{mt} is an estimate of the transportation cost to deliver gasoline from the refinery to market m (about 1/3 cents per liter in Québec City), and T_{mt} is the sum of federal and provincial taxes. Since most stations pay a wholesale price below w_t through negotiated discounts, the MEP is an upper bound on the marginal cost of selling gasoline. The price floor is determined and posted on the Régie's website every Monday.

If a firm observes rivals charging below the floor, it can sue for financial compensation based on *excessive and unreasonable commercial practices*. The floor was adopted following an earlier price war in 1996. According to the Régie, the war was caused by predatory pricing by the major retailing chains, and the floor was implemented by the Québec government in an effort to protect small independent retailers.[11]

Since the MEP only accounts for taxes and transportation costs, retail prices at the MEP would most likely not cover the stations' fixed operating costs. This is especially problematic for independent retailers paying higher wholesale prices. In situations where an investigation has proven that firms repeatedly price below or at the floor in a specific region, the regulation stipulates that the Régie can impose an additional minimum margin on top of the floor of around $0.03 per

---

[11] In fact, the 1996 price war was more likely the result of excess capacity in the industry and the decision by Ultramar, Québec's largest retailer, to institute a low-price guarantee. An investigation by the Competition Bureau of Canada did not find any evidence of predatory behavior. For further discussion of Quebec's price floor, see Carranza, Clark, and Houde (2015).

liter. This minimum margin has the objective of helping smaller retailers survive. It also allows the Régie to indirectly compensate stations following a price war.

7.3 PREWAR COLLUSIVE EQUILIBRIUM

The heavy presence of branded independents in Québec City's retail gasoline market in the late 1990s led to the development of a hub-and-spoke arrangement in which upstream branded suppliers coordinated "zone pricing" between their own downstream retailers and independent branded stations operating in a given neighborhood.[12] Integrated, company-owned stations had incentive to keep prices high and to abstain from business stealing. On the other hand, branded independents had reason to undercut the arrangement, especially toward the end of their contracts with the upstream firm. Suppliers have the right to terminate cross-lease contracts if they can demonstrate that the retailer lowered its price for reasons other than to respond to "normal" competitive pressures. However, demonstrating that a particular retailer initiated a price war requires costly monitoring by the supplier, which leads to a standard principal–agent problem: with imperfect monitoring, independent stations have a clear incentive to initiate price wars by undercutting their rivals, reducing overall profits for upstream suppliers. Despite this, coordination was maintained throughout the late 1990s as branded independents chose the future stream of profits provided by contract renewal over those from deviation.

Suppliers influenced prices charged by independent station owners and softened retail competition by using nonlinear wholesale price schemes and by offering price-support clauses of the sort described in the previous section. By controlling retail prices for all affiliated stations and by internalizing business-stealing externalities, upstream suppliers facilitate coordination via a sort of resale-price

---

[12] An industry report prepared by the Conference Board of Canada in 2000 also discusses the fact that many Canadian cities exhibit uniform or zone-pricing strategies. See The Conference Board (2001).

maintenance (RPM) pricing scheme operating through repeated interactions with independent retailers. Although RPM is illegal per se in Canada, a tacit arrangement between firms with similar results can be achieved if there are repeated interactions and if the threat of punishment is large enough. Punishment can take the form of price wars and/or threat of contract termination.

The resulting equilibrium reached by retailers and suppliers in Québec City between 1997 and 1999 featured high margins for retailers, of 5.64 cpl on average (9 percent of the average price).[13] The market was also characterized by relatively uniform prices within neighborhoods. The median interquartile range of prices within neighborhoods was 0.30 cpl compared to 0.94 cpl across all of Québec City and surrounding area. To further test for zone pricing, we use data on stations' prices and characteristics to investigate the contribution of different factors (station size, amenities, neighborhood and brand) to the cross-sectional variance of margins in the prewar period.[14] Our results show that geographical location (neighborhood) is the most important factor of the margin's variance, accounting for 47.7 percent of the total variation. Amenities, size, and brand account for just 2.5 percent, 1.8 percent, and 4.3 percent, respectively.

7.4 THE PRICE WAR

In January of 2000, conditions in Québec City's retail gasoline market changed drastically when one independent station broke ranks and unilaterally lowered its price. Figure 7.2a plots the modal price along with the price floor around the year 2000. The late 1990s were a period of historically high oil prices during which price levels kept rising due

---

[13] Source: Régie de l'énergie du Québec price survey.
[14] Specifically, after calculating the average across time, we decompose the cross-sectional margin variance as $Var(margin_i) = Var(\hat{\gamma}_i^{neighborhood}) + Var(\hat{\gamma}_i^{amenities}) + Var(\hat{\gamma}_i^{brand}) + \hat{\beta}^2 Var(size_i) + Var(\hat{e}_i) + Cov$, where $\hat{\gamma}$ are fixed effects estimates and Cov is the sum of pairwise covariances between components. *Amenities* is a categorical variable indicating the presence of convenience store, repair shop and/or carwash. *Neighborhood* is the three-digit zip number. *Size* refers to the number of islands.

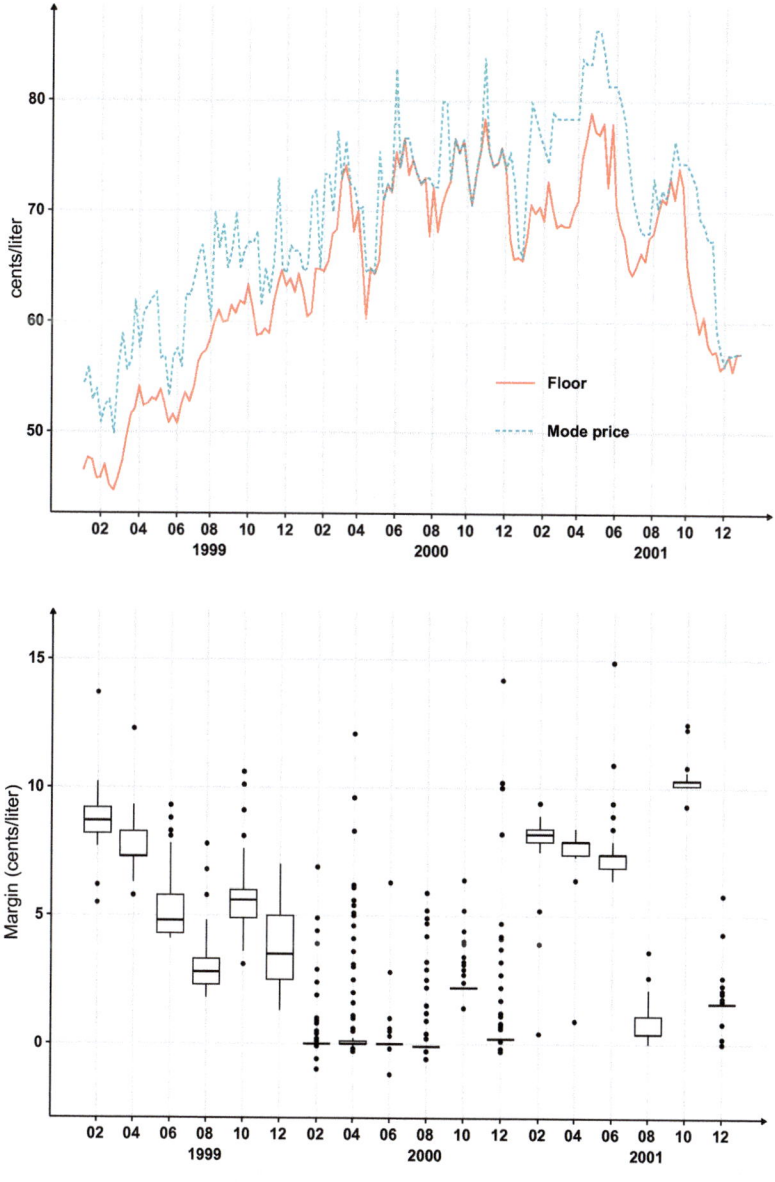

FIGURE 7.2 Evolution of retail prices, margins, and sales around the 2000 price war in Québec City.

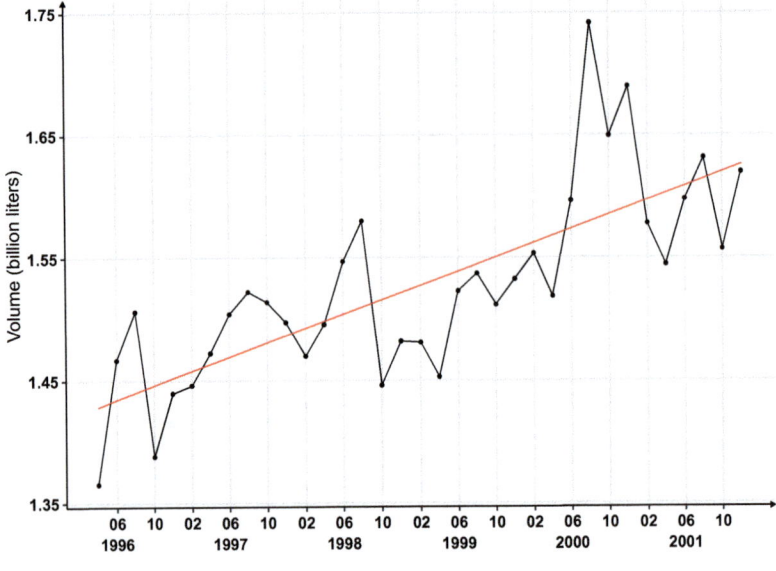

FIGURE 7.2 (cont.)

to increases in the rack (wholesale) price and only reached a maximum at the beginning of 2001. It is, therefore, likely that demand for individual stations was more elastic than usual since consumers had greater incentive to search for better prices, making it difficult to sustain a collusive equilibrium. As can be seen from the figure, prices were well above the floor throughout 1999 before falling to the floor at the start of 2000.

The abrupt change in equilibrium prices is even more evident when looking at the distribution of margins. In Figure 7.2b we use a whisker plot representation of the observed margins to highlight how, during the six bimonthly periods of 2000, the market exhibited little margin dispersion, and the vast majority of stations posted a price equal to the price floor.[15] As can be seen from the figure, margins are

---

[15] For each time period represented by a whisker plot, the lower, middle and upper edge of the box correspond to the first, second and third quartile of the distribution. The lines extending above and below the box cover all observations that are not considered outliers. Dots above and below represent outliers.

much higher and dispersion much lower in the periods before and after the price war, consistent with an equilibrium featuring tacit or explicit coordination. Finally, Figure 7.2c illustrates that the decrease in margins during the price war had a positive impact on aggregate sales volume. Starting in the third bimonthly period of 2000, we observe a large increase in aggregate sales when compared to the sales trend observed since 1996.

These three figures highlight the severity and impact of the price war that started during the first two months of 2000. They also clearly delineate its time span until the first month of 2001, when margins recovered to prewar levels or higher. In what follows, we analyze the causes and consequences of the price war that took place in Québec City between January and December 2000.

7.4.1 Causes

On December 13th 2000, the Association of Independent Gasoline Retailers (Association québécoise des indépendants du pétrole or AQUIP) filed a complaint with the Régie based on its responsibility for enforcing the price floor regulation. Independent retailers, led by the owner of the Eko chain of gas stations, asked the Régie to investigate violations of the regulation preventing stations from posting a price at or below the MEP. The goal of the investigation was twofold, first to determine if a violation of the law on petroleum products had occurred, and second, to evaluate whether the price war caused sufficient damages to justify raising the floor. The investigation focused on the period between September and November 2000.

The investigation report identified the existence of price-support clauses offered to branded independent stations by major upstream suppliers as a root cause of the price war. Testimony from a manager at *Couche-Tard*, the largest convenience-store chain in Québec, established a direct link between the price-support clause and the occurrence of the price war. The magnitude of the negotiated minimum margin varied across retailers based on market conditions at the time the contract was signed. Since gross margins were relatively high between 1996 and 1998, stations that were near the end of their contacts in 2000 enjoyed minimum margins that were between 3 and 5 cpl. The manager also stated that minimum-margin clauses above 3 cpl were phased out in the late 1990s. In 2000, differences in the size of the minimum margin across retailers created an opportunity for some station owners to benefit from asymmetric contracts, as retailers with more generous price supports could sustain zero margins for longer periods and gain market share over others with less generous support from suppliers.

The manager summarized the incentives for firms with minimum-margin clauses above 3 cpl and near the end of their contracts as follows: *"a site that it knows it is going to close within two years [...] decides to treat itself at the expense of the market and limit competition for the sole purpose of increasing, tripling and quadrupling its volume to obtain the maximum remuneration."*[16] Testimony from the Couche-Tard manager and other witnesses refers to one such "deviant" station operating in a suburb of Québec City. This station changed its banner at the end of 2000, and according to witnesses, benefited from a larger-than-average minimum-margin clause during the price-war period. Multiple witnesses confirmed that this station posted a price equal to the MEP continuously between January and December 2000. The end of this low-price strategy coincided with the beginning of the Régie investigation.

This discussion highlights the fact that price-support clauses expose suppliers to an important moral hazard risk – when the market price is such that the retail margin that an independent station would earn is close to, or lower than, the minimum margin, it has a unilateral incentive to lower its price in order to increase its volume. When this occurs, the supplier increases its payment to the station (lease

---

[16] Translated from *"un site qu'elle sait qu'elle va fermer dans deux ans avec l'un de ces raffineurs-là et décide de payer une traite au marché et de nuire à la concurrence dans le seul but uniquement d'augmenter, de tripler et de quadrupler son volume pour aller chercher le maximum de rémunération."* See Régie (2000).

price + minimum margin) and effectively offers a subsidy or "price support" to the retailer. One industry expert, interviewed during the investigation, summarized the cost to suppliers as follows: *"The price reductions may be costless to the retailer, but they are not costless to the refiner. And therefore, if the retailer is pricing in an inappropriate manner, economically inappropriate, from the perspective of the supplier, there is a clear incentive for the refiner to opt out of or change the contractual arrangement."*[17]

7.4.2 Dissemination

In order to provide a deeper understanding of how the price war disseminated across Québec City's neighborhoods, we document the evolution of the geographical allocation of gas sales. In Figure 7.3 we present a heatmap for Québec City of the difference in cumulative sales between 1999 and 2000 for different time periods. For comparison purposes, we use volume shares instead of levels and represent positive share differences with red and negative differences using blue. The median station had a volume share of 0.3 percent at the end of 1999. Figure 7.3a illustrates the change in shares for the first two months of the price war relative to the same period of the previous year. An area in the district of Charlesbourg at the North end of Québec City (red circle) stands out with some stations having considerably larger share gains and their aggregate sales share increasing by 0.28 percentage points in 2000 relative to the same period in 1999.[18,19] Of particular note is a Petro Canada station that achieved a 5-fold increase in sales relative to the same period in 1999. As mentioned above, from the testimony during the Régie investigation we know that the deviant station was located in one of the suburbs of the city and was not an unbranded station. Since the Charlesbourg Petro Canada station is a clear outlier in cumulative volume-share

---

[17] Interview of John D. Todd in Régie (2000).
[18] The specific area we refer to is Forward Sortation Area G1G.
[19] For comparison, the standard deviation of share difference from 1997 to 1998 and 1998 to 1999 is 0.21 percentage points.

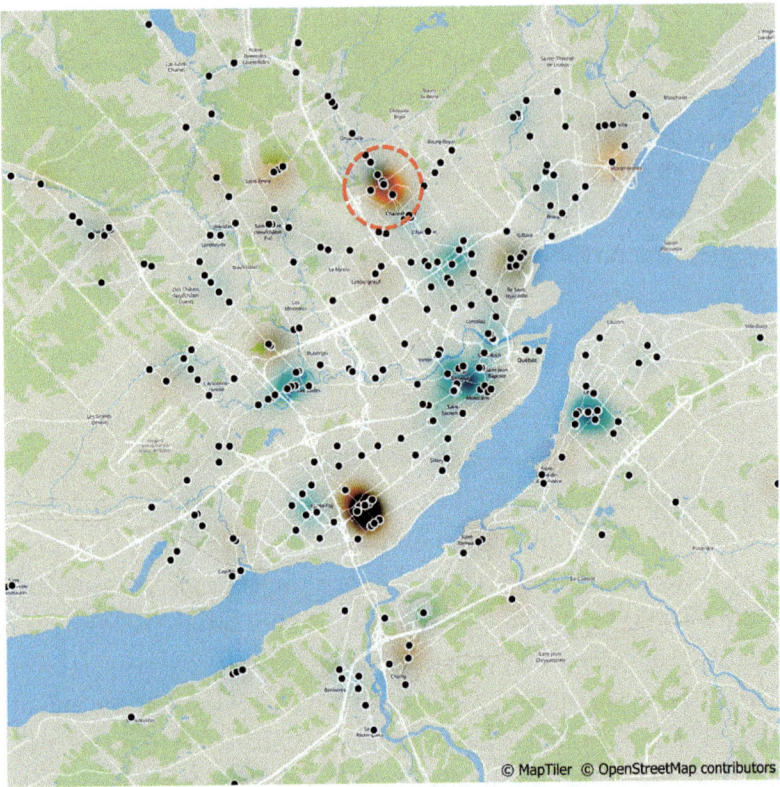

FIGURE 7.3 Difference in share of cumulative sales between 1999 and 2000.

difference during the first two months of 2000 and maintains an elevated cumulative sale share difference throughout the year, we strongly suspect that it is the deviant.

In Figure 7.3b we compare sales shares during the first six months of 1999 and 2000. At this stage of the price war, stations not only in Charlesbourg but also in other neighborhoods located along commuting paths started to experience sale shares significantly higher than those observed during the same period of the previous year. For example, stations in Sainte-Foy, which is located just on the Québec City side of the bridge (red circle) used by commuters coming from the South shore to the city, had an aggregate share increase of

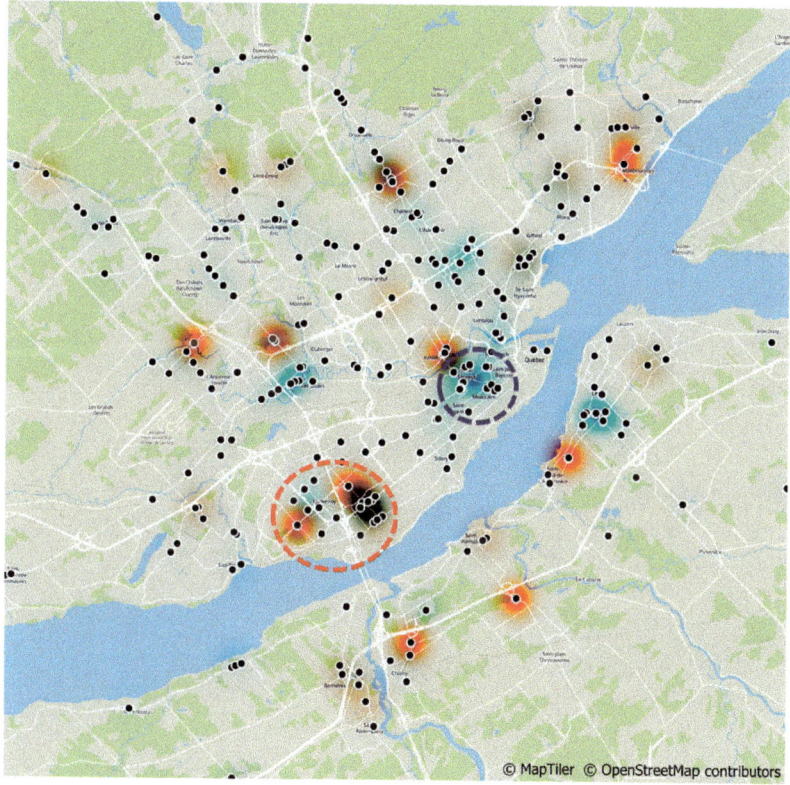

FIGURE 7.3 (cont.)

0.45 percentage points in the first semester. On the other hand, stations located in the downtown core (blue circle), just to the East of Sainte-Foy, were underperforming and losing an aggregate of 0.84 percentage points in market share at the end of the semester. Finally, we can see from Figure 7.3c, which covers the first ten months of the year, that the same trend continued until the end of the price war. Stations located along the entry points to Québec City (red circle) featured higher yearly sales than the previous year, while stations located inside the city (blue circle) experienced a decrease in share relative to the previous year, with the city core suffering a decrease of 1.73 percentage points in sales share.

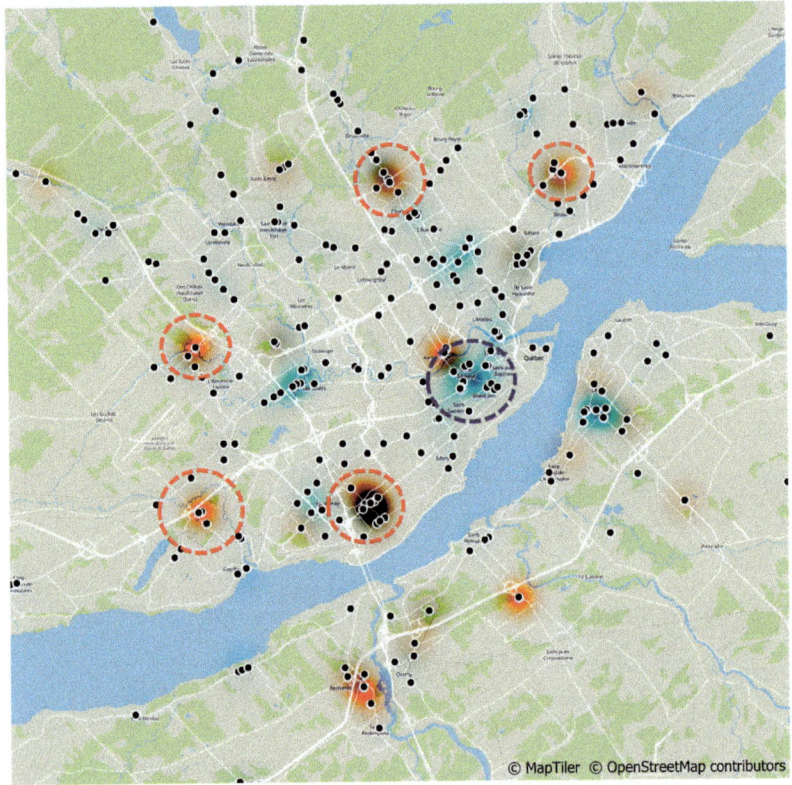

FIGURE 7.3 (cont.)

7.5 LENGTH OF THE WAR

The price war lasted for almost an entire year, coming to an end only in November of that year when the government finally intervened.[20] The persistence of the war raises questions about the difficulties faced by retailers that may have been trying to restart collusion.

Using rich daily price and quantity information for the largest independent retail chain in Québec City, Eko, we are able to illustrate one such attempt to restart coordination. In Figure 7.4 we plot margins and volume for Eko stations during the first three weeks of

---

[20] This is longer than the price wars described in Porter (1985) for instance.

RETAIL GASOLINE IN CANADA 209

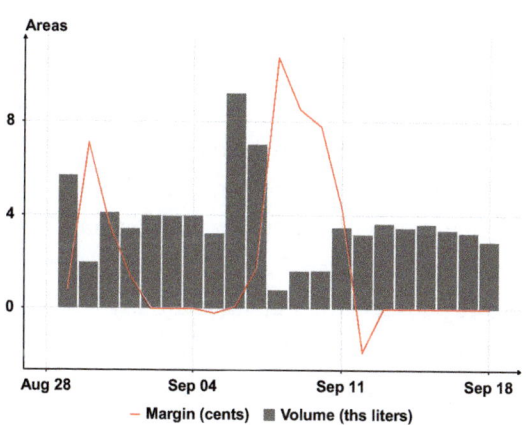

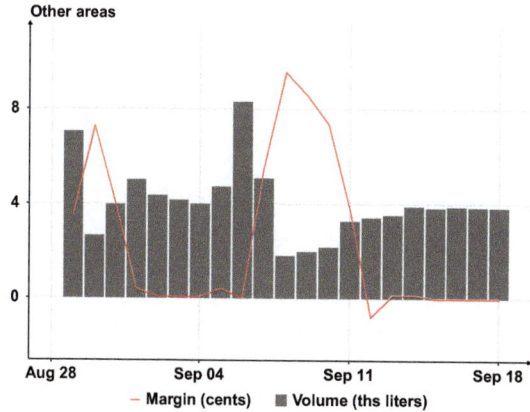

FIGURE 7.4 Eko stations' daily margins and sales during the price-war period.
Notes: Areas are Charlesbourg, Levis, Saint-Foy, and Beauport.

September 2000. On September 5, we observe a stark increase in the average sales (gray bars) at Eko stations, which we conjecture likely reflects an attempt by nearby stations to restart coordination by increasing prices above the floor. In the following days, Eko stations increased margins (red line) above zero in what was likely a response to this price-increase attempt. However, this increase had a severe impact on the stations' immediate sales, with daily volume decreasing to a level that was less than half of what is observed during days when stations charged at the price floor. After only four days, Eko stations started to reduce margins back to zero, which resulted in daily gasoline volume recovering to the level observed before the event. The speed and intensity at which sales responded to the increase in margins highlight the considerable cost that stations incur when unilaterally setting margins above market. Finally, by contrasting the average demand response between Eko stations located in the entryway areas and stations located elsewhere, the graph is also suggestive that restarting costs can differ substantially depending on the local market structure faced by each station.

Two factors, in particular, may explain why restarting collusion was challenging in this setting: (i) demand was very elastic and (ii) one of the leading firms operated under a low-price guarantee. These market features may have posed challenges for any firm or station trying to unilaterally increase its price above the market price, since it would lose too much volume.[21]

7.5.1 Price Elasticity

To quantify the loss in sales for stations from raising their prices, in Table 7.1 we measure the demand response to price changes while controlling for other demand determinants. In column (1), we regress log sales on log prices using the Eko data. In column (2), we provide validation to our result by running a similar regression but in another dataset, the Kent Marketing data. The findings imply short-run elasticities of −6 using the Eko data (i.e., a 1 percent increase in price implies a 6 percent decrease in sales) and −8 using Kent, suggesting that consumers are well-informed about the distribution of gasoline prices across the market and react accordingly. The demand response is even more striking when we evaluate the impact of posting a price

---

[21] The difficulties faced by these retailers trying to restart collusion are similar to those faced by firms attempting to get collusion off the ground in the first place. For instance, Igami and Sugaya (2022) document that vitamin C margins took roughly three years after the beginning of the collusive arrangement to achieve stability. Alé-Chilet (2018) and Byrne and deRoos (2019) also find evidence of a slow and costly adjustment to coordination.

Table 7.1 *Demand response to prices during price-war period*

	log(sales)		
	1	2	3
log(price)	−6.141	−8.074	
	(0.668)	(1.082)	
2 cent or more above market price			−0.459
			(0.043)
2 cent or more above market price × entryway area			−0.206
			(0.105)
Data source	Eko	Kent	Eko
Time FE	Week+Day of Week	Bimonth	Week+Day of Week
Individual FE	Station	FSA+Brand	Station
Adj. R^2	0.343	0.607	0.254
Num. obs.	2531	1744	2639

Notes: Sales and Price refer to unleaded gasoline sold during 2000. Market price is defined as the mode price of the last Régie price survey. Additional control variables: in model 1, log(price) of the closest station in the last Régie survey, dummies for the previous and next day price change sign; in model 2, log(price) of the closest station in Kent, number of islands and dummy for convenience store; in model 3, price 2 cents below market price, plus interaction with the number of stations in a 500 meters range. Heteroscedasticity robust standard errors. FSA corresponds to the first three digits of the station's zip code.

two cents above the market price. In column (3), we quantify that such a price difference had an average impact on sales of around −36 percent for Eko stations.[22] Moreover, using a dummy variable for geographical areas located along Québec City's entryways, we found an even higher response of drivers to above-market prices of −49 percent. Corroborating the findings from Figure 7.4, the regression

---

[22] Based on column (3), $\Delta Sales/Sales = \exp(-0.459) - 1$.

results suggest that retail chains face substantial losses in sales if they try to restart coordination by unilaterally raising prices away from the competitive equilibrium, and that this is especially true in highly competitive areas such as the entryways.

The estimated sales response implies a large opportunity cost for stations from trying to sustain above-floor prices. Using the results from column (3) in Table 7.1, we compute the difference in daily profit from charging 5 cents above the floor vs charging at the floor and receiving a price-support clause of 3 cents.[23] In this case, stations located at entryways would have suffered a short-term opportunity cost of around $18,636 per day from not increasing sales and receiving the price support, which corresponds to 14 percent of their daily profit. The stations located in Québec City's downtown core, on the other hand, would have experienced an increase in profits of around $6,302, or 5 percent of daily profit, in the short term.

7.5.2 Low-Price Guarantees

Ultramar is the largest chain of branded retailers in the province of Québec. It is vertically integrated, operating the only refinery in the Québec City region. Its head office maintains price-setting control through a combination of lessee retailers acting under commission and company-owned stores.

In the summer of 1996, Ultramar instituted a low-price guarantee policy known as Valeur-Plus (or ValuePlus). Each Ultramar station was required to list the lowest price among stations located within *close proximity*. To operationalize the guarantee, Ultramar employed a team of regional representatives who were responsible for establishing and adjusting prices. The company also put in place a centralized pricing center that monitored prices across the province and provided a free phone line through which rival stations and consumers could report discrepancies. From Table 7.2 we can see that the policy

---

[23] The average margin from stations that charged 2 cents above market price was 5.6 cents.

Table 7.2 *Fraction of stations pricing at the minimum*

Year	1991	1992	1993	1994	1995	1996	1997	1998	1999	2000	2001
Ultramar	0.36	0.32	0.40	0.62	0.73	0.92	0.92	0.83	0.92	0.94	0.94
Petro Canada	0.20	0.37	0.55	0.63	0.76	0.62	0.73	0.87	0.73	0.83	0.76
Shell	0.27	0.51	0.49	0.65	0.61	0.47	0.61	0.69	0.57	0.73	0.75

Notes: To compute the fraction for a given brand we: locate for each station that are inside a 1km circular range; find the minimum retail price for unleaded gasoline inside the range, count the number of stations belonging to the chain that price at the minimum in its range, and divide by the total number of stations with price information.

immediately changed the way that Ultramar set prices. The table presents the fraction of Ultramar stations that charge a price below any other station within a 1km radius.[24] In the early 1990s, this fraction was at most 40 percent. It increased somewhat in 1994 and 1995, before jumping sharply in 1996 to more than 90 percent, at which point it stabilized. For comparison purposes, we show the same information for two of the other main chains, Petro Canada and Shell. We see a similar increase in 1993 and 1994, but there was no big jump in 1996 as there was for Ultramar.

The low-price guarantee, together with highly elastic demand, made it difficult for other stations to raise their prices much above those of a nearby Ultramar station in an effort to restart coordination.[25] The announcement of the low-price guarantee policy likely provided a clear signal for price-sensitive but uninformed consumers, and for other chains about the willingness of Ultramar to engage in fierce competition.[26] Moreover, since it was not clear what was the definition of *close proximity* used by Ultramar to establish the reference neighborhood for each of its stations, the policy created uncertainty for some nearby rivals as to whether the local Ultramar station would actually follow on a price increase. Finally, it would also have been common knowledge across retailers that Ultramar would not be leading any attempt to raise prices.

7.6   AFTEREFFECTS

The conclusion of the Québec City price war coincided with the request by AQUIP for a Régie-led investigation into violation of the price floor regulation. The investigation was initiated in January 2001 and lasted until July of the same year. It determined that the severity and geographical extent of the price war justified government

---

[24] Price information is from the Kent Marketing survey.
[25] Studying the cartels uncovered in nearby cities, Clark and Houde (2013) provide evidence that even small delays in price matching by Ultramar implied large transfers between retailers.
[26] See Moorthy and Winter (2006) for a discussion of the effects of price-matching guarantees on price information in an environment with search costs.

intervention. The final report states that *"it [the Regie] intends to send a clear message to market participants that market aberrations are not tolerated and that the rationalization of the market must continue according to the rules of free competition for the benefit of consumers."*[27] The Régie then decided to raise the price floor by 3 cpl between September and November of 2001. Later, in a 2004 report it produced, the Régie analyzed the market and concluded that the intervention had been successful at *"preventing prolonged periods of price war."* From Figure 7.2a we can establish that prices started to move away from the floor toward a more elevated level in December 2000, and especially into 2001. The margins observed after the price war are even higher than those achieved by the within-brand hub-and-spoke arrangements that characterized the prewar period.[28] Despite the increase in margins, dispersion was minimal in 2001, shrinking to almost zero by the end of the year.

In Figure 7.5 we use another whisker plot to provide further details on the timing and size of the recovery. The figure shows that the high margins and limited dispersion that developed in 2001 persisted in Québec City well after the end of the price war. We combine three of our data sets to provide a comprehensive overview of pricing before, during, and after the war.[29] From the figure it is clear that margins are very elevated and that prices are nearly uniform. In fact,

---

[27] See Régie (2000).

[28] It should be noted that the retail gasoline price level increased by 15.5 percent in real terms from 1997 to 2003. This increase was, for the most part, due to increases in the rack price. The high price levels probably had a negative impact on margins. Even so, firms manage to charge markups higher than those observed before the price war.

[29] Unlike in Figure 7.2b, which uses all of the 306 stations from the Kent Marketing data set, here we focus on a restricted set of stations. The reason for this is that we do not have access to the Kent Marketing data after 2001 and therefore, to study dispersion in the period after the price war we must incorporate data from the Régie and MJ Ervin. Since these data sets survey a smaller number of stations than does Kent Marketing, we restrict the number of Kent stations we consider for our analysis in an effort to be sure that any differences in dispersion over time that we identify are not driven by the greater number of stations in the Kent survey. More specifically, the Régie surveys only thirteen stations and so, for consistency, we use information from just thirteen stations in the Kent sample, taking one station for each of the Régie stations. In each case we take the closest Kent station.

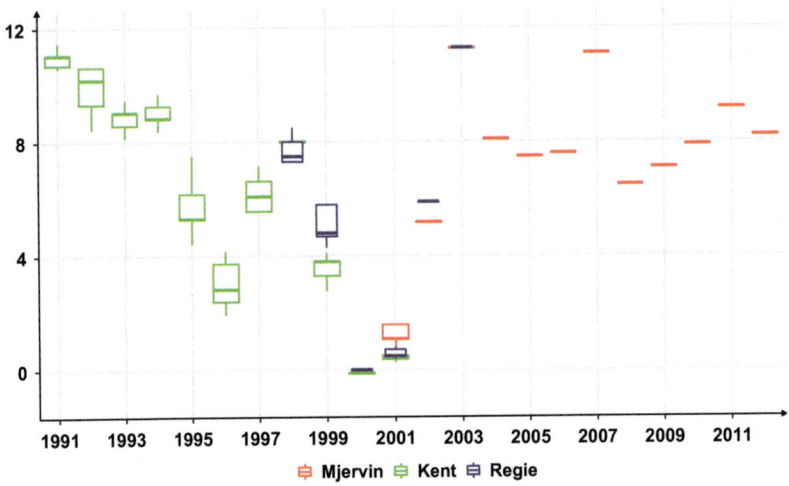

FIGURE 7.5 Evolution of margin dispersion.
Notes: For comparison, we select Kent observations only from stations that are closest to stations surveyed by Régie. Margins are surveyed around the last week of August of each year.

at least among the thirteen stations surveyed by the Régie, pricing is uniform starting in 2002. Since the Régie data only go until 2003, we also use the MJ Ervin survey of fifteen (possibly different) stations that covers the 2001 to 2012 period to see whether uniformity and high margins persist. Indeed we find that there is no dispersion at all through to the end of the sample, and that margins are quite high, although they do fall somewhat in 2008.

These postwar pricing patterns are consistent with those observed in the retail gasoline markets in four nearby cities where a Competition Bureau investigation uncovered evidence of an alleged hard-core cartel. The Bureau's investigation focused on the retail gasoline markets of four cities in the province of Québec: Magog, Sherbrooke, Thetford Mines, and Victoriaville; and culminated with the issuing of search warrants in 2006, after which margins fell sharply. Evidence suggests that it was not only stations in the four target markets that reacted to the Bureau investigation, but that similar patterns can be detected in a number of other nearby markets in the Eastern part of the province, including Québec City. In contrast, cities in the Western part of the province experienced no margin adjustment at this time.[30] These findings, while suggestive of collusion being widespread in the province, are not conclusive, since, to our knowledge, the Competition Bureau investigation was not extended to markets outside of the four cities investigated. As a result, there exists no direct evidence of explicit coordination among players outside these four markets and other reasons can explain the similarities in pricing.

Using the price data for other cities in the province, we can investigate these patterns further. To see whether pricing in other markets was similar to Québec City pricing, in Figure 7.6a we plot the difference between the modal price in Québec City and station-level posted prices for stations located across the Central and Eastern part of the province, including Québec City stations. The figure shows that, starting just after the price war, pricing in the central-east markets began to follow Québec City pricing – the difference between prices surveyed at other stations in the region and the modal Québec City price, falls to zero. In other words, these stations feature the same high prices as in Québec City. Among these markets is Sherbrooke, one of the markets targeted in the Competition Bureau investigation. Consistent with margin collapse in response to the Bureau investigation, all of the Eastern markets we consider here appear to move in the same direction. In contrast, Figure 7.6b shows that the same patterns do not exist in the city of Montréal, located at the west part of the province. Following the price war, there are considerable differences between prices at Montréal stations and the modal price in Québec City and these persist or even become larger in later years.

---

[30] See Clark and Houde (2014) who use micro-level price data to study the impact on margins and adjustment asymmetry of the collapse of the cartels following the Competition Bureau investigation in 2005 and 2006. See also Erutku and Hildebrand (2010) who estimate the collusion overcharges in the Sherbrooke market. Their results show that following the announcement of the Bureau investigation, prices decreased by nearly 2 cpl relative to Montréal, but not at all relative to Quebec City.

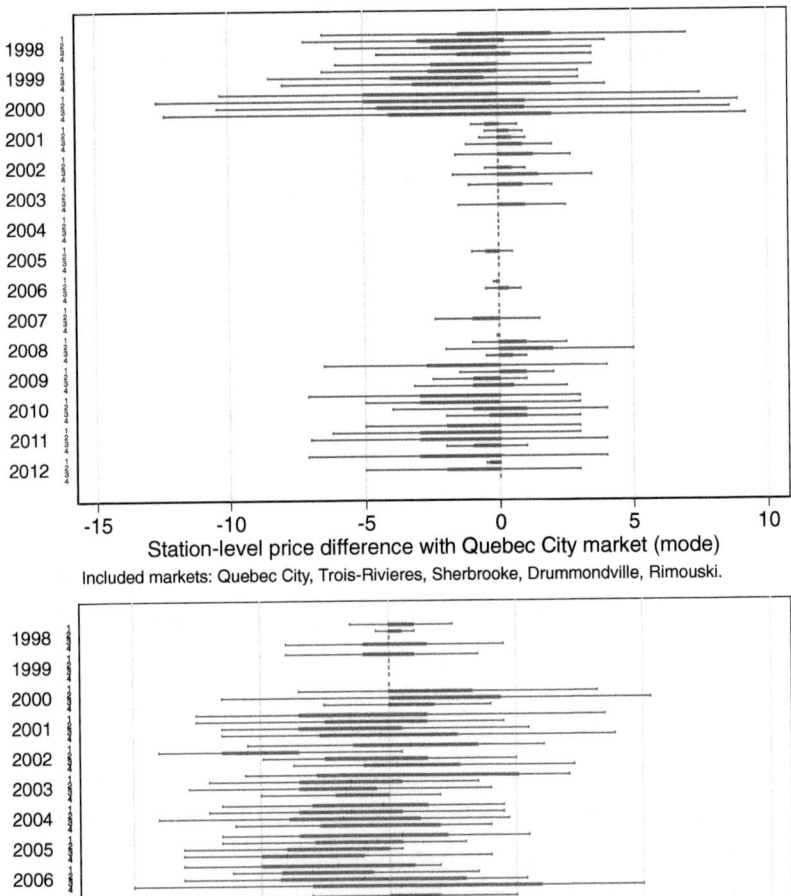

FIGURE 7.6 Distribution of gasoline prices in the south and east regions of Québec relative to the modal price in Québec City.
Notes: Each observation corresponds to the difference between the station-level posted price and the modal price in Québec City on the same survey date.

Comparing margins between 2002 and 2006 we find that they were 6.45 cpl in Québec City and only 4.06 cpl in Montréal.

Note that from Figure 7.6a we can see that, starting in 2008, differences relative to Québec City begin to arise again suggesting that, in the years after the Bureau investigation, the market seems to have been disrupted.

7.7 CONCLUSION

We provide an investigation into the price war that occurred in Québec City's retail gasoline market between two episodes of price coordination. Our analysis identifies two main market features that influenced the origin and duration of the price war: (i) the existence of nonlinear contracts and (ii) low-price guarantees. The former is identified as the root cause of the price war as it created asymmetric margins between gas stations, inducing those with low margins to defect, while the latter, in conjunction with elevated demand elasticity, helps to explain its prolonged duration. Gasoline markets are far from alone among retail markets in being characterized by these two features and so it is worth understanding the ways in which they contribute to the sustainability of collusive arrangements. The role of low-price guarantees is particularly compelling, since not only can they lead to longer lasting price wars, but they can also allow periods of price stability to persist longer.

7A APPENDIX

The documents from the Régie de lénergie can be found here: www.regie-energie.qc.ca/audiences/3457-00/index.html.

They include information related to the motion requesting the inclusion of the fixed amount for operating costs in the minimum price provided for in subsection 59 (2) of the Act respecting the Régie de l'énergie (R-3457-2000).

For the purpose of this case study, we base our understanding of the facts with respect to the alleged retail-gasoline cartel that arose in certain markets in the province of Québec in the years after the price war mostly on documents prepared by the Competition Bureau.

We were given a copy of the 52-page affidavit of Mr. Pierre-Yves Guay of the Competition Bureau dated May 16, 2006 in file no 500-26-039962-067 of the Superior Court of Québec, district of Montréal. From the Court, we received copies of the three annexes attached to the affidavit of Mr. Guay. Annex A is a 143-page document which contains mostly reported wiretap telephone conversations with respect to the region of Victoriaville; Annex B is a 45-page document which contains mostly reported wiretap telephone conversations with respect to the region of Thetford Mines; Annex C is a 121-page document which contains mostly reported wiretap telephone conversation with respect to the regions of Sherbrooke and Magog. We will refer to the affidavit of Mr. Guay and its three annexes as the "Competition Bureau documents." We also found information on the actions taken by the Competition Bureau on its website. These documents are analysed and reported on more extensively in Clark and Houde (2013) and Clark and Houde (2014).

REFERENCES

Alé-Chilet, J. (2018) "Gradually Rebuilding a Relationship: The Emergence of Collusion in Retail Pharmacies in Chile." Working paper, Bar Ilan University.

Byrne, D. and N. deRoos (2019) "Learning to Coordinate: A Study in Retail Gasoline." *American Economic Review* 109, 591–619.

Carranza, J. E., R. Clark, and J.-F. Houde (2015) "Price Controls and Market Structure: Evidence from Gasoline Retail Markets." *The Journal of Industrial Economics* 63 (1), 152–198.

Clark, R. and J.-F. Houde (2013) "Collusion with Asymmetric Retailers: Evidence from a Gasoline Price Fixing Case." *American Economic Journal: Microeconomics* 5 (3), 97–123.

Clark, R. and J.-F. Houde (2014) "The Effect of Explicit Communication on Pricing: Evidence from the Collapse of a Gasoline Cartel." *Journal of Industrial Economics* 62, 191–228.

Erutku, C. and V. Hildebrand (2010) "Conspiracy at the Pump." *Journal of Law & Economics* 53, 223–237.

Faber, R. and M. Janssen (2019) "On the Effects of Suggested Prices in Gasoline Markets." *The Scandinavian Journal of Economics* 121, 676–705.

Foros, Ø. and F. Steen (2013) "Vertical Control and Price Cycles in Gasoline Retailing." *The Scandinavian Journal of Economics 115*, 640–661.

Houde, J.-F. (2012) "Spatial Differentiation and Vertical Mergers in Retail Markets for Gasoline." *American Economic Review 102*, 2147–2182.

Igami, M. and T. Sugaya (2022) "Measuring the Incentive to Collude: The Vitamin Cartels, 1990–1999." *Review of Economic Studies 89* (3), 1460–1494.

Moorthy, S. and R. A. Winter (2006, June) "Price-Matching Guarantees." *The RAND Journal of Economics 37* (2), 449–465.

Porter, R. H. (1985) "On the Incidence and Duration of Price Wars." *The Journal of Industrial Economics 33* (4), 415–426.

Régie (2000) *Requête demandant l'inclusion du montant fixé au titre des coûts d'exploitation dans le prix minimum prévu au paragraphe 59 (2) de la Loi sur la Régie de l'énergie (R-3457-2000)*.

Rey, P. and T. Vergé (2008) "Economics of Vertical Restraints." *Handbook of Antitrust Economics 353*, 390.

The Conference Board (2001) *The Final Fifteen Feet of Hose: The Canadian Gasoline Industry in the Year 2000*. Ottawa: Conference Board of Canada.

Wang, Z. (2009) "(Mixed) Strategy in Oligopoly Pricing: Evidence from Gasoline Price Cycles before and under a Timing Regulation." *Journal of Political Economy 117* (6).

8 Coordinated Rebate Reductions and Semi-collusion

*Retail Gasoline in Sweden**

Frode Steen and Lars Sørgard

8.1 INTRODUCTION

In the fall of 1999, five oil companies in the Swedish retail market for gasoline and diesel made a joint effort to change the price structure facing their final consumers at the pump. For large corporate customers that received a negotiated rebate on the public pump price, such as transport and taxi companies, they jointly eliminated those rebates, while at the same time reducing the pump prices for all customers. According to the firms, their clean out of rebates was exactly offset by the lower pump prices, so there was no net effect on their corporate customers' costs. All other customers with no rebates – who just paid pump prices – were then claimed to be better off. If all that is true, then the coordinated adjustment in rebates and pump prices would have been beneficial to consumers: customers who did not receive rebates benefited and other customers were not worse off, as they were fully compensated for the elimination of their rebates.

Based on detailed communication concerning their collective clean out of rebates in late 1999, the five firms were convicted in 2005 for violation of the prohibition against anticompetitive cooperation. During the investigation, one of the parties presented the aforementioned rationale for cleaning out rebates and claimed the collective intervention had been necessary and had improved

---

* We are indebted to Joseph Harrington and Maarten Pieter Schinkel for very helpful comments to an earlier draft. Professor Steen wrote an expert report on behalf of the Swedish Competition Authority in this case and was also an expert witness in court. Professor Sørgard was not involved in the case.

consumer welfare by lowering pump prices for regular customers. In this case study, we show that there can indeed in theory be some merits to such an argument by applying a model of semi-collusion in which firms collude on one variable (here, pump prices) and compete on another variable (here, rebates). The competition in rebates could result in excessively high pump prices in order to maintain sufficiently high net prices paid by those customers with rebates. The companies managed to raise pump prices by (tacit) collusion on that dimension of competition. Under such circumstances, a clean out of rebates under semi-collusion could, in theory, have led to a lowering of the pump prices, possibly even enhancing consumer welfare.

While this outcome of no harm to consumers is theoretically possible, our analysis finds it unlikely. We explain the potential mechanism at work in the Swedish gasoline cartel as presented by the parties and show that there are strict assumptions that must hold for such a claim of no consumer harm to be valid. Moreover, it turns out that the oil companies, according to evidence from a secret meeting between the parties' representatives, planned all along to adjust the pump prices, but not to lower the margin on the pump prices. In fact, they planned to exploit changes in input prices, that normally would lead to corresponding changes in pump prices, to camouflage a coordinated return to the initial margin on pump prices from before the drop in pump prices associated with the elimination of rebates. We provide supportive empirical analysis for such a return of the pump price margin to its initial level, and we also find support for a similar price pattern a few years earlier, when the firms had a similar clean out of rebates. Thus, in contrast to what the parties claimed, large customers who lost their rebates were worse off, while small customers only experienced a short period of lower pump prices, before prices returned to their initial level.

In this case study, we begin by describing the market in question and the cartel behavior in Section 8.2. In Section 8.3, we discuss the possible rationale for why this behavior might not be harmful to consumers, supplemented by an appendix with a simple formal model. In Section 8.4, we describe how the clean out of rebates affected the pump prices, both in late 1999 as well as in 1995 when similar behavior by the firms was observed. In Section 8.5, we conclude and offer some takeaways from this case.

8.2 THE SWEDISH GASOLINE CARTEL

The Swedish Competition Authority (SCA) conducted a dawn raid on December 16, 1999, at the premises of the firms Statoil, OK-Q8, Shell, Preem and Hydro that together at that time served more than 90 percent of the Swedish retail market for gasoline and diesel.[1] They found evidence that the oil companies had taken part in a number of meetings in the period from August to November 1999. In the meetings, the participants had exchanged information on each firm's current and future pricing policy. The normal form of rivalry between them had been competition on rebates for large customers who would then be supplied exclusively by one firm. After more than four years with escalating rebates, the companies met to coordinate a rebate reduction, which led the SCA to conclude that it was a cartel infringement.[2] The case went through two levels of the court system before the companies in the Swedish Market Court were ultimately fined the substantial sum of SEK 112 million.[3]

Price setting in this market consists of a mixture of a pump price that is applicable to all consumers and rebates to some large customers under contract, such as major transport companies with many vehicles that purchase large quantities of gasoline. The net price for a large customer is the regular pump price less the rebate it

---

[1] See Swedish Competition Authority (2000), figure 1.
[2] See Swedish Competition Authority (2000).
[3] See the verdict by the Swedish Market Court from February 22, 2005 (2005:7 Dnr A 2/03). There were five companies sharing almost the whole market, and all five participated in the cartel meetings: Statoil (SEK 50 mill), OK-Q8 (SEK 25 mill), Shell (SEK 20 mill), Preem (SEK 10 mill) and Hydro (SEK 7 mill) (fines in parentheses). Statoil received the highest fine since it took the initiative to start the meetings, and was also the largest firm. The total fines are more than twice the amount of what was decided by the Stockholm District Court (SEK 52 million), but still far below the total fines of approximately half a billion SEK that the SCA had proposed.

receives. Since large consumers pay the pump price minus the rebate, competition on rebates can partly be offset by raising the pump price. The pump price is transparent and displayed at the gasoline station. It is common knowledge that firms in the retail gasoline industry follow their rivals' price movements very closely, and that pump prices can change every day and even more often than that.[4] The rebate, however, is typically private between the seller and the buyer and, consequently, each seller lacks full information about the rebate given by a rival. In addition, the pump price is much more flexible than the rebate. While pump prices can change daily, the rebate is set for a contract period that typically lasts for half a year or more.

According to the Swedish Market Court's 2005 verdict (hereafter referred to as "the verdict", 37) price competition between the firms mainly takes place in relation to the rebates they offer:

> ... there is a connection between the pump price and the escalating rebate levels and ... this, in turn, entails periodically recurring rebate adjustments. The firms have explained that the reason for the escalation of rebates is the fierce competition, and the main competitive instrument, at least in the short run, is the rebates that firms offer to their customers.

Such a remediating of rebates had in fact been undertaken by the firms in 1990 and 1995. It is not, however, known whether the firms communicated prior to these remediations.[5]

In 1999, the rebates were once again reduced. This time it was clearly proven that representatives of the firms had several meetings in the period from August 13 to November 23, both before and after the rebate reduction was implemented on November 1. The gasoline companies stated publicly in October 1999 that they would reduce all

---

[4] See Foros and Steen (2013) for a description of the changes in the pump prices in the Swedish market for gasoline and diesel.

[5] The remediation of rebates in 1990 and 1995 is described briefly in the subpoena SCA submitted to Stockholm District Court (page 20), see Swedish Competition Authority (2000). Note that we have no data on the 1990 event.

rebates by SEK 0.15, but that they would also reduce the pump prices by the same amount at the same time. However, a closer look at the details of the case reveals this description is at best incomplete. The SCA alleged that the firms' representatives discussed both the development in pump prices and the reduction of rebates at their initial meetings. Compromising information found with the companies reveals among other things that their plan was never to lower the margin on pump prices in the long run, but to camouflage a return to normal margins on pump prices in a period with a decrease in the world market price and then a corresponding fall in the pump prices.[6] The cartel's real intentions are illustrated in Figure 8.1, which is an illustration of a drawing made by one of the representatives at one of the first meetings between the firms that was discovered.

The sketch shows the wholesale price of gasoline, called Platt, as the black line, and the normal and coordinated pump price development as the red and green lines, respectively. Clearly, a gradual decrease in the input price of gasoline (the Platt price) was expected in late fall 1999. As a result, it was anticipated that, but for the coordination, the pump price would be adjusted downward in several stages, which is illustrated by the stepwise short-dashed red line. The illustration then shows how the oil companies' common plan was to replace the normal gradual stepwise change in the pump prices with a large immediate drop, shown by the stepwise long-dashed green line. This would have been at the same time (September 30) that the rebates were to be reduced by an equal amount. If the latter were to take place, large customers would apparently not be negatively affected since the reduction in rebates would be exactly offset by a simultaneous reduction in pump prices.

---

[6] This is explained in the subpoena SCA sent to Stockholm District Court (reference in Footnote 1), see paragraph 116: "The reason that the companies planned to carry out the discount clean-up during the autumn was that a decreasing world market price would make it easier for companies to return to the normal price – and thereby achieve the average target margin – than when the world market price rises. The reason was that more negative reactions from customers could be expected in the latter case because a return to the normal price must then take place through price increases."

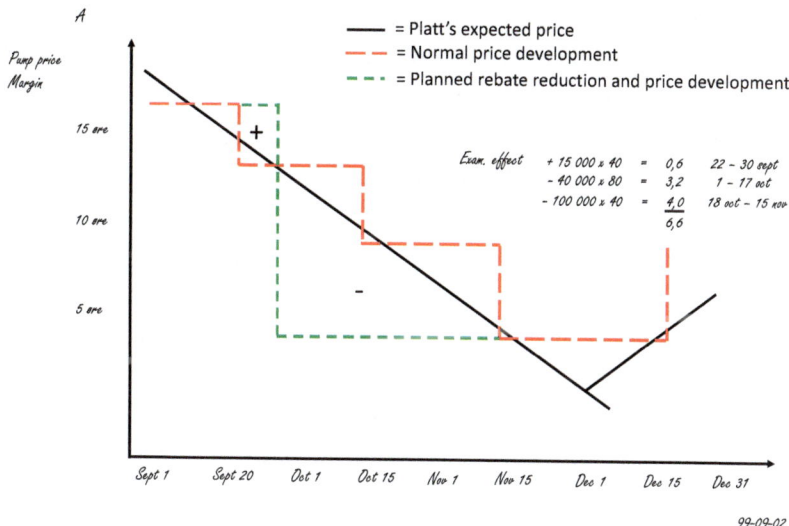

FIGURE 8.1 Development in pump prices: Illustration of a drawing by a firm representative made for internal use during a cartel meeting.[7]

Figure 8.1 also makes clear that the reduction in pump prices was expected by the companies to happen in any case. In fact, the plan included a delay in the first expected drop in the pump price (as the green dashed line extends a little longer on the original price level than the red dashed line), and then a substantial reduction in the pump price at some point, which was to be linked to the remediation of rebates. The drop in the green line September 30 then represents the reduction in rebates, which are to be identical to the corresponding drop in pump prices on that date. This would imply there would be no reduction in pump prices for almost a month longer than normal, even though the input price would have decreased during that period.

After just over a month, according to this illustration, the margin on pump prices was to return to the same level as it had been

---

[7] The figure was shown and discussed in court. The illustration was slightly changed from the original the illustration, in order to make it clearer. The colors were added by the authors. Note, though, that the illustration is reproduced mostly "as it was," including a rather confusing mixture of margins and prices on the vertical axis.

prior to the drop in the pump price in late September, when the rebate reduction was scheduled to take place (see the overlap of green and red lines in early November in Figure 8.1). There is also a back-of-the-envelope calculation in the upper right-hand corner of the illustration showing a net loss for the firms during that period when only considering changes in pump prices. However, after returning to the same margin on pump prices as would otherwise have applied, a net positive effect for the firms is projected. By executing this plan, they will have managed to maintain the margin on pump prices, and at the same time reduced the rebates.

Consumers that were receiving rebates would therefore be worse off in the long run compared to before the rebate remediation, despite the decline in pump prices. Consumers would first experience a short-term loss from the pump prices remaining high, followed by a short-term gain from the large price reduction. After that, the plan was to return the pump price associated with the "normal" margin, meaning that those consumers would no longer gain from the projected drop in price (see Footnote 6 from the SCA subpoena to the District Court). In sum, the illustration indicates that the plan was not to implement a permanent reduction in the margin on pump prices. After less than a month, they would return to the margin on pump prices before the SEK 0.15 rebate reduction.

This reconstruction of events and plans concerning both changes in rebates and pump prices was entered as evidence in the Swedish District Court, in first instance court proceedings. In its verdict in the second court proceedings, in the Market Court, they focused on the firms' coordination of the rebate remediation. As part of the evidence the court refers to notes taken by some of the firms' representatives who took part in the meeting (The verdict, 15). Information obtained from interrogations of participants from the meetings indicates that they discussed the rebates in detail:

> During the interrogations, it has emerged that the discussions regarding the discount restructuring had a far greater degree of

concreteness than what the companies wanted to acknowledge, and that not an insignificant part of the meetings was devoted to the discount clean out.

The court also recognized that the gasoline industry is quite transparent. There could, for example, be a price leader in the market, resulting in parallel pricing behaviour on pump prices. Obviously, and as accepted by the court, a rebate reduction could have been achieved if, for example, the largest firm had moved forward on their own and publicly announced rebate reductions, but this would prove costly in terms of the loss of customers and market share. The firms therefore tried to make sure that they all undertook the reduction at the same time:

> ... within the framework of their cooperation, the companies sought to ensure that they were not deceived by their competitors, see for example B W's notes on "There is a need for a trigger that initiates a reduction" and "the letter from OK-Q8 will be sent next week – Wednesday".

During the meetings, the representative had also shared information on rebate structures in relation to different customer groups as well as details on what should be considered maximum rebates.[8] According to the SCA, the companies also discussed the necessity of a "truce" for a period around and after the rebate reduction. The SCA was not, however, able to prove this in court.[9]

The verdict (27) states that the information the firms exchanged at the meetings could add value for them:

> In light of the above, it becomes almost obvious that the purpose of the meetings and contacts and exchange of information has been to seek to influence or obtain information about the competitors' behaviour before and during the discount clean out, e.g., by stating

---

[8] See the verdict, 25 second paragraph.   [9] See the verdict, 27 second paragraph.

the behaviour you yourself have decided to apply or considered applying to the market.

The court concluded that the firms had a common understanding ("concerted practice") concerning the rebate reduction. It found that the meetings must have had an anticompetitive purpose, and that the coordination made it possible to share information about future behaviour that would most likely have helped the cartel members to achieve a more "effective" rebate reduction. In that respect, this behaviour was a violation by object of TFEU Article 101 (Identical to § 6 in the Swedish Competition Act).

In the District court, (the appeal body before it was appealed to the higher Market court), the SCA argued on the basis of the illustration in Figure 8.1 that the plan agreed on at these meetings had all along been to change not only rebates but also pump prices, so that consumer welfare would have been reduced. However, in the Market court, the SCA did not claim that the firms also changed the pump prices, and that there was a link between pump prices and rebates. One reason why the SCA did not argue for a link between the pump prices and rebates was that this mechanism was not decisive for concluding that the firms' behavior was a violation of the relevant competition law. Direct communication between rivals on prices, in this case a reduction of future rebates, is a violation by object of competition law – analogous to a violation of Article 101 in TFEU – and thereby an infringement as such, without a need for proving any actual effect on prices.

The parties nevertheless put forward an efficiency defence for their coordinated reduction of the rebates, based on off-setting changes in the pump prices. While the argument put forward by the parties appealed to a basis – that exists in theory – for rebutting the claimed violation, the likelihood for success is small once a violation by object is established. Since the off-setting price reductions claim was part of the parties' defence, the SCA had to comment on it, and therefore expert witnesses from both sides presented economic analysis in court for and against the argument.

8.3 A POSSIBLE THEORY OF NO CONSUMER HARM

Firms setting list prices and offering some of their customers rebates on the list prices, as in the Swedish retail gasoline and diesel market, is something we observe in other markets as well.[10] The list price and the size of the rebate are both a choice variable for firms. By competing on one, while colluding on the other, companies might end up with a so-called semi-collusive outcome.[11] If one of these choice variables is transparent and flexible, as pump prices are in this case, so that it can easily be monitored by all firms and adjusted by the firm, then there is potential for collusion on this particular choice variable. To elaborate on this point, think about a firm's incentive to deviate from such a high price. On the one hand, it is tempting because it leads to business stealing when the firm sets a price slightly below the rivals' prices. On the other hand, it may trigger fierce price competition in the future. If prices are transparent and firms can change those prices quickly, any deviation could lead to a quick response from the rivals. The short run gain from deviating would then be limited, and it might not be worthwhile for the firm to deviate and then trigger imminent and tough price competition.

Rebates, however, are typically negotiated bilaterally between a firm and an individual large customer and therefore are less observable. Since usually all firms take part in the competition for winning a large customer, a firm that does not win a contract can infer something about the rebate the rival must have offered to secure the contract. Presumably, the rival's rebate was higher than what the firm proposed.

---

[10] See Harrington and Ye (2019) for some examples of firms that coordinated on list prices but not on rebates or discounts.

[11] See, for example, Schmalensee (1994), Steen and Sørgard (2009), Schinkel and Spiegel (2017), and Basso, Ross, and Shadarevian (2021) on various models of semi-collusion. From these studies of semi-collusion, it is difficult to draw general and robust lessons when there is a regime shift from semi-collusion to full collusion as is the issue in this case.

However, in contrast to list prices, the firm will not have exact information about the rival's rebate. In addition, because it is costly to negotiate, a rebate contract typically lasts longer, so rebates are less frequently modified. All of this can make it tempting for a firm to compete, rather than comply with some collusive rebate. Its deviation from that collusive rebate will not necessarily or at least immediately be learned by rival firms and, even if they did find out, it is not possible for them to quickly retaliate by increasing their rebates.

Pertinent to this analysis, a complicating market characteristic is that there are two distinctly different types of consumers. The firms compete on offering rebates to only one type of consumers, and they can set an individual rebate to each of those consumers. The latter can be explained by transaction costs. For small consumers, certainly individual consumers and small firms, it is too costly relative to the possible benefit for an oil company to individually negotiate a rebate with each of them. Consequently, those consumers typically pay the list price. For large buyers with significant demand, the oil companies' benefit can justify the cost of negotiating a rebate.

In line with the differences in consumer types just outlined, a semi-collusive outcome with (tacit) collusion on list prices and competition on rebates may have been the initial "normal" situation in the market under investigation. A semi-collusion model therefore has merit for understanding the cartel in this particular case. It can take account not only of the shift from competition to collusion on rebates, but also of the interaction between the coordination on reduction in rebates and the setting of the pump prices. Indeed one of the party's expert witnesses applied a model of semi-collusion to make the argument that the reductions in rebates were offset by corresponding reductions in pump prices.[12] We agree that the semi-collusive model can be well suited in this case, but disagree on how the model was applied.

---

[12] The expert witness referred to the semi-collusion model in Steen and Sørgard (2003). The model was applied to explain the rebates given to large customers in the Norwegian airline industry in the period 1997–2001. However, this was a pure theoretical argument not backed by any data.

First of all, it is remarkable that they put forth semi-collusion on pump prices as the "normal" form of pricing. It implies admittance of the parties engaging in a form of collusion, though one that is different from that which they were charged in the case (which was about coordinating on rebates). However, tacit collusion on pump prices is well known in several national markets. As indicated in Foros and Steen (2013), this is likely also in the Swedish petrol market. Tacit collusion is very often legal, and in that respect, it is not so risky for the parties to claim semi-collusion where they tacitly collude on pump prices.

Another feature of the semi-collusion model relevant to this particular market is that the interplay between collusion on pump prices and competition on rebates may lead to a price structure that is detrimental to the sellers' profit. To see why, suppose that without any rebates, the firms achieve perfect collusion by setting the monopoly pump price. Now suppose they introduce rebates to some customers and at the same time the pump price is increased. By lifting the pump price, they prevent the net price (pump price minus the rebate) to fall too far below the monopoly price for those customers with rebates. This is beneficial for the firms. But at the same time, it leads to a price above monopoly price for those customers without rebates who pay the pump price. Firms have to balance the change in revenues from those two groups of consumers. A price above the monopoly price for the group with no rebates can be optimal given that it helps to increase the revenues from the other group with a net price below the monopoly price.[13]

---

[13] To understand the mechanism, see the simple model presented in Appendix A. As an illustration, let us assume the monopoly pump price is 10 for both groups of consumers and the costs are 8. Let us assume some customers receive 2 in rebates, deducted from the pump price. By lifting the pump price to 11, it can increase revenues from the group receiving a rebate (they then pay 9 in net price instead of 8), but at the same time increases the price to the other customers with no rebates to a net price of 11. It can be shown that this can be profitable, despite the fact that the customers with no rebates pay a price above the monopoly price. The firm must balance the below monopoly price for one group against the above monopoly price for the other group.

In trying to counteract high rebates due to tough competition for large customers, companies can end up with unprofitably high prices for those customers with no secret rebates who pay only the list prices. A clean out of rebates, in an episode in which the firms shift from competing on rebates to colluding on rebates, can in such a situation indeed lead to a reduction in pump prices. The reason is that the initial rationale for a high pump price – price above the monopoly price for the no-rebate customers – is no longer present when the firms are also coordinating on rebates. The reason is that pump prices are no longer an instrument for lifting the net price paid by large customers. It can then be optimal to reduce the pump prices upon eliminating rebates, since the pump prices were driven up only because of the high rebates to large customers. The resulting combination of lower rebates and lower pump prices could benefit all consumers in total, as claimed by the parties' expert when invoking the semi-collusion model. This is true even if the large customers are not fully compensated for the reduction in rebates, as long as the gain for customers with no rebate through lower pump prices more than offsets the net loss for the large customers.

This argument is not universally valid, however, for strict conditions must be met for it to hold and result in no consumer harm. The firms must at the outset have achieved perfect or almost perfect semi-collusion on pump prices for the off-setting price reductions to take place.

Under the semi-collusion theory with less than perfect collusion, the collusive price can take any value between the competitive (or static Nash equilibrium) price and the monopoly price. Taking that into account, it is not necessarily the case that the colluding companies would always prefer to set a lower pump price after cleaning out their rebates. It will depend on the level of the pump price before the clean out, which with imperfect collusion can be lower than the monopoly price. Let us assume this is true. Then none of the customers pay a price at the outset that is above their monopoly price. When rebates are removed, there are no above-monopoly-price to fix. So, the incentives to lower the pump prices are not present.

The price path described in Figure 8.1 shows that there were no plans to reduce the margin on pump prices, that is, no plans to lower pump prices after remediation of rebates. This observation is consistent with pump prices before the reduction in rebates not being above the monopoly price. In such a case, the firms did not have an incentive to lower pump prices when rebates were cleaned out. In fact, by reducing rebates and maintaining the same margin on pump prices, they achieved a higher net price in the market and thereby were able to implement a higher (and more profitable) collusive price. This shows that the claim by the parties, that a drop in pump prices had offset the clean out of rebates, is not supported by the data.

As indicated in the quotation from page 37 of the Swedish Market Court's verdict, it is possible that rebates escalated as large firms received ever increasing rebates over time. Escaping from this high rebate trap would require coordination by firms to do it jointly and simultaneously, for if one firm unilaterally reduces its rebates, it would lose its large customers to rivals. This coordination is exactly what happened in the fall of 1999. The oil companies managed to achieve a common understanding of simultaneous rebate reduction.[14] As a result, the industry moved from a situation with collusive behavior on pump prices and competitive behavior on rebates, to a situation with collusion on both dimensions. While firms did eliminate the rebates, it did not reduce the pump prices to their previous net levels.

8.4 QUANTITATIVE EVIDENCE

Data collected by the SCA that was used in this case by one of the authors (Steen) appears to support the SCA's claim that the parties

---

[14] Note that our reasoning can explain their incentives to move from an equilibrium with rebates to an equilibrium with a removal of rebates.

FIGURE 8.2 Rebate reduction illustration from November 1999: Actual price development for gasoline in 1999 (daily data) and the predicted "normal" price.

indeed were able to return to their original margins on the pump prices. Figure 8.2 illustrates how, despite the reduced rebates, pump prices quickly returned to the level they were predicted to reach had the cartel not taken place, and were not lower, as the parties claimed. The estimated "normal" price path is based on an econometric model that is explained below. Although the input prices did not fall in this period (contrary to the expectation of the companies at the time Figure 8.1 was drawn), it can be seen from Figure 8.2 that on approximately November 1, that is roughly a month after the drop in pump prices that accompanied the rebate reduction, the pump price returned to its predicted normal level.[15]

A variety of econometric models were put forward by experts to substantiate and criticize the predicted but for price path, showing

---

[15] The international input price for gasoline (the Platt price), as with other international resource prices, is typically known to follow a unit root process – or random walk. Thus, it is difficult to predict such prices, and the increasing variance and randomness typically dominate deterministic predictions for such prices. One could speculate whether the lack of a negative trend in the Platt price made it easier for the competition authorities to spot the oil companies' strategy, though it were the public announcements on rebate reductions that triggered the case.

that prices and margins followed the pattern the firms had planned.[16] Prices and margins were above the "normal" level during the months prior to the rebate reduction, fell below after the rebate reduction day, only then to move up toward their normal level during the months after the reduction in the rebates. This "return" pattern, however, was hard to show with a significant degree of statistical precision, and several of the defendants' specifications typically showed even more statistical uncertainty (larger standard errors) for the period around the rebate reduction. Hence, the hypothesis that price movements were due to random variation could not be reasonably dismissed.

An intriguing point in this case is that the dawn raid on December 16 interrupted the potential "return process" whereby "normal margins" were to be recovered. Figure 8.2 suggests a recovery process, but it is difficult to show the recovery was statistically significant (and not just random short-run dynamics). This was largely due to the short amount of time between the rebate reduction and the dawn raid. Furthermore, the companies had the incentive from the ongoing litigation to potentially make sure there would be no "return process," thus keeping prices lower than they would otherwise have done. In the process, several econometric models were presented, but the statistical tests' precision of a potential significant return to the normal level is dependent on the length of the data period included after the rebate reduction.

Another interesting discovery in the case was the companies appeared to have reduced their rebates in a similar manner in May 1995. Though this rebate reduction was never investigated as potentially collusive, several of the SCA's experts found that it was

---

[16] The typical model was price or margin as the dependent variable, with tax and wholesale price as the major independent (explanatory) variables. In addition, several different trends and macro control variables were included as explanatory variables. Several of the models were dynamic in the sense that they included lags of both dependent and independent variables as explanatory variables, while some models were purely static models (no lagged variables). All models produced an estimate of the predicted normal price or margin which was compared to the actual price or margin.

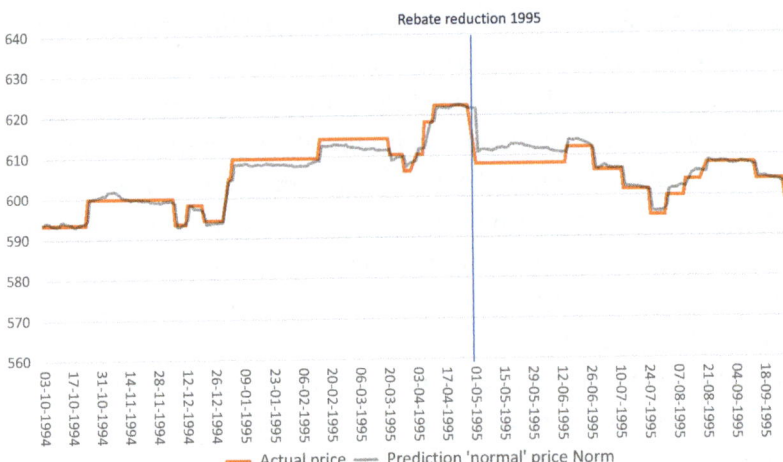

FIGURE 8.3 Rebate reduction illustration May 1995: Actual prices and predicted "normal" prices (daily prices).

robust and relevant enough to use as collaborative evidence for the price pattern before and after the 1999 rebate reduction. Since the 1995 incident was allowed to play out without any interference from the competition authority, it did not suffer from a lack of relevant data post the restoration and, as a result, a precisely measured return to the normal price could be shown econometrically. Figure 8.3 illustrates that then too the actual price was back to its long-run level around July 1995. It is also clear that prices were above their long-run level prior to May, and below in May and June. This episode, however, was not admissible in the case, for there was no evidence the cartel was operating at that time.

The "normal" price prediction in Figures 8.2 and 8.3 come from a dynamic econometric model, estimated using daily data for the period April 1, 1993–March 31, 2000, and presented before the court.[17] The price model was formulated to capture the long-run steady state development

---

[17] The model controls for current and lagged versions of the tax variable and the wholesale price. In addition, the gasoline price enters as a lagged explanatory variable.

in gasoline prices, while at the same time allowing for short-run dynamics. The estimated model allowed for price deviations three months prior to and four months after the rebate reduction months in 1995 and 1999. Hence, allowing the stepwise deviations in the "normal" price shown in Figures 8.2 and 8.3. In addition to controls for trend, seasonality, and a price war in October 1993, major determinants of the gasoline retail price were included which are the wholesale price and taxes.[18]

The results are reasonable as both point estimates and dynamics are in line with earlier results for the Swedish market, see for example, Asplund et al. (2000)[19] as well as studies of other countries' gasoline markets.[20] We observe an interesting pattern with positive and significant deviations from the "normal level" prior to the reduction month. We find a reduction of SEK 0.15 in the reduction month (equal to the agreed-upon rebate reduction). In the two months after the rebate reduction, deviations are significant but smaller and negative. Finally, in the third and fourth months after the rebate reduction, both negative estimates are smaller in magnitude and their significance is low. Hence, the results suggest a return to the "normal level" after two to three months. This is also illustrated in Figure 8.4, where the "normal" price level is zero, and deviations are shown through the graph.

The "normal" price predictions behind the pattern illustrated in Figures 8.2 and 8.4 both rely on price data for more than a hundred

---

[18] The data was obtained from one of the large oil companies in Sweden. The tax figures are public data, and the wholesale price corresponds to the Rotterdam spot price for gasoline translated to SEK. All data was provided by the SCA. The detailed results can be obtained from the authors on request.

[19] For instance, we find full pass-through of the tax rate both in the short run and the long run, whereas the wholesale price is only partly passed through in the short run. These findings are reasonable because, while changes in the wholesale price cannot be anticipated, changes in tax can, suggesting that whereas changes in wholesale prices take some time to be fully implemented in the retail price, tax changes have an immediate impact. The models survived tests of autocorrelation, and had a relatively high statistical fit (R^2).

[20] There exists a large literature on pass-through of wholesale costs and gasoline retail prices, e.g., Borenstein, Cameron, and Gilbert (1997), Johnson (2002), Verlinda (2008), Apergis and Vouzavalis (2018), and Byrne (2019). For a recent study of cost pass-through in the Swedish gasoline market, see Rrukaj and Steen (2022).

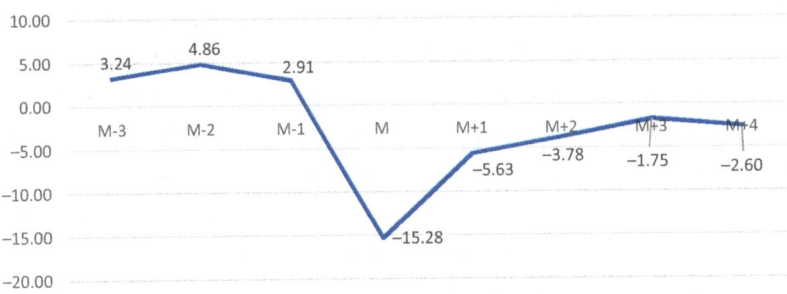

FIGURE 8.4 Price development as suggested by the dynamic price model.

days after the dawn raid and depend on price deviations during a rebate restoration from 1995.[21] Reducing the data used to a sample ending at the dawn raid, in order to avoid the interruption, effectively implied that the monthly deviations taking place more than one month after the 1999 rebate reduction (second, third, and fourth months), are statistically identified only from what happened after the rebate reduction in 1995. Hence, beyond the positive deviations prior to the rebate reduction, the statistical evidence is determined more or less fully from the earlier restoration in 1995. Since we do not have unbiased information on the prices for the period after the 1999 dawn raid in December, the data needed to identify effects taking place more than one and a half months after the 1999 restoration are not necessarily unbiased. Thus, if one reduces the dataset and excludes price data after December 16, 1999, it is the 1995 data that identifies deviations for the last two to three monthly indicators. Hence, it remains difficult to disentangle what the cartel's price path would have been without interference by the dawn raids and subsequent investigations of possible net price overcharges. Nevertheless, the picture that emerges is that, even though the firms had offset the

---

[21] During the case, several more models with various controls were introduced, for instance GDP and the share of serviced gasoline stations. In addition, much more complicated lag structures could be imposed to obtain different conclusions, something that did in fact take place during the case. The econometric evidence proved as confusing as it was enlightening for the judges.

clean out of their rebates with lower pump prices for a few months in the fall of 1999, they quickly returned to the initial margin on pump prices. We found a similar pattern in 1995 when a clean out of rebates took place during an uninterrupted period of full collusion. Hence, we conclude the theoretical "waterbed effect" proposed by the parties – whereby pump prices fall an amount equal to the decline of rebates – did not materialize, clearly not in 1995, but probably not in 1999 either.

8.5 SOME LESSONS LEARNED

This cartel episode is an example of a phenomenon that we see in other cartel cases as well, which is that firms collude on one dimension while they continue to compete along other dimensions. In this particular market, the normal mode of competition seems to be that firms collude on pump prices, which are list prices that only some of their customers pay, and earn a positive margin on that price. A relatively high price-cost margin on pump prices gives the firms an incentive to compete to capture larger consumers by offering them rebates. Pump prices are transparent and can change very often, so there is the potential for semi-collusion on pump prices, which seems to have been done by the oil companies.

Rebates, on the other hand, are not so transparent and are less frequently adjusted, and therefore have a more limited potential for collusion. They are the more natural dimension of competition. Rebates offered to specific customers are an example of the extra effort made by each firm to steal sales from its rivals. This effect can easily escalate and seemingly did so in this market. To get out of this dilemma, the firms coordinated to remove these rebates as well. The evidence showed that the firms initially competed on rebates, but then held several meetings to discuss the dampening of competition with respect to rebates. As a result, they managed to coordinate their behaviour and simultaneously removed the rebates.

A first lesson learned can be that competition agencies should be careful to monitor for semi-collusion (here, on pump prices), and be aware a move to an equilibrium that is even more harmful for consumers. Semi-collusion is typically not beneficial for consumers, and certainly full collusion is not. Combinations of competition dimensions that differ in their level of transparency would be something a competition authority may be suspicious of. They should have in mind that the existence of semi-collusion can put firms in a position in which they are induced to engage in full collusion.

Our case raises a general question concerning the possible substitution between competition on one dimension and at the same time collusion on another, and whether elimination of competition along one price dimension leads to a countervailing price effect along another price dimension. There are several markets with a combination of list prices for all consumers and individual rebates or discounts for some consumers, as we have seen in this particular case.

A second lesson learned from our case study is that in such markets there is, in theory, an argument – in line with what one of the parties claimed – for a "waterbed effect," where a clean out of rebates can lead to a lower list price. But, as we explained, such an outcome hinges on some strict conditions being satisfied, in particular, that the list prices for those consumers with no rebates are above the monopoly price. We find that in our case, contrary to what some of the parties claimed, there was no "waterbed effect." Rebates were cleaned out, without any effect on the pump prices in the long run.

Unfortunately, there are only a few theoretical and empirical studies of this type of cartel behavior in the economic literature.[22] There is a need for further research on this potential waterbed effect, as well as other theoretical and empirical studies that might help us to better understand the potential for other mechanisms that may lead

---

[22] Harrington and Ye (2019) analyses collusion on list prices while leaving sellers to set their final prices. Their model, though, applies to an intermediate goods market and focuses on how high list prices can signal to the buyer a high cost. This mechanism is very different from the one we are looking at and does not capture the situation with two distinctly different types of consumers as we focus on. The case study by Zhiqi Chen in this volume on the air cargo cartel shows collusion on surcharges and competition on base prices also harms consumers.

to consumer harm associated with such a cartel behavior. As explained above, any waterbed effect depends crucially on the details of the particular market under investigation.

A third lesson learned is that, whether we economists like it or not, the case must be analysed and presented in such a way that it fits into the courts' approach in such cases. Neither the theoretical reasoning nor the econometric evidence we have described were decisive in the court's verdict. The conclusion that the coordinated rebate clean out was a violation of the prohibition of anticompetitive behaviour was based on evidence showing the cartel members had communicated on the planned rebate reduction. This approach is in line with case law on cartels in Europe, where direct communication between rivals regarding commercially sensitive information, such as prices, is a violation by object of TFEU Article 101 (Identical to § 6 in the Swedish Competition Act). According to this legal doctrine, the crucial question is whether the parties have been in contact concerning information related to their competitive strategy. Communication on a rebate clean-out is, according to this approach, a violation by object, and there is no need for an effects-based approach to conclude there is a violation of competition law. Since neither the change in pump prices, nor the potential return of the "normal" margin were pertinent for the court's conclusion (after all, explicit communication among the cartel members was documented), the court did not opine on the presence of a waterbed effect.

A fourth lesson learned from this episode is that, even in cases where a "by object" approach is enough to obtain a conviction according to case law, the competition agency should do a full analysis of the cartel mechanism. First, this is about setting the right priorities. If a full analysis reveals that it is most likely that the behaviour was beneficial for the consumers, then the agency would – hopefully – not give priority to such a case. Second, the agency will be better prepared for the court proceedings. For this case, such an analysis would probably have better prepared them for the defendants' (somewhat expected) claim of a "waterbed" effect.

A fifth lesson learned is that a dawn raid can influence how a cartel plan plays out, which can destroy potential evidence. Although the final verdict was not based on an effects-based approach, the debate between the economic experts in this case clearly points to a number of challenges when calculating possible effects. The pattern in the estimated deviations from the "normal price" (see Figure 8.4) is quite suggestive, and the size of the parameter estimates is in fact probably more convincing than the discussion of individual parameters' significance. Indeed, it appeared to be a clear pattern where prices deviate less and less from the "normal price" as time goes by. However, the short post-cartel period obviously reduced the precision of the estimated parameters and, as we saw above, the results depended on also using data from the 1995 rebate reduction. This illustrates that a dawn raid carried out quite early on, which is obviously important for finding conclusive document evidence, can undermine the finding of economic evidence, since the marke data after the raid are likely to be biased.

APPENDIX 8A   SIMPLE THEORY OF SEMI-COLLUSION[23]

We assume there are two firms and both serve two consumer groups. In line with that observed in the Swedish gasoline market, firms set one price that is valid for both consumer groups, which we will refer to as the *pump price*. To illustrate the mechanisms at work, let us simply assume the firms set a collusive pump price that is the same for both consumer groups. This implies the pump price is above the level of a static Nash equilibrium price. We refrain from discussing challenges for the cartel members when setting this price, and simply assume they set a pump price that maximizes their joint profit. With no rebates, we will refer to this as pure price fixing. The price is denoted P^M and is the monopoly price.

There are two types of consumers. Type A consumers are large, and they write a contract with the selling firm specifying a particular rebate. The net price they pay is the pump price minus the rebate. Type B consumers have smaller purchases and can be thought of as ordinary private households. As they do not

---

[23] Our simple model of semi-collusion draws on Steen and Sørgard (2002). For a more general discussion of semi-collusion, see Steen and Sørgard (2009) and Basso *et al.* (2021).

receive rebates, their net price is identical to the pump price. One interpretation is that there are transaction costs depending on the type of customer, implying that negotiations are only viable for large customers (typically, firms) but not for small customers (typically, households). Since both firms compete for large customers, we assume they can infer something about what is the minimum rebate offered even if the firm does not succeed in winning all of the large customers. Since large customer contracts are negotiated for longer periods as well as infrequently, the firms will thus not be able to exactly infer the rebate.

The firms compete to capture the Type A consumers by offering them rebates. For simplicity, we assume there is only one type A consumer. Let P denote the pump price set for both groups of consumers, and, correspondingly, R_i is the discount offered to the type A consumer by firm i, where $i = 1,2$. D_j is the quantity consumed by type j consumers, where $j = A, B$. To simplify further, we assume the price elasticity of demand is identical in those two consumer groups. It implies that the monopoly price, given identical marginal costs for those two groups, is identical in both consumer groups.

Pump prices are monitored closely by rivals and they change very often, typically several times each day. The contracts on rebates, though, have a much longer duration and they last typically for one year. Contracts with consumers for rebates are then more long-term decisions than the decisions on pump price. In line with this fact, we assume that when the firms agree on the pump price, they know there is a contract with the Type A consumer concerning discounts and each firm either knows exactly (the one who won the contract) or infers the size of the rebate. This implies that discounts are exogenous and known to the firms when they decide to fix the pump price. We assume the following sequence of decisions:

- Stage 1: Firms 1 and 2 compete by offering discounts R_1 and R_2 for the Type A consumer to maximize individual profit, and the Type A consumer writes a contract with one of them.
- Stage 2: Firms 1 and 2 collude by setting the pump price P to maximize joint profit.

At Stage 2, Firms 1 and 2 maximize joint profits by setting P – the pump price applicable to both groups of consumers. The net price paid by the Type A consumer served by firm i, where $i = 1,2$, can be defined as $P_A = P - R_i$, while the net price paid by Type B consumers is equal to $P_B = P$. Given they maximize joint profits, they encounter the following maximization problem at stage 2:

$$\max_P \pi = (P - R_i - MC)D_A(P - R_i) + (P - MC)D_B(P). \qquad (1)$$

To find the optimal price and rebate, we start by considering the optimal pump price at stage 2. For a given rebate, the optimal pump price is defined by:

$$D_A + D_B + \frac{\partial D_A}{\partial P}[P - R_i - MC] + \frac{\partial D_B}{\partial P}[P - MC] = 0. \quad (2)$$

If no discounts are given ($R_i = 0$), we have pure price fixing with $P_A = P_B = P$. It is then obvious that the price with pure price fixing, $P = P^M$, is the monopoly price assuming a uniform price across both consumer types. If $R_i > 0$, then this is no longer true. The net price paid by the Type A consumer is lower, and the first-order condition concerning the pump price P is no longer met as long as $P = P^M$.

If $R_i > 0$, it follows that Equation (2) can only be met if $P > P^M$. We see from (2) that $R_i > 0$ is analogous to an increase in marginal cost for supplying the Type A consumer. The higher is the marginal cost, the higher is the monopoly price for that particular consumer group. When the firms have offered discounts on the pump price, they can partly offset the price reduction by increasing the pump price. By doing so, they increase the net price paid by the Type A consumer. On the other hand, such a price increase will be detrimental to the revenues earned on Type B consumers, since the price will be further increased compared to the optimal price for Type B consumers.

Let us now consider Stage 1 of the game. Firms 1 and 2 set the rebate for the Type A consumer simultaneously. There is by assumption no coordination. If $R_i > P - MC$, then each of them will find it profitable to undercut the rival by setting a marginally higher discount in order to try to win the contract. Note that there is no effect on the outcome of Stage 2 since the discount is (almost) identical to the one with no undercutting. This implies there is an incentive to undercut unless $R_i = P - MC$. The prices we observe are thus as follows:

- Price for Type A consumer: $P_A^I \equiv P_A^0 = P^M - R^0 = MC < P^M$
- Price for Type B consumers: $P_B^I > P^M$

In this simple model, we can see the pump price can be distorted upward. The pump price is above the standard monopoly price for Type B consumers. According to this reasoning, it is possible that, had the rebates been removed, the firms have an incentive to reduce their pump prices.

However, whether a clean out of rebates would lead to lower pump prices depends on the initial collusive price. In our simple model, we assume that without any rebates, the firms succeed in achieving perfect collusion by setting the monopoly pump price. As is well known, with an imperfect cartel, the collusive price can be anything between the static Nash equilibrium and the monopoly price. Taking that into account, it is not necessarily the case that they would always prefer to set a lower pump price after eliminating all rebates. It depends on the pump price before the clean out, which with imperfect collusion might be lower than the monopoly price. The firms might in such a case prefer to reduce the rebates without lowering the pump price.

REFERENCES

Apergis, N., and Vouzavalis, G. (2018) "Asymmetric Pass through of Oil Prices to Gasoline Prices: Evidence from a New Country Sample." *Energy Policy*, 114, 519–528.

Asplund, M., Eriksson, R., and Friberg, R. (2000) "Price Adjustments by a Gasoline Retail Chain." *Scandinavian Journal of Economics*, 102 (1), 101–121.

Basso, L. J., T. W. Ross and V. Shadarevian (2021) "The Welfare Effects and Stability of Semicollusion," University of British Columbia.

Borenstein, S., Cameron, C., and Gilbert, R. (1997) "Do Gasoline Prices Respond Asymmetrically to Crude Oil Price Changes?" *Quarterly Journal of Economics*, 112(1), 305–339.

Byrne, D. P. (2019) "Gasoline Pricing in the Country and the City." *Review of Industrial Organization*, 55, (2), 209–235.

Foros, Ø. and F. Steen (2013) "Retail Pricing, Vertical Control, and Competition in the Swedish Gasoline Market," Report 2013:5, Swedish Competition Authority.

Harrington, J. E. Jr. and L. Ye (2019) "Collusion through Coordination of Announcements," *The Journal of Industrial Economics*, 67(2), 209–241.

Johnson, R. N. (2002) "Search Costs, Lags and Prices at the Pump." *Review of Industrial Organization*, 20, (1), 33–50.

Ljung, G., & Box, G. (1979) "On Measure of Lack of Fit in Time Series Models," *Biometrika*, 66, 265–270.

Rrukaj, R. and F. Steen (2024) *Asymmetric Cost Transmission and Market Power: An Examination of the Swedish Retail Gasoline Market*. WP NHH.

Schinkel, M. P. and Y. Spiegel (2017) "Can Collusion Promote Sustainable Consumption and Production?" *International Journal of Industrial Organization*, 53, 371–398.

Schmalensee, R. (1992) "Sunk Costs and Market Structure: A Review Article," *The Journal of Industrial Economics*, 40(2), 125–134.

Steen, F. and L. Sørgard (2002) "From a Regulated to a Private Monopoly: The Deregulation of the Norwegian Airline Industry," *Swedish Economic Policy Review*, 9, 191–221.

Steen, F. and L. Sørgard (2009) "Semicollusion," *Foundation and Trends in Microeconomics*, 5(3), 153–228.

Swedish Competition Authority (2000) "'Ansøkan om stamning,' Subpoena to the District Court, Document 2000-06-29." (www.konkurrensverket.se/globalas sets/dokument/konkurrens/beslut/stamningsansokan/00-060~1.pdf)

Verlinda, J. A. (2008) "Do Rockets Rise Faster and Feathers Fall Slower in an Atmosphere of Local Market Power? Evidence from the Retail Gasoline Market." *Journal of Industrial Economics*, 56(3), 581–612.

9 Average Bid Auction Format Facilitates Bidding Rings
Construction Tenders in Italy
Francesco Decarolis

9.1 INTRODUCTION

For relatively standardized products and services – such as many construction projects (e.g., road paving) or the provision of a commodity (e.g., generic drugs) – a common procurement procedure is to conduct an auction. One popular auction design has suppliers submit bids and the procurer awards the contract to the bidder who submitted the lowest bid and pays the bidder a price equal to their bid. Referring to it as the low-price auction, it is intended to produce intense competition – as each bidder is incentivized to undercut anticipated competing bids in order to win – with the contract being supplied by the lowest-cost supplier at a bid near its cost.

In practice, there are at least two forces that can interfere with the low-price auction performing to the satisfaction of the procurer. First, the winning bidder may be able to offer the lowest bid only because it intends to compromise on the quality of the product or service. The procurer may well have been better off awarding the contract to a company offering a higher price but with higher quality. Second, the winning bidder may have submitted a bid that it does not intend to abide by. Rather, it plans to renegotiate a higher price at a later stage when the procurer is inclined to make the price concession rather than run the procurement auction again. For both of these reasons, the procurer may not want to award the contract to the supplier that has submitted the lowest bid.[1] Nevertheless, low-price

---

[1] This problem is the well-known limit of competition in environments with "incomplete contracts" and, to address it, the academic literature has recently

auctions are commonly used due to their simplicity, transparency, and that they do incentivize price competition.

Toward addressing these potential weaknesses to the low-price auction, an alternative auction design has emerged: the average bid auction (ABA). With details to come later in the case study, the ABA, roughly speaking, awards the contract to the bidder whose bid is nearest to the average bid (or perhaps a trimmed average bid where the very lowest and very highest bids are eliminated prior to calculating the average bid). The intent is to avoid awarding the contract to unrealistically low bids which may come with low quality or plans of ex post renegotiation. While not common in the United States – though it has been used by the Florida Department of Transportation and the New York State Procurement Agency – the ABA is present in the public procurement regulations of many countries, including Chile, China, Colombia, Italy, Japan, Peru, Switzerland, and Taiwan (Decarolis, 2018).

Usage of the ABA format has been advocated by the civil engineering literature (Ioannou and Leu, 1993) and major institutions (European Commission, 2002) as a suitable auction format for public procurement purposes, for the reasons given. However, the literature that developed the ABA did not adequately consider the strategic (or game-theoretic) implications of the design on bidding. It was implicitly assumed that firms would continue to submit the same bids as in low price auctions and it did not consider how firms would adapt their behaviour to respond to the incentives created by changing the rules of the auction. Under that assumption on bidding, the ABA, by design, is expected to result in the procurer paying a somewhat higher price – as they will pay close to the average bid rather than the lowest bid – though presumably in exchange for higher quality and less risk of renegotiation. However, in practice, the procurer could end up paying a significantly higher price, because bidders stop competing and

proposed interesting mechanisms that better balance competition at the auction stage with ex post performance (Lopomo et al., 2022).

instead form a cartel whereby they coordinate on submitting high bids. As this case study will describe, the average bid auction format is fertile ground for collusion and, as a result, it does not perform as intended.

Our examination of collusion at ABAs will focus on the tendering of public work projects by the County and Municipality of Turin between 2000 and 2003. Unbeknownst at the time but later revealed in a criminal investigation, there were subgroups of construction firms who formed cartels. They coordinated and manipulated their bids to enhance their chance of winning the contract at an inflated price. The case study draws on the court case to describe how the design of the auction contributed to the formation, operation, and stability of these cartels.[2] Moreover, we will show that by understanding how cartels operate under different market arrangements like the ABA, it is possible to improve cartel enforcement in terms of both enhancing the detection of cartels and redesigning procurement procedures to make them more immune to collusive activities. While the latter is well-known within the literature on "market design" (Roth 2002, 2018), its practical relevance is not fully recognized as reflected by the persistence of ill-conceived market designs such as the ABA.

In Section 9.2, the ABA is explained along with how it affects competitive bidding and facilitates collusion. Section 9.3 describes the formation of cartels in the Turin procurement case. Its operation and effect are covered in Section 9.4, while an assessment of cartel stability along with the cartel's demise are presented in Section 9.5. Section 9.6 turns to offering ideas on how to detect cartels that might be operating at an ABA. Section 9.7 concludes with a description of the main lessons to be learned about cartels and anti-cartel enforcement.

---

[2] Turin Court of Justice, First Criminal Section, 28/4/2008, case N.2549/06. The material in this case is partly based on the academic article of Conley and Decarolis (2016).

9.2 AVERAGE BID AUCTION: RULES AND BIDDING INCENTIVES

9.2.1 Auction Rules

The rules by which the ABA works can be illustrated in the context of Italian public contracts. Potential suppliers are informed through the announcement of a tender which states the maximum price that can be charged (i.e., the government procurer's reserve price which is typically the engineering cost estimate) and that the bid to be submitted is the percentage discount off the reserve price for the contract. With the low-price auction, the contract would be awarded to the bidder submitting the highest discount (or, equivalently, the lowest price). The determination of the winning bidder in the ABA is quite different. In the case of the Turin ABA format, the procurer first sorts bidders' submitted discounts from the highest to the lowest. Next, the highest 10 percent and the lowest 10 percent of the discounts are discarded. For the remaining 80 percent of the bids, the average discount is calculated (call this A1). Now, calculate the average discount of those discounts above A1 (still excluding the top 10 percent of discounts), and call that A2. The winner of the auction is the firm with the highest discount among those discounts lower than A2. In case there is a tie, a fair lottery determines which of the bidders with a winning bid is awarded the contract. For fulfilling the contract, the winner is paid a price equal to the winning bid; that is, the reserve price minus the discount it bid.

An example is helpful to illustrate the above description. As shown in the leftmost column in Figure 9.1, there are nineteen bids which are expressed as percentage discounts off the reserve price. In the second column (from the left), the lowest and the highest 10 percent of bids (depicted in red) are discarded and then the average bid A1 is calculated. In the third column, the average of the bids above A1 is calculated which is A2. Finally, in the fourth column (the rightmost column), all bids above A2 are discarded (depicted in red) and the winning bid is the highest one below A2 (depicted in green).

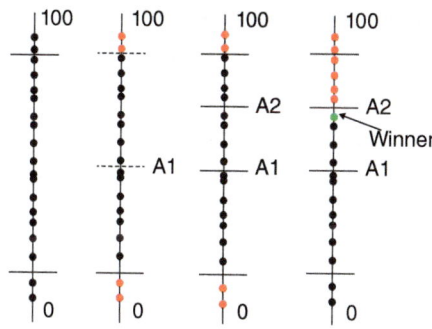

FIGURE 9.1 Example of an ABA with nineteen bids.

Consequently, the winning bidder in the ABA did not offer the highest discount. By the auction's design, bids higher than A2, which is the average of the bids above the average, cannot win. In the specific example, for instance, the contract is awarded to the firm that submitted the seventh-highest discount.

9.2.2 Competitive Bidding

Prior to examining how the rules of the ABA facilitate collusion, it is useful to describe what bids look like under competition. We'll do so by first describing competitive bidding with the more standard low-price auction and examine how bidding incentives change when the contract is allocated using the ABA. It will make for an easier discussion if we think about a bid being the price that the firm would be paid if it is awarded the contract (where the price is the reserve price less the offered discount).[3]

In submitting a bid, a firm is assumed to do so with the objective of maximizing its expected profit. Expected profit is the product of two terms: 1) the profit the firm earns should it win the auction; and 2) the probability that it wins the auction. In both the low-price auction and ABA formats, the profit earned in the event of winning is the same: the firm's bid (which is the price it receives) minus its cost of

---

[3] For the formal equilibrium analysis of these two auction formats under competition and collusion, see Decarolis (2018).

fulfilling the contract. Where the two formats differ is how a firm's bid affects the probability of winning. With the low-price auction, a firm faces a trade-off: bidding a lower price increases the likelihood that its price is the lowest and thus wins the auction, but the realized profit is lower should it win. The optimal bidding strategy balances these two forces and the net effect is that a firm bids above its cost (so it has some profit in the event it wins) but not too much above (in order to have a reasonable chance of winning). How much it raises its bid above its cost will depend on how competitive the auction is expected to be. More competition – as reflected in more bidders or rival bidders have lower cost (and thus willing to bid lower) – will cause a bidder to set a lower bid. All that is good for the procurer.

Bidding incentives are very different with the ABA. While a firm's profit from winning is higher when its bid is higher, the probability of winning is higher only when its bid is closer to the average bid. One implication is that a bidder wants to avoid having a relatively low bid because it will then be far away from the average bid and thus have little chance of winning the auction. (For example, in the Turin format, a bidder would have zero chance of winning if its price is in the bottom 10 percent.) Thus, a bidder does not want to be too aggressive as it is a lose–lose proposition, for it delivers a low probability of winning the auction and low profit should it win. A firm will want to bid near the conjectured average bid of other bidders, at least as long as that bid is above the firm's cost. To do otherwise would create little chance of winning the auction.

For the ABA format, bidding will depend very much on what firms expect will be the average bid. If they feel the average bid will be low then all will bid low in order to be close to the conjectured average. If they feel the average bid will be high then all will bid high. There is not that general force driving bids down as in the low-price auction because the incentive is to bid like everyone else, rather than to undercut everyone else's bids. Returning to the Turin procurement auction where bids take the form of discounts off the reserve price, competition could result in all bidders submitting relatively large discounts (which is desirable for the procurer) or submitting relatively small discounts, perhaps even zero (which is undesirable for the procurer as they end up paying a price close to their reserve price).

9.2.3 Collusive Bidding

Let us now turn to how the auction rules affect collusion. For the low-price auction, competition drives firms to bid low prices (or, equivalently, high discounts) in order to increase their chances of winning. The appeal of collusion is that firms could all be better off if they were to inflate their bids (or, equivalently, depress their discounts) and take turns winning (bid rotation) or sharing profits through subcontracting (which is particularly feasible with construction projects) or direct side payments. While a collusive agreement is then collectively attractive, is it stable? That is, will firms find it in their individual best interests to comply? When another cartel member is designated to win the current auction, a firm is supposed to submit a price exceeding the price of the designated winner (typically known as a "cover bid") in order to ensure it loses. However, it may be tempted to deviate from the collusive agreement and just undercut the designated winner's price so as to win the contract. That temptation can periodically lead to deviations and affect the extent and duration of collusion.

In contrast, there is no such challenge to cartel stability with the ABA format. Suppose that competitive bidding is resulting in firms believing that submitted prices are relatively low. Thus, in order to have a chance to win, a bidder must then submit a relatively low price in order for it to be close to the average bid. Now consider firms forming a cartel. All they need to do is to agree to all submit high prices. That will reap higher profits – just as with the low-price auction – but there will be no temptation to deviate. A firm that thinks about submitting a higher or lower price will move their bid farther away from the average bid and thus *reduce* its chances of winning. The ABA format thus makes collusion less difficult because cartel stability is greater as a result of its design.

The ABA format also creates an incentive for a subset of firms to form a cartel in order to increase their chances of winning. This is true whether other bidders are competing or colluding. If a sufficiently large number of firms form a coalition, they can move the average bid (such as A2 in the Turin format) up or down in a manner to cause their bids to be closer to the average bid than the bids of firms outside of their coalition (Decarolis, 2018). Even if the winning bid is decreased (because the average bid is decreased) so the price received is lower, the coalition members can benefit because each has a higher likelihood of winning when their coordinated manipulation of bids moves the average bid closer to their bids. As a result, a group of competing bidders can respond to the formation of a collusive subgroup by also colluding as a subgroup and earn higher profit.

To underscore this point, let us explain how collusion by a subset of firms can be profitable even when competitive bidding has very low discounts and thus very high prices. Suppose, under competition, all firms submit a zero discount (thus proposing to be paid the highest price to complete the job). Individually, no firm has an incentive to offer a positive discount because that will cause its bid to be farther away from the average bid. However, a coalition of firms can raise their profit by coordinating on a positive discount. To see how this can happen, consider the following example: there are fifty firms bidding with a reserve price equal to €300,000.[4] If all firms offer a zero discount, each firm has an expected revenue of €6,000 (since the probability of winning for each firm is 1/50). Suppose that seven firms form a cartel. One of them submits a small discount of, say, 1 percent, and the other six submit discounts of, say, 5 percent. By the rules of the Turin ABA, the top 10 percent of the bids are eliminated (which means five of the 5 percent discounts) and the bottom 10 percent of the bids are eliminated (which means five of the 0 percent discounts). This leave thirty-eight bids with a zero discount, one bid with a

[4] The choice of these values approximates those in the prototypical ABA from the court case in Turin.

1 percent discount, and one bid with a 5 percent discount (where the latter two are from the cartel). The average of those discounts is a 0.15 percent discount (which is A1). The discounts above A1 – which are the 1 and 5 percent discounts – have an average of 3 percent (which is A2). The winning discount is 1 percent as it is the highest discount just below A2. Thus, the cartel member with the 1 percent discount wins for sure. If the seven cartel members randomly determine who would be the designated winner then the expected revenue for a cartel member is $(1/7)*(1-0.01)*300,000 = €42,429$ which is far above its expected revenue of €6,000 by not colluding. This simple calculation illustrates a striking point: the design of the ABA creates a powerful incentive for cartel formation.

The civil engineering literature (Ioannou and Leu, 1993) that developed the ABA did not consider the strategic (or game-theoretic) considerations described above. It was implicitly assumed that firms would continue to submit the same bids and it did not consider how firms would adapt their behaviour to respond to the incentives created by changing the rules of the auction. However, it is naïve to think that a change in the auction rules would not affect how firms bid or the likelihood that they would form a cartel, or several competing cartels, and coordinate and coordinate their bids.

A series of studies of the ABA format documents how bidders strategically adjusted their behavior to the auction format. For example, Decarolis (2018) reports that when a law reform in Italy allowed public buyers to (temporarily) abandon ABA in favor of low-price auctions, this triggered changes in the bidding behavior. Given its attractive features for collusion, we should expect that the ABA bolsters cartel formation. Exactly how is more nuanced, but the fundamental intuition is simple: a bidder in the ABA can coordinate with other bidders to manipulate the location of the threshold that determines the winner. Since jointly manipulating a threshold that is based on an average of the bids is relatively easy, bid coordination helps the bidders because the expected payoffs will typically increase due to the higher probability of winning the auction.

In the many years since various government procurers in Italy adopted the ABA format in 1998, documented episodes of collusion have abounded. However, none is more effective in illustrating the perverse connection between ABAs and cartel activity than that of the Turin Court of Justice, first Criminal Section, April 28, 2008, sentence N. 2549/06 R.G. This case involves an unusually large number of firms, ninety-five, with multiple cartels operating simultaneously within the same market. Indeed, so powerful were the incentives created by the ABA format for cartel formation that eight cartels emerged and started to compete against each other in manipulating the auctions.

9.3 CARTEL BIRTH AND FORMATION

The ruling by the Turin Court of Justice contains valuable material to understand what led to cartel formation. This material includes both detailed data about all the bids in nearly 300 ABAs (from the inception of this system, until the cartel were discovered) and confessions of some of the firms' owners and managers, as well as the email exchanges and phone call conversations captured by the police during an investigation phase that lasted more than two years. The picture that emerges is essentially the following. An anticorruption crackdown in the early 1990s lead the Italian parliament to pass a public procurement law centered around having transparent low-price auctions. Soon enough, however, the perverse effects of excessive competition described at the start of the case study kicked in, which lead to the adoption of the ABA format starting in 1998. After some fine-tuning, the ABA format described in Section 9.2.1 was implemented in 2000.

In the Court case, several of the defendants argued explicitly that it was the introduction of the ABA that "forced" them to form cartels. Their argument was basically as follows. A large cartel of firms from the South of Italy started bidding in the ABAs held by the County and Municipality of Turin. This cartel was sufficiently large that, through the coordination of its members' bids, it was able to secure winning the project in nearly all the auctions. Local firms were then obliged to either accept working as subcontractors or stay out of all public contracts. The response was the formation of other cartels, mostly composed of local firms based in the Turin area, intended to give them a better chance of winning these auctions. Bruno Bresciani, owner and general manager of one of the colluding firms, testified having made the following remark about the first meeting in which his cartel was formed:

> At the first meeting they said: "Why should we kill ourselves and let those coming from the outside laugh at us?" Here [in Turin] firms from the South were coming and getting the jobs, setting the averages, they used to come with 20, 30 or 40 bids, they used to get the jobs and then what was left for us?

The co-existence of multiple cartels that compete (and sometimes also cooperated) in the same auction is a rather unique feature of the cartel episode studied here. From what can be derived from the court materials, these cartels where closely connected to the municipalities where the firms were located; specifically, firms in the same city pooled together to form bidding rings. This underscores the importance of "proximity" both in a geographical and a social sense; being "close" to each other allowed the firms to meet and coordinate on their illegal activities. That public procurement auctions took place frequently across many thousands of public buyers (there is a total of approximately 35,000 public buyers in Italy) created the need to meet frequently to coordinate on which auctions to enter and how to bid.

9.4 CARTEL OPERATION AND EFFECT

Mr. Bresciani was found guilty of having rigged ninety-four average bid auctions along with other related crimes, and was sentenced to seven years of jail in 2008.[5] He was one of the two leading members of

---

[5] In the Italian jurisdiction, bid rigging that involves public contracts is a crime ("turbativa d'asta").

a cartel known as San Mauro because most of the cartel members were headquartered in the municipality of San Mauro Torinese, which is a small city near Turin. At sentencing, the court explained that the members of the San Mauro cartel regularly coordinated their actions to manipulate ABAs in the Turin area. In particular, they: (i) determined the bids that each member was to submit, (ii) collected data about potentially interesting ABAs and about rival firms' strategies through a shared entity (a firm consortium, "Consorzio Imprenditori Subalpini"), (iii) decided on which ABAs to enter, (iv) determined the designated winner, (v) coordinated actions with two of the other cartels to limit competition, (vi) secured the help of firms outside the cartels when the expected number of bids required to pilot the ABA was particularly high, and (vii) implemented rotation and subcontracting schemes to remunerate cartel members.

Overall, the eight cartels were very successful in their activity. Despite representing no more than 10 percent of the firms in the market, they won about 80 percent of all auctions held in the Piedmont region between 2000 and 2003. One cartel was composed of firms that were already part of an economically powerful consortium ("Cooperative") operating in the North-east of Italy: its core was composed of nineteen firms, but only a few of them were the designated winners in the Turin area ABAs. The other cartel members helped these firms in exchange for reciprocation in ABAs held in different geographic areas where they had interest.

All other cartels were formed by firms geographically close to each other, which is a reminder of the importance that geographical proximity plays in lowering coordination costs among cartel members. Indeed, the extent of coordination activity required by a cartel to operate successfully is extensive, as the aforementioned list provided by Mr. Bresciani and other cartel members illustrates. Three crucial dimensions of coordination are participation, bidding, and subcontracting. We now turn to describe each one of these activities, while emphasizing how the rules of the ABA shaped the specific strategies undertaken by the cartels.

9.4.1 Participation

ABAs tend to have higher participation than low-price auctions. In the latter, competition drives up the winning discount. Thus, only firms with very competitive cost structures can participate in the tender with a reasonable chance of winning. On the contrary, in ABAs, the lowering of discounts allows even highly inefficient companies to participate with the expectation of a profit after being awarded a contract. This implies that ABAs should have higher participation, which is confirmed by the data. By exploiting some regulatory changes in Italy that alternated the two auction formats, it was found that the number of offers per tender went from about sixty offers for ABAs (on average, but with peaks from 100 to 300 offers) to about seven offers for low-price auctions (for the exact same type of contracts and in the same geographical areas).

With such a large number of participants, it comes as no surprise that cartels needed to coordinate the participation of a large number of firms. The size of the cartels as assessed in the court case ranged from six to nineteen firms. But not all firms could bid in all ABAs as rules about financial and technical capacity restrict participation. Generally, the larger the project size (as measured by the engineering estimate), the more restrictive are the participation requirements. As a result, cartels needed to exert substantial effort in mobilizing all of their members eligible to bid to participate, and then accurately estimating the number of total bidders in each auction. A related point of interest is that if a single firm could control multiple bids, this would be valuable in the context of an ABA as it could better manipulate the average bid. However, as regulations in Italy prohibited a firm from submitting more than one bid, several firms gamed the system by creating shadow subsidiaries (shills) so that they could submit several bids. The fact that, despite the costs of setting up a new firm, multiple suppliers did create shill firms (often formally owned by a relative of the "mother company" owner) testifies to the powerful and distorted incentives created by ABAs.

9.4.2 Bidding

The second coordination activity involves joint bidding. Here the cartels operated in ways that are both sophisticated and remarkably close to what the relevant economic models predict. In particular, they coordinated their price bids by clustering them either on relatively high values (to move the average bid upward) or on relatively low values (to move the average bid downward), but never combining high and low bids within the same auction (which would cancel out the effects of these bids on the average bid).

The choice of whether to manipulate the average upward or downward was, according to the confessions reported in the court case, the result of fairly complex calculations: if successful, downward manipulations lead to a lower winning discount and, hence, higher profits, but the nuances of how the threshold is determined make downward manipulations harder (in the sense of requiring more bids) than the upward ones (indeed, recall from the previous discussion that the threshold A2 is calculated by looking only at those discounts above A1).

A common bid rigging strategy used by a cartel is illustrated in Figure 9.2, which reports all of the bids submitted in one of the ABAs that was part of the court case. Bids (i.e., discounts to be applied to the reserve price) are on the vertical axis, and firms are ordered on the horizontal axis from the lowest (on the left) to the highest discount (on the right). Two features are worth noting. First, most bids are concentrated around 18 percent. We know why from the court case. In order to infer what other bidders might be thinking about the value of A2, bidders rely on the observation of past auctions. Since past auctions in Turin used to have A2 close to 18 percent, this value is a natural guess of where other bidders are expecting A2 to lie.

Notice that this belief is self-fulfilling: if all bidders bid close to 18 percent because they believe others believe A2 will be close to 18 percent, then A2 will indeed be close to 18 percent. But now let's bring into this picture strategic behavior by a cartel. A cartel knowing that

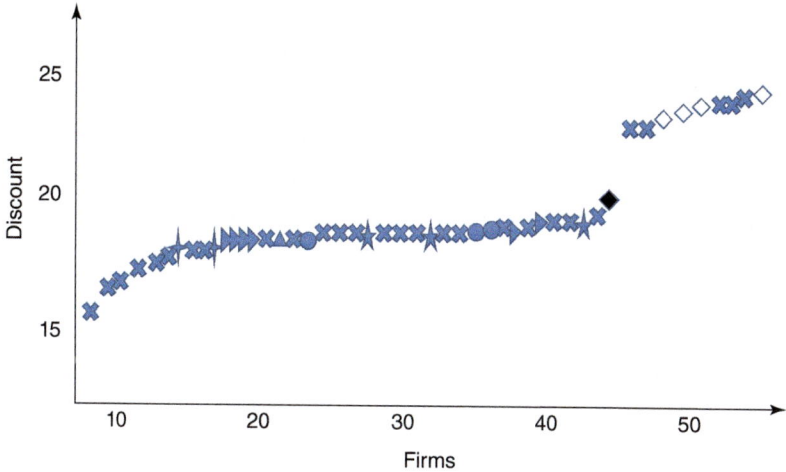

FIGURE 9.2 Bids from an ABA in the Turin trial case.
Note: Discounts offered in one ABA. The horizontal axis marks all the fifty-six bidders that participated in this auction, while the vertical axis reports the discount they offered. The firms are sorted to be in increasing order of the discount offered. Almost all bidders are offered a discount close to 18 percent. The different symbols mark different cartels, but the symbol x indicates noncoordinating firms. The diamond symbol, ◇, is used for the bids of the winning cartel: the dark, full diamond represents the winner's bid, while the hollow diamonds represent the nonwinning members of this cartel. The nine highest discounts comply with the description of "supporting bids" presented in the text. This figure and its note are reproduced from Conley and Decarolis (2016).

most other bidders will bid close to 18 percent and having an estimate of about sixty bidders participating can figure out how to manipulate A2 so that the cartels' bids are closer to (and just above) A2 so a cartel member has a good chance of winning the auction.

In Figure 9.2, different cartels are marked with different symbols – stars, triangles, circles, and diamonds – with an X representing a non-cartel firm. Let us focus on the "diamond" cartel which has five members with the lowest bid proving to be the winning bid (depicted as the black diamond). The bid of the black diamond is somewhere near 20 percent. Why did this firm offer a discount distinctly above 18 percent? Because its cartel was manipulating A2 upward by placing several very high bids (the four other diamonds) at discounts close to 25 percent. This example is revealing not only of a cartel's strategic conduct, but also of its effect on non-cartel firms who are surely worse off as a result, as the cartel has lowered those firms' probability of winning and forced up the winning discount which reduces a non-cartel member's profit should they be so fortunate as to win.[6]

There is the question of how many bids should the cartel place and where exactly should the cartel's designated winner place its bid. These are quite complex calculations that are conducted under uncertainty about who is participating and what they are (expected to be) bidding. In the case of Figure 9.2, the cartel was successful in its strategy because they correctly figured out that with nearly sixty participants and only five of the cartel firms qualified to bid in this ABA, they needed to secure the help of some other firms outside the cartel. Consequently, they shopped around for five firms outside of the cartel to submit bids; these are the five X's in Figure 9.2 that are next to the four diamonds.[7]

9.4.3 Subcontracting, Rotation, and Side Payments

With the ABA, there is extensive use of subcontractors which is only partly due to cartel activities. Recall that ABAs induce high participation as even highly inefficient firms have a chance of winning by properly guessing A2 and bidding near it (as long as they are not so inefficient that their cost exceeds A2). But, when this happens, the inefficient firm might find it more profitable to resell the contract via subcontracting to a more efficient firm for execution. Moving to subcontracting by a cartel, the motives are twofold. On the one hand, subcontracts awarded to cartel members are one of the methods for

---

[6] The analysis in Conley and Decarolis (2016) offers a quantification of the effects of the cartels in terms of damages for both the public administration and the noncolluding firms.

[7] Most likely the other cartels that participated in this auction were unable to manipulate a sufficiently large number of bids to secure an effective manipulation strategy and, hence, resorted to bidding close to the reference value of 18 percent.

implementing side payments which help ensure the stability of the cartel agreement. On the other hand, subcontracts awarded to firms outside the cartel can be justified by either reselling the contract to more productive firms or repaying outside firms for their help in manipulating A2 (as discussed in connection with Figure 9.2).

While all eight cartels followed the same bid and entry coordination strategies, they differed in how they shared rents. Most of the cartels used bid rotation schemes (designating different winners across different auctions), but some cartels also extensively used subcontracting and, in the case of one cartel, even cash transfers between members were routinely used. Nevertheless, despite the broad set of tools that the cartels had to sustain their illegal agreement, complaints from cartel members about not being sufficiently rewarded through subcontracts or rotation were among the causes that ultimately led to the authorities discovering the cartels.

9.5 CARTEL STABILITY AND DEATH

Cartels among bidders in the Turin procurement auctions were long lasting, but not fully stable. These cartels lasted for about five years until the police arrested a large number of individuals implicated in the cartel in the winter of 2003. However, during the previous years of activity, the cartels' members were regularly changing, as it grew by co-opting formerly independent firms and shrunk as members abandoned the cartel over the sharing of the cartel's profits.

The case documents reveal the tensions that existed inside the cartels. They needed a large number of members to effectively manipulate A2, but maintaining cartel discipline was difficult with a large number of members as they all wanted to win some auctions. Rotation of the designated winner was preferred to receiving subcontracts or side payments because, only by winning some contracts, firms could earn the qualification points needed to be eligible to participate in future auctions. This led to various episodes of noncompliance with the cartel agreement. An interesting act of deviation involved the "informants" (as they were referred to in the court case) who were cartel members that sold information about their cartel's bidding strategy to rival cartels. Sometimes they did so before leaving their cartel and transitioning to a rival cartel, but some of the cases appear to be driven by pure grievance about how their own cartel was treating them. This situation proved to be important during the judicial trial. Although the police investigation was started on the basis of the complaint from the public buyer (the city of Turin) who had noticed systematic coordination in the bid and participation of several firms, the hard feelings among several cartel members led several of them to confess their crimes and report the cartels' illegal activities.

The conviction of many cartel members in this case, as well as the fact that the city of Turin passed a law switching from the ABA to low-price auctions, likely terminated cartel activities for some time. However, ABAs are still widely used in Italy (even Turin has returned to this auction format) and collusion is likely to be still occurring.

9.6 CARTEL DETECTION

Given that the cartel behavior, as we have argued, at an ABA has several distinguished features, can we use that information to design a method for detecting cartels? The study of Conley and Decarolis (2011) is motivated precisely by this question and its answer is that it is indeed possible. Since the kind of behavior (in terms of both bids and participation) of colluding firms differs substantially from that of firms outside the group, statistical tests can be designed to capture these differences and detect (potential) cartels. The metrics for identifying participation and bidding patterns are motivated by how colluding firms can coordinate their bids to manipulate the thresholds that determine the awarding of the contract.

The basic idea is to compare the behaviour of a suspected cartel to that of "comparable" reference groups of plausibly competing firms, and then assess whether the behaviour of the suspected cartel is sufficiently different relative to that of this reference group in the sense that their behaviour is very unlikely based on the empirical distribution generated by the reference groups. For instance, consider

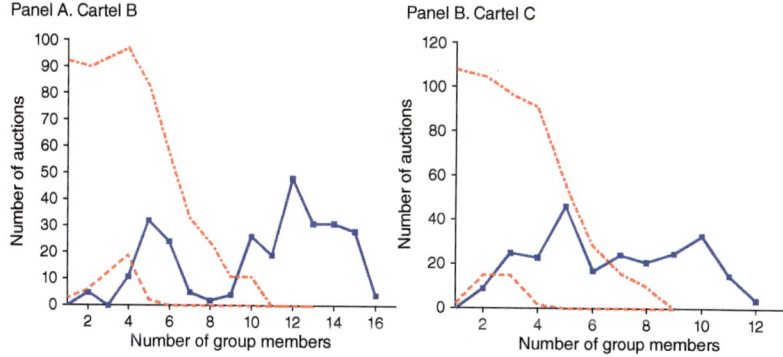

FIGURE 9.3 Outcomes of the participation test for two cartels.
Note: the figure is an adaptation from figure 2 in Conley and Decarolis (2016). It illustrates the outcomes of participation tests for two cartels: Cartel B on the left and Cartel C on the right. The solid, blue line represents on the Y axis the number of auctions jointly entered by the cartel members of different size (the size is on the X axis). The red, dashed line is the 5th percentile of the reference distribution. The red, dash-dot line is the 95th percentile of the reference distribution.

a test for joint participation: cartel members attend the same auctions to effectively manipulate A2. Hence, for colluding firms, their frequency of jointly participating in the same auctions should be substantially higher than the frequency of joint participation of a random group of firms (conditional on observable firm characteristics that contribute to determine participation, like firm location relative to the worksite and their legal qualification to participate). By repeatedly sampling random groups of firms that are comparable to those in the cartel and calculating their observed frequency of joint participation, we can construct a reference distribution for joint participation and assess whether or not the likelihood of joint participation of the suspect group is low relative to this reference distribution.

To clarify how the test works, Figure 9.3 reports the outcomes of the test for two of the Turin cartels. This figure shows how exactly one is able to statistically distinguish between competition and collusion based on participation in multiple ABAs. The red lines are the 5th and 95th percentiles of the number of auctions jointly participated by a random group of firms of the same group size with the same firm characteristics as the firms in the suspected cartel (whose joint bidding patterns are described by the solid blue line).

Consider Panel A where the suspected cartel (Cartel B) has at most sixteen of its members simultaneously participating in the same auctions and this happens in five of the auctions in the data set. In comparison, the value of the 95th percentile of the reference distribution for the case of joint participation by sixteen-member groups is zero. Stated differently: given a candidate cartel that has N members and observing the characteristics of these N firms in terms of their geographical location and eligibility to bid, we can construct, say, 1,000 other N-member groups by drawing the group traits in a way that matches the firms in the cartel (again in terms of location and eligibility requirements). Then we can calculate how many times the N-firm cartel has all of its members jointly participating in the ABAs as present in the data. We can do the same calculation for each one of the simulated 1,000 groups. Based on the latter, we can calculate the 5th and 95th percentiles of joint bidding as the reference distribution in the test statistics.

Based on the theoretical prediction that a cartel strategy entails joint participation, we predict that a cartel will have a frequency of joint participation that is higher than that of the 95th percentile of the reference distribution for the largest group sizes and lower than the 5th percentile of the reference distribution for the smallest group sizes. In Panel A of Figure 9.3, if we consider cases in which the cartel participates with all of its sixteen members, the frequency of joint participation is indeed higher than that of the reference distribution. The same is true when we consider the joint participation involving fifteen, fourteen, thirteen, twelve, eleven or ten of the cartel members. Hence, for all of the instances of the largest group sizes, it is indeed the case that the joint participation by cartel members is higher than the 95th percentile of the reference distribution. Such joint participation is highly unlikely in the absence of a cartel. The tests (one for each of the cartel sizes from ten to sixteen) indicates coordinated entry into these auctions.

Similarly, when we look at the smallest group sizes, the theory indicates that a cartel should not have its members jointly participate in small numbers (for, if participation is costly, doing so is wasteful as the chances of manipulating A2 to their benefit is small). The evidence in Panel A indicates that this is indeed the case for Cartel B, as participation by a single cartel member (or by two, three or four members) is less frequent than the 5th percentile of the reference distribution. Therefore, these participation tests do confirm coordinated entry by the cartel firms. Finally, Panel A shows that for groups of intermediate size (between five and nine members), there is no statistical difference between the joint participation of the cartel and that of the reference distribution (i.e., the value observed for the cartel is within the interval between the 5th and 95th percentiles of the reference distribution). Such a pattern is in line with the theoretical predictions because it is for the smallest and largest group sizes that we expect a cartel to follow behaviour that distinguishes it from a group of noncolluding firms.

In Panel B, the same patterns can be observed for a different cartel (Cartel C). The differences in the red and blue lines between panels A and B are due to the fact that the two cartels have different sizes and are composed of members with different characteristics, thus determining the construction of different groups of firms as part of their reference distribution.

A similar test can be constructed for bidding by exploiting the property explained earlier that cartel members should pool bids on the same side of the bid distribution, either all submit relatively high bids or all submit relatively low bids. The interested reader is referred to Conley and Decarolis (2016) where the test for the presence of cartel-using bids is described.

When applied to the data set of auctions that were part of the Turin case, the bidding and participation tests manage to replicate almost perfectly the structure of the cartels detected by the police investigation. Even more interestingly, when the tests are applied to a larger dataset of ABAs from 2005 to 2010 which were not part of the case, the tests also identify a large number of potentials cartels. Strikingly, a conservative estimate of their penetration is that at least 50 percent of ABAs entailed bids that were rigged by cartels.

9.7 CONCLUSIONS

The insights developed through the discussion of the Turin cartel case involving average bid auctions (ABA) in Italy should make clear how the procurement rules can affect cartel formation. An important lesson for procurers therefore is to always consider how their procurement procedure affects bidding incentives under both competition and collusion and the incentive for firms to form a stable and profitable cartel. The ABA format is clearly not a great advance over lowest price auctions when the risks of it inducing collusion are taken into account. A second main insight from the case study is that an understanding of the cartel's response to the procurement procedure can guide its detection. For the ABA format, the frequency of joint participation becomes a relevant statistic to raise suspicion of collusion. Given the large number of settings where both points are relevant, it is highly conceivable that more cartel cases will emerge in the future and that statistical tests similar to those described here can contribute to their detection.

REFERENCES

Abrantes-Metz, R., and P. Bajari (2012) "Screens for Conspiracies and Their Multiple Applications," *Competition Policy International Journal*, 8(1), 177–183.

Baranek, B., L. Musolff, and V. Titl (2021) "Detection of Collusive Networks in E-procurement," working paper Princeton University.

Chassang, S. and J. Ortner (2019) "Collusion in Auctions with Constrained Bids: Theory and Evidence from Public Procurement," *Journal of Political Economy*, 127, 2269–2300.

Conley, T., and F. Decarolis (2016) "Detecting Bidders Groups in Collusive Auctions," *American Economic Journal: Microeconomics*, 8(2), 1–38.

Curto, V., L. Einav, J. Levin, and J. Bhattacharya (2021) "Can Health Insurance Competition Work? Evidence from Medicare Advantage," *Journal of Political Economy*, 129(2), 570–606.

Decarolis, F. (2015) "Medicare Part D: Are Insurers Gaming the Low Income Subsidy Design?" *American Economic Review*, 105(4), 1547–1580.

Decarolis, F. (2018) "Comparing Procurement Auctions," *International Economic Review*, 59(2), 391–419.

Decarolis, F., M. Polyakova and S. Ryan (2020) "Subsidy Design in Privately Provided Social Insurance: Lessons from Medicare Part D," *Journal of Political Economy*, 128(5), 1712–1752.

European Commission (2002) "Prevention, Detection and Elimination of Abnormally Low Tenders in the European Construction Industry," Enterprise and Industry Report.

Hendricks, K. and R. Porter (1988) "An Empirical Study of an Auction with Asymmetric Information," *American Economic Review*, 78, 865–883.

Ioannou, P. G., and S.-S. Leu (1993) "Average-Bid Method. Competitive Bidding Strategy," *Journal of Construction Engineering and Management*, 119(1), 131–147.

Kastl, J. and A. Hortacsu (2012) "Valuing Dealers' Information Advantage: A Study of Canadian Treasury Auctions," *Econometrica*, 80(6), 2511–2542.

Kawai, K. and J. Nakabayashi (2022) "Detecting Large-Scale Collusion in Procurement Auctions," *Journal of Political Economy*, 130, 1585–1629.

Klemperer, P. (2002) "What Really Matters in Auction Design," *Journal of Economic Perspectives*, 16 (1): 169–189.

Lopomo, P., N. Persico and A. Villa (2022) "Optimal Procurement with Quality Concerns," working paper Northwestern University.

Myerson, R. (1981) "Optimal Auction Design," *Mathematics of Operations Research*, 6, 58–73.

Porter, R. H. and J. D. Zona (1993) "Detection of Bid Rigging in Procurement Auctions," *Journal of Political Economy*, 101, 518–538.

Porter, R. H. and J. D. Zona (1999) "Ohio School Milk Markets: An Analysis of Bidding," *RAND Journal of Economics*, 30, 263–288.

Roth, A. (2002) "The Economist as Engineer: Game Theory, Experimentation, and Computation Tools for Design Economics," *Econometrica*, 70(4), 1341–1378.

Roth, A. (2018) "Marketplaces, Markets, and Market Design," *American Economic Review*, 108(7): 1609–1658.

Schurter, K. (2020) "Identification and inference in first-price auctions with collusion," working paper, University of Chicago.

10 The Challenges of Cartelization with Many Products and Ongoing Technological Advancements
*Liquid Crystal Displays Worldwide**

Dennis Carlton, Mark Israel, Ian MacSwain, and Allan Shampine

10.1 INTRODUCTION

The liquid crystal display (LCD) cartel is an interesting case study of both the strong incentives that arise in an oligopoly to limit competition, and thus raise prices and profits, and also of the practical difficulties that can limit the success of such activity, even in the presence of frequent meetings by a large number of competitors over the course of years.

It is difficult to overstate the breadth of the conspiracy, which potentially impacted all uses of LCD panels. LCD panels were (and are) used in monitors, laptop computers, televisions, and phones, as well as other applications. However, during the relevant period, the sizes and quality of the panels changed significantly (both within a given application, as well as across applications), leading to the extreme breadth of the cartel, but also presenting challenges for how the cartel would accommodate the regular introduction of new and better products.

Given multiple guilty pleas, the existence of price-fixing activity is not in doubt, and the cartel activities have been documented with cooperation from some participants and through discovery in

---

* Compass Lexecon was retained on behalf of the joint defense group In re TFT-LCD (Flat Panel) Antitrust Litigation and related litigations. Dennis Carlton testified on behalf of Defendants. The authors would like to thank Joseph Harrington and Maarten Pieter Schinkel for their insightful review and comments.

extensive litigation. For example, the cartel was exposed by Samsung under an amnesty arrangement.[1] Many firms in the industry entered guilty pleas in various forums, including Chi Mei, Chunghwa, Epson, HannStar, Hitachi, LG Display, and Sharp.[2]

Governments imposed billions of dollars of fines, which in some cases were reduced in exchange for cooperation by the companies.[3] For example, LG paid $400 million to the US Department of Justice (DOJ), €215 million to the European Competition Commission (ECC), and ₩65.52 billion to the Korean Fair Trade Commission (KFTC); CMO paid $220 million, €300 million, and ₩1.55 billion, respectively; AUO paid $500 million, €116.8 million, and ₩28.53 billion, respectively; and Samsung as a cooperator paid nothing to the DOJ or ECC, but still paid ₩97.29 billion to the KFTC.[4] More than twenty

---

[1] See, e.g., European Commission press release, "Antitrust: Commission fines six LCD panel producers €648 million for pricing fixing cartel," December 8, 2010, https://ec.europa.eu/commission/presscorner/detail/es/IP_10_1685.

[2] See, e.g., Plea Agreements in *United States of America* v. *Chi Mei Optoelectronics*, February 2, 2010; *United States of America* v. *Chunghwa Picture Tubes, Ltd.*, November 10, 2008; *United States of America* v. *Epson Imaging Devices Corporation*, October 23, 2009; *United States of America* v. *HannStar Display Corporation*, June 29, 2010; *United States of America* v. *Hitachi Displays Ltd.*, May 17, 2009; *United States of America* v. *LG Display Company, ltd. and LG Display America, Inc.*, December 8, 2008; and *United States of America* v. *Sharp*, December 8, 2008.

[3] See, e.g., Plea Agreements in *United States of America* v. *Chi Mei Optoelectronics*, February 2, 2010; *United States of America* v. *Chunghwa Picture Tubes, Ltd.*, November 10, 2008; *United States of America* v. *Epson Imaging Devices Corporation*, October 23, 2009; *United States of America* v. *HannStar Display Corporation*, June 29, 2010; *United States of America* v. *Hitachi Displays Ltd.*, May 17, 2009; *United States of America* v. *LG Display Company, ltd. and LG Display America, Inc.*, December 8, 2008; and *United States of America* v. *Sharp*, December 8, 2008. European Commission press release, "Antitrust: Commission fines six LCD panel producers €648 million for pricing fixing cartel," December 8, 2010, https://ec.europa.eu/commission/presscorner/detail/es/IP_10_1685.

[4] See, e.g., Plea Agreements in *United States of America* v. *Chi Mei Optoelectronics*, February 2, 2010; *United States of America* v. *Chunghwa Picture Tubes, Ltd.*, November 10, 2008; *United States of America* v. *Epson Imaging Devices Corporation*, October 23, 2009; *United States of America* v. *HannStar Display Corporation*, June 29, 2010; *United States of America* v. *Hitachi Displays Ltd.*, May 17, 2009; *United States of America* v. *LG Display Company, ltd. and LG Display America, Inc.*, December 8, 2008; and *United States of America* v. *Sharp*, December 8, 2008. European Commission press release, "Antitrust: Commission

executives were criminally indicted in the USA alone.[5] Civil litigation followed alleging an even broader conspiracy than that alleged by the governments. Massive private settlements and court verdicts, again totaling in the billions of dollars, followed. Indirect purchasers in US civil litigation obtained $1.1 billion in settlement, and direct purchasers obtained $473 million in settlement, not including opt-out plaintiffs and defendants that did not settle.[6]

The cartel conduct claims varied, but cartel activity started as early as 1996 and continued until 2006.[7] The specific dates and participants were subject to dispute. For example, civil plaintiffs claimed a single, overarching conspiracy involving many defendants,[8] but the DOJ claimed multiple smaller conspiracies starting at different times.[9] While there were multiple guilty pleas, the specifics of what was pled also varied. For example, Korean and Taiwanese conspirators pled guilty to a conspiracy starting in 2001, but Japanese conspirators pled guilty to separate conspiracies at different periods of time,[10] and Toshiba, a defendant in much of the civil litigation, never pled guilty

fines six LCD panel producers €648 million for pricing fixing cartel," December 8, 2010, https://ec.europa.eu/commission/presscorner/detail/es/IP_10_1685. *Taiwan-Based AU Optronics Corporation Sentenced to Pay $500 Million for Role in LCD Price-Fixing Conspiracy*, September 20, 2012, www.justice.gov/opa/pr/taiwan-based-au-optronics-corporation-sentenced-pay-500-million-criminal-fine-role-lcd-price#:~:text=WASHINGTON%20%E2%80%94%20AU%20Optronics%20Corporation%2C%20a,panels%20sold%20worldwide%2C%20the%20Department.

[5] See Plea Agreements, *supra* note 2.
[6] See, e.g., LCD Flat Panel Indirect Purchase Antitrust Settlement for $1.1 billion, available at www.srgllc.com/us/en/settlements/electronics/lcd-indirect-purchaser; and LCD Flat Panel Direct Purchaser Antitrust Settlement for $473 million, available at www.srgllc.com/us/en/settlements/electronics/lcd-direct-purchaser.
[7] See, e.g., Complaint, Dell Inc. v. Sharp Corp. et al., (In re TFT-LCD (Flat Panel) Antitrust Litig.), March 12, 2010, 2.
[8] See, e.g., Complaint, Dell Inc. v. Sharp Corp. et al., (In re TFT-LCD (Flat Panel) Antitrust Litig.), March 12, 2010, 2.
[9] Expert Report of Professor Dennis W. Carlton, February 23, 2012, Redacted, available in Dell's Daubert Motion, Case 3:07-md-01827-SI, Document 7222, filed November 20, 2012 ("Carlton 2/2012 Redacted Report"), ¶ 68.
[10] Carlton (2012), ¶ 68.

at all.[11] This case study refers generally to participants and conspirators, but that should be understood as alleged participants as the precise list of participants was subject to dispute and not all firms accused admitted liability.

Overall, while it is clear that firms attempted to raise prices above competitive levels, the evidence shows that the effect was at most small as a percentage of price. This raises two questions. First, why was the cartel relatively ineffective? Second, given how ineffective the cartel was, why did the firms persist in meeting for so long? Did they think they were having a larger effect than they were, or expect the effect to grow over time?

This case study begins with a description of the industry and of the operations of the cartel, then turns to why the characteristics of the industry made it so difficult for a cartel to significantly raise prices across the wide breadth of product types being sold. Finally, it concludes with a discussion as to why the cartel persisted in light of those difficulties, and what the experiences of the LCD cartel teach us about cartel operations more generally.

10.2 DESCRIPTION OF THE INDUSTRY

An LCD panel is an electronic display device that operates by applying an electrical charge to a layer of liquid crystal, thereby inducing changes in its optical properties. LCD panels are used in a variety of products, including computer monitors, notebook computers, flat-panel televisions (TVs), and mobile devices, such as mobile phones, digital cameras, camcorders, and portable electronic games.[12]

---

[11] In at least one private litigation, Toshiba was found not liable. "Best Buy wins and loses LCD price fixing trial," September 9, 2013, available at www.lexology.com/library/detail.aspx?g=d2e09b80-821e-4ce9-b3e8-c36d9d57b69a.

[12] A TFT-LCD panel combined with a backlight unit, some electronic circuitry, and other components is referred to as a TFT-LCD "module." A TFT-LCD panel may be sold as a panel, a module, or embodied in a further-finished product such as a computer monitor. In this case study, raw panels and modules are referred to collectively as "panels."

The discussion in this case study centers primarily on TFT-LCD panels, made with a particular LCD technology that became ubiquitous in many products, and which were the subject of the various plea deals with the DOJ. During the relevant period, TFT-LCD panels became the dominant technology for monitors, laptop screens, television screens, and cell phone screens.[13] A TFT-LCD panel is composed of a layer of liquid crystal encapsulated between two glass substrates. One glass substrate has an array of thin film transistors and circuitry. The other glass substrate has color filters. When stimulated by an electrical charge, liquid crystals change the properties of light passing through the color filters, allowing an image to appear on the screen. TFT-LCDs are distinguished from earlier passive matrix technologies by the presence of a transistor at each pixel, the smallest picture element in a panel. Color and brightness at each pixel are electronically adjusted through manipulation of the optical properties of the liquid crystal via the transistor. Standard names have been adopted for several display resolutions (e.g., a configuration with 1,024 horizontal pixels by 768 vertical pixels is referred as a "1024x768" resolution, or "Extended Graphics Array" (XGA) display). From here on, we will refer to TFT-LCD panels simply as LCD panels.

LCD panels are produced in multibillion dollar fabrication plants, or "fabs," where each fab is equipped to handle a particular size of "motherglass," the sheets of glass that are cut to become multiple monitor panels, laptop panels, TV panels, etc.[14] Discussed in more detail below, as technology improved, successive generations of fabs were able to accommodate larger and larger sheets of motherglass, allowing for larger panels, improved efficiency, and lower unit costs.[15] For example, the size of motherglass for fabs at the beginning

---

[13] See, e.g., CDW, "LED vs. LCD Monitors – The Key Differences," www.cdw.com/content/cdw/en/articles/hardware/led-vs-lcd-computer-monitors.html; Abt, "TV Buying Guide," www.abt.com/learn/tv-buying-guide. The only difference between LCD and LED screens is the backlighting used for the panel, not the liquid crystal itself.

[14] Carlton (2012), 68–69.   [15] Carlton (2012), 68–69.

of the alleged cartel period was just over 1,000 square feet, and by the end of the alleged cartel period the most modern fabs could handle motherglass of over 18,000 square feet. Throughout the relevant period, cartel members built new fabs which continually added production capacity to the industry, as well as the ability to make larger and cheaper LCD panels. Notably, a decision by any firm not to build a new fab would not just have resulted in less capacity for that firm, it would have left them behind technologically – working with an older, higher-cost generation of fab.

An LCD panel is an intermediate good. Panel manufacturers do not sell panels directly to end consumers, but instead panels are sold to manufacturers that use the panels as an input into final goods, such as televisions, notebook computers, computer monitors, and mobile phones, which are in turn sold to end consumers. The allegations in this cartel are fixing the prices of LCD panels, not of finished goods. Therefore, the complicated manufacturing and distribution chain, including vertically integrated manufacturers who controlled much of the process, allow for many levels where any anticompetitive increase of LCD panel prices could be absorbed (or hidden) before reaching consumers, complicating attempts to use retail prices and pass through rates as a way to monitor adherence to pricing of LCD panels.

When discussing the LCD cartel, it is useful to group LCD panels into three broad categories made up of panels that are clearly distinct in their characteristics and primary manufacturers and, most importantly for the analysis of prices and alleged cartel effects, exhibit distinct pricing patterns. The three product categories are: 1) TV panels, which are generally larger than 20" diagonal; 2) monitor/notebook panels, which are generally between 10" and 20" diagonal (although there are examples of notebook panels below 10" and monitor panels over 20"); and 3) small panels used in mobile phones and other small devices. Significant differences remain even within these three groups. For example, within the monitor and notebook panel group, LCD monitor panels are simpler to make than LCD laptop

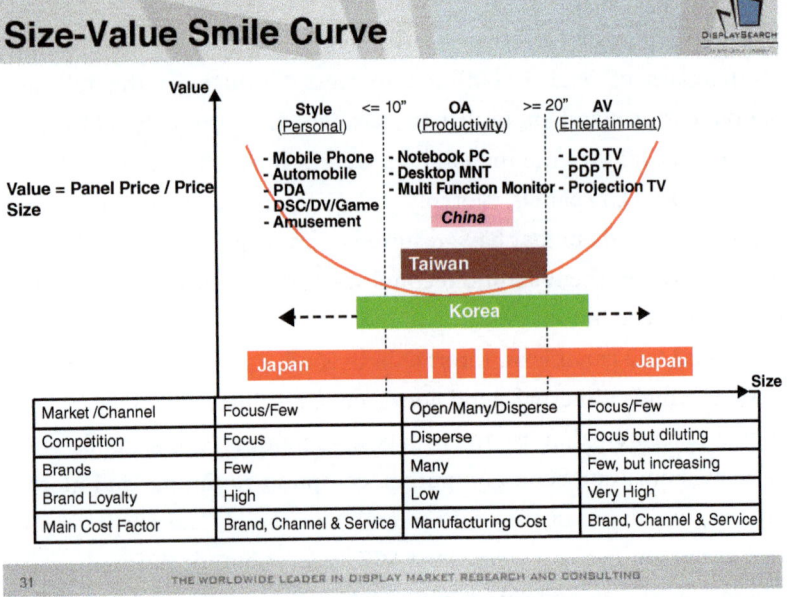

FIGURE 10.1 LCD panel value curve.[16]

panels as, for example, the laptop panels are designed for lower power consumption. Similarly, LCD monitor panels represent the vast majority of the functionality and cost of the finished product – a stand-alone LCD monitor – whereas a laptop panel is a part of a more complex finished product – a laptop computer with an integrated LCD screen.

As shown in Figure 10.1, "value" (measured as panel price/panel size) differs by category of panel, with both small panels (for mobile phones, automotive applications, hand-held video game consoles, and other uses) and larger panels for TVs having greater value per square inch than medium-sized panels for monitors and notebooks. This pattern follows from the fact that it is technically more difficult to produce very small panels and very large panels than to produce medium-sized panels. In addition, the main producers vary by size,

---

[16] Carlton (2012), 13. Figure drawn from David Hsieh (2005), 31.

with Taiwanese and (by the end of the cartel period) Chinese producers primarily focusing on the medium-sized monitor and notebook panels, Korean producers making the whole range of sizes, and Japanese producers primarily focusing on the higher-valued small and large panels. Figure 10.1 also lists several other differences across categories, including the fact that the main cost factors vary by category of panel.

Within the three main categories, panels can be distinguished by several additional characteristics, including application types, an array of sizes and resolutions, and other characteristics.

The range of applications for TFT-LCD panels includes not just the major applications discussed above (TVs, monitors/notebooks, and mobile phones), but also applications such as portable DVD players, GPS navigation systems, MP3 players, video cameras, digital still cameras, portable medical devices, refrigerators, car displays, and ATM displays. Figure 10.2 illustrates the breadth of panel applications in 2005, both for TFT-LCD panels and some alternative types of flat-panel displays.

Panel sizes and resolutions also do not fall into just a few size and resolution categories. Data produced by defendants during litigation contained more than 120 different panel sizes, ranging from less than 1 inch to 82 inches. In addition, there are over 25 different display standards, which combine with sizes to produce well over 300 unique display standard and size combinations sold by the alleged cartel members.[17]

Differentiation across panels, however, ranges far beyond size and resolution. Other relevant dimensions of differentiation include viewing angle, contrast, brightness, glare, refresh rates, color quality, response time, cosmetic specifications, "greenness," and thickness. Panel characteristics vary in importance depending on the application.[18] For

---

[17] Carlton (2012), 934.
[18] Carlton (2012), 935. See also, the general discussion of relevant characteristics in David Hsieh, "LCD Demand, Panels, Substrates All Move from Large to Larger,"

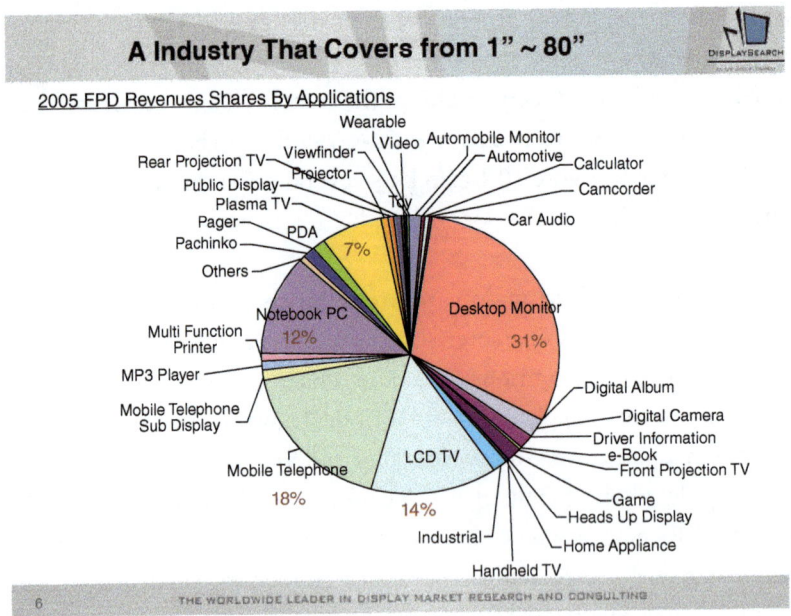

FIGURE 10.2 2005 flat-panel display shares by application.[19]

example, there are important differences in weight, size, and power consumption between monitor panels (which are relatively stationary and always plugged into a power source) and notebook computer panels (which are portable and often not plugged into a power source). As another example, in order to compete with other TV display technologies such as Plasma Display Panel (PDP), LCD panels for TVs generally require higher contrast ratios (how bright and dark images can be), wider viewing angles (LCD images can fade when viewed from off-center), and faster response times (how long it takes a pixel to change colors) than panels used for monitors.[20] Similarly, automotive

    DisplaySearch Trends, Spring 2006; Richard Chu, "Sharp," ING Barings, July 26, 2001, 13.
[19] Carlton (2012), 15. Figure drawn from David Hsieh, "Flat Panel Display Market Outlook," Shanghai Intl. Industry Fair, *DisplaySearch*, November 5, 2005 at 6.
[20] See, e.g., Steve Kindig, "LED-LCD vs. Plasma," *Crutchfield's*, www.crutchfield.com/S-21PTs4k4ZHh/learn/learningcenter/home/tv_flatpanel.html.

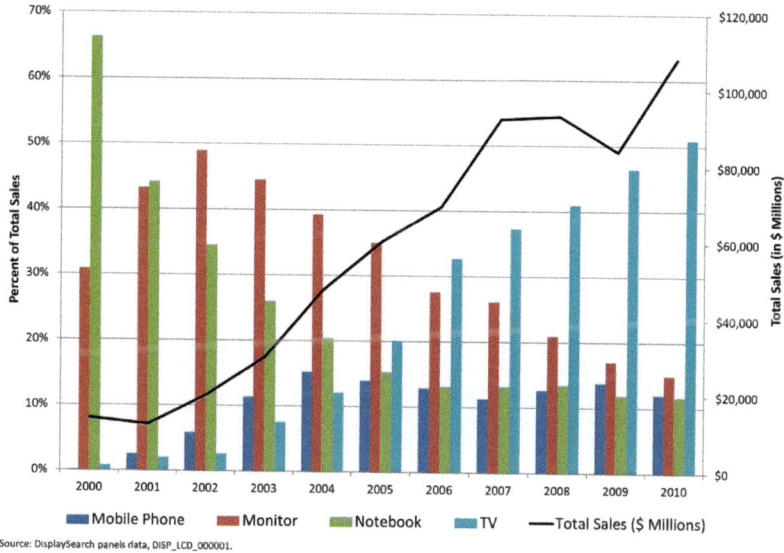

FIGURE 10.3 LCD sales and shares by application.[21]

applications require higher tolerances to temperature extremes than do other applications.[22]

The three main categories of LCD panels grew rapidly, but on sharply different timelines. Panels for notebooks, then monitors, were the first main LCD products, with over $4 billion in annual sales each for notebook computers and for monitors, as early as 2000. Figure 10.3 shows total LCD panel sales over time and how the shares of the categories changed.

These shifts were driven in large part by shifts from the older CRT technologies, which differed by application. For example, CRTs were never used for mobile phones or laptops, but they were commonplace for monitors and televisions. Figure 10.4 shows the sales for LCD and CRT monitors over time, with more LCD monitors being sold by 2004 and CRT monitors effectively disappearing by 2009. The same pattern holds true for televisions.

[21] Carlton (2012), 18. [22] Carlton (2012), 935.

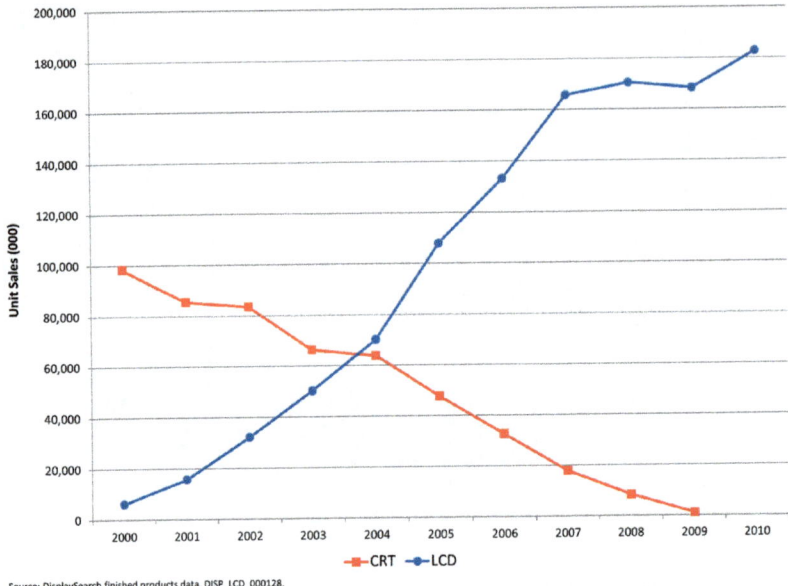

FIGURE 10.4 LCD vs. CRT monitor unit sales.[23]

10.3 PRICE TRENDS

The industry is characterized by sharply declining prices. Those declining prices have been driven in large part by investments in successive "generations" of fabs designed to handle successively larger-sized motherglass, which allows more panels and larger-sized panels to be formed from a single sheet.[24] (Fabs are discussed in more detail later.) However, although there is general agreement that TFT-LCD prices declined over the relevant period of time, analysts differ in their characterization of those price declines. Indeed, what exactly happened to prices and how to measure changes in prices over time was at the heart of some of the trial debates.

Figure 10.5 shows the average monthly panel price for one of the most popular products, the 17" SXGA monitor from January

---

[23] Carlton (2012), 22.
[24] See Jeongsik Lee, Byung-Cheol Kim, Young-Mo Lim (2011), "Dynamic competition in technological investments: An empirical examination of the LCD panel industry," *International Journal of Industrial Organization*, 29:718–728 at 720.

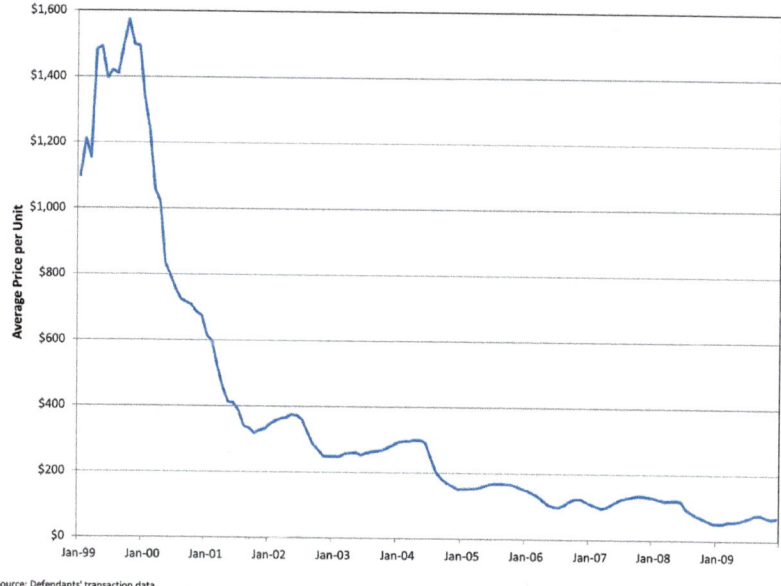

FIGURE 10.5 17″ SXGA monitor panel average price.[25]

1999 through 2010. There is an initial increase in price in 1999 followed by a decline. (As discussed above, some allegations contend that the conspiracy began prior to 1999.)

10.4 ORGANIZATION OF THE CARTEL

The primary meetings of the LCD cartel were called "Crystal Meetings."[26] Figure 10.6 reports their frequency over the life of the cartel. Those meetings, which often involved senior executives, occurred between two and eight times a quarter, mostly in Taiwan.[27]

---

[25] Carlton (2012), 30.
[26] See, e.g., *Complaint, Dell Inc. v. Sharp Corp. et al.*, (In re TFT-LCD (Flat Panel) Antitrust Litig.), March 12, 2010, 23; European Commission, Case AT.39437-TV and computer monitor tubes, Commission Decision of 5.12.2012, available at https://ec.europa.eu/competition/antitrust/cases/dec_docs/39437/39437_7332_3.pdf;
[27] Expert Report of B, Douglas Bernheim, Ph.D., Concerning Target Corp., Sears, Roebuck and Co., Kmart Corp., Old Comp Inc., Good Guys, Inc., Radioshack Corp. and Newegg Inc., December 15, 2011, Redacted, available in Sharp's Daubert Motion, Case 3:07-md-01827-SI, Document 7843-2, filed May 3, 2013 ("Bernheim, 2011), 19–20.

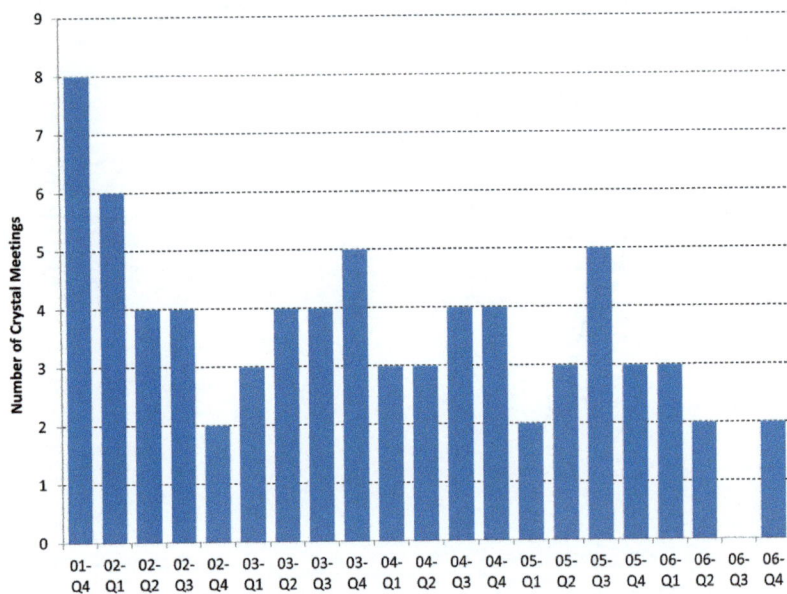

FIGURE 10.6 Instances of Crystal Meetings.[28]

The parties went to great lengths to maintain secrecy. For example, one internal message stated that after the DRAM price-fixing cases, the LCD conspirators "need to pay more attention to security internally and otherwise, and must try to refrain from written communication which would leave trails."[29] As a Samsung deponent noted, "everyone knows that this is illegal."[30]

The meetings consisted primarily of discussions of products, prices, price targets, and price floors.[31] In addition, documents mention attempts to implement supply restrictions by promising to delay investment in new capacity, slow ramp-up for new production lines, or reduce production on existing lines.[32] Not every topic was discussed at every meeting, nor were the employees or cartel members represented consistently across meetings. There were meetings with

---

[28] Bernheim (2011), figure 9.   [29] Bernheim (2011), ¶ 45.
[30] Bernheim (2011), ¶ 46.   [31] Carlton (2012), 42–46; Bernheim (2011), § III.B.
[32] Bernheim (2011), § III.B.

CEOs and senior executives that focused on overall pricing agreements and supply restrictions, meetings with sales and marketing managers that focused on pricing and product information, and meetings with account managers that focused on pricing for specific customers.[33] Not all meetings were attended by all alleged cartel members.[34]

Figures 10.7 and 10.8 provide two examples of spreadsheets used by the cartel to set targets for LCD production and pricing, respectively, by month and manufacturer. As discussed later, however, actual sales prices often differed from those discussed at the meetings.

These spreadsheets illustrate an important theme – the discussions focused on a few particular types of display, but there were many other types that were not discussed, and there were no standard formulae for relating prices across types of display or varying quality dimensions, other than some ad hoc decisions on relative prices of varying sizes (e.g., "15″ XGA = 14.1″ XGA+$45; NBPC: 15″ SXGA+ = 15″ XGA+$30; NBPC: 15″ XGA [sic] = Monitor 15″ XGA+$15″[35]). Typically, there would be a range of target prices or price floors discussed, or possibly production levels, with the products being discussed at the application/size/resolution level, and sometimes just at the application/size level.

Given the large number of product variants available for sale, and the large number of dimensions on which those products differed one from another, it was likely impractical to do more than focus on the most commonly sold variants and to provide general guidance. As one example, two notebook panels with the same size and resolution might have substantially different refresh rates, viewing angles, weights, and thicknesses. The record does not show formulaic adjustment for such differences by participants, which is not surprising given the sheer number of quality dimensions and the fact that any

---

[33] Bernheim (2011), 19.
[34] Bernheim (2011), ¶ 55 ("In a September 14, 2001 cartel meeting attended by senior executives from the four Taiwanese defendants...").
[35] Bernheim (2011), ¶ 56, quoting December 11, 2001 Crystal Meeting minutes.

	2004	Jan	Feb	Mar	Q1	New Apr	May	Jun	Q2	Jul	Aug	Sep	Q3	Oct (R)	Nov (R)	12月
	Breakdown	7,891	7,832	8,454	24,177	8,558	8,740	8,726	26,024	8,245	8,114	8,642	25,001	9,702	10,544	
AUO	Total 6 TFT Vendors															
	Total(Kpcs)	1,200	1,332	1,440	3,972	1,454	1,548	1,500	4,502	1,530	1,270	1,510	4,310	1,690	1,890	
	NB Total	320	340	360	1,020	395	420	390	1,205	400	390	410	1,200	440	495	
	14" XGA	90	100	100	290	130	130	100	360	100	100	120	320	130	160	
	15" XGA	175	170	170	515	180	180	165	525	160	170	180	510	180	180	
	15" SXGA+	25	35	35	95	30	50	50	130	25	20	20	65	20	20	
	15.4" WXGA						5	15	20	35	50	20	105	50	65	
	Others (8"/10"/12"/15.2")	30	35	55	120	55	55	60	170	80	50	70	200	60	70	
	MNT Total	828	880	950	2,650	968	1,020	1,015	3,003	1,015	795	950	2,760	1,050	1,210	
	15"	190	180	210	580	225	240	240	705	280	190	190	660	150	170	
	17"	500	500	500	1,500	510	530	560	1,600	575	490	580	1,645	660	730	
	19"	130	200	210	540	210	220	210	640	155	110	170	435	210	275	
	others			30	30	23	30	5	58	5	5	10	20	30	35	
	TV Total	60	112	130	302	91	108	95	294	115	85	150	350	200	185	
	TV 20"	45	70	88	203	45	45	35	125	30	30	55	115	80	70	
	TV 14"/15"/17"	15	28	28	71	35	45	40	120	65	45	75	185	90	80	
	TV 26"		8	8	16	8	10	7	25	10	5	15	30	20	20	
	TV 30"		6	6	12	3	8	13	24	10	5	5	20	10	15	
	TV 32"															
	TV 37"															
CMO	Total	994	991	1,194	3,179	1,219	1,238	1,195	3,652	1,041	1,131	1,155	3,327	1,270	1,323	
	NB Total	409	360	422	1,191	389	436	375	1,200	288	323	294	905	343	345	
	12" + 12W	97	110	104	311	97	152	120	369	54	46	82	182	68	74	
	14" XGA	78	71	110	259	117	115	110	342	101	124	54	279	97	107	
	15" XGA															
	15" SXGA+															
	15.4" Wide	14	-	26	44	8	11	15	34	3	-	18	21	30	24	
	17"W		4		4						-	-	-	-	-	
	IDT	220	175	182	577	167	158	130	455	130	153	140	423	148	140	
	MNT Total	512	544	655	1,711	688	857	666	2,011	603	618	696	1,917	726	727	
	15"	143	161	178	482	178	191	165	534	106	155	106	367	108	60	
	17"	235	250	327	812	387	331	360	1,078	411	396	480	1,287	568	554	
	18"															
	19"	128	127	150	405	123	135	125	383	86	67	110	263	50	113	
	20"	6	6	12	12	16	16	16	16							
	TV Total	73	87	117	277	142	145	154	441	150	190	165	505	201	251	
	TV 20"	48	54	57	159	66	87	76	229	76	82	55	213	65	80	
	TV 23"															70	
	TV 27"	12	15	26	53	22	33	31	86	28	53	30	111	43	60	
	TV 30"	13	18	34	65	29	25	22	76	21	23	35	79	40	40	
	TV 32"															1	
	TV Others (small)					25	-	25	50	25	32	45	102	53		
	>32"															
CPT	Total	807	901	906	2,614	912	915	916	2,743	782	756	858	2,396	920	927	

FIGURE 10.7 Example of a spreadsheet memorializing production figures. Bernheim (2011), figures 10 and 11.

Display Size	Vendor	2004				Date: 2004/5/
		Jan	Feb	Mar	Apr	May
15" XGA	CPT	220-225	220-225	225-230	230-235	230-235
	AUO	220-225	220-225	230	230-235	230-235
	CMO	220	225	225-230	230-235	230-235
	HSD	230-235	230-235	245	250	255
	SEC	220	220	220	230	235
	LGP	210-215	210-215	220	230	233-235
17" SXGA	AUO / TN	285-290	290	290	293-298	295-300
	CMO / TN	285-290	285-290	290	290-295	290-295
	CPT	285-290	285-290	285-290	300	300
	LGP	288-292	288-292	292-310	295-310	295-310
	SEC / TN	310	310	290	310	310
	HSD					295
18" SXGA	QDI					
	CMO / MVA	340	350	EOL	EOL	
19" SXGA	LGP / IPS					
	CMO	415-420	415-420	415-420	415-420	415-420
	AUO	415	415	415	415-420	415-420
	SEC	415	415	415	415	415
	LGP	410	410	410	410	410
19" TN	LPL	390		390	390	390
17" Wide	LGP	300	300	290-300	310-320	320-330
	SEC	340	340	340	330	330
20" UXGA	AUO	570	570	570	570	550
	LPL	575	570	570	560	510-530
	SEC (21")	620	620	650	650	650
	CMO	570	570	570	570	545
20" TV	CMO	420-230	420-430	400	390-400	390-400
	LGP	420	420	420	410	400
22" TV	AUO	420	420	410	405	400
	SEC	850?	800	800	800	650
23" TV	CMO					700
	HSD					
	LPL	710	670	670	650-670	650
			710	710	690-700	680-690
26" TV	SEC	1000	1000	1000	900	800
	LPL			810	800	790
	AUO	800	800	780	750-780	700

FIGURE 10.8 Example of a spreadsheet memorializing prices. Bernheim (2011), figures 10 and 11.

287

given quality dimension may vary continuously (e.g., weight and thickness may vary in small increments, and the relation to price may be nonlinear).

Turning back to the degree to which various products were discussed in meetings, Table 10.1 illustrates that, over the course of the Crystal Meetings, less than 50 percent of monitor and notebook panel sales consisted of application/size combinations for which there had been documented discussions regarding the price to charge in the month in which the panel was sold. Restricting this figure to months for which there were discussions of a panel's specific application/size/*display resolution* combination would further reduce this number. Even including all sales of application/size combinations for which there had been a price discussion corresponding to one of the preceding six months yields only 67 percent of total monitor and notebook panel revenue. Therefore, for long stretches of time during the relevant period, the prices for many of the LCD panel products were not discussed at the cartel meetings, leaving large portions of the cartel members' sales without explicit price guidance.

Application/size is a relatively high level at which to discuss prices given the number of varying quality dimensions, and, in fact transaction prices varied widely around the discussed target prices. Figure 10.9 illustrates prices discussed at Crystal Meetings for 15" monitors but with no display resolution information provided, and compares the range of the discussed prices with actual transaction prices. Transaction prices show an enormous range around the prices discussed in Crystal Meetings.

Even when a specific resolution was discussed, transaction prices still show an enormous range around the prices discussed in Crystal Meetings. Figure 10.10 shows prices communicated at Crystal Meetings and actual transaction prices for 15" notebook panels with XGA resolution. Again, this range is not surprising in light of the large degree of product variation available even at the application/size/resolution level. To the extent the average monthly prices were not too far away from discussed prices, that could be consistent with the targets

Table 10.1 *Revenue of monitor and notebook panels around the time of Crystal Meeting price discussions*[36]

Application	Size	Revenue ($ millions)		
		Month of discussed price	Month of discussed price and the two months after	Month of discussed price and the five months after
Monitor	15"	$6,939	$7,974	$8,762
Monitor	17"	$10,520	$13,485	$15,221
Monitor	17.1"	$11	$24	$44
Monitor	18"	$118	$135	$158
Monitor	18.1"	$200	$309	$481
Monitor	19"	$3,699	$5,300	$6,823
Monitor	20"	$9	$11	$18
Monitor	20.1"	$219	$429	$620
Monitor	21"	$14	$52	$80
Monitor	21.3"	$6	$8	$15
Monitor	22"	$0	$0	$0
Monitor	23"	$14	$35	$50
Monitor	24"	$15	$62	$156
Monitor	30"	$0	$0	$1
Discussed Monitors Total		**$21,766**	**$27,825**	**$32,429**
Notebook	12"	$10	$26	$40
Notebook	12.1"	$492	$737	$909
Notebook	13.3"	$127	$194	$207
Notebook	14"	$81	$214	$382
Notebook	14.1"	$3,764	$4,361	$4,880
Notebook	15"	$5,244	$6,358	$7,323
Notebook	15.2"	$83	$124	$175
Notebook	15.4"	$1,811	$2,584	$3,500
Notebook	17"	$6	$21	$48
Notebook	17.1"	$26	$34	$74
Discussed Notebooks Total		**$11,646**	**$14,653**	**$17,538**

[36] Carlton (2012), Figure IV-2.

Table 10.1 (cont.)

		Revenue ($ millions)		
Application	Size	Month of discussed price	Month of discussed price and the two months after	Month of discussed price and the five months after
Other Monitors	10.4"–30"	$21,769	$15,710	$11,106
Other Notebooks	10"–20.1"	$19,253	$16,246	$13,361
Non-Discussed Panels Total		$41,022	$31,955	$24,467
Grand Total		$74,434	$74,434	$74,434
Discussed Monitors Share		50%	64%	74%
Discussed Notebooks Share		38%	47%	57%
Discussed Panels Share		45%	57%	67%

having some effect, or at least cartel members believing they were having some effect. That is, although the average actual monthly prices were typically below the target prices, cartel members may have believed that they were sometimes close to the target prices and that absent their activities actual prices would have been even lower.

While there is substantial dispersion in prices at the application/size and application/size/resolution level, in general, average actual transaction prices tended to be below the average discussed price, and were often below the lowest discussed price. Table 10.2 shows the share of industry revenue at transaction prices below the midpoint or lowest price communicated at the Crystal Meetings. The dispersion is likely driven in large part by differences in quality, but those differences also make it difficult to detect price reductions by cartel members due to the difficulty in holding quality constant for any comparisons.

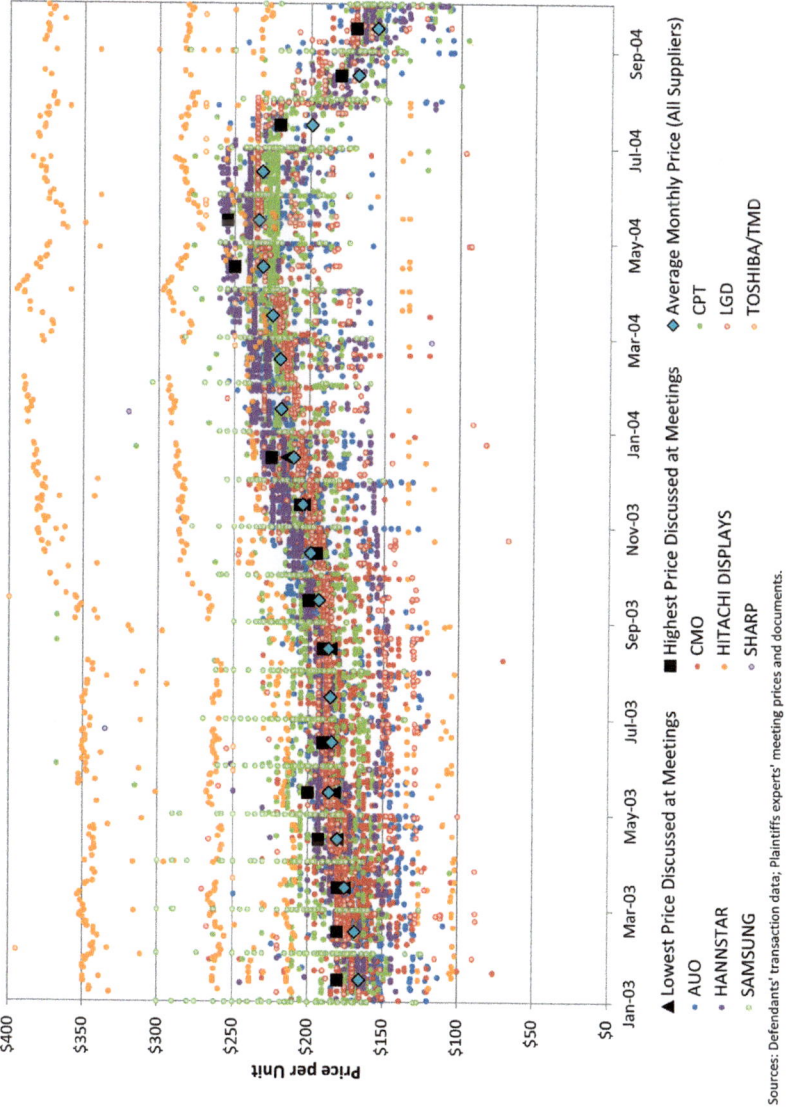

FIGURE 10.9 Prices communicated at Crystal Meetings and actual transaction prices, 15" monitor (no display resolution information discussed).
Carlton (2012), figure IV-1.

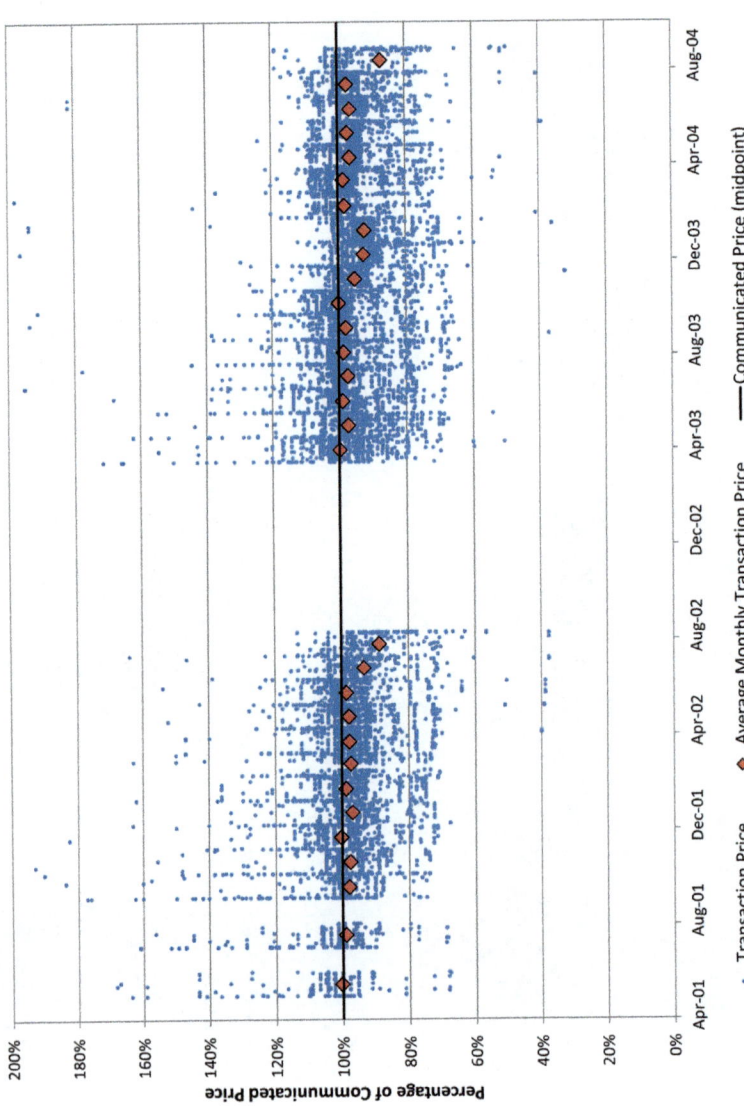

FIGURE 10.10 Prices communicated at Crystal Meetings and actual transaction prices, 15″ monitor, XGA resolution. Carlton (2012), figure IV-7.

Table 10.2 *Share of industry revenue at transaction prices below midpoint or lowest price communicated at Crystal Meetings, by panel*[37]

Panel	Revenue below midpoint communicated price (%)	Revenue below lowest communicated price (%)
MT 17" SXGA	57.7	34.7
MT 15" XGA	63.3	38.8
MT 19" SXGA	64.3	47.3
NB 14.1" XGA	66.6	48.3
NB 15.0" XGA	63.3	41.8
NB 15.4" WIDE	52.4	34.2
MT 20.1" WIDE	15.4	8.6
NB 12.1" XGA	77.0	64.6
MT 18.1" SXGA	80.2	79.8
NB 15" SXGA+	58.1	32.0
NB 13.3" XGA	38.0	35.8
NB 14.1" SXGA+	60.4	60.4
NB 12.1" SVGA	70.4	70.4
NB 17" WIDE	84.8	84.7
MT 24" WIDE	77.7	77.7
NB 14" WIDE	97.0	97.0
NB 15.2" WIDE	8.2	8.2
MT 19" WIDE	95.4	0.2
MT 23" WIDE	99.8	83.6
NB 15" SXGA	92.6	92.5
NB 15" UXGA	53.2	28.2
MT 21.3" UXGA	0.5	0.5
NB 14" XGA	100.0	100.0
MT 18" SXGA	67.7	53.3
MT 21" WIDE	74.0	74.0
MT 17" WIDE	52.0	39.2
Average for panels with display information	**61.3**	**39.5**

[37] Carlton (2012), table IV-3.

Table 10.2 (cont.)

Panel	Revenue below midpoint communicated price (%)	Revenue below lowest communicated price (%)
MT 17"	66.7	52.6
MT 15"	65.6	58.7
MT 19"	49.1	31.2
NB 14.1"	43.5	27.0
NB 15"	54.6	41.9
NB 15.4"	62.8	46.0
NB 12.1"	83.3	74.0
NB 13.3"	57.3	54.0
MT 18.1"	43.9	41.7
NB 17.1"	81.1	81.1
NB 14"	32.5	22.9
NB 17"	3.0	1.2
NB 15.2"	48.4	48.4
MT 17.1"	94.5	94.5
MT 18"	53.1	46.1
NB 12"	69.3	65.6
MT 20"	0.0	0.0
Average for panels without display information	**59.5**	**46.4**

In contrast to some other cartels, the LCD cartel did not engage in explicit allocation of customers, territories, or shares among cartel participants, nor did it have any direct enforcement mechanism.[38] That is, the cartel was alleged to have enforced price targets only by the knowledge that not adhering to them would likely cause "price-slashing" behavior.[39] In the vitamins cartel, for example, participants were assigned production shares equal to their market shares prior to the cartel's formation.[40] If a vitamin firm sold too much in a given

---

[38] See Bernheim (2011), ¶¶ 76–77. [39] See Bernheim (2011), ¶¶ 76–78.
[40] Carlton and Perloff (2005), 142–143. See also, Carlton (2012), ¶ 124.

year, it could be required to buy supplies from the other firms to restore the original sales allocation.[41]

10.5 DIFFICULTIES FACED BY THE CARTEL[42]

In many ways, the LCD industry was a particularly difficult one to cartelize in order to raise price, as there were many elements present known to hinder cartel efforts. The wide range of quality dimensions and how the cartel attempted to deal with those has been discussed above, but there were other difficulties faced by the cartel as well.

10.5.1 Rapid Technological Change and Capacity Expansion

Industries experiencing rapid technological change will generally find it more difficult to maintain a price-fixing agreement, particularly when the changes lead to lower costs, forcing other firms to invest to keep up. Here, LCD production technology evolved dramatically during the cartel period, vastly increasing production capacity and output, lowering costs, improving quality, and allowing new and bigger products. The fabrication plants (or "fabs") were extremely expensive, taking years to build and costing billions of dollars.[43] As technology changed over time, new and better generations of fabs were introduced, each allowing larger motherglass than the prior generation. At the beginning of the alleged cartel period, 3rd generation fabs of the time were able to handle motherglass of 550mm x 650mm, or approximately 1,172 square feet. By the end of the relevant period, 8th generation fabs were able to use motherglass of 2,200mm x 2,500mm, or approximately 18,045 square feet.[44] Figure 10.11 shows the evolution of LCD panel fab generations over time.

---

[41] Carlton and Perloff (2005), 143.
[42] Unless otherwise noted, this section draws on the Carlton (2012).
[43] See, e.g., Expert Report of Mohan Rao Ph.D., December 15, 2011, Redacted, available in Hannstar Display's Daubert Motion, Case 3:07-md-01827-SI, Document 7226-2, filed November 21, 2012, ¶ 9, noting a Generation 6 fab cost approximately $3.3 billion, and a Generation 7 fab cost approximately $5.3 billion.
[44] Carlton (2012), 68–69; Samsung Display Newsroom, "Mother Glass & Generation," http://global.samsungdisplay.com/28976/.

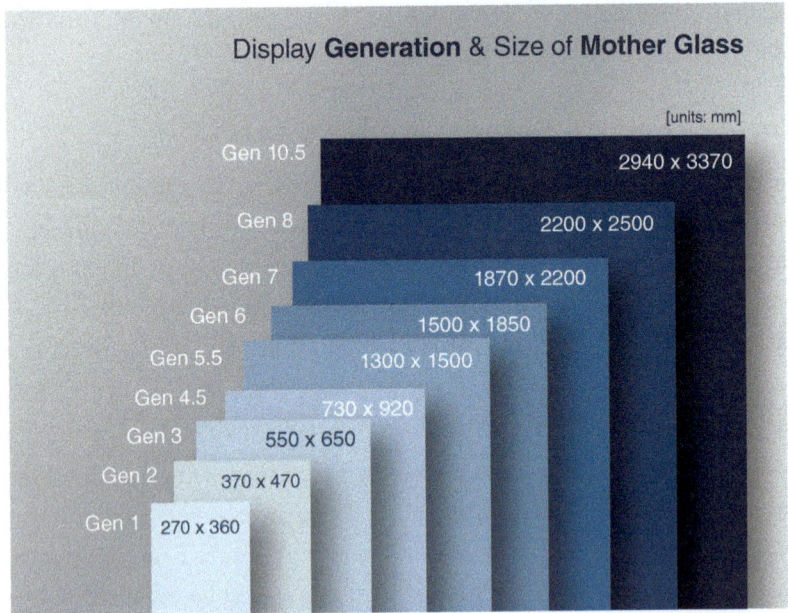

FIGURE 10.11 LCD panel fab generations and motherglass size.[45]

As a result of LCD manufacturers building new and better fabs over time, multiple generations of plants were in operation at any given time, meaning that different cartel participants had different production costs, those costs were steadily falling over time, and firms had incentives to increase production up to capacity because marginal costs were low relative to the fixed costs of building the fab. Of course, the firms also had a desire to avoid price being driven down to marginal cost and to earn a return on fabs costing billions of dollars.

Furthermore, production costs were not static even within a generation of fab. Firms learned how to better use their new facilities over time, so ongoing production resulted in learning by doing that reduced costs. This fact produced incentives to increase production not only to cover the enormous costs of creating the fab, but because

---

[45] Samsung Display Newsroom, "Mother Glass & Generation," http://global.samsungdisplay.com/28976/.

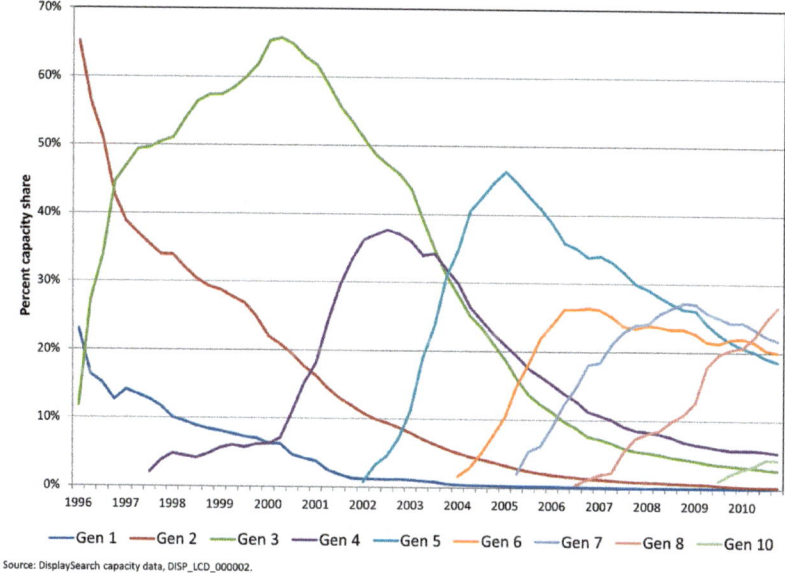

FIGURE 10.12 Share of TFT-LCD capacity by fab generation.[46]

doing so reduced the costs of future production. This phenomenon further complicated matters for the cartel.[47]

Figure 10.12 depicts the share of LCD capacity by technology generation, illustrating the evolution of the technology and cost structures over time.

The building of new fabs expanded total production capacity, which further complicated efforts to maintain a cartel. Between entry and expansion by existing producers, total industry production capacity increased drastically. Between 1999 and 2006, capacity went from about 212k square meters of glass per month to about 5,950k – a roughly 30-fold increase, as seen in Figure 10.13.[48] While there were some claims that the cartel attempted to limit capacity expansion, it is clear that capacity nonetheless increased at a rapid rate.

[46] Carlton (2012), 70. [47] See, e.g., Carlton (2012), ¶ 101.
[48] Carlton (2012), 82–83.

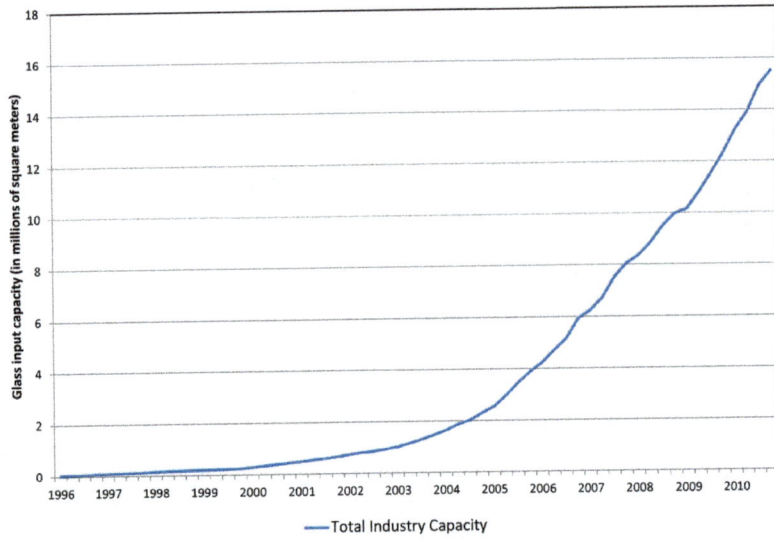

FIGURE 10.13 Quarterly industry capacity.[49]

10.5.2 *Product Differentiation and Customer Customization*

Price-fixing agreements are expected to be generally less successful and stable when they attempt to cover a wide variety of differentiated products. In such a situation, the cartel must determine relative prices for various goods with different demand conditions and production costs. The more differentiation, the more difficult is this undertaking. Also, differentiation means more products and thereby more prices to be fixed, and the cartel must monitor all of these prices. This greatly complicates the problem of detecting cheating on cartel agreements. Finally, extensive product differentiation can provide a way for firms to cheat on a price-fixing agreement by adjusting the product characteristics and quality rather than the nominal price. As discussed above, the cartel attempted to address this difficulty by focusing on a set of more commonly sold products.

[49] Carlton (2012), figure V-6.

Product customization for individual customers is a specific example of product differentiation that may be particularly difficult to monitor as the product specifications may be unique to the customer and hence difficult to compare with other products. (As discussed next, it is also the case that prices with individual customers are often privately negotiated; however, as discussed above, some meetings did discuss individual customers.)

New panels were also introduced with great frequency, further complicating efforts to coordinate. For example, a 15″ monitor panel with the XGA image resolution was one of the top selling panels during the 1999–2006 period and was frequently discussed at the Crystal Meetings. But one manufacturer began selling a slightly larger panel – 15.1″ – at a similar price. Since that panel was larger, that could be interpreted as a reduction in the quality-adjusted price. However, it does not appear that variant size was discussed at the Crystal Meetings, nor was it even tracked by industry sources.[50]

And, of course, new products and ever larger monitor and television screens were regularly being introduced, which further complicated LCD panel product comparisons. For example, it is fairly straightforward to understand that between two TV panels, one 32″ and one 40″ that are otherwise identical in quality, the 40″ TV should be more expensive than the 32″ one. However, if an LCD panel producer introduces a 32″ TV with improved resolution, it is less clear how the price of that television relates to the 40″ TV at the older, lower resolution.

10.5.3 *Individual, Private Negotiations*

The LCD industry is also characterized by private negotiations over prices, and it is especially difficult for a cartel to monitor prices where buyers and sellers trade through privately negotiated contracts containing both price terms and product specifications. Cartel members did discuss individual customers at some meetings, but individually

---

[50] Carlton (2012), 76.

negotiated contracts can be difficult to monitor, and manufacturers may be able to give hidden discounts by adjusting non-price contractual terms. For example, rebates or very favorable payment terms may allow for effective price discounting that is difficult for other cartel members to detect. Moreover, many buyers in this industry were purchasing multiple products from the producers, as original equipment manufacturers (OEMs) sometimes manufactured ranges of products including monitors, laptop computers, TVs, and cell phones. A privately negotiated contract concerning multiple products involves many contract terms that a seller could use to offer a potential price discount that cartel members could not readily detect.

In the LCD industry, buyers also differed widely in purchase volumes, bargaining power, and specification requirements, resulting in substantial price dispersion.[51] Individual negotiations with large buyers were commonplace. Those negotiations might be for products made to certain specifications that would *only* be sold to a specific buyer like, for example, Nokia who obtained LCD panels designed specifically for use for Nokia phones. Other firms such as Dell accounted for substantial fractions of total monitor or notebook panel purchases and negotiated for specified quality characteristics as well as discounts. The presence of large buyers, individual negotiations, and many quality dimensions all facilitate cheating and thus hinder the effectiveness of cartel agreements to elevate price.

10.5.4 Substantial Entry

The entry of new firms in an industry is often disruptive to a cartel.[52] Here, literally dozens of firms entered between 1999 and 2010. In particular, a number of Taiwanese firms entered and rapidly increased production, including Quanta, HannStar, CPT, CMO, AUO, Giantplus, Infovision, GMP, Optrex, TPO Toppoly, and

---

[51] Carlton (2012), 55–62.
[52] See, Margaret C. Levenstein and Valerie Y. Suslow (2004), "Studies of Cartel Stability: A Comparison of Methodological Approaches," in Peter Z. Grossman, ed., *How Cartels Endure and How They Fail*, table 1.11.

Innolux. Collectively, these entrants went from about 5 percent of industry revenues to over 35 percent in just six years.[53]

Although entry can disrupt cartels by adding firms outside the cartel, the cartel addressed that difficulty here by incorporating the Taiwanese entrants into the cartel. Taiwanese manufacturers AUO, CMO, CPT, and HannStar all pled guilty to some form of price conspiracy, similar to the allegations for which Korean manufacturers Samsung and LG Display also pled guilty. However, one effect of the entry was that the Taiwanese entrants had lower costs than existing Japanese producers, leading the Japanese producers to differentiate themselves by focusing almost exclusively on high-end products like large, high-resolution televisions and small cell phone panels (see Figure 10.1). The entry did, however, increase the number of firms across which coordination was required, as discussed next.

10.5.5 Large Numbers of Firms in an Unconcentrated Industry

Implementing and maintaining a cartel is more difficult when there are a larger number of firms participating in the cartel.[54] This is because the more firms that participate in a cartel, the more complex are the tasks of reaching agreements and monitoring compliance with such price-fixing agreements. For the LCD cartel, at least a dozen separate firms were alleged to have participated in the agreements.

The large number of firms involved is related to the fact that the LCD industry has a large number of producers and is relatively unconcentrated. For example, the HHI for the industry averaged less than 1,100 between 2001 and 2006, and it did not exceed 1,253 – levels that the Horizontal Merger Guidelines characterize as "unconcentrated."[55]

Table 10.3 summarizes the shares of industry participants over time.[56]

---

[53] Carlton (2012), 81.   [54] Levenstein and Suslow (2004), 34.
[55] U.S. Department of Justice and the Federal Trade Commission (2010), "Horizontal Merger Guidelines," § 5.3, www.justice.gov/atr/horizontal-merger-guidelines-08192010#5c.
[56] Carlton (2012), 79.

Table 10.3 Share of industry revenues by manufacturer (all applications)

TFT-LCD supplier	1999 (%)	2000 (%)	2001 (%)	2002 (%)	2003 (%)	2004 (%)	2005 (%)	2006 (%)	2007 (%)	2008 (%)	2009 (%)	2010 (%)
AUO	1.95	3.18	7.57	8.51	10.51	10.75	11.73	13.62	16.70	15.15	13.97	14.03
Acer				2.67								
Alps							0.03	0.01				
BOE Hydis	1.90	2.63	2.90	3.44	2.46	1.41	1.94	1.55	1.49	1.12	1.04	0.99
BYD									0.08	0.15	0.18	0.23
CMO	0.12	2.41	4.76	6.62	8.62	7.94	8.42	8.86	10.23	11.55	11.81	2.77
CPT	2.82	3.20	4.29	5.56	5.16	4.89	4.17	4.97	5.10	3.75	2.17	2.37
Casio		0.24	1.20	0.94	1.33	1.06	0.88	0.64	0.52	0.32	0.17	0.04
Chimei Innolux												10.60
EDT						0.01	0.01	0.00	0.00	0.00	0.00	0.00
Epson						1.06	3.82	2.78	1.81	1.57	0.87	0.15
Fujitsu	2.95	2.52	1.35	0.68	0.39	0.25	0.03					
GBM						0.11	0.02					
GiantPlus								0.04	0.05	0.28	0.48	0.36
HannStar		1.87	3.81	4.69	3.16	2.47	2.88	2.57	2.66	1.95	1.80	1.61
Hitachi	11.34	10.11	7.26	5.71	4.54	3.70	1.96	1.80	1.60	1.90	1.53	1.34
Hyundai					0.08	0.01	0.03	0.00	0.01	0.00		

	C1	C2	C3	C4	C5	C6	C7	C8	C9	C10	C11	C12
IPSAlpha								0.37	1.20	1.64	1.42	0.34
Infovision								0.05	0.52	0.45	0.80	0.96
Innolux						0.00	1.10	1.93	1.95	1.62	2.24	0.64
Kyocera							0.02	0.02	0.06	0.08	0.05	0.11
LG Display	16.87	14.66	15.39	14.67	17.76	15.85	16.56	15.99	16.90	16.70	20.16	21.44
LG Innotek						0.69	0.94	0.52	0.43	0.40	0.36	0.10
Matsushita	3.07	2.37										
Mitsubishi/ADI	3.73	2.93	0.79	0.06	0.64	0.23	0.19	0.19	0.18	0.12	0.12	0.14
NEC	8.16	6.54	1.65	1.12	1.09	0.68	0.68	0.34	0.26	0.21	0.18	0.17
Optrex			3.83	1.99	0.16	0.30	0.36	0.29	0.14	0.15	0.12	0.18
Ortus				0.02								0.13
Others		0.02	0.11	0.10	0.33	0.38	1.13	0.52	0.26	0.08	0.06	0.13
PVI									0.15	0.22	0.38	0.54
Panasonic LCD												1.33
Philips	1.13											
Philips Kobe			0.09	0.14	0.53	0.60	0.92	0.51				
Quanta		1.21	0.44	2.70	2.66	3.80	3.19	2.22	0.26	0.22		
SII					0.03	0.46	0.38	0.34			0.11	
ST LCD		0.15	2.15	1.69	2.55	1.82	1.40					0.08
SVA NEC						0.00	0.87	1.17	1.12	0.90	0.20	0.00
Samsung	20.95	21.57	19.60	16.51	18.21	20.48	19.28	21.55	20.69	22.11	24.54	22.77

Table 10.3 (cont.)

TFT-LCD supplier	1999 (%)	2000 (%)	2001 (%)	2002 (%)	2003 (%)	2004 (%)	2005 (%)	2006 (%)	2007 (%)	2008 (%)	2009 (%)	2010 (%)
Sanyo	4.82	3.90	3.68	3.22	2.48	1.58						
Sharp	9.65	8.33	10.08	10.30	9.53	12.70	11.14	10.55	9.70	10.92	9.07	10.72
Sony	5.42	5.34	4.29	2.62			0.18	1.50	1.11	1.10	0.65	1.18
TMDisplay				5.30	7.74	5.87	4.27	3.78	2.91	2.91	2.30	2.02
TPO								0.74	1.09	1.18	1.19	0.15
Tianma										0.06	0.63	1.01
Toppoly					0.05	0.89	1.33	0.50	0.10			
Toshiba	5.11	5.06	3.13	0.55								
Truly									0.40	0.63	0.68	0.72
Unipac		1.76	1.61	0.18								
Wintek						0.00	0.14	0.05	0.32	0.56	0.73	0.63
Total Share of Suppliers with less than 5% share	22%	28%	40%	27%	22%	26%	33%	29%	21%	24%	20%	20%
- Number of suppliers with less than 5% share	9	14	17	17	16	24	27	28	27	28	27	30

Table 10.3 illustrates several points. First, it shows the entry by multiple firms, some of which became substantial suppliers. Second, it shows that there were many firms in the industry. Third, it shows that firms' revenue shares changed substantially over time, a feature which is known to be disruptive to cartel stability. Shifting shares make it difficult for a cartel to reach initial terms of agreement and undermines stability as the cartel members' interests can diverge over time. This difficulty follows because a cartel agreement involves a reduction in aggregate output in return for higher prices which translates into elevated aggregate profit, but the relative costs and benefits to the members change if their relative shares change. Large shifts in share on a regular basis can also increase the difficulty in detection of cheating – is a change in share due to demand fluctuations or another firm cheating on the alleged cartel price?

The share changes among LCD cartel members were significant. For example, Figure 10.14 tracks revenue shares for monitors for a number of accused cartel members.[57] Over time, several firms entered and obtained substantial shares, while others saw their shares fall substantially. Sharp, for example, went from the second highest share in 1999 to zero in 2006.

10.5.6 Vertical Integration by Cartel Members

Finally, another potential problem with the ability of a cartel to elevate price is that if some firms are vertically integrated, it may be difficult for the cartel to determine at what point in the distribution chain cheating occurs.[58] That is, if cartel members are not only selling LCD panels to phone, monitor, and television manufacturers, but are themselves making phones, monitors, or televisions using their own LCD panels, the cartel member can cheat on an agreement to fix the price of the panels by not increasing the price for the finished product. This ability to cheat and avoid detection is most likely when the price-fixed input accounts for a small fraction of the total price of

---

[57] Carlton (2012), 87. [58] Carlton and Perloff (2005), 136–139.

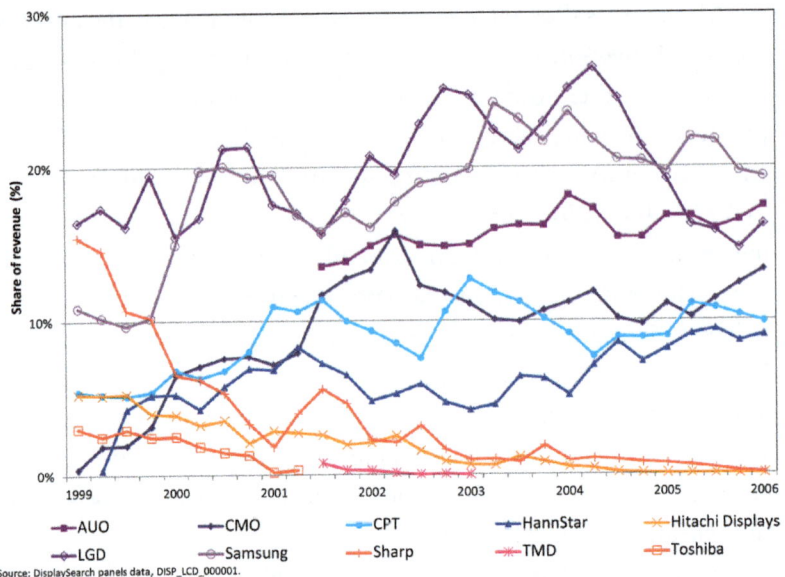

FIGURE 10.14 Alleged cartel member revenue shares, monitors.

the finished product, as is the case for the LCD panel costs as a share of the total retail price of many of the final LCD products. The cartel members included vertically integrated makers of televisions, phones, computer monitors, and laptop computers.

10.6 EVALUATING EVIDENCE ON THE OVERALL EFFECTIVENESS OF THE CARTEL

We know that the LCD panel cartel met frequently and extensively to set product prices, but there are also reasons to believe that industry conditions likely made it difficult to coordinate, monitor, and enforce a cartel. What evidence is there on how effective the cartel ended up being over the alleged conspiracy period?

In order to assess the effectiveness of the cartel in elevating prices during the alleged conspiracy period, one must compare actual prices to the prices that would have arisen in the absence of the cartel. Plaintiffs pointed to an initial increase in average prices around 1999. See, for example, Figure 10.15 which uses price indices calculated by

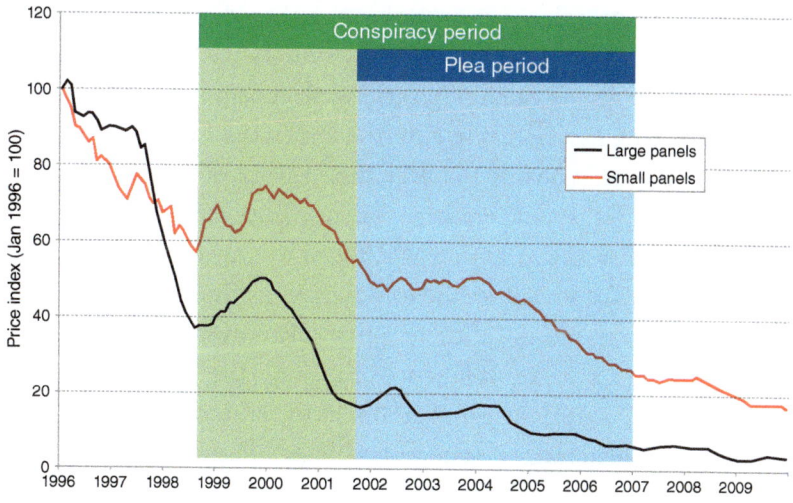

FIGURE 10.15 Plaintiff LCD price indices.[59]

an economic expert for one group of plaintiffs, a downward trend in which appears to be reversed at the start of the conspiracy period.[60] But, in assessing the magnitude of effect, a relevant question is whether that initial price increase, even if attributable to the cartel, applied over the entire period of the alleged conspiracy, as plaintiffs alleged, or instead was just a temporary moment of cartel success that disappeared afterward. Moreover, price patterns for many individual products were substantially different than the price indices.[61]

One might hope that an econometric model could sort out these matters. However, in a rapidly changing industry such as this one, obtaining a stable econometric model to estimate overcharges based on price data proved to be extremely challenging. The econometric analyses presented in the various litigations involving LCD panels reached very different conclusions, with plaintiffs' experts generally finding double digit percentage increases on average, and defendants' experts generally finding statistically insignificant low single digit

---

[59] Bernheim (2011), 11.   [60] Bernheim (2011), 11.
[61] See, e.g., Figures III-3 through III-10, Carlton (2012), 35–41.

(under 2 percent) price increases over the alleged conspiracy period, thereby being consistent with no effect.[62]

Another way to examine a cartel's effect on prices is to examine price-cost margins before and after the end of the cartel. Among the most basic predictions of the economic theory of cartels is that a successful cartel should generate higher price-cost margins than would otherwise occur. One would therefore expect, all else equal, that the price-cost margin would be significantly lower after the cartel ended relative to during the conspiracy. However, there does not appear to be a large difference between the margins during (2005–2006) and after the cartel (2007–2008), as shown in Table 10.4, based on the defendants' transaction data.[63] See also Figure 10.16 which reports average price / cost over the same period for the various applications (notebooks, monitors, phones, and televisions), where the vertical reference line indicates the end of the cartel damages period (as claimed in litigation). These time series give little reason to believe that prices were increased during the conspiracy period.

This evidence does not necessarily mean the cartel had no effect: Measuring margins can be difficult as data for cost measures that correspond to economic marginal costs are rarely available; it might take some time for price adjustments to occur; and other factors may be affecting margins over time. However, it does indicate that the cartel may have failed to raise prices at all and, in any event, was likely unable to have raised prices by a large percentage amount across the entire volume of commerce. While this is not surprising in light of the difficulties faced by the cartel, it does raise the question as to why the cartel members persisted in the face of such difficulties and apparent lack of success.

---

[62] See, e.g., Bernheim (2011), 57 (reporting overcharges between 17.8 percent and 25.5 percent), Carlton (2012), 151 (reporting statistically insignificant overcharges ranging from −0.7 percent to 1.9 percent).

[63] Carlton (2012), 126–127.

Table 10.4 *Average price/cost for alleged conspiracy period and post period*[64]

Application	Period	Total revenue	Total cost	Revenue / costs
Mobile	2005–2006 (Cartel)	2,573,624,298	2,187,112,098	1.18
	2007–2008 (Post)	2,640,432,487	2,292,449,762	1.15
Monitor	2005–2006 (Cartel)	18,353,136,798	16,722,625,665	1.10
	2007–2008 (Post)	23,015,042,040	18,745,544,004	1.23
Notebook	2005–2006 (Cartel)	9,648,819,860	9,041,280,565	1.07
	2007–2008 (Post)	17,549,122,990	14,537,271,579	1.21
TV	2005–2006 (Cartel)	11,495,929,870	10,753,013,692	1.07
	2007–2008 (Post)	19,905,020,200	18,501,287,967	1.08
Total	2005–2006 (Cartel)	42,071,510,825	38,704,032,020	1.09
	2007–2008 (Post)	63,109,617,717	54,076,553,312	1.17

10.7 WHY DID THE CARTEL CONTINUE TO OPERATE?

If the cartel either failed to raise average prices at all, or alternatively raised average prices by only a small amount (under 2 percent), why then did it continue to operate? First, it is important to put such a finding into context. It is well known that there have been many cartels that continued to operate even though they were ineffective

[64] Carlton (2012), 126–127.

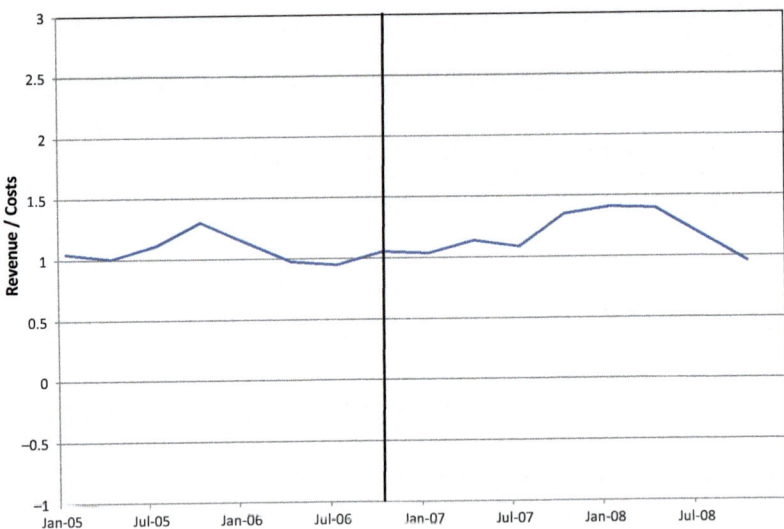

Source: Defendants' sales data.

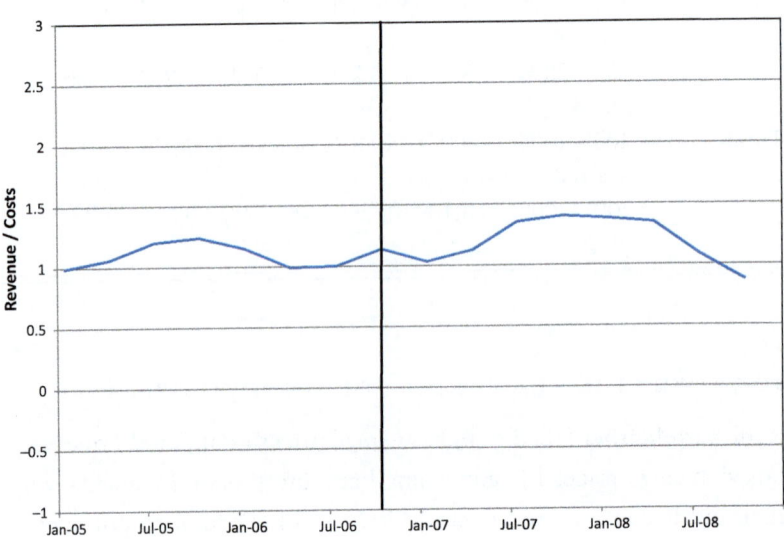

Source: Defendants' sales data.

FIGURE 10.16 Average price/cost for notebook, monitor, television, and phone panels.[65]

[65] Carlton (2012), 123–126.

LIQUID CRYSTAL DISPLAYS WORLDWIDE 311

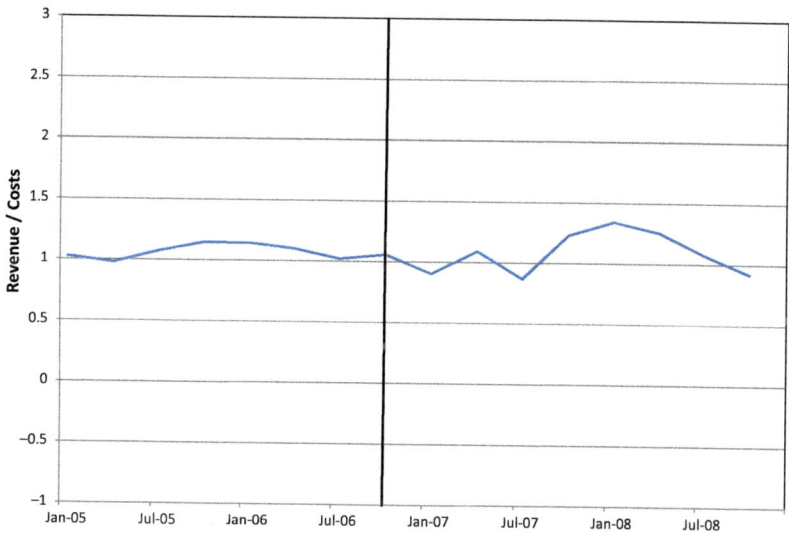

Source: Defendants' sales data.

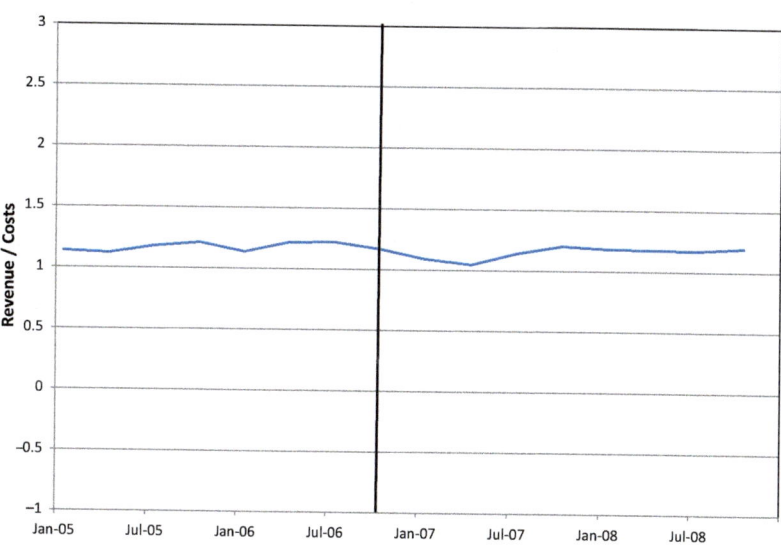

Source: Defendants' sales data.

FIGURE 10.16 (cont.)

and failed to raise average prices.⁶⁶ Similarly, some cartels have had a relatively brief peak effectiveness well in excess of their average effectiveness, so a brief period of success followed by significantly less (or any) effect would not be surprising.⁶⁷ Thus a finding that the LCD cartel may have failed to raise prices at all or was unsuccessful in significantly raising prices for all products over an extended period is not a peculiar one. The rationale for a cartel continuing under such circumstances can be based on either a misperception by participants of the cartel's success or the hope that the cartel might succeed in the future. In the case of the LCD cartel, as discussed earlier, there was an increase in price at the very beginning of the alleged cartel and that might have been, either properly or improperly, construed to mean that the cartel had the capability of achieving some success. That it soon failed to exploit that potential may have gone unnoticed by the companies that participated in the conspiracy.

The findings that many cartels fail to elevate average prices, or to sustain peak overcharges, highlight that when evaluating a cartel there is a critical difference between the existence of an agreement and its effectiveness. When there is evidence of meetings (e.g., detailed notes from meetings) and guilty pleas, there may be no doubt as to the presence of agreement – but that still leaves the question of the actual success of the agreement in raising prices. Even though a cartel may be viewed as relatively unsuccessful if it fails to elevate prices by a large percentage, cartel participants are not focused on percentage increases in price and would view a cartel as a success if it increased total profits by a large amount in dollar terms. For example, two businesses can produce equal profits even when one has low

---

[66] See, e.g., John Connor, "Price Fixing Overcharges: Legal and Economic Evidence," in Richard Zerbe, John Kirkwood, ed., *Research in Law and Economics*, v. 22, 2007, 59–153, table 5, noting 50 cartels with zero or negative overcharges and 111 with overcharges between 0.1 and 9.9 percent. Connor equates an "ineffective" cartel with zero percent overcharges (FN 56).

[67] See, e.g., John Connor, "Price Fixing Overcharges: Legal and Economic Evidence," in Richard Zerbe, John Kirkwood, ed., *Research in Law and Economics*, v. 22, 2007, figure 9.

margins and the other has high margins if the low margin business has sufficiently high volumes. The same applies to cartels. A higher percentage overcharge will, all else equal, be preferred by cartel participants, but a cartel imposing a small percentage overcharge on a large volume of commerce can generate larger absolute profits for its participants than a cartel imposing a high percentage overcharge on a small volume of commerce.[68] As mentioned, the defendant's econometric estimates indicated at most a small average overcharge (below 2 percent) that might well have been zero given the statistical uncertainty in the estimate. But even if the small overcharge of 2 percent were the correct number, the resulting profits from the cartel would have been material. If LCD panel sales totaled approximately $159 billion over the relevant conspiracy period,[69] even a 2 percent average overcharge would have resulted in incremental revenues to the conspirators exceeding $3 billion.

10.8 LESSONS ON CARTEL OPERATIONS

The LCD cartel offers several useful lessons with respect to both the difficulties cartels can face to be successful and the efforts cartels can go to overcome these difficulties given the large potential profits. Faced with the challenge of getting many cartel members to agree on prices for a large number of products differing along a wide array of uses and quality characteristics in the face of constant technological change, the cartel tried to address the difficulty in coordinating prices and monitoring compliance in a number of ways.

First, the cartel met frequently and focused on target prices for a limited number of products at any given time, and chose to focus on products with relatively large revenues. That is, instead of trying to

---

[68] A small percentage average overcharge on a large volume of commerce is consistent with a zero overcharge on most products but a significant overcharge on a few products. Regardless of how the overcharge is distributed across products, the point is that a small average overcharge on a large volume of commerce can lead to a substantial increase in profits.

[69] Carlton (2012), ¶ 65.

coordinate a dozen manufacturers' prices across hundreds of different products, the cartel focused only on the highest selling products, and at a degree of aggregation not reflecting all quality characteristics – usually the most common size and resolution combinations of laptop, monitor, and TV panels. This strategy traded increased risk of evasion of price targets for tractability and coverage of a broader group of products. The participants may also have hoped that targeting one group of products would impact other substitute products as well. By successfully raising the price of one product in a product line, *ceteris paribus*, even independent pricing of other products in that line would mean higher prices.

Second, the cartel attempted to reduce overall production for broad categories of products. This approach attempted to sidestep the complexities posed by the large number of differentiated products and simply raise prices by limiting overall output.

Ultimately, neither approach was particularly successful in the sense of producing large percentage increases in prices across all products for the entire cartel period, but both were sensible means for a cartel to try and deal with the challenges the industry structure posed to them.

One important lesson from the LCD cartel is confirmation of the finding that cartels can form even in industries that, on their face, would not appear conducive to the operation of a successful cartel.[70] Especially when a large volume of commerce is involved, the hope for even a small increase in price may provide sufficient incentive for firms to attempt to conspire. Furthermore, the potential harm to consumers and society from a cartel may actually be greater in those industries than in some other industries that might appear to offer

---

[70] See, e.g., Margaret C. Levenstein and Valerie Y. Suslow (2006), "What Determines Cartel Success?" *Journal of Economic Literature*, 44(1); Richard A. Posner, *Antitrust Law*, Second ed. Chicago: University of Chicago, 2001, 54 ("But while it is true that firms would not participate in price-fixing conspiracies if they were sure they would not succeed, they may sometimes be mistaken, and such mistakes, even if rare, could account for a large proportion of the small number of price-fixing cases that the public enforcement agencies bring.")

more fruitful ground for a successful conspiracy. This too is a function of the volume of commerce involved. The lesson for enforcement agencies is to use potential harm to consumers and deadweight loss in prioritizing cartel enforcement actions. The absolute harm in an industry with a large volume of commerce but a small increase in price can be larger than the harm in an industry with a small volume of commerce and a large increase in price.

REFERENCES

Carlton, D. W. and Perloff J. M. (2005) Modern Industrial Organization, 4th edition.

Chu, R. (2001) "Sharp," ING Barings, July 26.

Complaint, Dell Inc. v. Sharp Corp. et al. (2010) "(In re TFT-LCD (Flat Panel) Antitrust Litig.)," March 12.

Connor, J. (2007) "Price Fixing Overcharges: Legal and Economic Evidence," in Richard Zerbe, and John Kirkwood, eds., Research in Law and Economics, v. 22. JAI Press Inc.

European Commission press release, (2010) "Antitrust: Commission fines six LCD panel producers €648 million for pricing fixing cartel," December 8, https://ec.europa.eu/commission/presscorner/detail/es/IP_10_1685.

European Commission, (2012) "Case AT.39437-TV and computer monitor tubes, Commission Decision of 5.12.2012," https://ec.europa.eu/competition/antitrust/cases/dec_docs/39437/39437_7332_3.pdf.

Expert Report of B. Douglas Bernheim, Ph.D. (2011) "Concerning Target Corp., Sears, Roebuck and Co., Kmart Corp., Old Comp Inc., Good Guys, Inc., Radioshack Corp. and Newegg Inc., December 15," Redacted, available in Sharp's Daubert Motion, Case 3:07-md-01827-SI, Document 7843-2, filed May 3, 2013 ("Bernheim Redacted Report").

Expert Report of Mohan Rao Ph.D., December 15 (2011) Redacted, available in Hannstar Display's Daubert Motion, Case 3:07-md-01827-SI, Document 7226-2, filed November 21, 2012.

Expert Report of Professor Dennis W. Carlton, February 23 (2012) Redacted, available in Dell's Daubert Motion, Case 3:07-md-01827-SI, Document 7222, filed November 20, 2012 ("Carlton 2/2012 Redacted Report").

Hsieh, D. (2005) "Flat Panel Display Market Outlook," Shanghai Intl. Industry Fair, DisplaySearch, November 5.

Hsieh, D. (2006) "LCD Demand, Panels, Substrates All Move from Large to Larger," DisplaySearch Trends, Spring.

Kindig, S. "LED-LCD vs. Plasma," Crutchfield's, www.crutchfield.com/S-21PTs4k4ZHh/learn/learningcenter/home/tv_flatpanel.html.

Kindig, S. "LCD Flat Panel Direct Purchaser Antitrust Settlement for $473 million," www.srgllc.com/us/en/settlements/electronics/lcd-direct-purchaser.

Kindig, S. LCD Flat Panel Indirect Purchase Antitrust Settlement for $1.1 billion," www.srgllc.com/us/en/settlements/electronics/lcd-indirect-purchaser.

Lee, J., K., B.-C. Kim, and Y.-M. Lim. (2011) "Dynamic competition in technological investments: An empirical examination of the LCD panel industry," *International Journal of Industrial Organization*, 29:718–728.

Levenstein M. C. and V. Y. Suslow (2004) "Studies of Cartel Stability: A Comparison of Methodological Approaches," in Peter Z. Grossman, ed., *How Cartels Endure and How They Fail*, Edward Elgar Publishing.

Levenstein M. C. and V. Y. Suslow (2006) "What Determines Cartel Success?" *Journal of Economic Literature*, 44(1).

Plea Agreement in United States of America v. Chunghwa Picture Tubes, Ltd., January 16 (2009) www.justice.gov/atr/case-document/plea-agreement-71.

Plea Agreement in United States of America v. Epson Imaging Devices Corporation, October 23 (2009) www.justice.gov/atr/case-document/plea-agreement-115.

Plea Agreement in United States of America v. Hitachi Displays Ltd., May 26 (2009), www.justice.gov/atr/case-document/plea-agreement-163.

Plea Agreement in United States of America v. Chi Mei Optoelectronics, February 8 (2010) www.justice.gov/atr/case-document/plea-agreement-67.

Plea Agreement in United States of America v. HannStar Display Corporation, August 5 (2010) www.justice.gov/atr/case-document/plea-agreement-154.

Posner, R. A. (2001) *Antitrust Law, Second ed.* Chicago: University of Chicago.

Samsung Display Newsroom (2021) "Mother Glass & Generation," http://global.samsungdisplay.com/28976/.

U.S. Department of Justice (2008) "LG, Sharp, Chunghwa Agree to Plead Guilty, Pay Total of $585 Million in Fines for Participating in LCD Price-fixing Conspiracies," www.justice.gov/archive/opa/pr/2008/November/08-at-1002.html.

U.S. Department of Justice and the Federal Trade Commission (2010), "Horizontal Merger Guidelines," § 5.3, www.justice.gov/atr/horizontal-merger-guidelines-08192010#5c.

U.S. Department of Justice (2012) "Taiwan-Based AU Optronics Corporation Sentenced to Pay $500 Million for Role in LCD Price-Fixing Conspiracy," www.justice.gov/opa/pr/taiwan-based-au-optronics-corporation-sentenced-pay-500-million-criminal-fine-role-lcd-price.

11 Two Cartels in the Supply Chain
Raw Tobacco in Spain*

Thilo Klein, Helder Vasconcelos, and Elena Zoido

This is a case study of two cartels that operated simultaneously in the Spanish raw tobacco market between 1996 and 2001. The first cartel was established in February 1996 and operated on the seller side of the market. It was set up by the three agricultural unions that managed contract negotiations for the tobacco producers ("the producer representatives' cartel"). The second cartel, on the buyer side, was formed shortly after by the purchasers of raw tobacco ("the processors' cartel"): it formally commenced its operations on March 13, 1996. Both cartels carried on their restrictive practices at least until August 10, 2001.[1]

The European Commission ("EC") started proceedings against both cartels with an *ex officio* investigation – based on information it held[2] – between October 3 and 5, 2001.[3] On October 20, 2004, the EC issued its decision ("Decision"), sanctioning the undertakings involved in the two cartels for their operations between March 13, 1996 and October 3, 2001 (the "infringement").

---

* Daniel George, Ishwara Hegde, Jussi Kerttula, Giulio Paltrinieri, and David Galindo Peinado provided excellent research assistance. The authors have not advised any of the parties involved in this case. This case study relies exclusively on information found in the EC decision and other publicly available sources and data.
[1] See EC Decision (2004), relating to a proceeding under Article 81(1) of the EC Treaty – Case COMP/C.38.238/B.2 – *Raw tobacco Spain*, page 100 (Article 1). It should also be highlighted that, according to para. 4 of the same decision, the processors also informed the Commission that, as of October 3, 2001, they had put an end to their practices.
[2] Appeal Judgment of the General Court, July 19, 2012, para. 9. Available at: https://eur-lex.europa.eu/legal-content/ES/TXT/HTML/?uri=CELEX:62010CJ0628&from=SL#c-ECR_62010CJ0628_ES_01-E0001.
[3] See EC Decision (2004), relating to a proceeding under Article 81(1) of the EC Treaty – Case COMP/C.38.238/B.2 – *Raw tobacco Spain*, para. 3.

In this study, we first summarize essential facts of the Spanish raw tobacco market, including an overview of the relevant regulatory framework at the time. We then describe the *modus operandi* of the two cartels and assess the likely reasons why the cartels formed and the effectiveness of both cartels.

Our main findings can be summarized as follows. First, the formation of the cartels was triggered and facilitated by government regulation, implemented both at the EU and national Spanish levels, that aimed at establishing fair prices for tobacco producers, including through a system of production quotas. The Spanish government favored industry-wide negotiations and established a system of standard contracts that promoted collective bargaining by the tobacco producers, which encouraged the formation of the cartel on the seller side. The processors' cartel then likely formed shortly after to counterbalance the producer representatives' cartel, following changes in the regulatory regime that introduced competition among the processors.

Second, the case shows the difficulties of achieving effective collusion and the importance of establishing monitoring processes and compensation mechanisms. Both cartels benefited from regulatory support. However, the processors' cartel was ineffective in the first two years of the infringement period, despite the high level of market concentration and intense monitoring. This is reflected in a failure to adhere to price and volume agreements and the fact that the prices the processors paid to the producers kept increasing. The processors' cartel only became effective once an internal compensation mechanism that created the incentives necessary for processors to comply with the collusive outcome had been put in place.

11.1 BASIC MARKET FACTS

11.1.1 Spanish Tobacco: Product and Supply Chain

In Spain, cultivation of tobacco is largely concentrated in the Extremadura region, which accounted for 84 percent of the landmass dedicated to tobacco production in 2000.[4] Five varieties of tobacco leaves are grown: (i) Virginia (flue-cured, group I); (ii) Burley E (light air-cured, group II); (iii) Burley F (fermented, dark air-cured, group III); (iv) Havana (dark air-cured); and (v) Kentucky (fire-cured, group IV). Raw tobacco is used in the production of cigarettes, cigars, pipe, and chewing tobacco. During the infringement period, Spain accounted for 12 percent of European production and was the third-largest producer of tobacco in Europe, after Greece and Italy. The existence of price regulation and coordination suggest that Spanish tobacco prices to some extent formed independently.[5]

Figure 11.1 reports the production volumes of the different tobacco varieties produced in Extremadura in the period between 1985 and 2005. The most relevant variety was Virginia, accounting for 73 percent of average total volume. The other varieties were more expensive.[6]

As illustrated in Figure 11.2, the tobacco supply chain encompasses four steps. The first step is growing raw tobacco leaves. The second step consists of the first processing of the tobacco leaves, which includes the removal of impurities and sorting.[7] This is followed by a second processing stage, which includes blending and threshing.[8] The final step is the manufacturing of consumer products, like cigarettes and cigars.

11.1.2 Producers

At the time of the infringement, there were over 5,000 raw tobacco producers in Spain.[9] Almost all producers (approximately 99.7

---

[4] Decision (2004), para. 35.
[5] Regulatory constraints may have prevented full arbitrage. The whole purpose of European regulation was to ensure (via a quota-subsidy scheme) that producers could get more than the world market price. In addition, the fact that a Spanish cartel formed is already indicative of its usefulness in affecting prices.
[6] Approximately 30 tonnes of the Kentucky variety were produced each year in Extremadura between 1996 and 2006, corresponding to less than 0.1 percent of total yearly production.
[7] Decision (2004), paras. 26–28.   [8] Decision (2004), paras. 26–28.
[9] Decision (2004), table 11.1.

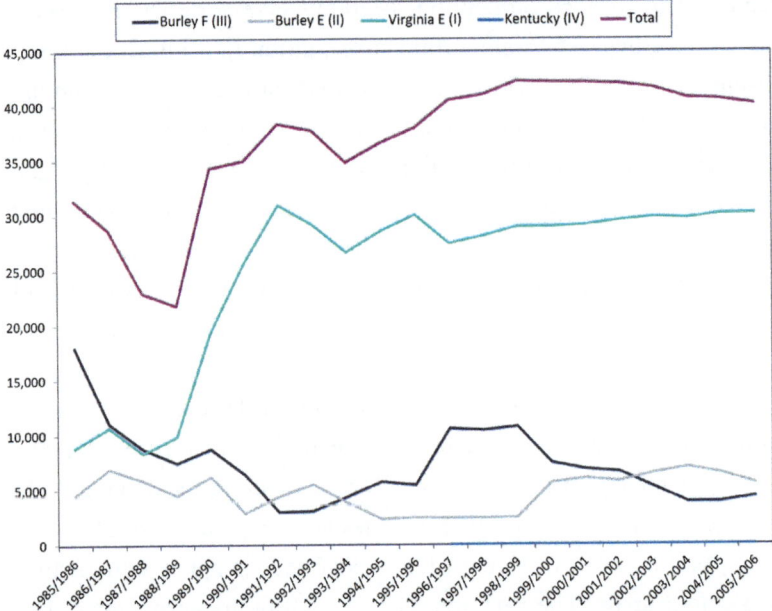

FIGURE 11.1 Volume of tobacco produced in Extremadura between 1985 and 2005 (tons).
Notes: Kentucky represents approximately 0.07 percent of total tobacco production each year.
Source: Authors based on data from the University of Extremadura.

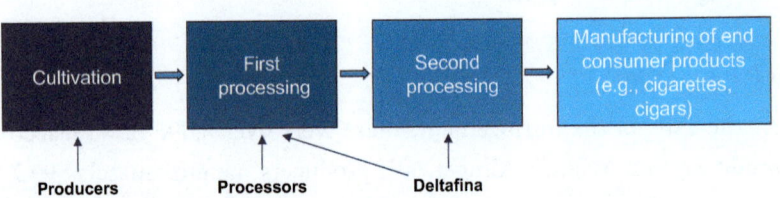

Source: Authors' analysis based on EC decision and "Mesa del Tabaco" 2015 Report.

FIGURE 11.2 Raw tobacco supply chain.
Source: Authors' analysis based on EC decision and "Mesa del Tabaco" 2015 Report.

percent) were members of one of ten raw tobacco producer groups, the *agrupaciones de productores de tabaco* ("APAs"). In addition, virtually all producers were linked to three agricultural branches or union organizations, the *organizaciones profesionales agrarias* ("OPAs"), or to the confederation of agricultural cooperatives ("CCAE").[10]

The three agricultural unions and the CCAE are collectively referred to as "the producer representatives." One of the critical roles of the producer representatives is to negotiate selling terms with the processors on behalf of groups of individual producers.

11.1.3 Processors

All processors in Spain at the time were part of the cartel. At the first processing stage, Compañía Española de Tabaco en Rama ("Cetarsa") was the state monopoly until 1990 and it still held a 90 percent market share in the 1993/94 marketing year.[11] Most of its tobacco sales were made to other processors and international dealers.[12]

Cetarsa had significant spare capacity, which it provided on contract to other processors. There were only three other first processors operating in the market at the time of the infringement:

- World Wide Tobacco España (WWTE), which carried out all the processing of the raw tobacco it bought from Spanish producers itself.[13]
- Agroexpansión, which did not possess all the equipment to process tobacco and therefore had processing contracts with another processor (unnamed in the decision, but most likely Cetarsa).[14]
- TAES, a sister company of Deltafina, which had virtually no equipment for the processing of tobacco and thus signed processing contracts with two other processors.[15]

---

[10] Decision (2004), paras. 33 and 34.
[11] The Decision refers to "marketing years" to reflect the tobacco growing and cultivation process. For example, in marketing year 1994/95, raw tobacco is planted between February and May 1994, cultivated between August and the first months of 1995, and marketed in 1995. As the standard contract negotiations occur before planting (which is 1994 in our example), we refer to 1994 as the pertinent year for the cartel activity, even though final prices with individual producers may not be agreed until cultivation is complete (in our example, 1995).
[12] Decision (2004), para. 20.   [13] Decision (2004), para. 25.
[14] Decision (2004), para. 22.   [15] Decision (2004), para. 27.

Table 11.1 *Processor market shares in Extremadura, 1997–2001*

Firm	1997 (%)	1998 (%)	1999 (%)	2000 (%)	2001 (%)
Agroexpansión	16.6	16.7	14.6	17.2	15.5
Cetarsa	62.8	63.0	66.7	65.1	67.3
TAES	2.5	1.8	2.5	1.9	1.6
WWTE	18.0	18.5	16.2	17.6	15.6

Source: Authors based on data from the University of Extremadura and Dossier Tabaco (Revista Rural).

Apart from the four Spanish processors, Deltafina, a subsidiary of the Universal Corporation and sister company[16] of TAES,[17] was sanctioned in the Decision for its role in the processors' cartel. Although Deltafina did not directly participate in the Spanish tobacco processing market, the EC found that it played a "preponderant role" in the processors' cartel, by virtue of it being the largest buyer of tobacco in Spain and, more importantly, for taking an active leadership role in the organization of the activities of the processors.[18] Table 11.1 presents the market shares of the first processors between 1997 and 2001.

11.2 REGULATION

The production of raw tobacco and its sale to processors are heavily regulated at the European Union level. The Common Market Organization ("CMO") in Raw Tobacco was established in 1970 and revised several times in the 1990s.[19] The CMO's main aim was to stabilize the tobacco market by controlling supply and providing a fair

---

[16] A sister company is a company that shares its parent company (in this case, the Universal Corporation) with another company (in this case, TAES).

[17] Decision (2004), para. 19.

[18] Summary decision, section 8, para. 1. Available here: https://eur-lex.europa.eu/legal-content/EN/TXT/PDF/?uri=CELEX:32007D0236. The General Court eventually dismissed the accusation of Deltafina being a leader. See here for more information: https://curia.europa.eu/jcms/upload/docs/application/pdf/2010-09/cp100079en.pdf; Coelho (2011), p.276.

[19] It was replaced in 1992 by a new regulation that was substantially amended in 1998; see Decision (2004), para. 39.

standard of living for tobacco farmers. For this purpose, the Spanish government used a system of premiums (or subsidies) for raw tobacco producers, and in 1995 put a quota system in place, and imposed certain rules on contract formation.

Notably, from 1999, the pricing schedules which served as guidelines for the final prices to be paid to producers were submitted jointly by the representatives of the producers and processors to the Spanish Ministry of Agriculture, that is, there was an industry-wide price agreement with knowledge of and approval by the government. Indeed, as mentioned in the summary of the decision:[20]

> Although the applicable national rules did not require the producer representatives and the processors to agree jointly on the price brackets and the additional conditions, the standard "cultivation contracts" negotiated between 1995 and 1998 mentioned that all the producer representatives would negotiate jointly with each individual processor the price schedules and the additional conditions relating to the sale of tobacco. In 1999 the Agriculture Ministry even approved the price schedules that had already been negotiated jointly by all the producer representatives and the four processors. These schedules were annexed to the "standard" contract published in the Official Gazette that year. Lastly, in 2000 and 2001 the Agriculture Ministry invited the representatives of the two sectors to a number of meetings – some of which were held at the Ministry itself – with a view to agreeing on the price schedules. In so doing, the Ministry did at least encourage the producers to press ahead with their joint negotiations on those schedules.

11.2.1 Producer Premium Scheme

The subsidies that tobacco producers could receive on their crop were substantial. Over the infringement period, the premiums constituted

---

[20] See summary of the decision published on April 19, 2007 in the Official Journal of the European Union (available at: https://eur-lex.europa.eu/eli/dec/2007/236/oj), page 5, section 9.2 (point (ii)).

approximately 84 percent of their total revenues.[21] Initially, these premiums were paid out to the raw tobacco processors, who were contractually obliged to pass them on to the producers. Since 1995, member states could opt for paying the premiums directly to the producers or through the processors. Spain chose the latter option and continued to pay the processors, who were then to pass the premium on to the producers through the cultivation contracts.[22] A subsequent reform in 1998 established that member states would pay the premiums directly to producers (and also that part of the premium would vary according to quality).

11.2.2 Quotas

From 1992 onward, the CMO also imposed controls on the production of tobacco by each member state, introducing a quota system for the processing of raw tobacco.[23] In principle, premiums were only paid for tobacco production within the quota, reducing incentives to exceed it. In addition, producers and producer organizations and producer groups were also given the freedom to contract freely with the processing company of their choice, effectively ending Cetarsa's monopoly on the processing side.[24]

The member states were required to allocate these quotas to processors established on their territory. By the end of the 1994/95 marketing year, the CMO was amended, and these quotas became production quotas in all member states. It was the raw tobacco

---

[21] Source: Authors' analysis based on data from the EC decision (para. 38) and Juan José Manzanero Iniesta e Inocencio Blanco Martín, "Tabaco," page 23. Available at www.unex.es/conoce-la-uex/centros/eia/archivos/iag/2005/2005_05%20La%20agricultura%20extremena.%20Informe%202005.pdf.

[22] Decision (2004), para. 42: "The processors undertook in the cultivation contracts concluded by them with the producer groups ... to pay to the producers at the time of delivery of the tobacco – in addition to the purchase price – an amount equal to the premium."

[23] Council Regulation (EEC) No 2075/92 of June 30, 1992.

[24] Minutes of the testimony before the Senate of the Chairman of Cetarsa, Mr. Gerardo Entrena Cuesta, on December 15, 1994. Available at: www.senado.es/web/actividadparlamentaria/iniciativas/detalleiniciativa/index.html?id1=713&id2=000264&legis=5.

producers and, since 1999, their groups (APAs) or the producers that were not members of a group that was allocated a quota under the scheme.[25]

11.2.3 Supply Contracts

Tobacco seeds were sown between February and May each year. Around April, the processor and producer groups met to discuss the standard contracts. In May, the land was fertilized, and the plants were treated. The processor and producer groups also met to discuss cultivation contracts during this time. The harvest took place between August and December, but it was not unusual that it continued during the first months of the following year. During the harvest, producers sold raw tobacco at cultivation prices that were based on the prices previously agreed upon in the cultivation contracts.

As part of the CMO regulation, rules on the cultivation contracts made in advance of the harvest season between producers and individual processors were introduced in 1995 and developed further in 1998.[26] Producers could not obtain the premium if they did not agree to a contract. The cultivation contracts had to be closed by May 30 of each year – far ahead of the harvest – and required specifying the price to be paid for the tobacco, depending on the grade.

Some additional rules and practices applied specifically in Spain. Between 1982 and 2000, the regulatory framework for agricultural activities allowed standard templates of cultivation contracts to be submitted for the Agriculture Ministry's approval. In the tobacco sector, these standard contracts were jointly negotiated by processors and producer representatives and served as the reference for the cultivation contracts to be negotiated between processors and producers, either by each producer group or by the individual producers not associated with any group.[27]

[25] Decision (2004), para. 41.   [26] Decision (2004), para. 50.
[27] Decision (2004), para. 53.

Under Spanish law, the standard contracts could be submitted to the Ministry both by producers and processors. Approval of standard contracts made the parties eligible for agricultural loans and insurance in Spain. It was mandatory for the standard contracts to include:

- a guaranteed minimum price schedule to be paid by the buyer per grade of variety for the marketing year, as negotiated by the OPAs; and
- the price that the producer must receive, as negotiated between the individual producer and the processor.[28]

This regulation was modified in 2000. The new law explicitly indicated that the prices should be negotiated individually by the parties for each cultivation contract.[29]

11.3 OPERATION, FORMATION, AND EFFECTIVENESS OF THE CARTELS

11.3.1 Formation

The formation of the processors' cartel, according to the Decision on March 13, 1996, followed a period of increasing competition between processors that was a direct consequence of the regulatory changes at the EU level and their implementation by the Spanish government. In particular, Cetarsa formally lost its near-monopoly in processing (and a near-monopsony in the acquisition of raw tobacco) in 1993, when the CMO introduced a system of production quotas. The situation did not change immediately, and in fact Cetarsa's market share initially grew.[30] However, by the 1994/95 marketing year, competition among processors for raw tobacco purchases started to intensify.[31] In addition, raw tobacco prices started to increase in

---

[28] Decision (2004), para. 57. [29] Decision (2004), paras. 62–65.
[30] Minutes of the testimony before the Senate of the Chairman of Cetarsa op. cit. 19, at page 17: "In the 1993 harvest, with the quota attributed to the growers, we had the great satisfaction of seeing that, without any kind of recruitment – which others did – we increased our market share by 2 or 3 percent."
[31] Ibid, pages 17 and 18.

1995/96, making Spanish tobacco less competitive and leading to competitive disadvantages for processors on export markets.[32]

This situation, in combination with an institutional framework that favored industry-wide bargaining, triggered the formation of the processors' cartel, which had the explicit objective of stabilizing the market and, in particular, seeking "to avoid price escalation."[33]

The producer representatives' cartel began in February 1996 and continued until at least August 10, 2001.[34] Therefore, the processors' cartel was formed after the producers' cartel. While a timeline of the infringement can be established, we cannot be sure that there was a formal causal relationship between the two cartels given the limited publicly available information and the short time span separating their formations.

11.3.2 Operation

The activities of the two cartels were organized around the raw tobacco marketing year. Each cartel would have its own meetings and agreements, but there were joint cartel events. Figure 11.3 summarizes our understanding of what could be considered a typical year of interactions between the two cartels.

In the period before the negotiation of the standard contracts (January to April), processors met to agree on a maximum price for each tobacco variety to be negotiated with the producer groups. Volumes to be purchased by each processor from each producer group were also discussed. The processors cartel appears not to have concerned processed tobacco prices, as the emphasis in the Decision is on reduction of the raw tobacco prices paid to the producers. Furthermore, the producer representatives met to agree on (i) a minimum price for each tobacco variety; and (ii) the prices to be paid, depending on the quality.

---

[32] Decision (2004), para. 84. [33] Decision (2004), para. 85.
[34] See page 100 (Article 1) in the Decision (2004).

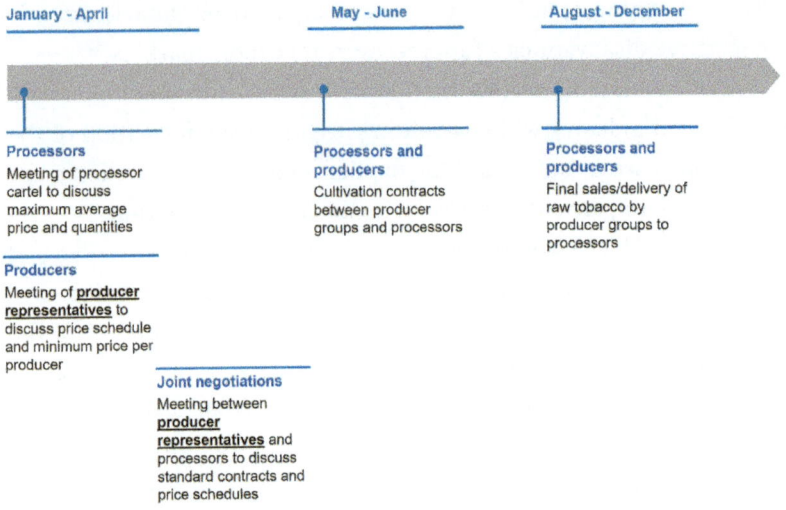

FIGURE 11.3 A typical year of negotiations between the two cartels.
Source: Authors based on EC decision.

Subsequently, in April and May, the negotiations of the standard contract between the processors' and the producers' representatives took place. Importantly, these discussions related not just to the wording of the standard contract, but also to the pricing schedules. In the later years of the infringement period, the price schedules were jointly agreed between producers and processors.

As mentioned, from 1999 onward, the pricing schedules were annexed to the standard contract submitted to the Spanish government and published in the Spanish Official Gazette (Boletín Oficial del Estado, "BOE"),[35] that is, there was an industry-wide price agreement with knowledge of and approval by the government.

---

[35] Decision (2004), para. 183. The BOE is the official gazette of the Kingdom of Spain. It publishes decrees by the Cortes Generales, Spain's Parliament (comprising the Senate and the Congress of Deputies) as well as orders enacted by the Spanish Autonomous Communities.

After the standard contract negotiations, between May and June, the cultivation contracts containing the purchase prices per quality grade for each variety and including the quantity commitments of the processors, were discussed between the processors and each producer group (or individual producers). From July to December, there were further contacts between the processors to exchange information on the terms of their respective cultivation contracts.

11.3.3 Effectiveness

The Decision reports that the processors' cartel was not very effective in the first two marketing years of its existence (1996/97 and 1997/98). In particular, the raw tobacco price and volume agreements concluded prior to the standard contract negotiations were subsequently not adhered to in the individual cultivation contract negotiations with producer groups. Individual processors tended to offer higher raw tobacco prices to secure supply. An immediate explanation for the cartel defection in these initial years was the lack of a punishment device. The payoff from deviating from the agreed price and volume had only upside with limited downside. Processors exceeded the maximum prices that were agreed among themselves with the aim of obtaining a higher market share. As a consequence, the stated goal of the processors' cartel – to limit increases of raw tobacco prices – was not achieved and prices continued to rise.[36] In particular, the prices that each processor subsequently negotiated with the producers' representatives show that none of them respected the agreements made at the beginning of the year. In addition, the processors kept Deltafina regularly informed of the failure to abide by the agreements.[37]

The situation changed in marketing year 1998/99 when the processors agreed on a formal monitoring process and a mechanism for compensation payments. At the start of each year, the processors

---

[36] See, for example, EC Decision (2004), paras. 139–140 and 144.
[37] Decision (2004), para. 112.

would agree on a maximum average price and a maximum quantity of each variety of tobacco that each of the processors could buy from producers within the cultivation contracts. Moreover, the processors that had paid the highest prices in 1997, namely Cetarsa and WWTE, agreed to reduce their buying prices in 1998. Whenever a processor exceeded its allocated quantity of tobacco, it had to compensate the processors that had not reached the target quantity in one of two ways: by paying compensation for tobacco purchases in excess of the target quantity, or by selling the excess quantities at the average price agreed to those processors that had suffered a shortfall with the producer groups in their cultivation contracts. Both the compensation to be paid by the processor who had exceeded its allocated quantity of tobacco and the selling price of these quantities were of the same magnitude and represented about 50 percent of the average prices paid to raw tobacco producers.

To assist in monitoring, bi-annual information exchanges among the members of the processors' cartel were introduced. The first of these two exchanges took place after the cultivation contracts between the processors and the producer groups were signed. Each processor communicated the total amounts it had agreed to purchase from each OPA to the other processor cartel members. This enabled members to monitor compliance with the agreed-upon purchase volume allocations. The second information exchange took place after the processors had purchased raw tobacco. As part of a self-reporting mechanism to verify compliance, representatives of the processors met and confirmed the quantities purchased and the prices paid by each processor. This was done by sharing their contracts and verifying purchases. The processors' cartel members did not rely on any third-party verification to check the quantities and prices.

According to the Decision, the new monitoring and compensation framework resulted in successful adherence to cartel prices and quantities from 1998 until 2001.[38] Moreover, starting in 1999, the

[38] Decision (2004), para. 168.

price schedules were even included in the approved standard contracts published in the Spanish Official Gazette. Those price schedules were then used in the individual cultivation contracts. This dissemination further contributed to the effectiveness and stability of the cartel arrangement.

11.3.4 Empirical Evidence

We have considered the evidence available in the public domain on prices and market shares to examine the impact of the cartel on market outcomes.

Data on the average price paid to the producers for each crop in the years from 1993 to 2016 is available in the public domain. Starting in 1993, Figure 11.4 shows the evolution of the prices paid to producers by tobacco variety in Spain. The solid vertical lines identify the

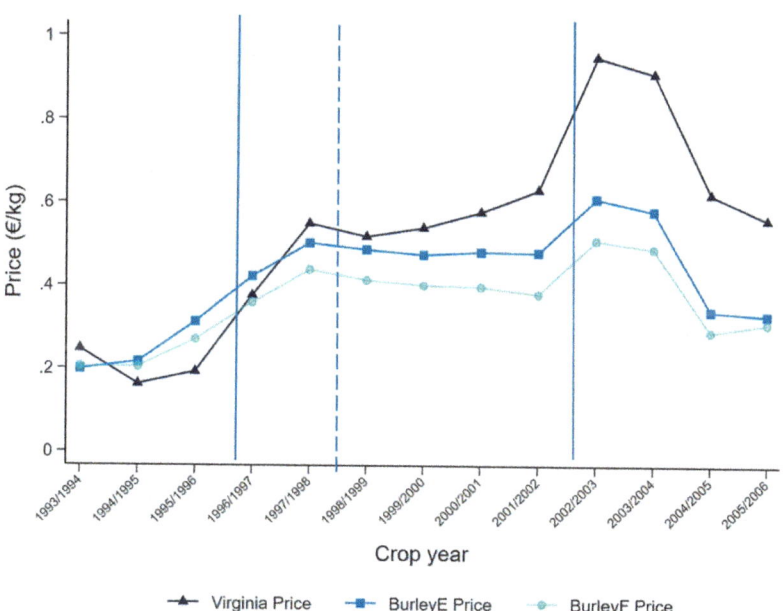

FIGURE 11.4 Prices paid to the producers, by tobacco variety.
Source: Authors' analysis based on the data described in the Annex.

beginning and the end of the infringement period, as reported in the Decision.

The chart shows four different phases in the evolution of prices. The first phase is prior to the start of the cartel. In 1994 and 1995, prices paid by processors to producers were on the rise. The second phase begins with the meetings among the processors. However, those initial meetings did not seem to achieve the objective of the processors' cartel as prices continued increasing in 1996 and 1997, as they had in previous years. The third phase is associated with the members of the processors' cartel realizing that the agreements were not being adhered to, which led them to introduce a monitoring and compensation system. We marked the start of this phase by a dotted vertical line. In the absence of a specific start date, the line has been placed mid 1998. We see that prices stabilized significantly from this point onward; in the case of the Burley varieties, they even decreased. In the fourth phase, prices increased significantly for the 2002/2003 crop, coinciding with the end of the cartel, as the EC carried out its dawn raids at the beginning of October 2001.

Table 11.2 shows some descriptive statistics of the prices paid to the producers, by tobacco variety, pre- and post-cartel, and in the two distinct phases in the cartel period (before and after 1998). It shows that price volatility (as measured by the coefficient of variation) in the first cartel subperiod was similar to the pre- and post cartel periods.

In contrast, prices in the 1998–2001 period were much more stable.[39] Although, on average, price levels for some varieties are similar within and outside the cartel period, the increased stability of prices during the second cartel subperiod is consistent with effective coordination.

---

[39] The lower coefficient of variation for price under collusion is consistent with behaviour observed in other cartels such as the frozen perch cartel (Abrantes-Metz et al. 2006).

Table 11.2 Summary of descriptive statistics on prices paid to the producers by variety

	Pre collusive period	1st cartel subperiod Exchange of information	2nd cartel subperiod Implementation of monitoring and compensation scheme	Post collusive period
Years	1993–1995	1996–1997	1998–2001	2001–2005
Virginia E				
Mean	0.2003	0.4625	0.5660	0.7600
Coefficient of variation	21.27	26.44	8.68	26.11
Burley E				
Mean	0.2424	0.4630	0.4810	0.4650
Coefficient of variation	25.32	12.21	1.03	32.40
Burley F				
Mean	0.2263	0.3990	0.3980	0.4000
Coefficient of variation	16.86	14.17	3.52	29.01

Source: Authors analysis based on the data described in the Annex.

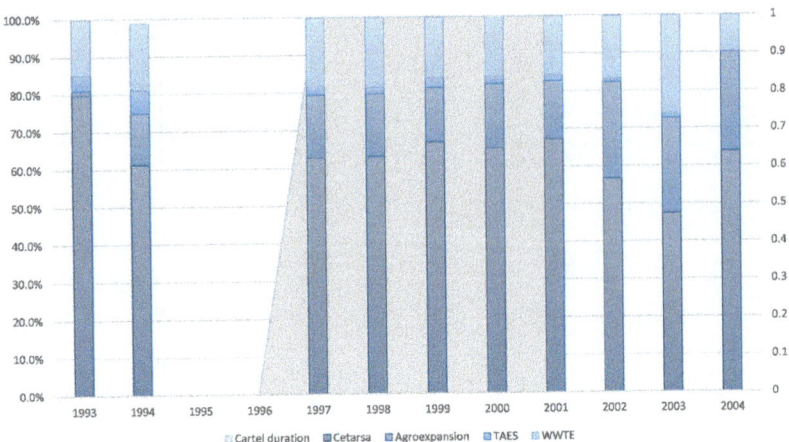

FIGURE 11.5 Processors' market shares for all the available years.
Source: Authors analysis based on data from the EC decision, Ministry statistics, a specialized magazine on agriculture (1999) and three press articles (2002, 2003 and 2004). See the Annex for detailed information on the sources.

It is important to be clear that the evolution of prices presented is merely suggestive of a correlation between the effectiveness of the cartel and the tobacco prices. Due to the lack of publicly available data on costs and other price determinants, we are unable to establish a clear causal link.

We have also considered the evolution of the processors' market shares, which are shown in Figure 11.5. The data are not available for every year, but an interesting pattern can still be observed. Prior to the cartel, Cetarsa's position as the former monopolist in tobacco processing eroded from 1993 to 1994, as other processors like WWT, TAES, and Agroexpansión gained market share. After the formation of the processors' cartel, we observe stable market shares from 1997 to 2001. In 2002, once the cartel was dismantled, the smaller processors gained market share again, at the expense of Cetarsa.

In sum, the data available on prices and market shares is consistent with the Decision's finding that, after the monitoring and compensation schemes were introduced in 1998, the processors' cartel was largely effective. This is consistent with previous findings, such as those of Levenstein and Suslow (2011), that many cartels adopt formal compensation rules and that cartels with such formal compensation mechanisms are significantly less likely to break up. The fact that the cartels only ended after an *ex officio* investigation by the EC, after which tobacco price rose again for a period, further attests to the stability of the cartels, as an intervention by the antitrust authorities was needed.

11.3.5 Other Aspects

The cartels took place in a market where regulation contributed to generate the rents that the cartels aimed at redistributing, and shaped the incentives of both producers and processors. At the same time, regulation may also have limited their impact on social welfare.

First, the quota system established by the government resulted in restricted supply, leading to increased prices and profitability. Thus, it is the regulatory intervention through quotas that primarily generated the scarcity rents, shaping market dynamics and influencing rent distribution and motivating the formation of the cartels.

The regulation implied that producers had incentives to reduce the production of tobacco, as they only obtained premiums on the tobacco produced within the quota. Further, no single producer group had an incentive to undercut the cartel price and gain market share. Hence, the regulation helped the producer cartel remain stable. At the same time, processors were incentivized to collaborate to keep the prices of raw tobacco from rising any further. This dual lever caused a scramble for rents on both sides of the market ultimately devolving in cartel activities on either side.

Second, in the context of a binding quota regime, it is likely that the cartel's influence would have been limited to redistributing rents between producers and processors, rather than causing substantial social welfare loss. Since quotas were allocated to producers and not to processors, the rents would have naturally accrued to the producers in the absence of any cartel behavior. This suggests that the social welfare loss resulting from the cartels may have been minimal, concentrated on the allocation of rents rather than on their overall magnitude.

11.4 CONCLUSION

The Spanish raw tobacco market shows how government regulation can inadvertently contribute to create collusion. The formation of the raw tobacco cartels was promoted by the CMO regulatory framework and changes thereof.

To begin with, the Spanish government favored the industry-wide negotiation of terms and promoted collective bargaining through the standard contracts system. Turning to the processors' cartel, its formation was likely triggered by changes in the CMO and the particularities of its implementation in Spain, which led to increased competition in the processing of raw tobacco. Before 1994, monopsony power allowed Cetarsa to purchase tobacco at very low prices. This changed when the quotas were instead allocated directly to producers which, given they now had alternative outlets, allowed them to command higher prices. These price increases caused by competition for raw tobacco purchases led processors to form their own cartel and coordinate on the prices they paid to the producers.

In sum, the regulatory context affects collusion dynamics. On the producer side, regulation encouraged coordinated activities that eventually led to a cartel. On the processor side, the government regulation gave competing buyers an incentive to coordinate their actions to keep prices from rising further. The presence of production quotas also made it easier for the processors to set up an enforcement mechanism, as there was a specified quantity that dictated the distribution of raw tobacco among themselves. Thus, the regulatory changes led to the two cartels arising in parallel, with each side seeking to maximize its share of the rents.

This suggests that cartel analysis should be tailored according to the regulatory context of the market. In a context where there are mandated quotas, the analysis should involve assessing cartel interactions in light of that regulation. In particular, when devising a subsidy scheme, one needs to be careful that rents do not get misappropriated through illicit means by other stages of the supply chain.

The raw tobacco case also attests to the difficulties of the self-enforcement of cartels and the importance of establishing an effective monitoring process and compensation mechanism for collusion to be effective. In its first two years, the processors' cartel was not effective; price and volume agreements were not adhered to and the prices they paid to producers kept increasing. The lack of effective collusion is especially remarkable given the high degree of market concentration – only four processors with one market leader – and intense monitoring. Furthermore, the quotas on the producer side also provided processors with an exogenously determined quantity to divide among themselves. In spite of these accommodating features, only when a compensation mechanism with a formal monitoring and information exchange procedure had been put in place did the processors' cartel achieve its goal. In contrast, the producer groups were successful in negotiating and adhering to a minimum average price. With a fixed quota for each producer, there was simply no incentive for any one producer to undercut the agreed-upon price.

A APPENDIX

Data sources

In this appendix we set out the data sources used in the case study. In particular, we show the sources from which we have collected the data for the analysis of prices paid to producers and the analysis of the processors' market shares.

Table 11.3 *Data sources for the analysis of prices paid to the producers*

Data period	Source type	Reference	Available at
1993–2000	EC Decision	Commission Decision of 20 October 2004 relating to a proceeding under Article 81(1) of the EC Treaty (Case COMP/C.38.238/B.2), 2007/236/EC.	https://ec.europa.eu/competition/antitrust/cases/dec_docs/38238/38238_249_1.pdf

Table 11.3 (cont.)

Data period	Source type	Reference	Available at
2001–2005	Journal article	Iniesta, J. J. M., & Martín, I. B. (2006). Tabaco. La agricultura y la ganadería extremeñas en…, (2005), 271–296	https://www.unex.es/ conoce-la-uex/ centros/eia/archivos/ iag/2005/2005_05%20 La%20agricultura%20 extremena.%20 Informe%202005.pdf
2006–2013	Ministry report	Ministry for Ecological Transition and the Demographic Challenge. (2013). Agricultura, Alimentación y Medio Ambiente en España 2013.	https://www.miteco .gob.es/content/dam/ miteco/es/ministerio/ servicios/ publicaciones/ Memoria-agricultura-2013_tcm30-84010 .pdf

Table 11.4 *Data sources for the computation of processors' market shares in Extremadura*

Data period	Source type	Reference	Available at
1993	Journal article	Martínez, J. S. (1994). La nueva OCM del tabaco crudo. La agricultura y la ganadería extremeñas en el sector del tabaco, (1993), 171–184.	https://www.unex.es/ conoce-la-uex/centros/ eia/archivos/iag/1993/ 1993_12%20La% 20nueva%20O.C.M.% 20del%20tabaco% 20crudo.pdf/view
1994	Journal article	Pérez Rubio, J. A. (1998). El nuevo escenario de la PAC y los agricultores tabaqueros.	https://www.mapa.gob .es/ministerio/pags/ biblioteca/revistas/pdf_ reeap/r184_03.pdf

Table 11.4 (cont.)

Data period	Source type	Reference	Available at
1997–1998	Journal article	Pérez, J. L. G. (1999). La nueva Organización Común de Mercado en el sector del tabaco. La agricultura y la ganadería extremeñas en..., (1998), 147–167	https://www.unex.es/ conoce-la-uex/centros/ eia/archivos/iag/1998/ 1998_11%20La% 20nueva% 20Organizacion% 20Comun%20de% 20Mercado%20en% 20el%20sector%20del %20tabaco.pdf
1999	Magazine article	Macías, J. C. (1999). Se inicia la transformación con una cantidad similar a la de 1998. Vida rural, 6 (95), 42–43.	https://www.mapa.gob .es/ministerio/pags/ biblioteca/revistas/pdf_ vrural/Vrural_1999_95_ 42_43.pdf
2000	Journal article	Pérez, J. L. G. (2001). La producción extremeña de tabaco. Análisis de las cosechas 1999 y 2000. La agricultura y la ganadería extremeñas en..., (2000), 141–160.	https://www.unex.es/ conoce-la-uex/centros/ eia/archivos/iag/2000/ 2000_8%20La% 20produccion% 20extremena%20de% 20tabaco.%20Analisis %20de%20las% 20cosechas%201999% 20y%202000.pdf
2001	EC Decision	Commission Decision of 20 October 2004 relating to a proceeding under Article 81(1) of the EC Treaty (Case COMP/C.38.238/ B.2), 2007/236/EC.	https://ec.europa.eu/ competition/antitrust/ cases/dec_docs/38238/ 38238_249_1.pdf

Table 11.4 (cont.)

Data period	Source type	Reference	Available at
2002	Newspaper article	Guerrero, A. (2003, April 7). "Ibertabaco abandona Cetarsa y se alía con World Wide Tobacco". El País.	https://cincodias.elpais.com/cincodias/2003/04/07/empresas/1049722788_850215.html
2003	Newspaper article	Guerrero, A. (2003, June 16). "La SEPI impide una posible entrada de la Junta de Extremadura en Cetarsa". El País.	https://cincodias.elpais.com/cincodias/2003/06/16/empresas/1055770783_850215.html
2004	Newspaper article	Cetarsa se relanza y procesará el 64% del tabaco español. (2004, July 02). el Periódico de Extremadura.	https://www.elperiodicoextremadura.com/economia/2004/07/02/cetarsa-relanza-procesara-64-tabaco-45630678.html?utm_source=mail&utm_me%E2%80%A6

REFERENCES

Abrantes-Metz, R. M., Froeb, L. M., Geweke, J., and Taylor, C. T. (2006) "A Variance Screen for Collusion," *International Journal of Industrial Organization*, 24(3), 467–486.

AFI, CEOE and Mesa del tabaco (2015) La importancia del sector tabaco en la economía Española, www.mesadeltabaco.es/files/Informe%20mesa%20del%20Tabaco.pdf.

Coelho, G. (2011) "Smoke without Fire – The Spanish Raw Tobacco Cartel Cases," *European Journal of Risk Regulation*, 2 (2), 275–278.

Commission Decision of October 20, (2004) "Relating to a proceeding under Article 81(1) of the EC Treaty (Case COMP/C.38.238/B.2), 2007/236/EC."

Dossier Tabaco (1999) "Revista Vida Rural, 15 de octubre. Judgment of the Court (Grand Chamber) of July 19, 2012 (Cases C-628/10 P and C-14/11 P)."

Levenstein, M. and Suslow, V. Y. (2011) "Breaking Up Is Hard to Do: Determinants of Cartel Duration," *The Journal of Law & Economics*, 54 (2), 455–492.

12 Is it Collusion or Competition behind Price Parallelism?

*Steel Manufacturing in Greece**

Yannis Katsoulacos and Marc Ivaldi

12.1 INTRODUCTION: BACKGROUND TO THE CASE, THE HCC INVESTIGATION AND ITS FINDINGS

12.1.1 Background

Following dawn raids in 2008,[1] the Hellenic Competition Commission (HCC) commenced an extensive investigation of the three Greek steel producers (SIDENOR, HALIVOURGIKI and HELLENIC HALIVOURGIA) and of their Industry Association (ENXE). This investigation was following (a) complaints from wholesalers[2] alleging that the producers were illegally colluding with

---

* The two authors acted as consultants to one of the three Greek steel manufacturers (SIDENOR). We are grateful for excellent research assistance, to Dr. Vasiliki Bageri, for the comments and suggestions and for the data provided, to the SIDENOR managers especially the Commercial Director Nikos Mariou, for providing in a very clear and succinct way detailed description of technical characteristics of production and of their mechanism of competitive price formation. Also to Prof. D. Tzouganatos and Dr N. Kosmidis who provided the legal defense for their excellent collaboration and comments. Last but not least we are grateful for the many constructive comments and suggestions by the two editors of this book. We note that Marc Ivaldi was responsible for the econometric analysis presented in Section 12.5 and Yannis Katsoulacos for the analyses in the other sections. Of course, all errors and ambiguities remain our own.

[1] The investigation continued until 2011, though much of our empirical analysis was based on data from 2002 to 2008. The Decision (no. 617) was taken in 2015 and concerned the *ex officio* investigation of the HCC to determine whether there was violation of articles 1 and 2 of law 703/11 or/and of law 3959/2011, and of articles 101 και 102 TFEU, in the production and the sale of the steel produced. Also it concerned the allegation with protocol number 3636/30.05.2008 for violation of these laws by IRON TENCO A.E. against the three steel companies mentioned in the text and also some steel wholesalers.

[2] Specifically, the company IRON TECNO. See Decision of HCC no.617/2015, 1–5. The complaint referred to "the common pricing policies of the three steel producers as manifested in the common, sudden and simultaneous change in their prices as a

respect to their pricing and (b) its own *ex officio* study of the Greek steel sector after widespread media reports of substantial common increases in prices. The objective was to investigate "the likelihood that there was a concerted practice between the three companies with respect to their pricing."[3] There was no hard evidence found of explicit collusive agreements between the three firms, however. Yet there was quite striking documented evidence of price parallelism during some specific periods (details are provided in Sections 1.2 and 1.3) and, specifically, evidence of the three firms changing their prices more or less simultaneously, which kept relative (list) prices more or less unchanged during the time that new list prices were announced by each firm. Accordingly, the HCC was concerned that the three steel producers were involved in tacit collusion or a concerted practice, possibly supported by their association ENXE,[4] that resulted in excessively high prices.

The three producers and ENXE categorically denied any involvement in price coordination, claiming that their behavior had always been independent and completely legal, that they were engaged in strong competition, and that the Greek steel market could not support collusive agreements. We were asked by SIDENOR to examine their claim that their behavior was not collusive and indeed could not be other than competitive. For this we used extensive economic analysis, detailed data about the evolution of prices in relation to costs, production and capacity levels, imports, and exports, and modeling of the structural conditions of the market, as well as econometric analysis.

In this case study, we draw on our findings to present a case of a mistaken allegation of collusion. We will explain, in the context of

---

result of a cartel-type agreement between them" (5). Also they concerned allegation of the three companies cooperating with a public sectoral R&D company (EVETAM), setting standards in the industry, that made, it was claimed, more difficult the importation of steel into Greece. Here we examine only the first allegation.

[3] Decision 617/2015, 3.

[4] Through information exchange. See p. 98 of Decision 617/2015. The HCC investigation focused on the potential existence of a concerted practice (102).

this case, that competition and collusion can be difficult to distinguish on the basis of observed patterns of price evolution which contain incidences of parallelism. Subsequently, we will discuss a number of ways through which a proper distinction can be achieved. In other words, our analysis of the Greek steel market serves to demonstrate how it can be shown that competitive behavior can provide a reasonable alternative explanation of the patterns of price and other market changes to that of tacit collusion.

The difficulty of correctly associating price parallelism with tacit collusion[5] is of course appreciated since the early landmark European case of Wood Pulp.[6] The HCC Decision recognizes this as the case that "has prescribed the relation between (legal) price parallelism and (illegal) concerted practice" (105). As observed by the Wood Pulp Decision, "when parallel behaviour can be explained with reasonable reasons other than those associated with the existence of collusion, in the conditions of the case under investigation, **the parallel behaviour cannot be considered illegal**, because it constitutes the legal consequence of (oligopolistic interaction)" (106). The allegations against the Greek steel producers were based on the assumption that the behavior of the Greek steel producers could not be explained other than as collusion, which we show to be false.

After a thorough examination of the steel market in Greece and of the behavior of the three producers, and taking into account the arguments put forward by the defendants and their consultants, the HCC considered in its Decision 617/2015 that there were no grounds to support the allegations of collusive behavior and decided to acquit the companies of this charge. To reach this conclusion the HCC relied on three considerations:

---

[5] See also the Decision 617/2015.
[6] Judgment of the Court of 27 September 1988. – *A. Ahlström Osakeyhtiö and Others* v. *Commission of the European Communities*. – Concerted practices between undertakings established in non-member countries affecting selling prices to purchasers established in the Community. – Joined cases 89, 104, 114, 116, 117 and 125 to 129/85.

(i) Market structure characteristics and demand fluctuations were not such as to create the conditions that, according to economic theory, are associated with a strong likelihood of collusion. Furthermore, a very high degree of transparency can be considered responsible for the quick adjustment in the prices of the rival producers to a change in the (list) price of one of them (112–115). We examine this consideration in the next subsection and in Section 12.3.
(ii) The evolution of prices and other market changes can be explained reasonably and plausibly as an outcome of competitive behavior, which implies, according to EU case law mentioned above, that parallelism cannot be considered illegal. We examine this in Sections 12.3 and 12.4.
(iii) Finally, the HCC established from the information it collected from the three companies that price parallelism did not, in by far most cases, involve *final prices* paid by their customers, which implied that there was competition between the producers through the use of discounts on their list prices (page 111 of the Decision).[7]

12.1.2 The HCC Investigation

In the context of procedures that it used to obtain detailed information about the three companies' pricing practices, the HCC undertook dawn raids in July 2008 at the offices of the three steel producers as well as of ENXE and nine wholesalers. It also collected information from extensive questionnaires sent to the producers, ENXE, the Greek Standardization Organization, and the Greek Statistical Office.[8] Preliminary findings of patterns of price parallelism that were identified motivated the HCC's subsequent investigation.[9]

Concerning pricing practices, as observed by the HCC in its Decision, two of the steel producers issue, as a matter of policy, list prices for all the steel products for all areas in Greece. Their clients are aware of these wholesale prices, and each customer can negotiate discounts that could be applied to its contract. The HCC found that the

---

[7] It should be mentioned here that our information did not extend to information on the level of final prices of the three producers.
[8] Decision 617/2015, 33–34.
[9] These preliminary findings were subsequently shown not to constitute an appropriate basis for supporting the allegation of a concerted practice, as mentioned in Section 12.1.1.

majority of *price adjustments to their clients by these two producers involved adjustments in the list prices.* Thus, for the period 2004–2011, one of the two producers adjusted its list prices seventy-five times and adjusted its prices through discounts twelve times. The other company had adjusted its list prices seventy-eight times and its prices through discounts five times. With regard to price parallelism, "both companies adjusted their prices either directly or through discounts, by the same amount, either on the same day or with a day difference 76 times."[10] The third company did not issue list prices. In order to compare its price adjustments to those of the other two companies, the HCC used the "price offers" made by the company during 2004–2008 (obtained during the dawn raid from the company's electronic files). In three days during 2008, it was found that "all three producers adjust their prices in a common way (simultaneously and by the same amount)."[11]

Concerning the adjustments in the list (or offer[12]) prices, the HCC notes that all firms described exactly the same process that justifies the high speed of adjustment (depicted in a diagram in page 64 of the Decision): "a change in the cost in the international or domestic market creates the need to adjust prices and this is announced immediately by one company or plant (within 1 hour), and the information is diffused quickly between competitors, so an announcement follows immediately by the other companies."[13]

12.1.3 Additional Remarks Regarding the Process of Price Formation

Some more remarks concerning the process of price formation and adjustments are useful here.[14] To start with, all three firms can get, from the same sources, the same detailed information each morning, at the same time, international and regional price levels and price

---

[10] Decision 617/2015, 61.   [11] Decision 617/2015, 63.
[12] As noted for two firms it is the lost prices and for the third the offer prices.
[13] Decision 617/2015, 63–64.
[14] The information in the remainder of this section was obtained from our own interviews of company representatives.

changes for each product type. This allows them to determine the maximum price that a Greek producer would be able to sell in the domestic market given the prices that Greek importers can purchase steel in other countries *and deliver* it to Greek customers.[15] Note that there are wholesalers that are pure importers of steel. This maximum price will be different for different countries. There will be such a maximum price related to imports from Italy, the country that can provide equivalent quality steel with the minimum differences in other conditions (e.g., credit) to that of Greek producers at minimum transport cost, and higher maximum prices related to other countries. The domestic producers operate in one of the most competitive regional markets in the world which includes Italy, Turkey, and Ukraine, all of whom are some of the largest producers and exporters of steel worldwide.

Focusing on a maximum import price, this *reference price* is common knowledge to all Greek producers and importers at any given time; it is determined outside the Greek market, and so they consider it as exogenous as far as they are concerned. Demand in Greece is too small to influence the import prices from Italy or Turkey, two very large international players in the steel market.[16] The demand faced by the domestic producers has a kink at the price level corresponding to the reference price of imports. Given total domestic demand at prices lower than this level, imports are given by total demand minus domestic production which depends on the capacity levels of the three producers. Along with the ex-works (EXW) export price,[17] the marginal production cost (the maximum of which determines "effective marginal cost") and the production capacities of the producers, we can determine the monopoly (or full collusion) price, the oligopolistic competitive price, and

---

[15] These prices are the ex-works prices in the country of origin, plus transport cost, plus various duties that have to be paid in the ports, plus the margin of the wholesalers.

[16] In 2011 Greek production was about 1.8 million metric tons (which covered domestic demand), compared to 30m in Italy, 35m in Turkey and 36m in Ukraine.

[17] This is the price that a Greek producer receives from exports net of any transport, port, shipping, and insurance costs that the buyer has to incur to get the steel to its location.

the efficient (perfectly competitive) price and corresponding output levels. The producers claimed that their prices were the oligopolistic competitive prices or, for short, "competitive prices."

The reference (import) price is changing when cost conditions change (especially the price of the main input, scrap, which takes up 60 percent of the final price, as well as other materials and energy) or there are changes in the factors that affect demand for steel regionally and internationally (primarily related to the construction industries). A change in the reference price induces a change in the competitive domestic list prices[18] announced by the producers to the wholesalers or other customers, who are seeking new contracts and trying to get the best deal. A change in domestic prices can also be induced by a change in domestic demand.

As noted above, the HCC Decision mentions that all companies explained in the same way why the competitive changes in list prices – independently set (as they claimed) – in response to changed market conditions, would be announced at about the same time.[19] We add here the importance in explaining the actions of wholesalers and other (direct) customers when a change in price is announced by one of the producers. They will immediately inform the other producers of this change in order to confirm this is an industry wide change, something which leads to the immediate announcement of price changes by the other producers. This action by wholesalers and other customers is necessary in order for them to ensure that:

(i) They cannot get a better deal from another producer or, in the case of a wholesaler facing a price fall, that it does not lose customers who get better deals from other producers;

---

[18] Or, as mentioned above, offer prices for one producer that does not issue list prices. As also noted, Greek producers may offer quantity discounts to their customers or, for example, provide credit or delivery facilitation.

[19] The decision to change prices may not be immediate as producers may wait a few days to confirm that the change in market conditions affecting the regional and international price levels are not temporary. This does not affect the argument that follows.

(ii) They know the current value of their stock;
(iii) They do not sell to their own customers (in case of wholesalers) at too low a price relative to the price that will prevail in the market.

However, given the asymmetries between the producers, these actions of wholesalers do not necessarily imply that the changes in prices will be the same, as the HCC notes that they are in a number of cases. As noted also below, this suggests that specific pieces of evidence are not sufficient for proving the presence or absence of collusion and that it is only the combination of the assessment of various considerations together that can allow a judgment.

12.2 MARKET ANALYSIS: DO MARKET CONDITIONS SUPPORT THE HYPOTHESIS OF A STRONG LIKELIHOOD OF TACIT COLLUSION?

12.2.1 Introduction

In this and the next section we present two approaches that were used to examine the hypothesis that there was tacit collusion between the three steel producers in the period under examination:

(i) Section 12.2 offers an investigation of the structural characteristics of the Greek market.
(ii) Section 12.3 involves an investigation that relies on a number of screen tests applied to the available data[20], on prices, costs, shares, capacities, domestic demand, volume of domestic sales, imports, and exports, in order to identify patterns in the evolution of the data that would be unlikely to hold in the presence of tacit collusion between the producers during 2002–2011. A model of Bertrand-Edgeworth (B-E) competition between three capacity-constrained sellers was used to describe the competitive market equilibrium and compare with the collusive outcome.
(iii) Section 12.4 provides further empirical evidence to support the main conclusions derived from the analyses presented in Sections 12.2–12.3. To do so, we estimate a differentiated-products oligopoly model while taking account of the competitive constraint imposed by the

[20] See for example, Harrington (2005, 2006) and Abrantez-Metz and Bajari (2009).

international steel market and then test which behavioral hypothesis – collusion or competition – best represents the functioning of the Greek steel market.

12.2.2 The Nature of Products

The investigation concerned three steel products: reinforcing steel in bars (known as rebar), common steel mesh, and steel jackets. These are complementary products of steel used in certain proportions in the construction industry. Rebar, being the main product and making up about 85 percent of total domestic production, is the focus of the econometric analysis. These products are to a large extent homogeneous, though there are attributes related to the products themselves and to the services provided by each of the firms that could make wholesalers and their customers treat firms as offering differentiated products; this is particularly true of imports with which it is easy to supply the Greek market mainly from Italy, Turkey, and to a lesser extent Ukraine and Egypt.[21] This is due to the fact that imports may not satisfy all the technical standards which are established by the Greek Standardization Organization (though this does not hold for Italy and other EU countries). Quality differentiation may be the result of differences in the purity of the main input used in steel production (scrap). The other main differentiating factors are:

(i) The credit conditions provided, which are usually better from Greek producers and may differ even between the latter;
(ii) The amount of time needed for delivery, especially at times when there is a trend of price reductions;
(iii) Exchange rate risks for imports from outside the EU;
(iv) Greek producers differ also in the range of varieties offered in order to satisfy customized orders as well as in various peripheral services offered depending on the size of their distribution network and sales force that

---

[21] Imports from other EU countries, for example, Spain, are certainly feasible too, at somewhat higher transport cost and, indeed, Greek producers have also been exporting in some periods to Spain.

can lower transaction costs and strengthen the perceived quality of purchasing by a specific producer.

According to available data, about 80 percent of the buyers purchase steel from all the different Greek producers which implies a significant degree of homogeneity but also the presence of some differentiating factors. Also, SIDENOR is able to charge a price per ton that is slightly above (by about 1–1.5 percent or 3–5 euros) that of the other Greek producers and the Greek producers can charge slightly higher prices than those of steel producers in other (especially non-EU) countries, without losing customers for the reasons mentioned above.

12.2.3 Structural Conditions

According to economic theory,[22] sustainable tacit collusion can occur if two necessary (though not sufficient) conditions hold:

A. Firms must all have the *incentive* to reach a common understanding concerning the prices to be charged;
B. The conditions in the market must be suitable for making coordination *feasible*. Specifically, there must be:
   (a) an ability to monitor the behavior of rivals;
   (b) a credible mechanism for deterring cheating;
   (c) conditions that allow the coordinated behavior to be sustainable.

We discuss the main conditions known to result in an incentive and an ability to collude and assess whether they apply to the Greek steel producers case to an extent that would give support to the hypothesis of illegal cooperation.

Incentives for Cooperation
The strength of the incentives for cooperation depends on the strength of the producers' common interests in the cooperative scenario, something that depends on the extent to which strategic objectives are

---

[22] See Ivaldi, Jullien, Rey, Seabright, Tirole (2003) for a succinct summary.

sufficiently aligned. Strong incentives will result under various conditions, but the following factors are particularly important:

(a) Cross-ownership: each firm has financial interests in the other firms even if these do not imply control of the other firms;
(b) There is significant symmetry between firms – in terms of market share, capacity, cost and demand conditions;
(c) Absence of "maverick" firms, that is, of firms that constrain effective coordination because they do not have the same incentives in cooperating.

None of the above factors was present in the Greek steel industry. The three companies did not (and do not) have financial interests in each other and so this significant factor that strengthens incentives to collude is absent.

When there are asymmetries, firms are *less likely* to "agree" on a common collusive price that is significantly higher than the competitive price; even when this is achieved, some firms are more likely to end up with strong incentives to deviate from the "agreement" and not to be equally disciplined by the prospect of punishment. While the demand conditions are broadly symmetric between the three companies, there have been quite strong asymmetries in market shares, mainly as a result of asymmetries in production capacities, and also asymmetries in cost between at least two of the companies.[23] These asymmetries weaken the incentives to collude especially when the total production capacity in the market is inadequate,[24] as it was in six out of the eight years in the market under examination.

In relation to asymmetries, it is also worth mentioning here the factor of "multi-market presence" (which is also relevant in the discussion on feasibility of tacit collusion below).[25] While multi-market presence can facilitate collusion when it is limiting asymmetries, this is not the case here: while there is presence in other markets of the Greek producers, this presence actually *increases* the asymmetries

---

[23] This was confirmed by the HCC Decision, 113–114.
[24] See Compte, Jenny, and Rey (2000) for an analysis of the effects on collusion of capacity levels.
[25] Bernheim and Whinston (1991) and Evans and Kessides (2001).

between them because the producers with the higher domestic market share have also the largest presence in other markets.

Maverick firms can be smaller firms that are in a phase of expansion of their production capacity, something that can lower significantly the collusive price and the share of profits of the other firms and hence lead to a breakdown of the tacit agreement. In the Greek steel market, one firm faced a significant capacity disadvantage in 2002 but managed to reverse this by internal growth – significant investments in increasing capacity (that often seemed not to make good economic sense to its rivals and other observers) – and thus increasing market share from 7 percent to 27 percent by 2009. Thus, the behavior of this firm during the period under consideration is consistent with that of a maverick firm.

Hence, we can conclude that the relevant structural conditions present in the Greek steel market in the years 2002–2011 *do not provide strong incentives* for collusive behavior, though we recognize that asymmetries between the producers are not generally incompatible with collusive behavior. This suggests that individual screen tests in isolation for proving collusion or no collusion can be of limited value. It is really the combination of various indicators, including a convincing set of alternative, competition explanations for observed behavior that should be decisive for a judgment.

Is Collusion Feasible?

(a) **Ability to monitor the behavior of rivals.** This depends on:

- The degree of market concentration, on market transparency, market stability, and predictability of demand evolution.

    The high concentration implied by the presence of just three firms that are active in the Greek steel market and the high degree of transparency (on which we will return in more detail below) facilitate the monitoring of rivals. However, market conditions were volatile during the period under investigation with domestic demand falling from 2050 tons in 2002 to 1800 tons in 2004, then rising to 2300 tons in 2006 and falling again to 1817 tons in 2008. The two declines in demand were anticipated as they followed the big increase induced by the Olympic Games (that took place in mid-2004) and the big increase induced by the change in the regulatory framework that affected favorably the Greek construction industry in 2005 and 2006.[26] Under such conditions, it was relatively difficult for the steel producers to achieve tacit collusion at least prior to the anticipated demand decreases.[27]

- Product differentiation and discount-based pricing[28]

    This could in principle affect the monitoring of rivals' behavior but we did not expect an adverse effect on monitoring in the Greek steel market where as mentioned above there are certainly no strong elements of product differentiation. On the other hand, as mentioned, the producers' competed rigorously on the basis of discounts off their announced list prices, which are very difficult for rivals to monitor.

- Asymmetries

    Given the high degree of market transparency, we did not expect that the asymmetries between the three steel producers would significantly affect monitoring of rivals.

(b) A credible mechanism for deterring cheating. While transparency and ability to monitor rivals' behavior, as well as the fact that prices are often adjusted (see also below) facilitate retaliation following deviation of a rival from the tacit agreement, the threat of retaliation was not credible because, for most of the period 2002 to 2008, the firms were facing capacity constraints in expanding production and costs increase very rapidly after production exceeds 75 perent of this capacity (see also below).

From the above it follows that, while the factors that affect the monitoring of rivals' behavior are not overall unfavorable to establishing a tacit agreement, there was not an effective mechanism of deterring deviations from this agreement and hence the likelihood of tacit collusion having been sustained was small.

(c) Conditions for the coordinated behavior to be sustainable. The conditions for sustainability were not satisfied:

- As already noted, one of the three firms could be characterized as maverick.
- Potential competition is strong. There are no legal or regulatory barriers to the entry of new firms or the expansion of smaller rivals in the domestic market though there is quite a significant sunk entry cost for the

---

[26] That reduced taxation on new building construction.
[27] See Haltiwanger and Harrington (1991).   [28] See Motta (2004) and Ross (1992).

establishment of a new plant. But it is worth mentioning that one of the three firms (Halivourgiki) exited the market in 1990 and re-entered without difficulty in 2000, while expanding its capacity and market share to 27 percent by 2008. However, potential competition is very strong because of the ease in importing steel to Greece; on average over the years 2002–2008 when the capacity of Greek firms was constrained in most years, imports made up about 15 percent of market supply. The availability of imports, with Greek wholesalers sometimes having been active only as importers, limits considerably the ability of Greek producers to jointly increase prices to supracompetitive levels since these are constrained by competition from other countries' producers.

- Significant buyers' power can reduce the sustainability of collusion.[29] In the Greek steel industry, while most buyers and wholesalers do not have significant power, their power is not always negligible. For example, a very large construction company accounted for 15 percent of Sidenor's sales and one wholesaler accounted for 10 percent.

Considering all the above factors we conclude that the likelihood of tacit collusion to be sustainable was low.

Overall, the conclusion from the above qualitative analysis is that there were weak or no incentives for collusion in the Greek steel market and, while there were some factors that could have been conducive to collusion, other factors constrained significantly the extent to which collusion could be feasible and sustainable in the period under examination. Of course, in and of itself, this does not prove that there was no collusion. Yet it indicates that structural market conditions in the Greek steel industry were more conducive to competitive than to collusive behavior.

12.3 LIKELIHOOD OF TACIT COLLUSION: SCREEN TESTS

As noted above, a number of screen tests were also applied to the available data on prices, costs, shares, capacities, domestic demand, volume of domestic sales, imports, and exports in order to identify patterns in the evolution of the data during 2002–2011. A model of Bertrand-Edgeworth (B-E) competition between the three capacity-constrained sellers was

---

[29] See, for example, Ivaldi et al. (2003), 53.

used to describe the competitive market equilibrium and compare it with the collusive outcome. The results are summarized below.

Conclusion 1

The Greek steel market faced excessive domestic demand (relative to total capacity of the three producers) in 2002–2003, excessive capacity in 2004, excessive demand in 2005–2006, and excessive capacity from 2007–2011. Despite these episodes of insufficient demand, two of the three producers invested heavily in new capacity during this period and Sidenor's investment was intended to reduce its costs. The increase in capacity is related to the elimination of imports, that fell from 18 percent in 2003 to 0.7 percent of domestic steel consumption in 2010. Domestic consumption is about the same in 2003 and 2007 but domestic consumption was significantly reduced after 2007 while capacity had at the same time significantly increased.[30] The behavior that led to the increase in capacity (especially by one of the firms that could be characterized as a maverick) is not compatible with sustainable tacit collusion but it is compatible with strong competition between the three producers.

Conclusion 2

As already mentioned and is clear from Table 12.1, the market shares of the three producers fluctuated over the period examined without a negative correlation, and these fluctuations in shares were not the same so relative market shares changed. This is another sign of strong competition between them for market share.[31]

---

[30] This increase in domestic capacity and significant reduction in demand meant that imports were squeezed out. Indeed, domestic demand fell significantly following the 2004 Olympic Games but, in anticipation, the government introduced a new law after the Games that lowered taxes on new building construction which led to a temporary increase in the demand for steel up to 2007.

[31] We remind the reader that domestic prices were kept just below the delivered prices of imports (otherwise imported steel could easily satisfy all domestic demand) and imports were equal to domestic consumption minus the production of the three Greek producers. When domestic capacity was still low relative to domestic

Table 12.1 *Product X market shares*

Undertaking	2002 (%)	2003 (%)	2004 (%)	2005 (%)	2006 (%)	2007 (%)	2008 (%)
Firm A	40	36	37	35	37	40	42
Firm B	31	34	33	33	27	30	25
Firm C	8	8	13	21	18	23	28
Imports	20	22	17	11	18	7	4

Source: Confidential industry data

Conclusion 3
Sidenor's delivered price in periods of excess capacity fell below the prices of imports from Italy and even Turkey, though when there is no excess capacity prices track or are a bit higher than those of these countries, indicating competitive behavior.

Conclusion 4
When we move from excessive demand to excessive capacity as happened between 2004 and 2007, the domestic ex-works ((EXW) prices converge to the export prices (the effective marginal cost), something consistent with competitive but not collusive behavior. Further, exactly as predicted by the model of competitive behavior, in period of excessive capacity there is a strong squeeze of the ex-work prices to marginal cost. This conclusion is strengthened when we calculate prices net of the cost of credit facilitation and of the unit avoidable cost, for then the margins are *negative* from 2008 onward.

Conclusion 5
Some other price-related screen tests for collusion are also relevant. These are the following[32] (the third test has been performed

demand, imports were quite significant but their share converged to zero as domestic capacity was increased and domestic demand was reduced.

[32] They are included in the survey of Abrantes-Metz and Bajari (2009) "Screens for Conspiracies and their Multiple Applications," *Antitrust*, Vol. 24.

by, for example, Abrantez-Metz R., L. Froeb, J Gewke, and C Taylor, 2005).[33]

Under collusive behavior, price increases do not appear to be explainable by increased costs. We observe that this is not true for domestic prices when taking into account that export prices constitute the effective marginal cost of domestic producers.

Under collusive behavior, discounts are eliminated which is something that has certainly never occurred in the market under investigation.

Prices tend to be stable under collusion and do not follow cost movements very closely. We calculated the mean, the standard deviation, and the coefficient of variation (CV = mean / standard deviation) of Sidenor's domestic final prices, domestic marginal production cost, and export EXW prices. Under competitive behavior, one expects the standard deviation and CV for domestic and EXW export prices and domestic marginal cost are quite close and this is indeed what we find. Actually, the standard deviation of final and EXW export prices are almost identical and the CVs of prices and marginal production cost are extremely close.[34]

The results in this and the two previous sections support the overall conclusion that the evolution of the market in the period 2002–2011 can be more satisfactorily interpreted in terms of a hypothesis of competition than a hypothesis of (tacit) collusion.

12.4 ECONOMETRIC ANALYSIS OF THE GREEK STEEL MARKET

In this section we offer further empirical evidence that the observed pricing in the Greek steel market at the time was not collusive. We consider a differentiated-products oligopoly model and show that the pricing patterns are consistent with competition and not with

---

[33] In "A Variance test for collusion," FTC Working Paper.
[34] The relevant table cannot be reproduced here as it contains confidential information.

monopoly. To that end we estimate both demand and supply sides of the industry before testing for collusion against competition. Although the main product is reasonably homogenous, the commercial practices of the different firms (as noted in Section 12.2) could introduce a significant level of differentiation, which we need to consider. This explains the choice of the model that we detail later.

In the sequel, for brevity, we name the three firms of the industry as A, B, and C, and we name the main product type (rebar) product X.

Before presenting the econometric analysis, let us first provide a description of the data made available to us.

12.4.1 Descriptive Analysis

The data, which covers the period 2002–2008, are complete for firm A and for the whole industry. They bear on the domestic prices of firm A, its domestic production levels and exports, its production capacities, the prices of raw material Y, the prices of international product X, the production capacities of competitors, and the level of Greek exports of product X. Some approximations of the market size are also available. However, we do not observe the prices of product X sold by competitors, nor do we have measures of any quality differences between the firms' products.

Market Figures

The three main competitors' domestic market shares during the period under investigation are reported in Table 12.1. Firm A's market share is the highest during the period under consideration, fluctuating between 35 percent in 2005 and 42 percent in 2008. The yearly difference in terms of market share between firm A and the second largest producer, namely firm B, is about 10 percent, except for 2005. The third producer, firm C, experiences a jump in its production level in 2004–2005 following the increase in its production capacities. Up to 2004, firm C's market share is lower than the market share of

FIGURE 12.1 Final prices vs. list and imported prices.
Source: Data on the industry provided by SIDENOR. The unit is euro per ton.

importers. Since 2005, this trend is reversed. Finally, observe a sharp drop in imports at the end of period.

The differences in market shares across competitors might be indicative of differentiation among their products, though they also reflect differences in capacity levels. In the absence of any differentiation, and keeping capacity unchanged, the industry should tend to a symmetric equilibrium. (See, however, Besanko and Doraszelski, 2004, on this point.)

Two types of prices are available for firm A: the list price and the final price.[35] Their evolution over the period are similar, as shown in Figure 12.1, but the list prices are significantly higher than the final prices. As the final prices are the prices actually paid by customers, they are more relevant than list prices in the analysis of the demand side of the market.

[35] See the end of Section 1.1 for a discussion relating to the pricing policies of the companies to list prices and final prices, where the latter are the list prices after discounts are applied.

The main importers of product X (Italy and Turkey) are referred to as country 2 and country 3; they compete with domestic firms' products. Although the final prices of firm A are often higher than the prices of importers, there remains a positive demand for the domestic products. The domestic firms might take advantage of their domestic position, differentiating their production of product X through commercial networks and marketing activities. In the sequel, we aggregate the importers (which, from here on, we refer to as the Representative Importer) and we use a weighted average of importers' prices for the price of imports.[36]

Consider now the quantities. The relevant quantities are firm A's production, both for domestic and international markets. We observe that firm A's domestic production decreases until 2004, then increases until 2007 (see Figure 12.2). There is a downturn starting in 2008. The level of imports and the total market size show roughly the same evolution, while the exports increase until 2005 and remain stable thereafter. Firm A's production capacities increase in 2006.

Discussion on Capacity Constraints[37]

A crucial issue related to identifying the market equilibrium is to characterize the level of capacity utilization (Figures 12.3 and 12.4). If one looks at the situation of firm A as presented in Figure 12.3, the level of capacity utilization is higher than 75 percent, which is considered the efficient level of production,[38] in all years except in 2003 and 2004; these latter years experience excess capacity.

Figure 12.4 displays how the capacity utilization has evolved during the period under investigation at the industry level. We observe only one year where there is excess capacity, specifically 2004. With 76.09 percent capacity utilized, the year 2008 is just at the

---

[36] We could have used the lowest price of importers prices and it would not affect the conclusions.
[37] Here we consider total capacity referring to physical capacities that can be directed to domestic sales or to exports.
[38] That is, the level of production at which unit cost minimization is achieved. The figure of 75 is based on information provided by the company directors.

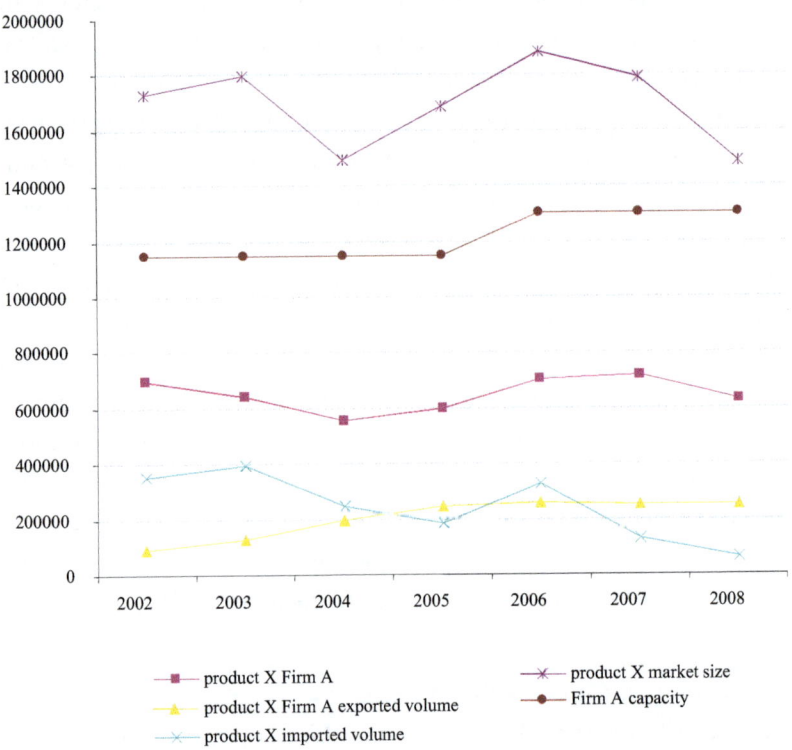

FIGURE 12.2 Domestic market size, level of productions, and capacities.
Source: Confidential data on the industry. The volumes are expressed in tons.

threshold for full capacity utilization. These are two specific years: 2004 follows a period of economic boom and 2008 is the beginning of the international downturn.

Given that we restricted attention to static equilibria (mainly because of limited time to develop the econometric analysis), we propose to apply a model for each period depending on a state of excess or full capacities.

12.4.2 Empirical Analysis

The empirical analysis is performed in four steps. In the first step, we build a mathematical representation of the working of the industry.

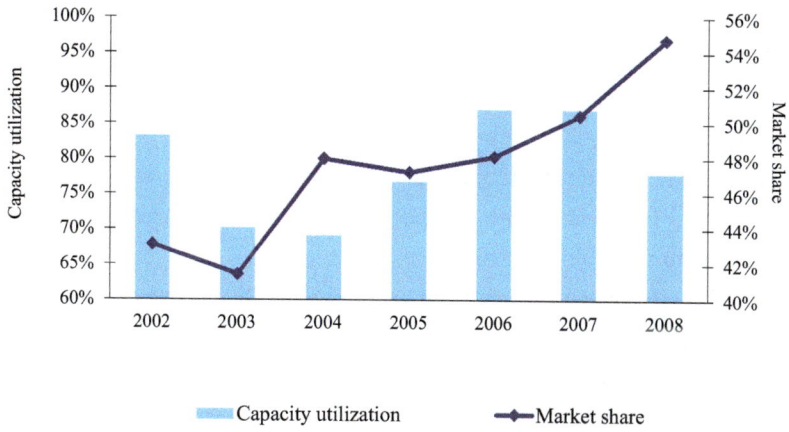

FIGURE 12.3 Capacity utilization and market share for firm A.
Source: Confidential data on the industry.

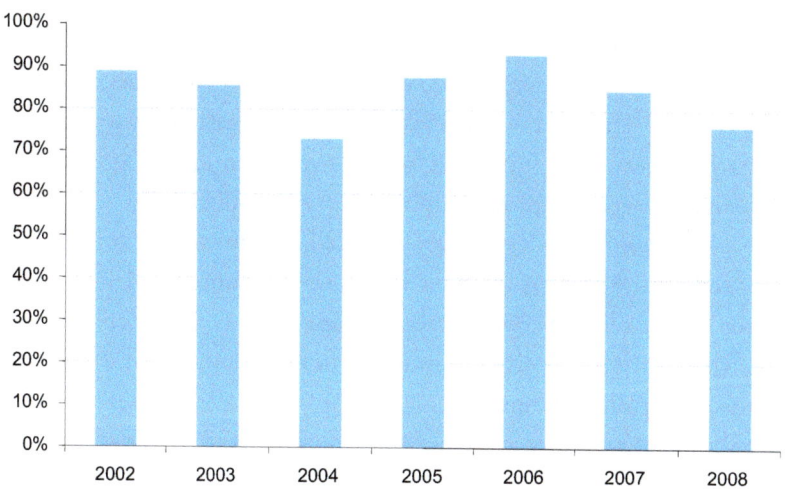

FIGURE 12.4 Capacity utilization at the industry level.
Source: Confidential data on the industry

The second step is devoted to the estimation of the model under the assumption that the market is competitive. The third step provides an estimation of the model when it is assumed that the main firms on the market form a cartel and, more specifically, are behaving like a monopoly. Finally, the fourth step consists in comparing the two estimations in their capacity to represent reality, that is, detecting which form of conduct – competition or collusion – is the most statistically adequate to represent the working of the market. The main result is that, in the industry under consideration and regarding the period of interest, the competition model statistically performs better than the collusion model.

The innovative part of our analysis lies in the use of a limited amount of information. Indeed, by assuming that the imports play the role of the outside alternative for the domestic customers and are provided by an importer with no strategic capacity in terms of price competition – which, we consider, are mild assumptions – we easily reach identification of a static Nash equilibrium based on a logit-type demand model. This adds to the originality and the specific interest of the proposed model.

Appendix 1 provides the model notation. The mathematical specification of the demand for product X is precisely described in Appendix 2. Appendix 3 describes the supply equations as well as the equations resulting from the firms' maximization program. The econometric specification is discussed in Appendix 4.

The estimation results are reported in Tables 12.8 and 12.9 in Appendix 5. We focus here on the main economic indicators that allow us to select between the different models and assumptions, i.e., whether the capacity constraint is or is not binding and whether firms' behavior is competitive or collusive. The economic indicators are the estimated own-price elasticities of demand, the level of estimated margins, and the estimated marginal cost in the case of nonbinding capacity constraints. Moreover, the sign of some of the parameters has to be checked for economic consistency. First, we discuss the estimated model under the assumption of binding capacity constraints. We compare the level of economic indicators obtained under the competitive assumption and under the assumption of coordinated practices. Second, we discuss the results of the models estimated under the assumption of nonbinding capacity constraints.

We compare the level of economic indicators obtained under the two behavioral assumptions. Finally, we present the results of a statistical standard test, the Vuong test, which is a specification test that is used to evaluate which of the conduct assumptions best represents the observed data.

Binding Capacity Constraints

Under the assumption of binding capacity constraints, the equilibrium is described by three equations: the demand addressed to firm A or to the monopoly, the demand addressed to the importer, and the markup. The estimated parameters of the competitive and coordinated models are reported in Table 12.8 of Appendix 5. All the parameters are statistically significant at the 1 percent or 5 percent level, whether competitive or coordinated behavior is considered. The parameters δ_i, $i = 0,1$, which reflect any own firms' characteristics, are positive, as well as the marginal utility of income, α.

Tables 12.2–12.7 report the values of the latter for the two models under competition and monopoly. Moreover, the parameters α_{GDP}, related to the GDP, are negative as expected since one it is natural for the marginal utility of income to decrease when income increases.

The own-price elasticities of demand belong to the interval $[-9.6, -6.17]$ in the case of competition (see Table 12.3). They are higher in absolute value in the case of coordination across the firms, as they belong to the interval $[-38.7, -8.5]$.

The estimated margins are reported in Table 12.4. Under the competitive assumption, the estimated margins belong to the interval

Table 12.2 *Estimated values of the marginal utility of income under the assumption of binding capacity constraints*

Year	2002	2003	2004	2005	2006	2007	2008
Competition	0.034	0.033	0.032	0.031	0.030	0.028	0.027
Monopoly	0.562	0.524	0.483	0.445	0.397	0.350	0.310

Table 12.3 Own-price elasticities of demand under the assumption of binding capacity constraints

YEAR	2002	2003	2004	2005	2006	2007	2008
# Obs	12	12	12	12	12	12	12
Competition							
Mean	−6.170	−7.112	−8.045	−7.799	−8.855	−8.241	−9.536
Std	0.542	0.735	1.198	1.214	0.928	1.051	3.311
Min	−7.006	−8.215	−9.663	−9.101	−10.970	−10.482	−18.331
Max	−5.359	−5.590	−5.661	−5.196	−7.552	−6.483	−5.841
Monopoly							
Mean	−35.029	−38.641	−32.250	−19.208	−33.334	−12.570	−8.511
Std	11.384	9.815	11.773	7.699	10.350	7.437	9.102
Min	−50.055	−51.462	−52.205	−36.118	−47.111	−28.418	−31.266
Max	−12.474	−19.871	−11.203	−7.972	−16.121	−1.246	0.000

Table 12.4 Estimated markups under the assumption of binding capacity constraints

YEAR	2002	2003	2004	2005	2006	2007	2008
# Obs	12	12	12	12	12	12	12/11
Competition							
Mean	49.541	47.465	50.916	50.828	54.280	59.515	66.105
Std	4.663	4.923	8.434	6.827	4.751	7.067	12.393
Min	40.675	40.923	42.299	42.019	45.497	50.884	44.981
Max	54.367	56.204	70.934	67.486	61.323	77.519	86.256
Monopoly							
Mean	10.045	9.372	14.608	23.563	15.877	69.825	150.156
Std	5.209	3.163	7.214	10.363	5.655	96.779	143.033
Min	6.126	6.620	7.692	11.905	9.888	17.247	26.751
Max	24.839	16.023	34.013	49.432	26.281	373.784	430.914

Table 12.5 Own-price elasticities of demand under the assumption of nonbinding capacity constraints

YEAR	2002	2003	2004	2005	2006	2007	2008
# Obs	12	12	12	12	12	12	12
Competition							
Mean	−1.098	−1.306	−1.529	−1.534	−1.819	−1.770	−2.132
Std	0.097	0.135	0.228	0.239	0.191	0.226	0.740
Min	−1.247	−1.508	−1.837	−1.790	−2.253	−2.252	−4.099
Max	−0.954	−1.026	−1.076	−1.022	−1.551	−1.393	−1.306
Monopoly							
Mean	−0.338	−0.400	−0.362	−0.234	−0.455	−0.195	−0.149
Std	0.110	0.102	0.132	0.094	0.141	0.115	0.159
Min	−0.483	−0.533	−0.586	−0.441	−0.643	−0.440	−0.547
Max	−0.120	−0.206	−0.126	−0.097	−0.220	−0.019	0.000

Source: Confidential data on the industry

Table 12.6 Markups under the assumption of nonbinding capacity constraints

YEAR	2002	2003	2004	2005	2006	2007	2008
# Obs	12	12	12	12	12	12	12
Competition							
Mean	35.908	45.016	58.202	51.084	55.763	58.186	71.591
Std	11.191	11.914	12.992	16.700	8.157	8.067	14.062
Min	24.798	20.991	34.372	19.199	45.360	41.613	49.331
Max	59.457	60.669	68.142	76.248	71.765	70.824	100.638
Monopoly							
Mean	−12.761	−5.370	21.168	0.084	15.541	13.077	40.287
Std	12.257	10.902	6.994	12.151	9.465	7.291	22.281
Min	−37.364	−27.310	7.524	−25.265	−7.451	2.709	−1.205
Max	3.603	7.356	34.019	20.603	24.182	25.600	68.994

Source: Confidential data on the industry

Table 12.7 Estimated marginal costs under the assumption of nonbinding capacity constraints

YEAR	2002	2003	2004	2005	2006	2007	2008
# Obs	12	12	12	12	12	12	12
Competition							
Mean	194.835	184.027	167.261	187.986	211.149	202.078	155.890
Std	35.850	41.656	50.433	54.945	40.627	38.566	58.688
Min	117.384	132.229	117.590	90.831	140.926	154.558	−5.258
Max	233.311	275.499	261.023	283.314	262.049	293.437	225.411
Monopoly							
Mean	341.539	351.560	315.618	386.084	401.275	419.642	334.338
Std	32.182	28.620	25.606	22.187	27.858	17.290	45.584
Min	306.098	315.612	264.952	341.396	365.031	385.501	259.327
Max	401.577	405.349	352.367	421.147	455.258	447.456	391.267

Source: Confidential data on the industry

[47.46, 66.11]. The margins increase during the period of consideration. Under the assumption of coordinated practices, the estimated margins belong to the interval [9.37, 150.15]. They do not exhibit a regular trend during the overall period. One expects that margins under coordinated practices would be higher than margins under competitive behavior. Our estimation shows contrary results except for the two last years of the period under consideration.

With respect to the main indicators, one can conclude the two models estimated under competition and monopoly are consistent with the main properties implied by economic theory. However, at this stage of our analysis, the relative values of own-price elasticity of demand and the relative values of the estimated margins favor the assumption of competition as a better approximation of the data.

Nonbinding Capacity Constraints
Under the assumption of nonbinding capacity constraints the equilibrium is described by four main equations: the demand addressed to firm A or to the monopoly, the demand addressed to the importer, the markup and the marginal cost equation; plus the additional total cost equation. The estimated parameters of the competitive and coordinated models are reported in Table 12.9 of Appendix 5. All the parameters are statistically significant at 1 percent level whether the competitive or coordinated behavior is considered, except the constant, β_{cst} in the total cost function and the parameter related to the interaction between raw material Y's price and product X's production in the total cost function, $\beta_{RM,Y}$. The parameters δ_i, $i = 0,1$, are positive, as well as the marginal utility of income, α. Notice that, contrary to the previous model, the marginal utility of income is constant over time.

The own-price elasticities of demand belong to the interval [−2.14, −1.09] in the case of competition. They are lower than one in absolute value in the case of coordination across firms, as they belong to the interval [−0.46, −0.14] (see Table 12.5). This result is fairly inconsistent with the results implied by economic theory related to monopoly (i.e., joint profit maximization). In the case of a monopoly, the own-price elasticity of demand has to be higher than one in absolute value, otherwise the markup equation leads to negative marginal costs. Even if Table 12.7 shows positive marginal costs both for competition and coordinated practices across firms, it means that the pricing equation under the monopoly assumption is poorly estimated, which explains why the estimated margins are unstable under this assumption (see Table 12.6).

Vuong Test as a Test of Model Selection

A standard statistical test to determine which of two models better fit the data is the Vuong test (see Gasmi, Laffont and Vuong, 1992). This test is based on the comparison of likelihood values of the estimated models, taking into account the variance-covariance matrix of the parameters and the estimated errors of the models. In our specific case, the Vuong test allows us to compare the assumptions of competition and coordinated practices.

If the Vuong test statistic is higher than 2, then the competitive assumption is a better approximation of the data. If the Vuong test statistics is lower than -2, then the assumption of coordinated practices across firms is a better approximation of the data. Finally, if the Vuong test statistics belongs to $[-2, 2]$, neither of the assumptions is statistically preferred to the other.

The Vuong test can only be applied when capacity constraints are binding since, only in this case, do the estimated models under competition and monopoly satisfy the economic conditions as explained above. In this case, the Vuong test statistics equals 2.19. From a statistical point of view, it means that the assumption of competition is preferred to the assumption of full coordinated practices. This result confirms the previous findings obtained through the analysis of the estimated economic indicators. Under the assumption of binding capacity constraints, the hypothesis of competition prevails over coordination.

12.5 CONCLUDING REMARKS

We have provided a comprehensive examination of the Greek steel market, with the objective to investigate whether it would be reasonable to consider the behavior of the three Greek producers of steel as tacitly collusive, as suspected by the HCC, or not, during the period 2002 to 2011.[39] This study has included undertaking qualitative analysis of the structural conditions of the market, explaining price formation and evolution on the basis of a Bertrand-Edgeworth model of the industry to assess whether the market data are or are not compatible with collusion, as well as with studying the phenomenon of price parallelism, investigating a number of collusion markers and, finally, undertaking econometric analysis. As noted above, the latter is innovative in the use of a limited amount of information. Specifically, the estimation of the model is performed based on data on the price and price from only one firm of the oligopoly, on the price and quantity of imports, and on some aggregated data related to the market, thanks to the model specification and the role of the international side of the market.

The analysis of this case study suggests that competition and collusion can be difficult to distinguish on the basis of observed patterns of price evolution which contain incidences of parallelism. A number of lessons emerge. Seemingly coordinated behavior such as simultaneous increases or decreases in prices can be the competitive response of producers to changes in import prices in conjunction with the information dissemination activities of wholesalers who have strong incentives to establish the new price levels of all producers. It is then important to establish whether, as was usually the case in the present case, the changes concern list prices and whether producers' changes in final prices, after the application of discounts, diverge.

In general, a competition authority, having in a preliminary investigation ascertained the facts in relation to the above

---

[39] 2002–2008 for the econometric analysis.

considerations and depending on its findings, could examine whether structural conditions and econometric analysis can provide more support to the hypothesis of collusion than to that of competitive behavior. A message that emerges is that pieces of circumstantial evidence and individual screen tests in isolation for proving collusion or no collusion can be of limited value. Particular individual red flags may be false alarms and mean something else. In such a case, it is really the combination of various indicators, pieces of evidence and analyses, including a convincing set of alternative, plausible competitive explanations for observed behavior that can be decisive for a judgment.

In this specific case study, it was found that, taking into account a multitude of complementary analyses and evidence, that the evolution of the Greek steel market in the period 2002–2011 can be more satisfactorily interpreted in terms of a hypothesis of competition. The HCC therefore was correct to ultimately drop its accusations against the Greek steel producers. That it took over eight years of investigation before the decision was finally reached only goes to show the importance of the lessons we draw from this case for future priority setting.

APPENDIX I   NOTATIONS

The product X is produced by three firms noted by $i = 1, 2, I = 3$ and by an importer indexed by the number 0.

The main notations are as follows:

- Domestic production capacity $= \overline{Q}_i$
- Domestic production $= q_i$
- Domestic price $= p_i$
- Export of firm $i = x_i$
- Total domestic production $= \sum_{i=1}^{I} q_i = q_d$
- Imports $= q_0$
- Import price $= p_i$
- International price $= W$
- Domestic market size $=$ sum of domestic production $+$ imports $= Q$
- Market share $= s_i = \dfrac{q_i}{q_0 + \sum_{i=1}^{I} q_i} = \dfrac{q_i}{q_0 + q_d} = \dfrac{q_i}{Q}$

APPENDIX 2 DEMAND MODEL

A typical buyer of product X has to choose among the three domestic firms or the importer to satisfy its demand. The logit specification of the demand is then adequate for this situation (see for instance Motta, 2004) It is written as

$$\ln s_i - \ln s_0 = \delta_i - \alpha p_i, \qquad (8)$$

where δ_i is the "quality" of the product sold by firm i and p_i is its price. For technical reason, one must assume that

$$\delta_0 - \alpha p_0 = 0. \qquad (9)$$

With this hypothesis, the model basically says that the market share of product i (or firm i) is a percentage of the market share of imports that represents an outside alternative to buying from a domestic producer, this percentage depending on the trade-off between quality and price determined by the parameter α, which is a rate of change between quality and money.

In the econometric model, the parameters δs have to be estimated as well as the parameter α.

Note that with this specification, the own-price elasticity ε_i is given by:

$$\varepsilon_i = -\frac{p_i}{q_i}\frac{\partial q_i}{\partial p_i} = \alpha p_i (1 - s_i). \qquad (10)$$

APPENDIX 3 SUPPLY SIDE

In the first place, assume that the industry is competitive. In this case, each firm sets her price and the quantity exported so as to maximize her profit, knowing that the other competitors are doing the same. Then the profit maximization is as follows:

$$\underset{p_i, x_i}{\text{Max}}\; p_i q_i + W x_i - C(q_i + x_i) \quad st \quad q_i + x_i \leq \bar{Q}_i. \qquad (11)$$

That is to say, each firm maximizes its profit defined as the difference between revenues and cost, where the revenues come from domestic sales and exports and where the cost is a function of the total production.

The first order conditions are:

$$q_i + \left(p_i - \frac{\partial C}{\partial q_i} - \lambda\right)\frac{\partial q_i}{\partial p_i} = 0,$$
$$W - \frac{\partial C}{\partial q_i} - \lambda = 0, \qquad (12)$$
$$(\bar{Q}_i - q_i - x_i)\lambda = 0,$$

where λ is the multiplier associated with the capacity condition.

There are different cases:

The capacity constraint is binding, in which case p_i is chosen so that:

$$\frac{(p_i - W)}{p_i} = \frac{1}{-\frac{p_i}{q_i}\frac{\partial q_i}{\partial p_i}}, \qquad (13)$$

and x_i is chosen as: $x_i = \overline{Q}_i - q_i$.

The capacity constraint is not binding, then $\lambda = 0$ and p_i and x_i are chosen so that:

$$\frac{(p_i - W)}{p_i} = \frac{1}{-\frac{p_i}{q_i}\frac{\partial q_i}{\partial p_i}}, \qquad (14)$$

and

$$\frac{\partial C}{\partial q_i} = W. \qquad (15)$$

In the second place, assume that, together, the different firms in the industry behave as a monopoly. In this case, the monopoly sets its price and the quantity exported so as to maximize its profit, just knowing that there is an importer which creates some competitive pressure. Then the profit maximization is as follows:

$$\operatorname*{Max}_{p, x} \; p q_d + W x_0 - C(q_d + x_0) \quad st \quad q_d + x_0 \leq \overline{Q}. \qquad (16)$$

The same type of equations holds in this case except that they apply at the industry level and not at the firm level.

APPENDIX 4 SPECIFICATION

A partial equilibrium on a product market is characterized by a system of equations related to both demand and supply of all firms. However, here the model is fully identified, thanks only to the description of demand and supply of firm A and the demand of the Importers on the domestic market.

Let index i be equal to A or to 0 when it refers to firm A or to the Representative Importer. Based on a logit-type specification, the demand function addressed to firm i is expressed as follows:

$$\ln(s_i) - \ln(s_0) = \delta_i - \alpha p_i + \zeta_i, \qquad (17)$$

where s_i is the market share of firm i on the product X domestic market, s_0 is the market share of the product X importer on this market, p_i is the price charged by firm i for one unit of the product, δ_i measures the observed "quality" of product

X sold by firm i, ζ_i measures the unobserved "quality" of product X sold by firm i, and α is the marginal utility of income. The market share of firm i is measured as:

$$s_i = \frac{q_i}{q_0 + q_d}, \qquad (18)$$

where q_i is the production level of firm i, q_d is the total domestic production (i.e., the sum of production levels of all domestic firms) on the market, and q_0 is the total amount of imports of product X.

Hence the demand for product X results from a trade-off between "quality" and price. The term denoted by δ allows for a differentiation across undertakings, which might be interpreted as reflecting any own firm's characteristics, in particular its capacity to react to new economic conditions. In the case of an exogenous shock, the demand would shift due to change in this term. As a matter of fact, this term is expressed as a function of a dummy variable which accounts for the specific aspects of year 2008 compared to the other years, as previously pointed out. Specifically, we write:

$$\delta_i = \left(\delta_{i,cst} + \delta_{i,2008} * dummy_{2008}\right), \qquad (19)$$

where $\delta_{i,cst}$ and $dummy_{2008}$ are parameters to be estimated.

The parameter α related to the price, defined as the marginal utility of income, might be interpreted as an exchange rate between one unit of quality and one monetary unit. Note that, by specifying this parameter as a function of country 1's GDP, that is to say,

$$\alpha = (\alpha_{cst} + \alpha_{GDP} * GDP), \qquad (20)$$

where α_{cst} and α_{GDP} are parameters to be estimated, we expect it to be positive and decreasing with GDP, reflecting a wealth effect, namely that a richer country is less sensitive to any change in money value.

Whatever the assumption, competition or collusion, two demand functions are estimated jointly in the model, the first one for firm i, firm A or the monopoly respectively, the second one for the importer.

The supply side of the economy is characterized by the markup of the firm, either firm A or the monopoly depending on the assumption related to the level of competition. One can show that the markup is a function of the own-price elasticity of demand; thus the markup is in particular a function of the parameter α described in the demand equation.

Each firm maximizes its profit defined as the difference between revenues and cost, where the revenues come from domestic sales and exports and where the cost is a function of the total production. On the domestic market, we assume that the firms compete in price. This choice is driven by the observed firms' behavior and is consistent with the heterogeneity of the firms' characteristics. On the international market, the firms take prices as given and compete in quantities.

Deriving the maximization program of the firm, one can show that the markup is expressed in terms of the product X export price rather than in terms of marginal costs of production. The expression of the markup is the following:

$$p_i - W = \frac{1}{\alpha(1 - s_i)}, \qquad (21)$$

where:

- p_i, s_i are respectively the price charged by firm i and its market share on product X domestic market;
- α is the marginal utility of income and its expression is identical to the one in the demand function;
- W is the price for exports, which is given for firm i.

Whatever the assumption, competition or collusion, the markup related to firm i is the only markup included in the model to be estimated. Under the assumption of binding capacity constraint, the markup equation perfectly describes the behavior of the firm and allows us to determine the optimal level of domestic production, while the level of exportation is deduced from the full capacity condition.

However, under the assumption of nonbinding capacity constraint, an additional equation is necessary to describe the strategic behavior of the firm, as both the level of domestic production and the level of exports have to be determined. This additional equation expresses that the marginal cost of production equals the export price (see also Sections 12.3–12.4). The marginal cost of production is expressed as a linear function of the raw material Y price and the total level of production (domestic production and exports). From an econometric perspective, both the equation related to the marginal cost of production and the equation related to the total cost of production will be included in the system to be estimated.

The specification for the total cost function is the following:

$$TC(y_i) = \beta_{cst} + \beta_{RM} \cdot p_{RM} + \beta_{RM,Y} \cdot p_{RM} \cdot y_i + \frac{1}{2}\beta_Y(y_i)^2 \qquad (22)$$

where

- y_i is the total production of product X, that is the sum over domestic production, q_i, and exports x_i. In the case of competition, q_i, and x_i are firm A's domestic production and exports respectively; in the case of monopoly, q_i, and x_i are respectively the total domestic production and the exports of all domestic firms;

- $TC(y_i)$ is the total cost to produce the quantity y_i;
- p_{RM} is the raw material (RM) Y price.

Given the specification of the total cost function, the marginal cost function is expressed:

$$MC(y_i) = \beta_{RM,Y} \cdot p_{RM} + \beta_Y y_i \qquad (23)$$

The equilibrium is characterized by equality between marginal cost and export price. Thus, under the assumption of nonbinding capacity constraints the following relationship holds for firm i:

$$W = \beta_{RM,Y} \cdot p_{RM} + \beta_Y y_i \qquad (24)$$

As explained previously, both this latter equation and the total cost function related to firm i are included in the model to be estimated.

APPENDIX 5 ESTIMATED PARAMETERS OF THE MODELS AND MAIN RELEVANT TEST STATISTICS

Table 12.8 Estimated parameters under the assumption of binding capacity constraints

	Competition				Monopoly			
Parameter	Estimate	Approx. Std Err	t Value	Approx. Pr > |t|	1st Stage R-Square	Estimate	Approx. Std Err	t Value	Approx. Pr > |t|	1st Stage R-Square
δ_0	12.143	0.711	17.08	<.0001	1.000	171.969	14.659	11.73	<.0001	1.000
$\delta_{0,2008}$	5.274	1.566	3.37	0.0012	1.000	37.942	12.729	2.98	0.0038	1.000
δ_1	13.357	0.702	19.04	<.0001	1.000	177.63	14.952	11.88	<.0001	1.000
$\delta_{1,2008}$	6.750	1.561	4.32	<.0001	1.000	29.792	12.740	2.34	0.0219	1.000
α_{cst}	0.049	0.009	5.70	<.0001	0.893	1.098	0.140	7.85	<.0001	0.827
α_{GDP}	-7.1E-7	3.1E-7	-2.29	0.0244	0.935	-3.0E-5	4.3E-6	-6.00	<.0001	0.867

Number of Observations
Used 83
Missing 1

Statistics for System
Objective 1.508 1.819
Objective*N 125.151 151.004

Notes: If Approx.Pr > |t| < 0.01 the corresponding parameter is statistically significant at level 1 percent; if 0.001< Approx.Pr > |t| < 0.05 the corresponding parameter is statistically significant at level 5 percent; If Approx.Pr > |t| > 0.1 the corresponding parameter is not statistically significant.

Table 12.9 Estimated parameters under the assumption of nonbinding capacity constraints

Parameter	Competition					Monopoly				
	Estimate	Approx. Std Err	t Value	Approx. Pr > |t|	1st Stage R-Square	Estimate	Approx. Std Err	t Value	Approx. Pr > |t|	1st Stage R-Square
δ_0	2.498	0.138	18.10	<.0001	1.000	2.263	0.130	17.41	<.0001	1.000
$\delta_{0,2008}$	0.921	0.161	5.74	<.0001	1.000	1.010	0.155	6.52	<.0001	1.000
δ_1	3.474	0.171	20.3	<.0001	1.000	3.858	0.166	23.31	<.0001	1.000
$\delta_{1,2008}$	2.348	0.294	7.99	<.0001	1.000	2.064	0.295	7.00	<.0001	1.000
α_{cst}	0.006	0.000	17.98	<.0001	0.971	0.005	0.000	18.06	<.0001	0.777
β_{cst}	1458633	1990910	0.73	0.4659	1.000	-8086291	8122373	-1.00	0.3225	1.000
β_{scrap}	124569	27293	4.56	<.0001	1.000	254065	90975	2.79	0.0066	1.000
$\beta_{scrap,Y}$	-0.318	0.350	-0.91	0.3658	0.891	-0.482	0.619	-0.78	0.4380	0.997
β_Y	0.003	0.001	6.30	<.0001	0.772	0.003	0.001	4.11	<.0001	0.988

Number of Observations
Used 82 82
Missing 2 2

Statistics for System
Objective 3.772 3.275
Objective*N 309.265 268.511

Notes: If Approx.Pr > |t| < 0.01 the corresponding parameter is statistically significant at level 1 percent; if 0.001< Approx.Pr > |t| < 0.05 the corresponding parameter is statistically significant at level 5 percent; If Approx.Pr > |t| > 0.1 the corresponding parameter is not statistically significant.

REFERENCES

Abrantez-Metz R. and P. Bajari (2009) "Screening for Conspiracies: Applications for Litigation, Pre-Litigation, Regulation and Internal Monitoring," https://papers.ssrn.com/sol3/papers.cfm?abstract_id=1357862.

Abrantez-Metz R., L. Froeb, J. Gewke, and C. Taylor (2005) "A Variance test for collusion," Working Paper 275 (ftc.gov).

Besanko D. and U. Doraszelski (2004) "Capacity Dynamics and Endogenous Asymmetries in Firm Size," *Rand Journal of Economics*, 35 (1), 23–49.

Bernheim B. D. and M. D. Whinston (1990) "Multimarket Contact and Collusive Behavior," *Rand Journal of Economics*, 21 (1), 1–26.

Compte O., J. Frederic, P. Rey (2000) "Capacity Constraints, Mergers and Collusion," *European Economic Review*, 46 (1), 1–29.

Evans W. N. and I. N. Kessides (2001) "Living by the 'Golden Rule': Multimarket Contact in the US Airline Industry," *Quarterly Journal of Economics*, 109 (2), 341–366.

Gasmi F., J. J. Laffont and Q. Vuong (1992) "Econometric Analysis of Collusive Behavior in a Soft Drink Market," *Journal of Economic and Management Strategy*, 1 (2) 277–311.

Haltiwanger J. and J. E. Harrington (1991) "The Impact of Cyclical Demand Movements on Collusive Behavior," *Rand Journal of Economics*, 22 (1), 89–106.

Harrington J. E. (2005) "Detecting Cartels," in Paolo Buccirossi ed., *Handbook of Antitrust Economics*, MIT Press.

Harrington J. E. (2006) "How do Cartels Operate?" *Foundations and Trends in Microeconomics*, now Publishers Inc.

Ivaldi M., B. Jullien, P. Rey, P. Seabright and J. Tirole (2003) "The Economics of Tacit Collusion," Microsoft Word – The Economics of Tacit Collusion Final Report July 16.doc (europa.eu).

Motta M. (2004) *Competition Policy: Theory and Practice*, Cambridge: Cambridge University Press.

Ross T. W. (1992) "Cartel Stability and product Differentiation," *International Journal of Industrial Organization*, 10 (1) 1–13.